WAR DIARY INDEX

Listing by Division
the full colour facsimile reprints of original
War Office documents. (WO95)

With bonus sample pages in full colour

The Naval & Military Press Ltd

Published by

The Naval & Military Press Ltd
Unit 5 Riverside, Brambleside
Bellbrook Industrial Estate
Uckfield, East Sussex
TN22 1QQ England

Tel: +44 (0)1825 749494

www.naval-military-press.com
www.nmarchive.com

ISBN: 9781783312375

In reprinting in facsimile from the original, any imperfections are inevitably reproduced and the quality may fall short of modern type and cartographic standards.

Title	Product Code	ISBN	Price
1 CAVALRY DIVISION			
1 CAVALRY DIVISION Headquarters, Branches and Services : 11 August 1914 - 31 December 1914 (First World War, War Diary, WO95/1096)	WD1096	9781474500098	£76.00
1 CAVALRY DIVISION Headquarters, Branches and Services General Staff : 1 January 1915 - 25 September 1919 (First World War, War Diary, WO95/1097)	WD1097	9781474500104	£85.00
1 CAVALRY DIVISION Headquarters, Branches and Services Adjutant and Quarter-Master General : 8 June 1914 - 31 December 1915 (First World War, War Diary, WO95/1098)	WD1098	9781474500111	£76.00
1 CAVALRY DIVISION Headquarters, Branches and Services Adjutant and Quarter-Master General : 1 January 1916 - 31 December 1917 (First World War, War Diary, WO95/1099)	WD1099	9781474500128	£51.00
1 CAVALRY DIVISION Headquarters, Branches and Services Adjutant and Quarter-Master General : 1 January 1918 - 31 December 1918 (First World War, War Diary, WO95/1100)	WD1100	9781474500135	£75.00
1 CAVALRY DIVISION Headquarters, Branches and Services Commander Royal Artillery : 10 August 1914 - 19 September 1919 (First World War, War Diary, WO95/1101/1)	WD1101_1	9781474500142	£58.00
1 CAVALRY DIVISION Headquarters, Branches and Services Royal Army Medical Corps Assistant Director Medical Services : 15 August 1914 - 12 October 1914 (First World War, War Diary, WO95/1101/2)	WD1101_2	9781474500159	£15.00
1 CAVALRY DIVISION Headquarters, Branches and Services Royal Army Ordnance Corps Assistant Director Ordnance Services and Veterinary Corps Assistant Director Veterinary Services : 10 August 1914 - 13 September 1919 (First World War, War Diary, WO95/1102)	WD1102	9781474500166	£81.00
1 CAVALRY DIVISION Divisional Troops 7 Brigade Royal Horse Artillery and Ammunition Column, 1 Field Squadron Royal Engineers and 1 Signal Squadron Royal Engineers : 4 August 1914 - 31 August 1919 (First World War, War Diary, WO95/1103)	WD1103	9781474500173	£76.00
1 CAVALRY DIVISION Divisional Troops 8 Light Armoured Battery, Cavalry Pioneer Battalion and Royal Army Medical Corps 1 Cavalry Field Ambulance : 5 August 1914 - 31 August 1919 (First World War, War Diary, WO95/1104)	WD1104	9781474500180	£42.00
1 CAVALRY DIVISION Divisional Troops Royal Army Medical Corps 3 Cavalry Field Ambulance, Royal Army Medical Corps 9 Cavalry Field Ambulance and 9 Sanitary Section : 13 August 1914 - 31 May 1917 (First World War, War Diary, WO95/1105)	WD1105	9781474500197	£78.00
1 CAVALRY DIVISION Divisional Troops Royal Army Veterinary Corps 1, 10 and 39 Mobile Veterinary Section : 5 August 1914 - 31 August 1919 (First World War, War Diary, WO95/1106)	WD1106	9781474500203	£61.00
1 CAVALRY DIVISION Divisional Troops Royal Army Service Corps Supply Column (57 Company A.S.C.), 1 Auxiliary Horse Transport Company (574 Company A.S.C.) and Ammunition Park (45 Company A.S.C.): 5 August 1914 - 20 February 1918 (First World War, War Diary	WD1107	9781474500210	£49.00
1 CAVALRY DIVISION 1 Cavalry Brigade Headquarters, I Battery Royal Horse Artillery and 1 Machine Gun Squadron : 4 August 1914 - 31 March 1919 (First World War, War Diary, WO95/1108)	WD1108	9781474500227	£60.00

Title	Product Code	ISBN	Price
1 CAVALRY DIVISION 1 Cavalry Brigade 2nd Dragoon Guards (Queen's Bays), 5th Dragoon Guards (Princess Charlotte's Own) and 11th (Prince Albert's Own) Hussars : 14 August 1914 - 15 February 1919 (First World War, War Diary, WO95/1109)	WD1109	9781474500234	£60.00
1 CAVALRY DIVISION 2 Cavalry Brigade Headquarters : 4 August 1914 - 31 March 1919 (First World War, War Diary, WO95/1110)	WD1110	9781474500241	£63.00
1 CAVALRY DIVISION 2 Cavalry Brigade 2 Machine Gun Squadron, 'H' and 'L' Battery Royal Horse Artillery and Brigade Pioneer Battalion : 5 August 1914 - 13 March 1917 (First World War, War Diary, WO95/1111)	WD1111	9781474500258	£33.00
1 CAVALRY DIVISION 2 Cavalry Brigade 4th Dragoon Guards (Royal Irish) : 15 August 1914 - 31 March 1919 (First World War, War Diary, WO95/1112)	WD1112	9781474500265	£60.00
1 CAVALRY DIVISION 2 Cavalry Brigade 18th (Queen Mary's Own Royal) Hussars and 9th Lancers (Queen's Royal) : 10 August 1914 - 31 March 1919 (First World War, War Diary, WO95/1113)	WD1113	9781474500272	£59.00
1 CAVALRY DIVISION 9 Cavalry Brigade Headquarters and 15th (The King's) Hussars : 14 April 1915 - 31 March 1919 (First World War, War Diary, WO95/1114)	WD1114	9781474500289	£69.00
1 CAVALRY DIVISION 9 Cavalry Brigade 8th (King's Royal Irish) Hussars and 19th (Queen Alexandra's Own Royal) Hussars: 6 April 1915 - 31 March 1919 (First World War, War Diary, WO95/1115)	WD1115	9781474500296	£53.00
1 CAVALRY DIVISION 9 Cavalry Brigade Bedford Yeomanry, 1/1 Warwickshire Battery Royal Horse Artillery, `Y' Battery Royal Horse Artillery, 9 Machine Gun Squadron and 9 Cavalry Pioneer Battalion : 1 October 1914 - 9 July 1917 (First World War, War Diary, WO	WD1116	9781474500302	£31.00

Title	Product Code	ISBN	Price
1 DIVISION			
1 DIVISION Headquarters, Branches and Services General Staff : 4 August 1914 - 28 February 1915 (First World War, War Diary, WO95/1227)	WD1227	9781474521659	£82.00
1 DIVISION Headquarters, Branches and Services General Staff : 1 January 1915 - 30 June 1915 (First World War, War Diary, WO95/1228)	WD1228	9781474502153	£64.00
1 DIVISION Headquarters, Branches and Services General Staff : 1 July 1915 - 30 September 1915 (First World War, War Diary, WO95/1229)	WD1229	9781474502160	£47.00
1 DIVISION Headquarters, Branches and Services General Staff : 1 October 1915 - 30 April 1916 (First World War, War Diary, WO95/1230)	WD1230	9781474502177	£46.00
1 DIVISION Headquarters, Branches and Services General Staff : 1 May 1916 - 31 December 1916 (First World War, War Diary, WO95/1231)	WD1231	9781474502184	£52.00
1 DIVISION Headquarters, Branches and Services General Staff : 1 January 1917 - 31 December 1917 (First World War, War Diary, WO95/1232)	WD1232	9781474502191	£44.00
1 DIVISION Headquarters, Branches and Services General Staff : 1 January 1918 - 5 June 1918 (First World War, War Diary, WO95/1233)	WD1233	9781474502207	£52.00
1 DIVISION Headquarters, Branches and Services General Staff : 1 July 1918 - 28 August 1919 (First World War, War Diary, WO95/1234)	WD1234	9781474502214	£54.00
1 DIVISION Headquarters, Branches and Services Adjutant and Quarter-Master General : 19 August 1914 - 31 December 1915 (First World War, War Diary, WO95/1235)	WD1235	9781474502221	£84.00
1 DIVISION Headquarters, Branches and Services Adjutant and Quarter-Master General : 1 January 1916 - 30 September 1917 (First World War, War Diary, WO95/1236)	WD1236	9781474502238	£65.00
1 DIVISION Headquarters, Branches and Services Adjutant and Quarter-Master General : 1 October 1917 - 11 August 1918 (First World War, War Diary, WO95/1237)	WD1237	9781474502245	£54.00
1 DIVISION Headquarters, Branches and Services Adjutant and Quarter-Master General : 1 August 1918 - 27 June 1919 (First World War, War Diary, WO95/1238)	WD1238	9781474502252	£57.00
1 DIVISION Headquarters, Branches and Services Commander Royal Artillery : 4 August 1914 - 30 November 1915 (First World War, War Diary, WO95/1239)	WD1239	9781474502269	£56.00
1 DIVISION Headquarters, Branches and Services Commander Royal Artillery : 1 January 1916 - 31 December 1917 (First World War, War Diary, WO95/1240)	WD1240	9781474502276	£59.00
1 DIVISION Headquarters, Branches and Services Commander Royal Artillery : 1 January 1918 - 30 August 1919 (First World War, War Diary, WO95/1241)	WD1241	9781474502283	£74.00
1 DIVISION Headquarters, Branches and Services Royal Army Medical Corps Assistant Director Medical Services : 14 September 1914 - 31 March 1915 (First World War, War Diary, WO95/1242A)	WD1242_A	9781474521666	£48.00
1 DIVISION Headquarters, Branches and Services Royal Army Medical Corps Assistant Director Medical Services : 1 April 1915 - 31 December 1915 (First World War, War Diary, WO95/1242B)	WD1242_B	9781474521673	£60.00
1 DIVISION Headquarters, Branches and Services Royal Army Medical Corps Assistant Director Medical Services : 1 January 1916 - 30 September 1919 (First World War, War Diary, WO95/1243)	WD1243	9781474521680	£75.00

Title	Product Code	ISBN	Price
1 DIVISION Headquarters, Branches and Services Commander Royal Engineers : 4 August 1914 - 31 December 1914 (First World War, War Diary, WO95/1244A)	WD1244_A	9781474502290	£76.00
1 DIVISION Headquarters, Branches and Services Commander Royal Engineers : 1 January 1915 - 30 April 1915 (First World War, War Diary, WO95/1244B)	WD1244_B	9781474521697	£16.00
1 DIVISION Headquarters, Branches and Services Commander Royal Engineers : 1 May 1915 - 30 April 1916 (First World War, War Diary, WO95/1245)	WD1245	9781474502306	£69.00
1 DIVISION Headquarters, Branches and Services Commander Royal Engineers : 1 May 1916 - 18 September 1919 (First World War, War Diary, WO95/1246)	WD1246	9781474521703	£64.00
1 DIVISION Headquarters, Branches and Services Deputy Assistant Director Ordnance Services and Assistant Director Veterinary Services : 4 August 1914 - 31 August 1919 (First World War, War Diary, WO95/1247)	WD1247	9781474502313	£76.00
1 DIVISION Divisional Troops `C' Squadron 15 Hussars, `B' Squadron Northumberland Hussars, Cyclist Company and 25 Brigade Royal Field Artillery: 4 August 1914 - 21 June 1916 (First World War, War Diary, WO95/1248)	WD1248	9781474502320	£43.00
1 DIVISION Divisional Troops 39 Brigade Royal Field Artillery : 4 August 1914 - 29 April 1919 (First World War, War Diary, WO95/1249)	WD1249	9781474502337	£47.00
1 DIVISION Divisional Troops 26 Brigade Royal Field Artillery : 1 August 1914 - 25 March 1917 (First World War, War Diary, WO95/1250/1)	WD1250_1	9781474502344	£19.00
1 DIVISION Divisional Troops 43 Brigade Royal Field Artillery : 4 August 1914 - 30 November 1914 (First World War, War Diary, WO95/1250/2)	WD1250_2	9781474502351	£24.00
1 DIVISION Divisional Troops Divisional Ammunition Column and Trench Mortar Batteries : 4 August 1914 - 31 July 1919 (First World War, War Diary, WO95/1251)	WD1251	9781474502368	£40.00
1 DIVISION Divisional Troops 23 Field Company Royal Engineers : 4 August 1914 - 30 April 1918 (First World War, War Diary, WO95/1252)	WD1252	9781474502375	£30.00
1 DIVISION Divisional Troops 26 Field Company Royal Engineers : 10 August 1914 - 30 April 1919 (First World War, War Diary, WO95/1253/1)	WD1253_1	9781474502382	£39.00
1 DIVISION Divisional Troops 409 Field Company Royal Engineers : 13 December 1914 - 31 January 1917 (First World War, War Diary, WO95/1253/2)	WD1253_2	9781474502399	£43.00
1 DIVISION Divisional Troops 409 Field Company Royal Engineers : 1 February 1917 - 30 September 1919 (First World War, War Diary, WO95/1254/1)	WD1254_1	9781474502405	£33.00
1 DIVISION Divisional Troops 75 Field Company Royal Engineers : 1 April 1919 - 23 September 1919 (First World War, War Diary, WO95/1254/2)	WD1254_2	9781474502412	£15.00
1 DIVISION Divisional Troops 76 Field Company Royal Engineers : 1 April 1919 - 31 August 1919 (First World War, War Diary, WO95/1254/3)	WD1254_3	9781474502429	£15.00
1 DIVISION Divisional Troops Divisional Signal Company : 5 August 1914 - 14 June 1919 (First World War, War Diary, WO95/1255)	WD1255	9781474502436	£54.00
1 DIVISION Divisional Troops 1 Battalion Machine Gun Corps : 1 March 1918 - 31 July 1919 (First World War, War Diary, WO95/1256/1)	WD1256_1	9781474502443	£21.00

Title	Product Code	ISBN	Price
1 DIVISION Divisional Troops 216 Machine Gun Company : 17 March 1917 - 28 February 1918 (First World War, War Diary, WO95/1256/2)	WD1256_2	9781474502450	£15.00
1 DIVISION Divisional Troops Welsh Regiment 1/6th Battalion Pioneers : 1 June 1916 - 1 April 1919 (First World War, War Diary, WO95/1256/3)	WD1256_3	9781474502467	£16.00
1 DIVISION Divisional Troops Royal Army Medical Corps 1 Field Ambulance : 5 August 1914 - 30 June 1919 (First World War, War Diary, WO95/1257)	WD1257	9781474502474	£38.00
1 DIVISION Divisional Troops Royal Army Medical Corps 2 Field Ambulance : 5 August 1914 - 28 August 1919 (First World War, War Diary, WO95/1258)	WD1258	9781474521710	£69.00
1 DIVISION Divisional Troops Royal Army Medical Corps 3 Field Ambulance : 5 August 1914 - 31 July 1915 (First World War, War Diary, WO95/1259/1)	WD1259_1	9781474502481	£15.00
1 DIVISION Divisional Troops Royal Army Medical Corps 141 Field Ambulance : 1 July 1916 - 21 September 1919 (First World War, War Diary, WO95/1259/2)	WD1259_2	9781474502498	£19.00
1 DIVISION Divisional Troops 13 Sanitary Section : 8 April 1915 - 31 March 1917 (First World War, War Diary, WO95/1259/3)	WD1259_3	9781474502504	£20.00
1 DIVISION Divisional Troops Royal Army Veterinary Corps 2 Mobile Veterinary Section : 4 August 1914 - 31 August 1919 (First World War, War Diary, WO95/1259/4)	WD1259_4	9781474502511	£23.00
1 DIVISION Divisional Troops Royal Army Service Corps Divisional Train (7, 13, 16, 36, Companies A.S.C.) : 17 August 1914 - 28 August 1919 (First World War, War Diary, WO95/1260)	WD1260	9781474502528	£38.00
1 DIVISION 1 Infantry Brigade Headquarters : 13 August 1914 - 31 December 1916 (First World War, War Diary, WO95/1261)	WD1261	9781474502535	£51.00
1 DIVISION 1 Infantry Brigade Headquarters : 1 January 1917 - 31 August 1919 (First World War, War Diary, WO95/1262)	WD1262	9781474502542	£44.00
1 DIVISION 1 Infantry Brigade Coldstream Guards 1 Battalion : 13 August 1914 - 31 July 1917 (First World War, War Diary, WO95/1263/1)	WD1263_1	9781474502559	£15.00
1 DIVISION 1 Infantry Brigade Scots Guards 1 Battalion : 4 August 1914 - 3 August 1915 (First World War, War Diary, WO95/1263/2)	WD1263_2	9781474502566	£15.00
1 DIVISION 1 Infantry Brigade Black Watch (Royal Highlanders) 1st Battalion : 4 August 1914 - 31 March 1919 (First World War, War Diary, WO95/1263/3)	WD1263_3	9781474502573	£27.00
1 DIVISION 1 Infantry Brigade Queen's Own Cameron Highlanders 1st Battalion : 1 October 1914 - 31 March 1919 (First World War, War Diary, WO95/1264)	WD1264	9781474502580	£66.00
1 DIVISION 1 Infantry Brigade Princess Charlotte of Wales's (Royal Berkshire Regiment) 8th Battalion, Gloucestershire Regiment 10th (Service) Battalion, Cheshire Regiment 4th Reserve Battalion, Cheshire Regiment 9th Battalion and Cheshire Regiment 52 Bat	WD1265	9781474502597	£42.00
1 DIVISION 1 Infantry Brigade Loyal North Lancashire Regiment 1st Battalion : 1 February 1918 - 16 April 1919 (First World War, War Diary, WO95/1266/1)	WD1266_1	9781474502603	£15.00
1 DIVISION 1 Infantry Brigade London Regiment 14th (County of London) Battalion (London Scottish) : 4 August 1914 - 31 January 1916 (First World War, War Diary, WO95/1266/2)	WD1266_2	9781474502610	£17.00

Title	Product Code	ISBN	Price
1 DIVISION 1 Infantry Brigade Trench Mortar Battery : 2 July 1917 - 31 December 1918 (First World War, War Diary, WO95/1266/3)	WD1266_3	9781474502627	£15.00
1 DIVISION 1 Infantry Brigade Machine Gun Company : 23 January 1916 - 28 February 1918 (First World War, War Diary, WO95/1266/4)	WD1266_4	9781474502634	£15.00
1 DIVISION 2 Infantry Brigade Headquarters : 4 August 1914 - 31 December 1916 (First World War, War Diary, WO95/1267)	WD1267	9781474502641	£51.00
1 DIVISION 2 Infantry Brigade Headquarters : 1 January 1917 - 31 December 1918 (First World War, War Diary, WO95/1268/1)	WD1268_1	9781474502658	£48.00
1 DIVISION 2 Infantry Brigade Headquarters : 1 January 1919 - 30 July 1919 (First World War, War Diary, WO95/1268/2)	WD1268_2	9781474502665	£15.00
1 DIVISION 2 Infantry Brigade Royal Sussex Regiment 2nd Battalion : 25 January 1914 - 12 April 1919 (First World War, War Diary, WO95/1269/1)	WD1269_1	9781474502672	£45.00
1 DIVISION 2 Infantry Brigade Royal Sussex Regiment 1/5 Battalion : 16 February 1915 - 29 August 1915 (First World War, War Diary, WO95/1269/2)	WD1269_2	9781474502689	£15.00
1 DIVISION 2 Infantry Brigade King's (Liverpool Regiment) 9th Battalion : 12 March 1915 - 31 December 1915 (First World War, War Diary, WO95/1269/3)	WD1269_3	9781474502696	£15.00
1 DIVISION 2 Infantry Brigade Loyal North Lancashire Regiment 1st Battalion : 5 August 1914 - 31 January 1918 (First World War, War Diary, WO95/1270)	WD1270	9781474502702	£39.00
1 DIVISION 2 Infantry Brigade Northamptonshire Regiment 1st Battalion : 12 August 1914 - 20 May 1919 (First World War, War Diary, WO95/1271)	WD1271	9781474502719	£29.00
1 DIVISION 2 Infantry Brigade King's Royal Rifle Corps 2nd Battalion : 4 August 1914 - 3 December 1916 (First World War, War Diary, WO95/1272)	WD1272	9781474502726	£65.00
1 DIVISION 2 Infantry Brigade King's Royal Rifle Corps 2nd Battalion, Welsh Regiment 51st Battalion, Welsh Regiment 52nd Battalion, Welsh Regiment 53rd Battalion, Trench Mortar Battery and Machine Gun Company : 26 January 1916 - 28 February 1918 (First	WD1273	9781474502733	£35.00
1 DIVISION 3 Infantry Brigade Headquarters : 12 August 1914 - 31 December 1914 (First World War, War Diary, WO95/1274)	WD1274	9781474502740	£61.00
1 DIVISION 3 Infantry Brigade Headquarters : 1 November 1914 - 30 June 1916 (First World War, War Diary, WO95/1275)	WD1275	9781474502757	£45.00
1 DIVISION 3 Infantry Brigade Headquarters : 1 July 1916 - 31 December 1917 (First World War, War Diary, WO95/1276)	WD1276	9781474502764	£42.00
1 DIVISION 3 Infantry Brigade Headquarters : 1 January 1918 - 26 August 1919 (First World War, War Diary, WO95/1277)	WD1277	9781474502771	£66.00
1 DIVISION 3 Infantry Brigade Gloucestershire Regiment 1st Battalion : 11 August 1914 - 30 April 1919 (First World War, War Diary, WO95/1278)	WD1278	9781474502788	£36.00
1 DIVISION 3 Infantry Brigade Royal Munster Fusiliers 2nd Battalion : 13 August 1914 - 31 January 1918 (First World War, War Diary, WO95/1279)	WD1279	9781474502795	£46.00
1 DIVISION 3 Infantry Brigade Queen's (Royal West Surrey Regiment) 1st Battalion : 4 August 1914 - 31 December 1914 (First World War, War Diary, WO95/1280/1)	WD1280_1	9781474502801	£15.00
1 DIVISION 3 Infantry Brigade Royal Welsh Fusiliers 4 Battalion : 5 November 1914 - 31 August 1915 (First World War, War Diary, WO95/1280/2)	WD1280_2	9781474502818	£15.00

Title	Product Code	ISBN	Price
1 DIVISION 3 Infantry Brigade South Wales Borderers 1st Battalion : 4 August 1914 - 11 June 1919 (First World War, War Diary, WO95/1280/3)	WD1280_3	9781474502825	£42.00
1 DIVISION 3 Infantry Brigade Welsh Regiment 2nd Battalion : 5 August 1914 - 30 April 1919 (First World War, War Diary, WO95/1281)	WD1281	9781474502832	£67.00
1 DIVISION 3 Infantry Brigade Welsh Regiment 1/6th Battalion, South Wales Borderers 51st, 52nd and 53rd (Grad) Battalions, Light Trench Mortar Battery and Machine Gun Company : 1 August 1915 - 28 February 1918 (First World War, War Diary, WO95/1282)	WD1282	9781474502849	£33.00

Title	Product Code	ISBN	Price
1 INDIAN CAVALRY DIVISION			
1 INDIAN CAVALRY DIVISION Headquarters, Branches and Services General Staff : 30 August 1914 - 31 August 1915 (First World War, War Diary, WO95/1167)	WD1167	9781474501347	£72.00
1 INDIAN CAVALRY DIVISION Headquarters, Branches and Services Adjutant and Quarter-Master General : 16 October 1914 - 31 December 1916 (First World War, War Diary, WO95/1168/1)	WD1168_1	9781474501354	£26.00
1 INDIAN CAVALRY DIVISION Headquarters, Branches and Services Royal Army Medical Corps Assistant Director Medical Services : 11 September 1914 - 31 December 1916 (First World War, War Diary, WO95/1168/2)	WD1168_2	9781474501361	£37.00
1 INDIAN CAVALRY DIVISION Headquarters, Branches and Services Commander Royal Engineers : 7 November 1914 - 28 February 1915 (First World War, War Diary, WO95/1169/1)	WD1169_1	9781474501378	£15.00
1 INDIAN CAVALRY DIVISION Headquarters, Branches and Services Royal Army Ordnance Corps Deputy Assistant Director Ordnance Services : 9 November 1914 - 30 December 1916 (First World War, War Diary, WO95/1169/2)	WD1169_2	9781474501385	£15.00
1 INDIAN CAVALRY DIVISION Headquarters, Branches and Services Royal Army Veterinary Corps Assistant Director Veterinary Services : 1 July 1916 - 31 December 1916 (First World War, War Diary, WO95/1169/3)	WD1169_3	9781474501392	£15.00
1 INDIAN CAVALRY DIVISION Headquarters, Branches and Services Royal Army Service Corps Assistant Director Supply and Transport : 11 September 1914 - 30 September 1916 (First World War, War Diary, WO95/1169/4)	WD1169_4	9781474501408	£15.00
1 INDIAN CAVALRY DIVISION Divisional Troops 1 Brigade Royal Horse Artillery : 2 September 1914 - 31 December 1916 (First World War, War Diary, WO95/1170/1)	WD1170_1	9781474501415	£15.00
1 INDIAN CAVALRY DIVISION Divisional Troops Rouse's Brigade Royal Horse Artillery : 1 September 1914 - 26 November 1914 (First World War, War Diary, WO95/1170/2)	WD1170_2	9781474501422	£15.00
1 INDIAN CAVALRY DIVISION Divisional Troops Divisional Ammunition Column : 31 August 1914 - 31 December 1916 (First World War, War Diary, WO95/1170/3)	WD1170_3	9781474501439	£15.00
1 INDIAN CAVALRY DIVISION Divisional Troops 1 Indian Field Squadron Royal Engineers : 2 February 1915 - 31 December 1916 (First World War, War Diary, WO95/1170/4)	WD1170_4	9781474501446	£15.00
1 INDIAN CAVALRY DIVISION Divisional Troops 2 Field Troop Sappers and Miners : 10 September 1914 - 30 November 1915 (First World War, War Diary, WO95/1170/5)	WD1170_5	9781474501453	£15.00
1 INDIAN CAVALRY DIVISION Divisional Troops Divisional Signal Squadron : 28 December 1914 - 31 December 1916 (First World War, War Diary, WO95/1170/6)	WD1170_6	9781474501460	£15.00
1 INDIAN CAVALRY DIVISION Divisional Troops Sialkot Cavalry Field Ambulance, 104 (Mhow) Cavalry Field Ambulance, Lucknow Cavalry Field Ambulance, Jodhpur Cavalry Field Ambulance and Divisional Sanitary Section : 1 September 1914 - 31 December 1915 (First	WD1171	9781474501477	£68.00

Title	Product Code	ISBN	Price
1 INDIAN CAVALRY DIVISION Divisional Troops Headquarters Army Service Corps. (426 Company A.S.C.), Supply Officer Army Service Corps, Auxiliary Horse Transport Company (577 Company A.S.C.), Divisional Ammunition Park (79 Company A.S.C.) and Divisional Amb	WD1172	9781474501484	£51.00
1 INDIAN CAVALRY DIVISION Divisional Troops Divisional Supply Column (89 Company A.S.C.) : 30 July 1914 - 30 September 1915 (First World War, War Diary, WO95/1173A)	WD1173_A	9781474521536	£59.00
1 INDIAN CAVALRY DIVISION Divisional Troops Divisional Supply Column (89 Company A.S.C.) : 1 October 1915 - 31 December 1916 (First World War, War Diary, WO95/1173B)	WD1173_B	9781474521543	£55.00
1 INDIAN CAVALRY DIVISION Lucknow Cavalry Brigade Headquarters : 11 August 1914 - 31 December 1916 (First World War, War Diary, WO95/1174/1)	WD1174_1	9781474501491	£17.00
1 INDIAN CAVALRY DIVISION Lucknow Cavalry Brigade Corps of Dragoons. 1st King's Dragoon Guards : 31 August 1914 - 31 December 1916 (First World War, War Diary, WO95/1174/2)	WD1174_2	9781474501507	£15.00
1 INDIAN CAVALRY DIVISION Lucknow Cavalry Brigade 29 Lancers : 10 August 1914 - 31 December 1916 (First World War, War Diary, WO95/1174/3)	WD1174_3	9781474501514	£15.00
1 INDIAN CAVALRY DIVISION Lucknow Cavalry Brigade 36 Jacobs Horse : 31 August 1914 - 31 December 1916 (First World War, War Diary, WO95/1174/4)	WD1174_4	9781474501521	£15.00
1 INDIAN CAVALRY DIVISION Lucknow Cavalry Brigade `U' Battery Royal Horse Artillery : 31 August 1914 - 31 December 1916 (First World War, War Diary, WO95/1175/1)	WD1175_1	9781474501538	£15.00
1 INDIAN CAVALRY DIVISION Lucknow Cavalry Brigade `G' Ammunition Column Royal Horse Artillery : 31 August 1914 - 27 March 1915 (First World War, War Diary, WO95/1175/2)	WD1175_2	9781474501545	£15.00
1 INDIAN CAVALRY DIVISION Lucknow Cavalry Brigade, Brigade Signal Troop : 3 August 1914 - 31 December 1916 (First World War, War Diary, WO95/1175/3)	WD1175_3	9781474501552	£15.00
1 INDIAN CAVALRY DIVISION Lucknow Cavalry Brigade Machine Gun Squadron : 12 January 1916 - 31 December 1916 (First World War, War Diary, WO95/1175/4)	WD1175_4	9781474501569	£15.00
1 INDIAN CAVALRY DIVISION Lucknow Cavalry Brigade Royal Army Veterinary Corps Mobile Veterinary Section : 20 November 1914 - 31 December 1916 (First World War, War Diary, WO95/1175/5)	WD1175_5	9781474501576	£15.00
1 INDIAN CAVALRY DIVISION Lucknow Cavalry Brigade, Brigade Supply Officer and Brigade Transport Officer : 30 July 1914 - 28 September 1916 (First World War, War Diary, WO95/1175/6)	WD1175_6	9781474501583	£15.00
1 INDIAN CAVALRY DIVISION Mhow Cavalry Brigade Headquarters, 2 Lancers (Gardner's Horse), 6th Dragoons (Inniskilling), 38 Central Indian Horse and `A' Battery (Chestnut Troop) Royal Horse Artillery : 8 January 1914 - 16 December 1916 (First World War, Wa	WD1176	9781474501590	£43.00
1 INDIAN CAVALRY DIVISION Mhow Cavalry Brigade, Brigade Signal Troop, Brigade Machine Gun Squadron, Mhow Pioneer Battalion, Royal Army Veterinary Corps Mobile Veterinary Section, Brigade Supply Officer and Brigade Transport Officer : 19 December 1914 - 30	WD1177	9781474501606	£22.00

Title	Product Code	ISBN	Price
1 INDIAN CAVALRY DIVISION Sialkot Cavalry Brigade Headquarters, 6 (King Edward's Own) Cavalry, 17th Lancers (Duke of Cambridge's Own) and 19 Lancers : 30 August 1914 - 31 December 1916 (First World War, War Diary, WO95/1178)	WD1178	9781474501613	£37.00
1 INDIAN CAVALRY DIVISION Sialkot Cavalry Brigade `Q' Battery Royal Horse Artillery, Brigade Signal Troop, Machine Gun Squadron, Royal Army Veterinary Corps Mobile Veterinary Section, Brigade Supply Officer and Brigade Transport Officer : 17 August 1914 -	WD1179	9781474501620	£36.00

Title	Product Code	ISBN	Price
11 DIVISION			
11 DIVISION Headquarters, Branches and Services General Staff : 1 July 1916 - 30 April 1917 (First World War, War Diary, WO95/1787)	WD1787	9781474507837	£34.00
11 DIVISION Headquarters, Branches and Services General Staff : 1 May 1917 - 31 August 1917 (First World War, War Diary, WO95/1788)	WD1788	9781474507844	£43.00
11 DIVISION Headquarters, Branches and Services General Staff : 1 September 1917 - 7 September 1917 (First World War, War Diary, WO95/1789)	WD1789	9781474507851	£34.00
11 DIVISION Headquarters, Branches and Services General Staff : 9 March 1917 - 31 October 1917 (First World War, War Diary, WO95/1790)	WD1790	9781474507868	£49.00
11 DIVISION Headquarters, Branches and Services General Staff : 1 January 1918 - 4 June 1918 (First World War, War Diary, WO95/1791)	WD1791	9781474507875	£53.00
11 DIVISION Headquarters, Branches and Services General Staff : 1 June 1918 - 30 June 1919 (First World War, War Diary, WO95/1792)	WD1792	9781474522755	£68.00
11 DIVISION Headquarters, Branches and Services Adjutant and Quarter-Master General : 20 January 1916 - 23 December 1917 (First World War, War Diary, WO95/1793)	WD1793	9781474507882	£55.00
11 DIVISION Headquarters, Branches and Services Adjutant and Quarter-Master General : 1 January 1918 - 31 October 1918 (First World War, War Diary, WO95/1794)	WD1794	9781474507899	£66.00
11 DIVISION Headquarters, Branches and Services Adjutant and Quarter-Master General : 1 November 1918 - 31 May 1919 (First World War, War Diary, WO95/1795)	WD1795	9781474522762	£78.00
11 DIVISION Headquarters, Branches and Services Commander Royal Artillery : 3 July 1916 - 2 December 1917 (First World War, War Diary, WO95/1796)	WD1796	9781474507905	£43.00
11 DIVISION Headquarters, Branches and Services Commander Royal Artillery : 1 January 1918 - 31 March 1919 (First World War, War Diary, WO95/1797)	WD1797	9781474507912	£52.00
11 DIVISION Headquarters, Branches and Services Royal Army Medical Corps Assistant Director Medical Services : 7 July 1916 - 30 April 1919 (First World War, War Diary, WO95/1798)	WD1798	9781474507929	£56.00
11 DIVISION Headquarters, Branches and Services Commander Royal Engineers, Royal Army Ordnance Corps Deputy Assistant Director Ordnance Services and Branches and Services Royal Army Veterinary Corps Deputy Assistant Director Veterinary Services : 28 June	WD1799	9781474507936	£31.00
11 DIVISION Divisional Troops 58 Brigade Royal Field Artillery : 2 July 1916 - 30 June 1917 (First World War, War Diary, WO95/1800)	WD1800	9781474507943	£38.00
11 DIVISION Divisional Troops 58 Brigade Royal Field Artillery : 1 October 1917 - 31 December 1918 (First World War, War Diary, WO95/1801)	WD1801	9781474507950	£59.00
11 DIVISION Divisional Troops 59 Brigade Royal Field Artillery, 60 Brigade Royal Field Artillery, 118 Brigade Royal Field Artillery, 133 Brigade Royal Field Artillery, Divisional Ammunition Column and Divisional Trench Mortar Batteries : 1 July 1916 - 30	WD1802	9781474507967	£48.00
11 DIVISION Divisional Troops 67 Field Company Royal Engineers, 68 Field Company Royal Engineers, 86 Field Company Royal Engineers and Divisional Signal Company : 1 June 1916 - 30 June 1919 (First World War, War Diary, WO95/1803)	WD1803	9781474507974	£38.00

Title	Product Code	ISBN	Price
11 DIVISION Divisional Troops East Yorkshire Regiment 6th Battalion Pioneers, 250 Machine Gun Company, Machine Gun Corps 11 Battalion and Divisional Train (479, 480, 481, 482, Companies A.S.C.) : 1 July 1916 - 31 May 1919 (First World War, War Diary, WO	WD1804	9781474522779	£58.00
11 DIVISION Divisional Troops Royal Army Medical Corps 33, 34 and 35 Field Ambulance, 21 Sanitary Section and 22 Mobile Veterinary Sections : 1 April 1916 - 11 April 1919 (First World War, War Diary, WO95/1805)	WD1805	9781474507981	£55.00
11 DIVISION 32 Infantry Brigade Headquarters : 1 July 1916 - 31 December 1916 (First World War, War Diary, WO95/1806)	WD1806	9781474507998	£49.00
11 DIVISION 32 Infantry Brigade Headquarters : 1 January 1915 - 30 September 1917 (First World War, War Diary, WO95/1807)	WD1807	9781474522786	£60.00
11 DIVISION 32 Infantry Brigade Headquarters : 1 October 1917 - 30 June 1919 (First World War, War Diary, WO95/1808)	WD1808	9781474508001	£59.00
11 DIVISION 32 Infantry Brigade Duke of Wellington's (West Riding Regiment) 8th Battalion, Prince of Wales's Own (West Yorkshire Regiment) 9th Battalion, Alexandra, Princess of Wales's Own (Yorkshire Regiment) 2nd Battalion, Alexandra, Princess of Wales'	WD1809	9781474508018	£48.00
11 DIVISION 33 Infantry Brigade Headquarters : 1 July 1916 - 30 June 1917 (First World War, War Diary, WO95/1810)	WD1810	9781474508025	£56.00
11 DIVISION 33 Infantry Brigade Headquarters : 1 July 1917 - 28 February 1918 (First World War, War Diary, WO95/1811)	WD1811	9781474508032	£40.00
11 DIVISION 33 Infantry Brigade Headquarters : 1 March 1918 - 30 June 1919 (First World War, War Diary, WO95/1812)	WD1812	9781474508049	£57.00
11 DIVISION 33 Infantry Brigade Sherwood Foresters (Nottinghamshire and Derbyshire Regiment) 9th Battalion : 1 July 1916 - 31 July 1917 (First World War, War Diary, WO95/1813)	WD1813	9781474508056	£52.00
11 DIVISION 33 Infantry Brigade Sherwood Foresters (Nottinghamshire and Derbyshire Regiment) 9th Battalion : 1 August 1917 - 31 December 1917 (First World War, War Diary, WO95/1814)	WD1814	9781474508063	£50.00
11 DIVISION 33 Infantry Brigade Sherwood Foresters (Nottinghamshire and Derbyshire Regiment) 9th Battalion : 1 January 1918 - 30 March 1919 (First World War, War Diary, WO95/1815)	WD1815	9781474508070	£54.00
11 DIVISION 33 Infantry Brigade South Staffordshire Regiment 7th Service Battalion : 28 June 1916 - 30 April 1919 (First World War, War Diary, WO95/1816)	WD1816	9781474508087	£46.00
11 DIVISION 33 Infantry Brigade Border Regiment 6th Battalion, Lincolnshire Regiment 6th Battalion, Brigade Machine Gun Company and Brigade Trench Mortar Battery : 1 July 1916 - 30 November 1916 (First World War, War Diary, WO95/1817)	WD1817	9781474508094	£43.00
11 DIVISION 34 Infantry Brigade Headquarters : 1 July 1916 - 31 December 1917 (First World War, War Diary, WO95/1818)	WD1818	9781474508100	£31.00
11 DIVISION 34 Infantry Brigade Headquarters : 1 January 1918 - 31 March 1919 (First World War, War Diary, WO95/1819)	WD1819	9781474508117	£34.00
11 DIVISION 34 Infantry Brigade Dorsetshire Regiment 5th Battalion and Lancashire Fusiliers 9th Battalion : 2 July 1916 - 21 February 1918 (First World War, War Diary, WO95/1820)	WD1820	9781474508124	£45.00

Title	Product Code	ISBN	Price
11 DIVISION 34 Infantry Brigade Manchester Regiment 11th Battalion, Northumberland Fusiliers 8th Battalion, Brigade Machine Gun Company and Brigade Trench Mortar Battery : 1 July 1916 - 31 August 1916 (First World War, War Diary, WO95/1821)	WD1821	9781474508131	£48.00

Title	Product Code	ISBN	Price
12 DIVISION			
12 DIVISION Headquarters, Branches and Services General Staff : 29 May 1915 - 31 December 1915 (First World War, War Diary, WO95/1822)	WD1822	9781474508148	£44.00
12 DIVISION Headquarters, Branches and Services General Staff : 1 January 1916 - 30 August 1916 (First World War, War Diary, WO95/1823)	WD1823	9781474508155	£46.00
12 DIVISION Headquarters, Branches and Services General Staff : 1 September 1916 - 30 June 1917 (First World War, War Diary, WO95/1824)	WD1824	9781474508162	£51.00
12 DIVISION Headquarters, Branches and Services General Staff : 1 July 1917 - 31 December 1917 (First World War, War Diary, WO95/1825)	WD1825	9781474522793	£64.00
12 DIVISION Headquarters, Branches and Services General Staff : 1 January 1918 - 3 July 1918 (First World War, War Diary, WO95/1826)	WD1826	9781474522809	£68.00
12 DIVISION Headquarters, Branches and Services General Staff : 1 August 1918 - 27 June 1919 (First World War, War Diary, WO95/1827)	WD1827	9781474508179	£28.00
12 DIVISION Headquarters, Branches and Services Adjutant and Quarter-Master General : 29 May 1915 - 27 June 1919 (First World War, War Diary, WO95/1828)	WD1828	9781474508186	£42.00
12 DIVISION Headquarters, Branches and Services Adjutant and Quarter-Master General Appendices : 2 June 1915 - 1 May 1917 (First World War, War Diary, WO95/1829)	WD1829	9781474508193	£62.00
12 DIVISION Headquarters, Branches and Services Adjutant and Quarter-Master General Appendices : 1 August 1916 - 30 April 1917 (First World War, War Diary, WO95/1830)	WD1830	9781474508209	£57.00
12 DIVISION Headquarters, Branches and Services Commander Royal Artillery : 25 May 1915 - 30 December 1916 (First World War, War Diary, WO95/1831)	WD1831	9781474508216	£43.00
12 DIVISION Headquarters, Branches and Services Commander Royal Artillery : 1 January 1917 - 31 December 1917 (First World War, War Diary, WO95/1832)	WD1832	9781474508223	£51.00
12 DIVISION Headquarters, Branches and Services Commander Royal Artillery : 1 January 1918 - 31 May 1919 (First World War, War Diary, WO95/1833)	WD1833	9781474508230	£30.00
12 DIVISION Headquarters, Branches and Services Royal Army Medical Corps Assistant Director Medical Services : 28 May 1915 - 30 November 1917 (First World War, War Diary, WO95/1834A)	WD1834_A	9781474522816	£52.00
12 DIVISION Headquarters, Branches and Services Royal Army Medical Corps Assistant Director Medical Services : 1 December 1917 - 31 May 1919 (First World War, War Diary, WO95/1834B)	WD1834_B	9781474522823	£44.00
12 DIVISION Headquarters, Branches and Services Commander Royal Engineers, Deputy Assistant Director Ordnance Services and Assistant Director Veterinary Services : 1 February 1915 - 31 March 1919 (First World War, War Diary, WO95/1835)	WD1835	9781474522830	£66.00
12 DIVISION Divisional Troops A Squadron King Edward's Horse, Divisional Cyclist Company and 62 Brigade Royal Field Artillery : 1 January 1915 - 31 December 1916 (First World War, War Diary, WO95/1836)	WD1836	9781474508247	£42.00
12 DIVISION Divisional Troops 62 Brigade Royal Field Artillery : 1 January 1917 - 5 June 1919 (First World War, War Diary, WO95/1837)	WD1837	9781474508254	£36.00

Title	Product Code	ISBN	Price
12 DIVISION Divisional Troops 63 Brigade Royal Field Artillery, 64 Brigade Royal Field Artillery and 65 Brigade Royal Field Artillery : 29 May 1915 - 31 August 1916 (First World War, War Diary, WO95/1838)	WD1838	9781474522847	£66.00
12 DIVISION Divisional Troops Divisional Trench Mortar Batteries and Divisional Ammunition Column : 2 June 1915 - 31 May 1919 (First World War, War Diary, WO95/1839)	WD1839	9781474508261	£50.00
12 DIVISION Divisional Troops 69 Field Company Royal Engineers and 70 Field Company Royal Engineers : 31 May 1915 - 10 May 1919 (First World War, War Diary, WO95/1840)	WD1840	9781474508278	£22.00
12 DIVISION Divisional Troops 87 Field Company Royal Engineers and Divisional Signal Company : 14 February 1915 - 20 June 1919 (First World War, War Diary, WO95/1841)	WD1841	9781474508285	£36.00
12 DIVISION Divisional Troops Northamptonshire Regiment 5th Battalion Pioneers, 198 Machine Gun Company, 235 Machine Gun Company and Machine Gun Corps 12 Battalion : 28 May 1915 - 1 May 1919 (First World War, War Diary, WO95/1842)	WD1842	9781474508292	£36.00
12 DIVISION Divisional Troops Royal Army Medical Corps 36 Field Ambulance and 37 Field Ambulance : 29 May 1915 - 30 April 1919 (First World War, War Diary, WO95/1843)	WD1843	9781474508308	£66.00
12 DIVISION Divisional Troops Royal Army Medical Corps 38 Field Ambulance, 23 Sanitary Section and Divisional Field Ambulance Workshop : 1 June 1914 - 31 January 1916 (First World War, War Diary, WO95/1844)	WD1844	9781474508315	£41.00
12 DIVISION Divisional Troops Royal Army Veterinary Corps 23 Mobile Veterinary Section and Divisional Train (116, 117, 118, 119 Companies A.S.C.) : 28 May 1915 - 31 May 1919 (First World War, War Diary, WO95/1845)	WD1845	9781474522854	£55.00
12 DIVISION 35 Infantry Brigade Headquarters : 1 September 1914 - 1 July 1916 (First World War, War Diary, WO95/1846)	WD1846	9781474508322	£51.00
12 DIVISION 35 Infantry Brigade Headquarters : 26 June 1916 - 31 December 1916 (First World War, War Diary, WO95/1847)	WD1847	9781474508339	£50.00
12 DIVISION 35 Infantry Brigade Headquarters : 1 January 1917 - 31 December 1917 (First World War, War Diary, WO95/1848)	WD1848	9781474508346	£39.00
12 DIVISION 35 Infantry Brigade Headquarters : 1 January 1918 - 31 May 1919 (First World War, War Diary, WO95/1849)	WD1849	9781474508353	£48.00
12 DIVISION 35 Infantry Brigade Princess Charlotte of Wales's (Royal Berkshire Regiment) 5th Battalion and Cambridgeshire Regiment 1st Battalion : 30 May 1915 - 10 May 1919 (First World War, War Diary, WO95/1850)	WD1850	9781474508360	£34.00
12 DIVISION 35 Infantry Brigade Essex Regiment 9th Battalion : 24 May 1915 - 8 May 1919 (First World War, War Diary, WO95/1851)	WD1851	9781474508377	£64.00
12 DIVISION 35 Infantry Brigade Suffolk Regiment 7th Battalion : 8 May 1915 - 31 May 1919 (First World War, War Diary, WO95/1852)	WD1852	9781474508384	£58.00
12 DIVISION 35 Infantry Brigade Norfolk Regiment 7th Battalion, Brigade Machine Gun Company and Brigade Trench Mortar Battery : 29 May 1915 - 8 May 1919 (First World War, War Diary, WO95/1853)	WD1853	9781474508391	£55.00
12 DIVISION 36 Infantry Brigade Headquarters : 31 May 1915 - 31 December 1917 (First World War, War Diary, WO95/1854)	WD1854	9781474508407	£46.00

Title	Product Code	ISBN	Price
12 DIVISION 36 Infantry Brigade Headquarters : 1 January 1918 - 18 June 1919 (First World War, War Diary, WO95/1855)	WD1855	9781474508414	£53.00
12 DIVISION 36 Infantry Brigade Princess Charlotte of Wales's (Royal Berkshire Regiment) 5th Battalion, Duke of Cambridge's Own (Middlesex Regiment) 11th Battalion and Royal Sussex Regiment 7th Battalion : 1 May 1915 - 16 June 1919 (First World War, War D	WD1856	9781474508421	£59.00
12 DIVISION 36 Infantry Brigade Royal Fusiliers (City of London Regiment) 8th and 9th Battalions, Brigade Machine Gun Company and Brigade Trench Mortar Battery : 26 May 1915 - 28 August 1916 (First World War, War Diary, WO95/1857)	WD1857	9781474508438	£52.00
12 DIVISION 37 Infantry Brigade Headquarters : 30 May 1915 - 17 June 1917 (First World War, War Diary, WO95/1858)	WD1858	9781474508445	£71.00
12 DIVISION 37 Infantry Brigade Headquarters : 1 July 1917 - 31 March 1919 (First World War, War Diary, WO95/1859)	WD1859	9781474508452	£60.00
12 DIVISION 37 Infantry Brigade Buffs (East Kent Regiment) 6th Battalion : 6 January 1915 - 31 March 1919 (First World War, War Diary, WO95/1860)	WD1860	9781474522861	£54.00
12 DIVISION 37 Infantry Brigade Queen's Own (Royal West Kent Regiment) 6th Battalion : 19 August 1914 - 31 December 1916 (First World War, War Diary, WO95/1861A)	WD1861_A	9781474522878	£41.00
12 DIVISION 37 Infantry Brigade Queen's Own (Royal West Kent Regiment) 6th Battalion : 1 January 1917 - 31 July 1919 (First World War, War Diary, WO95/1861B)	WD1861_B	9781474522885	£51.00
12 DIVISION 37 Infantry Brigade East Surrey Regiment 7th Battalion : 21 February 1915 - 5 February 1918 (First World War, War Diary, WO95/1862)	WD1862	9781474508469	£54.00
12 DIVISION 37 Infantry Brigade Queen's (Royal West Surrey Regiment) 6th Battalion, Brigade Machine Gun Company and Brigade Trench Mortar Battery : 6 May 1915 - 31 August 1916 (First World War, War Diary, WO95/1863)	WD1863	9781474508476	£64.00

Title	Product Code	ISBN	Price
14 DIVISION			
14 DIVISION Headquarters, Branches and Services General Staff : 1 June 1915 - 31 May 1916 (First World War, War Diary, WO95/1864A)	WD1864_A	9781474522892	£45.00
14 DIVISION Headquarters, Branches and Services General Staff : 3 October 1915 - 31 December 1915 (First World War, War Diary, WO95/1864B)	WD1864_B	9781474522908	£54.00
14 DIVISION Headquarters, Branches and Services General Staff : 1 January 1916 - 30 June 1916 (First World War, War Diary, WO95/1865)	WD1865	9781474508483	£63.00
14 DIVISION Headquarters, Branches and Services General Staff Appendices : 5 August 1916 - 2 September 1916 (First World War, War Diary, WO95/1866)	WD1866	9781474508490	£83.00
14 DIVISION Headquarters, Branches and Services General Staff : 1 July 1916 - 31 December 1916 (First World War, War Diary, WO95/1867)	WD1867	9781474522915	£85.00
14 DIVISION Headquarters, Branches and Services General Staff : 1 January 1917 - 28 February 1917 (First World War, War Diary, WO95/1868)	WD1868	9781474508506	£82.00
14 DIVISION Headquarters, Branches and Services General Staff : 7 February 1917 - 30 April 1917 (First World War, War Diary, WO95/1869)	WD1869	9781474508513	£67.00
14 DIVISION Headquarters, Branches and Services General Staff : 1 May 1917 - 31 July 1917 (First World War, War Diary, WO95/1870)	WD1870	9781474508520	£61.00
14 DIVISION Headquarters, Branches and Services General Staff : 1 August 1917 - 29 August 1917 (First World War, War Diary, WO95/1871)	WD1871	9781474508537	£68.00
14 DIVISION Headquarters, Branches and Services General Staff : 1 September 1917 - 2 October 1917 (First World War, War Diary, WO95/1872)	WD1872	9781474508544	£56.00
14 DIVISION Headquarters, Branches and Services General Staff : 1 October 1917 - 31 December 1917 (First World War, War Diary, WO95/1873)	WD1873	9781474508551	£48.00
14 DIVISION Headquarters, Branches and Services General Staff : 1 January 1918 - 11 March 1918 (First World War, War Diary, WO95/1874)	WD1874	9781474522922	£74.00
14 DIVISION Headquarters, Branches and Services General Staff : 1 April 1918 - 31 July 1918 (First World War, War Diary, WO95/1875)	WD1875	9781474508568	£74.00
14 DIVISION Headquarters, Branches and Services General Staff : 1 September 1916 - 31 August 1918 (First World War, War Diary, WO95/1876/1-2)	WD1876	9781474508575	£80.00
14 DIVISION Headquarters, Branches and Services General Staff : 1 October 1918 - 31 October 1918 (First World War, War Diary, WO95/1877A)	WD1877_A	9781474522939	£86.00
14 DIVISION Headquarters, Branches and Services General Staff : 1 November 1918 - 24 March 1919 (First World War, War Diary, WO95/1877B)	WD1877_B	9781474522946	£24.00
14 DIVISION Headquarters, Branches and Services Adjutant and Quarter-Master General : 11 May 1915 - 31 December 1915 (First World War, War Diary, WO95/1878)	WD1878	9781474508582	£47.00
14 DIVISION Headquarters, Branches and Services Adjutant and Quarter-Master General : 1 January 1916 - 30 September 1917 (First World War, War Diary, WO95/1879/1)	WD1879_1	9781474508599	£27.00

Title	Product Code	ISBN	Price
14 DIVISION Headquarters, Branches and Services Adjutant and Quarter-Master General : 1 January 1916 - 31 December 1916 (First World War, War Diary, WO95/1879/2)	WD1879_2	9781474508605	£28.00
14 DIVISION Headquarters, Branches and Services Adjutant and Quarter-Master General : 1 October 1917 - 1 July 1919 (First World War, War Diary, WO95/1880)	WD1880	9781474508612	£56.00
14 DIVISION Headquarters, Branches and Services Commander Royal Artillery : 1 February 1915 - 30 September 1916 (First World War, War Diary, WO95/1881)	WD1881	9781474522953	£65.00
14 DIVISION Headquarters, Branches and Services Commander Royal Artillery : 1 October 1916 - 31 August 1917 (First World War, War Diary, WO95/1882)	WD1882	9781474508629	£58.00
14 DIVISION Headquarters, Branches and Services Commander Royal Artillery : 1 September 1917 - 25 June 1919 (First World War, War Diary, WO95/1883)	WD1883	9781474522960	£68.00
14 DIVISION Headquarters, Branches and Services Royal Army Medical Corps Assistant Director Medical Services : 1 March 1915 - 30 November 1918 (First World War, War Diary, WO95/1884/1)	WD1884_1	9781474508636	£28.00
14 DIVISION Headquarters, Branches and Services Commander Royal Engineers : 19 May 1915 - 20 April 1919 (First World War, War Diary, WO95/1884/2)	WD1884_2	9781474508643	£19.00
14 DIVISION Headquarters, Branches and Services Royal Army Ordnance Corps Deputy Assistant Director Ordnance Services : 9 May 1915 - 31 May 1919 (First World War, War Diary, WO95/1885/1)	WD1885_1	9781474508650	£22.00
14 DIVISION Headquarters, Branches and Services Royal Army Veterinary Corps Assistant Director Veterinary Services : 1 May 1915 - 28 February 1919 (First World War, War Diary, WO95/1885/2)	WD1885_2	9781474508667	£23.00
14 DIVISION Divisional Troops D Squadron Duke of Lancaster's Own Yeomanry : 23 May 1915 - 31 May 1916 (First World War, War Diary, WO95/1886/1)	WD1886_1	9781474508674	£15.00
14 DIVISION Divisional Troops Divisional Cyclist Company : 1 July 1915 - 11 May 1916 (First World War, War Diary, WO95/1886/2)	WD1886_2	9781474508681	£15.00
14 DIVISION Divisional Troops 46 Brigade Royal Field Artillery : 19 May 1915 - 9 June 1919 (First World War, War Diary, WO95/1886/3)	WD1886_3	9781474508698	£36.00
14 DIVISION Divisional Troops 47 Brigade Royal Field Artillery, 48 Brigade Royal Field Artillery and 49 Brigade Royal Field Artillery : 18 May 1915 - 4 October 1916 (First World War, War Diary, WO95/1887)	WD1887	9781474508704	£62.00
14 DIVISION Divisional Troops Divisional Trench Mortar Batteries : 24 June 1915 - 29 January 1919 (First World War, War Diary, WO95/1888/1)	WD1888_1	9781474508711	£15.00
14 DIVISION Divisional Troops Divisional Ammunition Column : 10 May 1915 - 18 June 1919 (First World War, War Diary, WO95/1888/2)	WD1888_2	9781474508728	£15.00
14 DIVISION Divisional Troops 61 Field Company Royal Engineers : 20 May 1915 - 31 May 1919 (First World War, War Diary, WO95/1889/1)	WD1889_1	9781474508735	£17.00
14 DIVISION Divisional Troops 62 Field Company Royal Engineers : 20 May 1915 - 16 June 1919 (First World War, War Diary, WO95/1889/2)	WD1889_2	9781474508742	£15.00
14 DIVISION Divisional Troops 89 Field Company Royal Engineers : 22 May 1915 - 17 June 1919 (First World War, War Diary, WO95/1889/3)	WD1889_3	9781474508759	£23.00

Title	Product Code	ISBN	Price
14 DIVISION Divisional Troops Divisional Signal Company : 19 May 1915 - 31 May 1919 (First World War, War Diary, WO95/1890/1)	WD1890_1	9781474508766	£17.00
14 DIVISION Divisional Troops Machine Gun Corps 14 Battalion : 14 June 1918 - 28 February 1919 (First World War, War Diary, WO95/1890/2)	WD1890_2	9781474508773	£15.00
14 DIVISION Divisional Troops 224 Machine Gun Company : 12 November 1917 - 28 February 1918 (First World War, War Diary, WO95/1890/3)	WD1890_3	9781474508780	£15.00
14 DIVISION Divisional Troops 249 Machine Gun Company : 16 July 1917 - 20 October 1917 (First World War, War Diary, WO95/1890/4)	WD1890_4	9781474508797	£15.00
14 DIVISION Divisional Troops King's (Liverpool Regiment) 11th Battalion Pioneers : 17 May 1915 - 31 May 1918 (First World War, War Diary, WO95/1890/5)	WD1890_5	9781474508803	£17.00
14 DIVISION Divisional Troops Loyal North Lancashire Regiment 15th Battalion Pioneers : 1 June 1918 - 15 June 1919 (First World War, War Diary, WO95/1890/6)	WD1890_6	9781474508810	£15.00
14 DIVISION Divisional Troops Royal Army Medical Corps 42 and 43 Field Ambulance : 12 April 1915 - 31 May 1919 (First World War, War Diary, WO95/1891)	WD1891	9781474508827	£46.00
14 DIVISION Divisional Troops Royal Army Medical Corps 44 Field Ambulance : 20 May 1915 - 30 June 1919 (First World War, War Diary, WO95/1892/1)	WD1892_1	9781474508834	£29.00
14 DIVISION Divisional Troops 25 Sanitary Section : 21 May 1915 - 31 March 1917 (First World War, War Diary, WO95/1892/2)	WD1892_2	9781474508841	£15.00
14 DIVISION Divisional Troops Royal Army Medical Corps Divisional Field Ambulance Workshop Unit : 13 May 1915 - 31 March 1916 (First World War, War Diary, WO95/1892/3)	WD1892_3	9781474508858	£15.00
14 DIVISION Divisional Troops Royal Army Veterinary Corps 26 Mobile Veterinary Section : 21 May 1915 - 26 February 1919 (First World War, War Diary, WO95/1892/4)	WD1892_4	9781474508865	£19.00
14 DIVISION Divisional Troops Royal Army Service Corps Division Train (100, 101, 102, 103 Companies (A.S.C.) : 18 May 1915 - 24 June 1919 (First World War, War Diary, WO95/1893)	WD1893	9781474508872	£63.00
14 DIVISION 41 Infantry Brigade Headquarters : 17 May 1915 - 26 March 1919 (First World War, War Diary, WO95/1894)	WD1894	9781474522977	£71.00
14 DIVISION 41 Infantry Brigade Rifle Brigade (The Prince Consort's Own) 8th Battalion : 20 May 1915 - 31 July 1918 (First World War, War Diary, WO95/1895/1)	WD1895_1	9781474508889	£28.00
14 DIVISION 41 Infantry Brigade King's Royal Rifle Corps 8th Battalion : 18 May 1915 - 30 June 1918 (First World War, War Diary, WO95/1895/2)	WD1895_2	9781474508896	£27.00
14 DIVISION 41 Infantry Brigade Durham Light Infantry 29th Battalion : 19 June 1918 - 30 April 1919 (First World War, War Diary, WO95/1895/3)	WD1895_3	9781474508902	£15.00
14 DIVISION 41 Infantry Brigade London Regiment 33rd (City of London) Battalion : 7 June 1918 - 31 May 1919 (First World War, War Diary, WO95/1895/4)	WD1895_4	9781474508919	£15.00
14 DIVISION 41 Infantry Brigade Rifle Brigade (The Prince Consort's Own) 7th Battalion : 20 May 1915 - 31 May 1918 (First World War, War Diary, WO95/1896/1)	WD1896_1	9781474508926	£22.00

Title	Product Code	ISBN	Price
14 DIVISION 41 Infantry Brigade York and Lancaster Regiment 18th (Service) Battalion : 14 June 1918 - 31 May 1919 (First World War, War Diary, WO95/1896/2)	WD1896_2	9781474508933	£15.00
14 DIVISION 41 Infantry Brigade King's Royal Rifle Corps 7th Battalion : 18 May 1915 - 26 January 1918 (First World War, War Diary, WO95/1896/3)	WD1896_3	9781474508940	£18.00
14 DIVISION 41 Infantry Brigade, Brigade Machine Gun Company : 28 January 1916 - 28 February 1918 (First World War, War Diary, WO95/1896/4)	WD1896_4	9781474508957	£15.00
14 DIVISION 41 Infantry Brigade, Brigade Light Trench Mortar Battery : 24 July 1915 - 30 August 1916 (First World War, War Diary, WO95/1896/5)	WD1896_5	9781474508964	£15.00
14 DIVISION 41 Infantry Brigade, Brigade Light Trench Mortar Battery : 1 January 1919 - 17 February 1919 (First World War, War Diary, WO95/1896/6)	WD1896_6	9781474508971	£15.00
14 DIVISION 42 Infantry Brigade Headquarters : 19 May 1915 - 23 December 1916 (First World War, War Diary, WO95/1897)	WD1897	9781474508988	£51.00
14 DIVISION 42 Infantry Brigade Headquarters : 1 January 1917 - 31 October 1917 (First World War, War Diary, WO95/1898)	WD1898	9781474508995	£46.00
14 DIVISION 42 Infantry Brigade Headquarters : 1 November 1917 - 27 November 1917 (First World War, War Diary, WO95/1899)	WD1899	9781474509008	£40.00
14 DIVISION 42 Infantry Brigade Princess Louise's (Argyll & Sutherland Highlanders) 14th Battalion : 1 April 1918 - 6 June 1919 (First World War, War Diary, WO95/1900/1)	WD1900_1	9781474509015	£15.00
14 DIVISION 42 Infantry Brigade King's Royal Rifle Corps 9th Battalion : 11 May 1915 - 28 June 1918 (First World War, War Diary, WO95/1900/2)	WD1900_2	9781474509022	£46.00
14 DIVISION 42 Infantry Brigade Manchester Regiment 16th Battalion : 4 July 1918 - 6 June 1919 (First World War, War Diary, WO95/1900/3)	WD1900_3	9781474509039	£15.00
14 DIVISION 42 Infantry Brigade Oxfordshire and Buckinghamshire Light Infantry 5th Battalion : 18 May 1915 - 20 June 1918 (First World War, War Diary, WO95/1900/4)	WD1900_4	9781474509046	£22.00
14 DIVISION 42 Infantry Brigade Rifle Brigade (The Prince Consort's Own) 9th Battalion : 31 January 1915 - 31 July 1918 (First World War, War Diary, WO95/1901)	WD1901	9781474509053	£57.00
14 DIVISION 42 Infantry Brigade King's (Shropshire Light Infantry) 5th Battalion : 9 May 1915 - 7 February 1918 (First World War, War Diary, WO95/1902/1)	WD1902_1	9781474509060	£20.00
14 DIVISION 42 Infantry Brigade Duke of Edinburgh's (Wiltshire Regiment) 6th Battalion : 1 June 1918 - 9 June 1919 (First World War, War Diary, WO95/1902/2)	WD1902_2	9781474509077	£15.00
14 DIVISION 42 Infantry Brigade, Brigade Machine Gun Company : 1 March 1916 - 28 February 1918 (First World War, War Diary, WO95/1902/3)	WD1902_3	9781474509084	£15.00
14 DIVISION 42 Infantry Brigade, Brigade Trench Mortar Battery : 28 July 1915 - 31 August 1916 (First World War, War Diary, WO95/1902/4)	WD1902_4	9781474509091	£15.00
14 DIVISION 43 Infantry Brigade Headquarters and Prince Albert's (Somerset Light Infantry) 6th Battalion : 7 May 1915 - 31 December 1915 (First World War, War Diary, WO95/1903)	WD1903	9781474509107	£53.00
14 DIVISION 43 Infantry Brigade Headquarters : 1 January 1917 - 31 August 1917 (First World War, War Diary, WO95/1904)	WD1904	9781474509114	£58.00

Title	Product Code	ISBN	Price
14 DIVISION 43 Infantry Brigade Headquarters : 1 September 1917 - 25 March 1919 (First World War, War Diary, WO95/1905)	WD1905	9781474509121	£46.00
14 DIVISION 43 Infantry Brigade King's Own (Yorkshire Light Infantry) 6th Battalion : 20 May 1915 - 28 February 1918 (First World War, War Diary, WO95/1906)	WD1906	9781474522984	£65.00
14 DIVISION 43 Infantry Brigade Durham Light Infantry 10th Battalion : 21 May 1915 - 31 March 1917 (First World War, War Diary, WO95/1907)	WD1907	9781474509138	£70.00
14 DIVISION 43 Infantry Brigade Durham Light Infantry 10th Battalion : 1 January 1917 - 3 February 1918 (First World War, War Diary, WO95/1908/1)	WD1908_1	9781474509145	£39.00
14 DIVISION 43 Infantry Brigade Duke of Cornwall's Light Infantry 6th Battalion : 7 February 1915 - 20 February 1918 (First World War, War Diary, WO95/1908/2)	WD1908_2	9781474509152	£24.00
14 DIVISION 43 Infantry Brigade Prince Albert's (Somerset Light Infantry) 6th Battalion : 21 May 1915 - 31 May 1918 (First World War, War Diary, WO95/1909)	WD1909	9781474509169	£55.00
14 DIVISION 43 Infantry Brigade Highland Light Infantry 10th (Service) Battalion : 1 June 1918 - 13 June 1919 (First World War, War Diary, WO95/1910/1)	WD1910_1	9781474509176	£15.00
14 DIVISION 43 Infantry Brigade King's Royal Rifle Corps 7th Battalion : 2 February 1918 - 31 May 1918 (First World War, War Diary, WO95/1910/2)	WD1910_2	9781474509183	£15.00
14 DIVISION 43 Infantry Brigade Duke of Cambridge's Own (Middlesex Regiment) 20th Battalion : 1 June 1918 - 18 June 1919 (First World War, War Diary, WO95/1910/3)	WD1910_3	9781474509190	£21.00
14 DIVISION 43 Infantry Brigade Suffolk Regiment 12th Battalion : 1 June 1918 - 31 May 1919 (First World War, War Diary, WO95/1910/4)	WD1910_4	9781474509206	£15.00
14 DIVISION 43 Infantry Brigade, Brigade Machine Gun Company : 16 February 1916 - 28 February 1918 (First World War, War Diary, WO95/1910/5)	WD1910_5	9781474509213	£15.00
14 DIVISION 43 Infantry Brigade, Brigade Trench Mortar Battery : 21 August 1915 - 30 July 1916 (First World War, War Diary, WO95/1910/6)	WD1910_6	9781474509220	£15.00
14 DIVISION 43 Infantry Brigade, Brigade Trench Mortar Battery : 5 July 1918 - 30 September 1918 (First World War, War Diary, WO95/1910/7)	WD1910_7	9781474509237	£15.00

Title	Product Code	ISBN	Price
15 DIVISION			
15 DIVISION Headquarters, Branches and Services General Staff : 6 August 1915 - 24 December 1915 (First World War, War Diary, WO95/1911/1)	WD1911_1	9781474509244	£15.00
15 DIVISION Headquarters, Branches and Services General Staff : 3 July 1915 - 30 July 1915 (First World War, War Diary, WO95/1911/2)	WD1911_2	9781474509251	£15.00
15 DIVISION Headquarters, Branches and Services General Staff : 21 September 1915 - 25 October 1915 (First World War, War Diary, WO95/1911/3-4)	WD1911_3-4	9781474509268	£15.00
15 DIVISION Headquarters, Branches and Services General Staff : 1 September 1915 - 30 September 1915 (First World War, War Diary, WO95/1911/5)	WD1911_5	9781474509275	£24.00
15 DIVISION Headquarters, Branches and Services General Staff : 21 September 1915 - 13 October 1915 (First World War, War Diary, WO95/1911/6)	WD1911_6	9781474509282	£15.00
15 DIVISION Headquarters, Branches and Services General Staff : 1 June 1915 - 31 October 1915 (First World War, War Diary, WO95/1912)	WD1912	9781474509299	£64.00
15 DIVISION Headquarters, Branches and Services General Staff : 1 September 1916 - 30 September 1916 (First World War, War Diary, WO95/1913/1)	WD1913_1	9781474509305	£15.00
15 DIVISION Headquarters, Branches and Services General Staff : 7 August 1916 - 11 August 1917 (First World War, War Diary, WO95/1913/2)	WD1913_2	9781474509312	£15.00
15 DIVISION Headquarters, Branches and Services General Staff : 1 July 1916 - 31 December 1916 (First World War, War Diary, WO95/1913/3)	WD1913_3	9781474509329	£47.00
15 DIVISION Headquarters, Branches and Services General Staff : 1 January 1917 - 31 July 1917 (First World War, War Diary, WO95/1914)	WD1914	9781474522991	£64.00
15 DIVISION Headquarters, Branches and Services General Staff : 1 August 1917 - 30 June 1918 (First World War, War Diary, WO95/1915)	WD1915	9781474509336	£56.00
15 DIVISION Headquarters, Branches and Services General Staff : 1 July 1918 - 26 March 1919 (First World War, War Diary, WO95/1916)	WD1916	9781474509343	£40.00
15 DIVISION Headquarters, Branches and Services Adjutant and Quarter-Master General : 19 February 1916 - 31 July 1917 (First World War, War Diary, WO95/1917)	WD1917	9781474509350	£67.00
15 DIVISION Headquarters, Branches and Services Adjutant and Quarter-Master General : 1 August 1917 - 27 June 1919 (First World War, War Diary, WO95/1918)	WD1918	9781474509367	£53.00
15 DIVISION Headquarters, Branches and Services Commander Royal Artillery : 4 July 1915 - 9 June 1919 (First World War, War Diary, WO95/1919)	WD1919	9781474509374	£55.00
15 DIVISION Headquarters, Branches and Services Royal Army Medical Corps Assistant Director Medical Services : 7 July 1915 - 31 December 1916 (First World War, War Diary, WO95/1920)	WD1920	9781474523004	£77.00
15 DIVISION Headquarters, Branches and Services Commander Royal Engineers : 4 July 1915 - 30 June 1919 (First World War, War Diary, WO95/1921)	WD1921	9781474509381	£51.00
15 DIVISION Headquarters, Branches and Services Royal Army Ordnance Corps Deputy Assistant Director Ordnance Services : 4 July 1915 - 27 June 1919 (First World War, War Diary, WO95/1922/1)	WD1922_1	9781474509398	£15.00

Title	Product Code	ISBN	Price
15 DIVISION Headquarters, Branches and Services Royal Army Veterinary Corps Assistant Director Veterinary Services : 1 July 1915 - 2 April 1919 (First World War, War Diary, WO95/1922/2)	WD1922_2	9781474509404	£42.00
15 DIVISION Divisional Troops B Squadron 1/1 Westmorland and Cumberland Yeomanry : 19 June 1915 - 27 April 1917 (First World War, War Diary, WO95/1923/1)	WD1923_1	9781474509411	£15.00
15 DIVISION Divisional Troops Divisional Cyclist Company : 3 August 1915 - 29 May 1916 (First World War, War Diary, WO95/1923/2)	WD1923_2	9781474509428	£15.00
15 DIVISION Divisional Troops 70 Brigade Royal Field Artillery : 3 July 1915 - 28 February 1919 (First World War, War Diary, WO95/1923/3)	WD1923_3	9781474509435	£22.00
15 DIVISION Divisional Troops 71 Brigade Royal Field Artillery : 3 July 1915 - 31 May 1919 (First World War, War Diary, WO95/1923/4)	WD1923_4	9781474509442	£20.00
15 DIVISION Divisional Troops 72 Brigade Royal Field Artillery : 9 July 1915 - 31 December 1916 (First World War, War Diary, WO95/1924/1)	WD1924_1	9781474523011	£15.00
15 DIVISION Divisional Troops 73 Brigade Royal Field Artillery : 4 July 1915 - 2 December 1916 (First World War, War Diary, WO95/1924/2)	WD1924_2	9781474523028	£15.00
15 DIVISION Divisional Troops Divisional Trench Mortar Batteries : 1 July 1916 - 8 February 1919 (First World War, War Diary, WO95/1924/3)	WD1924_3	9781474523035	£15.00
15 DIVISION Divisional Troops Divisional Ammunition Column : 3 July 1915 - 30 May 1919 (First World War, War Diary, WO95/1924/4)	WD1924_4	9781474523042	£15.00
15 DIVISION Divisional Troops 73 Field Company Royal Engineers : 9 July 1915 - 26 June 1919 (First World War, War Diary, WO95/1925)	WD1925	9781474509459	£62.00
15 DIVISION Divisional Troops 74 Field Company Royal Engineers : 4 July 1915 - 30 June 1919 (First World War, War Diary, WO95/1926)	WD1926	9781474509466	£54.00
15 DIVISION Divisional Troops 91 Field Company Royal Engineers : 10 July 1915 - 30 June 1919 (First World War, War Diary, WO95/1927)	WD1927	9781474509473	£56.00
15 DIVISION Divisional Troops Divisional Signal Company : 4 July 1915 - 27 April 1917 (First World War, War Diary, WO95/1928)	WD1928	9781474509480	£45.00
15 DIVISION Divisional Troops Gordon Highlanders 9th Battalion : 7 July 1915 - 27 April 1918 (First World War, War Diary, WO95/1929)	WD1929	9781474523059	£80.00
15 DIVISION Divisional Troops Gordon Highlanders 9th Battalion : 3 May 1918 - 12 June 1919 (First World War, War Diary, WO95/1930/1)	WD1930_1	9781474509497	£46.00
15 DIVISION Divisional Troops Machine Gun Corps 15 Battalion Machine Gun Corps : 17 March 1918 - 31 March 1919 (First World War, War Diary, WO95/1930/2)	WD1930_2	9781474509503	£18.00
15 DIVISION Divisional Troops 225 Machine Gun Company : 10 July 1917 - 28 February 1918 (First World War, War Diary, WO95/1930/3)	WD1930_3	9781474509510	£15.00
15 DIVISION Divisional Troops Royal Army Medical Corps 45 and 46 Field Ambulance : 1 July 1915 - 2 July 1919 (First World War, War Diary, WO95/1931)	WD1931	9781474523066	£74.00
15 DIVISION Divisional Troops Royal Army Medical Corps 47 Field Ambulance : 9 July 1915 - 9 July 1919 (First World War, War Diary, WO95/1932/1)	WD1932_1	9781474509527	£24.00
15 DIVISION Divisional Troops 32 Sanitary Section : 1 August 1915 - 28 February 1917 (First World War, War Diary, WO95/1932/2)	WD1932_2	9781474509534	£15.00

Title	Product Code	ISBN	Price
15 DIVISION Divisional Troops Royal Army Medical Corps Divisional Field Ambulance Workshop Unit : 9 July 1915 - 31 March 1916 (First World War, War Diary, WO95/1932/3)	WD1932_3	9781474509541	£15.00
15 DIVISION Divisional Troops Royal Army Veterinary Corps 27 Mobile Veterinary Section and Royal Army Service Corps Divisional Train (138, 139, 140, 141 Companies A.S.C.) : 7 July 1915 - 17 July 1919 (First World War, War Diary, WO95/1933)	WD1933	9781474523073	£72.00
15 DIVISION 44 Infantry Brigade Headquarters : 7 July 1915 - 31 December 1916 (First World War, War Diary, WO95/1934)	WD1934	9781474523080	£89.00
15 DIVISION 44 Infantry Brigade Headquarters : 1 January 1917 - 31 December 1917 (First World War, War Diary, WO95/1935)	WD1935	9781474523097	£73.00
15 DIVISION 44 Infantry Brigade Headquarters : 1 January 1918 - 31 January 1918 (First World War, War Diary, WO95/1936)	WD1936	9781474523103	£76.00
15 DIVISION 44 Infantry Brigade Black Watch (Royal Highlanders) 4/5th (Angus and Dundee) Battalion (Territorial) and Black Watch (Royal Highlanders) 9th (Service) Battalion : 3 July 1915 - 31 March 1919 (First World War, War Diary, WO95/1937)	WD1937	9781474523110	£35.00
15 DIVISION 44 Infantry Brigade Gordon Highlanders 5th Battalion : 1 June 1918 - 28 February 1919 (First World War, War Diary, WO95/1938/1)	WD1938_1	9781474509558	£22.00
15 DIVISION 44 Infantry Brigade Gordon Highlanders 10th Battalion : 4 July 1915 - 12 May 1916 (First World War, War Diary, WO95/1938/2)	WD1938_2	9781474509565	£15.00
15 DIVISION 44 Infantry Brigade Gordon Highlanders 8/10th Battalion : 30 April 1916 - 17 August 1918 (First World War, War Diary, WO95/1938/3)	WD1938_3	9781474509572	£32.00
15 DIVISION 44 Infantry Brigade Seaforth Highlanders (Ross-shire Buffs, the Duke of Albany's) 8th Battalion : 4 July 1915 - 29 February 1916 (First World War, War Diary, WO95/1939/1)	WD1939_1	9781474509589	£15.00
15 DIVISION 44 Infantry Brigade Seaforth Highlanders (Ross-shire Buffs, the Duke of Albany's) 8th Battalion : 1 March 1916 - 31 July 1916 (First World War, War Diary, WO95/1939/2)	WD1939_2	9781474509596	£15.00
15 DIVISION 44 Infantry Brigade Seaforth Highlanders (Ross-shire Buffs, the Duke of Albany's) 8th Battalion : 1 August 1916 - 30 September 1916 (First World War, War Diary, WO95/1939/3)	WD1939_3	9781474509602	£17.00
15 DIVISION 44 Infantry Brigade Seaforth Highlanders (Ross-shire Buffs, the Duke of Albany's) 8th Battalion : 1 October 1916 - 31 December 1916 (First World War, War Diary, WO95/1939/4)	WD1939_4	9781474509619	£15.00
15 DIVISION 44 Infantry Brigade Seaforth Highlanders (Ross-shire Buffs, the Duke of Albany's) 8th Battalion : 1 January 1917 - 30 November 1917 (First World War, War Diary, WO95/1940A)	WD1940_A	9781474523127	£47.00
15 DIVISION 44 Infantry Brigade Seaforth Highlanders (Ross-shire Buffs, the Duke of Albany's) 8th Battalion : 1 December 1917 - 7 July 1919 (First World War, War Diary, WO95/1940B)	WD1940_B	9781474523134	£47.00
15 DIVISION 44 Infantry Brigade Queen's Own Cameron Highlanders 7th Battalion : 4 July 1915 - 14 August 1918 (First World War, War Diary, WO95/1941/1)	WD1941_1	9781474509626	£34.00
15 DIVISION 44 Infantry Brigade, Brigade Machine Gun Company : 1 March 1916 - 28 February 1918 (First World War, War Diary, WO95/1941/2)	WD1941_2	9781474509633	£20.00
15 DIVISION 44 Infantry Brigade, Brigade Trench Mortar Battery : 31 August 1915 - 30 August 1916 (First World War, War Diary, WO95/1941/3)	WD1941_3	9781474509640	£15.00

Title	Product Code	ISBN	Price
15 DIVISION 44 Infantry Brigade Royal Fusiliers (City of London Regiment) 3rd Battalion : 1 September 1918 - 30 September 1918 (First World War, War Diary, WO95/1941/4)	WD1941_4	9781474523141	£15.00
15 DIVISION 45 Infantry Brigade Headquarters : 8 July 1915 - 31 December 1916 (First World War, War Diary, WO95/1942)	WD1942	9781474509657	£55.00
15 DIVISION 45 Infantry Brigade Headquarters : 1 January 1917 - 10 July 1919 (First World War, War Diary, WO95/1943)	WD1943	9781474523158	£74.00
15 DIVISION 45 Infantry Brigade Princess Louise's (Argyll & Sutherland Highlanders) 1/8th Battalion and 11th Battalion : 4 July 1915 - 26 August 1918 (First World War, War Diary, WO95/1944)	WD1944	9781474523165	£37.00
15 DIVISION 45 Infantry Brigade Queen's Own Cameron Highlanders 6th Battalion : 8 July 1915 - 25 June 1919 (First World War, War Diary, WO95/1945)	WD1945	9781474523172	£74.00
15 DIVISION 45 Infantry Brigade Royal Scots (Lothian Regiment) 13th Battalion : 4 July 1915 - 15 June 1919 (First World War, War Diary, WO95/1946)	WD1946	9781474523189	£58.00
15 DIVISION 45 Infantry Brigade Royal Scots Fusiliers 7th Battalion : 28 March 1915 - 5 May 1916 (First World War, War Diary, WO95/1947/1)	WD1947_1	9781474509664	£15.00
15 DIVISION 45 Infantry Brigade Royal Scots Fusiliers 6/7th Battalion : 6 May 1916 - 31 January 1918 (First World War, War Diary, WO95/1947/2)	WD1947_2	9781474509671	£20.00
15 DIVISION 45 Infantry Brigade, Brigade Machine Gun Company : 1 June 1916 - 28 February 1918 (First World War, War Diary, WO95/1947/3)	WD1947_3	9781474509688	£22.00
15 DIVISION 45 Infantry Brigade, Brigade Trench Mortar Battery : 24 November 1915 - 31 August 1916 (First World War, War Diary, WO95/1947/4)	WD1947_4	9781474523196	£15.00
15 DIVISION 46 Infantry Brigade Headquarters : 4 July 1915 - 31 July 1916 (First World War, War Diary, WO95/1948)	WD1948	9781474509695	£59.00
15 DIVISION 46 Infantry Brigade Headquarters : 1 August 1916 - 31 March 1917 (First World War, War Diary, WO95/1949)	WD1949	9781474523202	£66.00
15 DIVISION 46 Infantry Brigade Headquarters : 1 April 1917 - 31 October 1918 (First World War, War Diary, WO95/1950)	WD1950	9781474523219	£56.00
15 DIVISION 46 Infantry Brigade Headquarters : 1 January 1918 - 27 June 1919 (First World War, War Diary, WO95/1951)	WD1951	9781474509701	£57.00
15 DIVISION 46 Infantry Brigade Highland Light Infantry 10/11th Battalion : 1 May 1916 - 31 May 1918 (First World War, War Diary, WO95/1952/1)	WD1952_1	9781474509718	£21.00
15 DIVISION 46 Infantry Brigade Highland Light Infantry 12th (Service) Battn : 4 July 1915 - 31 January 1918 (First World War, War Diary, WO95/1952/2)	WD1952_2	9781474509725	£23.00
15 DIVISION 46 Infantry Brigade King's Own Scottish Borderers 7th Battalion and 8th Battalion. : 4 July 1916 - 1 June 1919 (First World War, War Diary, WO95/1953/1-4)	WD1953_1-4	9781474523226	£61.00
15 DIVISION 46 Infantry Brigade Royal Scots (Lothian Regiment) 9th Battalion : 1 February 1918 - 31 May 1919 (First World War, War Diary, WO95/1954/1)	WD1954_1	9781474523233	£15.00
15 DIVISION 46 Infantry Brigade Cameronians (Scottish Rifles) 10th Battalion : 1 July 1915 - 31 August 1919 (First World War, War Diary, WO95/1954/2)	WD1954_2	9781474509732	£47.00

Title	Product Code	ISBN	Price
15 DIVISION 46 Infantry Brigade, Brigade Machine Gun Company : 7 February 1916 - 28 February 1918 (First World War, War Diary, WO95/1954/3)	WD1954_3	9781474509749	£15.00
15 DIVISION 46 Infantry Brigade, Brigade Trench Mortar Battery : 9 November 1915 - 31 August 1916 (First World War, War Diary, WO95/1954/4)	WD1954_4	9781474509756	£15.00

Title	Product Code	ISBN	Price
16 DIVISION			
16 DIVISION Headquarters, Branches and Services General Staff : 17 December 1915 - 30 April 1917 (First World War, War Diary, WO95/1955)	WD1955	9781474509763	£47.00
16 DIVISION Headquarters, Branches and Services General Staff : 1 April 1917 - 30 April 1919 (First World War, War Diary, WO95/1956)	WD1956	9781474523240	£67.00
16 DIVISION Headquarters, Branches and Services Adjutant and Quarter-Master General : 10 December 1915 - 30 November 1918 (First World War, War Diary, WO95/1957)	WD1957	9781474523257	£19.00
16 DIVISION Headquarters, Branches and Services Commander Royal Artillery : 1 January 1916 - 31 December 1916 (First World War, War Diary, WO95/1958)	WD1958	9781474509770	£66.00
16 DIVISION Headquarters, Branches and Services Commander Royal Artillery : 1 January 1917 - 25 December 1918 (First World War, War Diary, WO95/1959)	WD1959	9781474509787	£52.00
16 DIVISION Headquarters, Branches and Services Royal Army Medical Corps Assistant Director Medical Services : 18 December 1915 - 31 May 1919 (First World War, War Diary, WO95/1960)	WD1960	9781474509794	£48.00
16 DIVISION Headquarters, Branches and Services Commander Royal Engineers : 18 December 1915 - 25 June 1919 (First World War, War Diary, WO95/1961/1)	WD1961_1	9781474509800	£34.00
16 DIVISION Headquarters, Branches and Services Royal Army Ordnance Corps Deputy Assistant Director Ordnance Services : 21 January 1916 - 28 February 1919 (First World War, War Diary, WO95/1961/2)	WD1961_2	9781474509817	£15.00
16 DIVISION Headquarters, Branches and Services Royal Army Veterinary Corps Assistant Director Veterinary Services : 18 December 1915 - 28 February 1919 (First World War, War Diary, WO95/1961/3)	WD1961_3	9781474509824	£15.00
16 DIVISION Divisional Troops `C' Squadron South Irish Horse : 19 December 1915 - 31 May 1916 (First World War, War Diary, WO95/1962/1)	WD1962_1	9781474509831	£15.00
16 DIVISION Divisional Troops Divisional Cyclist Company : 18 December 1915 - 1 June 1916 (First World War, War Diary, WO95/1962/2)	WD1962_2	9781474509848	£15.00
16 DIVISION Divisional Troops 77 Brigade Royal Field Artillery : 1 October 1914 - 31 December 1916 (First World War, War Diary, WO95/1962/3)	WD1962_3	9781474509855	£15.00
16 DIVISION Divisional Troops 177 Brigade Royal Field Artillery : 16 February 1916 - 2 February 1919 (First World War, War Diary, WO95/1962/4)	WD1962_4	9781474523264	£57.00
16 DIVISION Divisional Troops 180 Brigade Royal Field Artillery : 16 February 1916 - 28 June 1919 (First World War, War Diary, WO95/1963/1)	WD1963_1	9781474523271	£24.00
16 DIVISION Divisional Troops 182 Brigade Royal Field Artillery : 10 February 1916 - 31 July 1916 (First World War, War Diary, WO95/1963/2)	WD1963_2	9781474509862	£15.00
16 DIVISION Divisional Troops Divisional Trench Mortar Batteries : 1 June 1916 - 21 August 1916 (First World War, War Diary, WO95/1963/3-4)	WD1963_3-4	9781474509879	£15.00
16 DIVISION Divisional Troops Divisional Ammunition Column : 29 November 1915 - 31 May 1919 (First World War, War Diary, WO95/1964)	WD1964	9781474523288	£60.00
16 DIVISION Divisional Troops 155 Field Company Royal Engineers : 4 August 1915 - 31 May 1919 (First World War, War Diary, WO95/1965/1)	WD1965_1	9781474523295	£25.00

Title	Product Code	ISBN	Price
16 DIVISION Divisional Troops 156 Field Company Royal Engineers : 29 July 1915 - 31 May 1919 (First World War, War Diary, WO95/1965/2)	WD1965_2	9781474509886	£15.00
16 DIVISION Divisional Troops 157 Field Company Royal Engineers : 19 December 1915 - 31 March 1919 (First World War, War Diary, WO95/1965/3)	WD1965_3	9781474509893	£17.00
16 DIVISION Divisional Troops Divisional Signal Company, Hampshire Regiment 11th Battalion (Service) Pioneers, Machine Gun Corps 16 Battalion and 269 Machine Gun Company : 17 December 1915 - 28 February 1918 (First World War, War Diary, WO95/1966)	WD1966	9781474523301	£73.00
16 DIVISION Divisional Troops Royal Army Medical Corps 111 Field Ambulance : 18 December 1915 - 30 April 1919 (First World War, War Diary, WO95/1967/1)	WD1967_1	9781474523318	£34.00
16 DIVISION Divisional Troops Royal Army Medical Corps 112 Field Ambulance : 19 December 1915 - 27 April 1919 (First World War, War Diary, WO95/1967/2)	WD1967_2	9781474509909	£27.00
16 DIVISION Divisional Troops Royal Army Medical Corps 113 Field Ambulance : 1 February 1916 - 30 April 1919 (First World War, War Diary, WO95/1967/3)	WD1967_3	9781474509916	£24.00
16 DIVISION Divisional Troops Royal Army Medical Corps Divisional Field Ambulance Workshop Unit : 1 December 1915 - 31 March 1916 (First World War, War Diary, WO95/1968/1)	WD1968_1	9781474509923	£15.00
16 DIVISION Divisional Troops 81 Sanitary Section : 18 December 1915 - 31 March 1917 (First World War, War Diary, WO95/1968/2)	WD1968_2	9781474509930	£15.00
16 DIVISION Divisional Troops Royal Army Veterinary Corps 47 Mobile Veterinary Section : 19 December 1915 - 30 September 1919 (First World War, War Diary, WO95/1968/3)	WD1968_3	9781474509947	£17.00
16 DIVISION Divisional Troops Royal Army Service Corps Divisional Train (142, 143, 144, 145 Companies A.S.C.) : 17 December 1915 - 31 May 1919 (First World War, War Diary, WO95/1968/4)	WD1968_4	9781474509954	£46.00
16 DIVISION 47 Infantry Brigade Headquarters : 23 November 1915 - 28 February 1919 (First World War, War Diary, WO95/1969)	WD1969	9781474509961	£41.00
16 DIVISION 47 Infantry Brigade Black Watch (Royal Highlanders) 9th (Service) Battalion : 1 May 1918 - 28 April 1919 (First World War, War Diary, WO95/1970/1)	WD1970_1	9781474509978	£15.00
16 DIVISION 47 Infantry Brigade Connaught Rangers 6th Battalion : 18 December 1915 - 31 July 1918 (First World War, War Diary, WO95/1970/2)	WD1970_2	9781474509985	£31.00
16 DIVISION 47 Infantry Brigade Royal Irish Regiment 6th Battalion : 17 December 1915 - 9 February 1918 (First World War, War Diary, WO95/1970/3)	WD1970_3	9781474509992	£15.00
16 DIVISION 47 Infantry Brigade Prince of Wales's Leinster Regiment (Royal Canadians) 7th Battalion : 16 December 1915 - 23 January 1918 (First World War, War Diary, WO95/1970/4)	WD1970_4	9781474510004	£16.00
16 DIVISION 47 Infantry Brigade Leicestershire Regiment 14th Battalion : 1 August 1918 - 30 April 1919 (First World War, War Diary, WO95/1970/5)	WD1970_5	9781474510011	£15.00
16 DIVISION 47 Infantry Brigade Royal Munster Fusiliers 1st Battalion : 1 November 1916 - 30 April 1918 (First World War, War Diary, WO95/1971/1)	WD1971_1	9781474510028	£20.00

Title	Product Code	ISBN	Price
16 DIVISION 47 Infantry Brigade Royal Munster Fusiliers 8th Battalion : 17 December 1915 - 23 November 1916 (First World War, War Diary, WO95/1971/2)	WD1971_2	9781474510035	£15.00
16 DIVISION 47 Infantry Brigade Welsh Regiment 18th Battalion : 27 July 1918 - 31 May 1919 (First World War, War Diary, WO95/1971/3)	WD1971_3	9781474510042	£15.00
16 DIVISION 47 Infantry Brigade, Brigade Machine Gun Company (24 April 1916 - 28 February 1918) and French Mortar Battery (9 November 1915 - 20 December 1915) : (First World War, War Diary, WO95/1971/4-5)	WD1971_4-5	9781474510059	£26.00
16 DIVISION 48 Infantry Brigade Headquarters : 19 December 1915 - 31 December 1916 (First World War, War Diary, WO95/1972)	WD1972	9781474523325	£65.00
16 DIVISION 48 Infantry Brigade Headquarters : 1 January 1917 - 25 April 1919 (First World War, War Diary, WO95/1973)	WD1973	9781474523332	£68.00
16 DIVISION 48 Infantry Brigade Royal Dublin Fusiliers 1st Battalion, 2nd Battalion, 8th Battalion, 9th Battalion, 8/9th Battalion and 10th Battalion : 11 December 1915 - 15 February 1918 (First World War, War Diary, WO95/1974)	WD1974	9781474523349	£77.00
16 DIVISION 48 Infantry Brigade Princess Victoria's (Royal Irish Fusiliers) 5th Battalion : 1 May 1918 - 9 June 1919 (First World War, War Diary, WO95/1975/1)	WD1975_1	9781474523356	£15.00
16 DIVISION 48 Infantry Brigade Royal Irish Rifles 7th Battalion : 19 December 1915 - 15 November 1917 (First World War, War Diary, WO95/1975/2)	WD1975_2	9781474510066	£15.00
16 DIVISION 48 Infantry Brigade Royal Munster Fusiliers 1st Battalion : 1 March 1916 - 31 October 1916 (First World War, War Diary, WO95/1975/3)	WD1975_3	9781474510073	£15.00
16 DIVISION 48 Infantry Brigade Royal Munster Fusiliers 2nd Battalion : 1 February 1918 - 31 May 1918 (First World War, War Diary, WO95/1975/4)	WD1975_4	9781474510080	£15.00
16 DIVISION 48 Infantry Brigade Royal Munster Fusiliers 9th Battalion : 20 December 1915 - 30 May 1916 (First World War, War Diary, WO95/1975/5)	WD1975_5	9781474510097	£15.00
16 DIVISION 48 Infantry Brigade Northumberland Fusiliers 22nd Battalion (Tyneside Scottish) : 1 August 1918 - 5 June 1919 (First World War, War Diary, WO95/1975/6)	WD1975_6	9781474510103	£15.00
16 DIVISION 48 Infantry Brigade Cameronians (Scottish Rifles) 18th Battalion : 1 August 1918 - 28 February 1919 (First World War, War Diary, WO95/1975/7)	WD1975_7	9781474510110	£15.00
16 DIVISION 48 Infantry Brigade, Brigade Machine Gun Company : 24 April 1916 - 28 February 1918 (First World War, War Diary, WO95/1975/8)	WD1975_8	9781474510127	£22.00
16 DIVISION 48 Infantry Brigade, Brigade Trench Mortar Battery : 31 October 1915 - 1 January 1916 (First World War, War Diary, WO95/1975/9)	WD1975_9	9781474510134	£15.00
16 DIVISION 49 Infantry Brigade Headquarters : 13 January 1916 - 30 April 1919 (First World War, War Diary, WO95/1976)	WD1976	9781474523363	£72.00
16 DIVISION 49 Infantry Brigade Gloucestershire Regiment 18th (Service) Battalion : 1 August 1918 - 31 May 1919 (First World War, War Diary, WO95/1977/1)	WD1977_1	9781474523370	£15.00

Title	Product Code	ISBN	Price
16 DIVISION 49 Infantry Brigade Royal Inniskilling Fusiliers 7th Battalion : 1 February 1916 - 31 August 1917 (First World War, War Diary, WO95/1977/2)	WD1977_2	9781474510141	£15.00
16 DIVISION 49 Infantry Brigade Royal Inniskilling Fusiliers 8th Battalion : 3 February 1916 - 23 August 1917 (First World War, War Diary, WO95/1977/3)	WD1977_3	9781474510158	£32.00
16 DIVISION 49 Infantry Brigade Royal Inniskilling Fusiliers 7/8th Battalion : 1 September 1917 - 31 May 1918 (First World War, War Diary, WO95/1977/4)	WD1977_4	9781474510165	£16.00
16 DIVISION 49 Infantry Brigade Princess Victoria's (Royal Irish Fusiliers) 7th Battalion, 8th Battalion, 7/8th Battalion and 11 Battalion : 1 February 1916 - 27 February 1918 (First World War, War Diary, WO95/1978)	WD1978	9781474510172	£35.00
16 DIVISION 49 Infantry Brigade Royal Irish Regiment 2nd Battalion : 23 April 1915 - 25 April 1915 (First World War, War Diary, WO95/1979/1)	WD1979_1	9781474510189	£25.00
16 DIVISION 49 Infantry Brigade Royal Irish Regiment 7th Battalion : 1 September 1917 - 31 May 1918 (First World War, War Diary, WO95/1979/2)	WD1979_2	9781474523387	£15.00
16 DIVISION 49 Infantry Brigade London Regiment 34th (County of London) Battalion : 1 July 1918 - 21 April 1919 (First World War, War Diary, WO95/1979/3)	WD1979_3	9781474523394	£15.00
16 DIVISION 49 Infantry Brigade Prince Albert's (Somerset Light Infantry) 6th Battalion : 1 March 1918 - 30 April 1919 (First World War, War Diary, WO95/1979/4)	WD1979_4	9781474510196	£15.00
16 DIVISION 49 Infantry Brigade, Brigade Machine Gun Company (1 May 1916 - 28 February 1918) and Brigade Trench Mortar Battery (10 November 1914 - 28 December) : (First World War, War Diary, WO95/1979/5)	WD1979_5-6	9781474510202	£15.00

Title	Product Code	ISBN	Price
17 DIVISION			
17 DIVISION Headquarters, Branches and Services General Staff : 20 July 1915 - 30 June 1916 (First World War, War Diary, WO95/1980)	WD1980	9781474510219	£56.00
17 DIVISION Headquarters, Branches and Services General Staff : 1 July 1916 - 30 April 1917 (First World War, War Diary, WO95/1981)	WD1981	9781474523400	£69.00
17 DIVISION Headquarters, Branches and Services General Staff : 1 May 1917 - 31 August 1917 (First World War, War Diary, WO95/1982)	WD1982	9781474523417	£61.00
17 DIVISION Headquarters, Branches and Services General Staff : 1 September 1917 - 31 December 1917 (First World War, War Diary, WO95/1983)	WD1983	9781474523424	£46.00
17 DIVISION Headquarters, Branches and Services General Staff : 1 January 1918 - 31 July 1918 (First World War, War Diary, WO95/1984)	WD1984	9781474510226	£63.00
17 DIVISION Headquarters, Branches and Services General Staff : 1 August 1918 - 28 February 1919 (First World War, War Diary, WO95/1985)	WD1985	9781474523431	£63.00
17 DIVISION Headquarters, Branches and Services Adjutant and Quarter-Master General : 4 July 1915 - 31 March 1919 (First World War, War Diary, WO95/1986)	WD1986	9781474523448	£64.00
17 DIVISION Headquarters, Branches and Services Commander Royal Artillery : 15 July 1915 - 31 December 1916 (First World War, War Diary, WO95/1987)	WD1987	9781474523455	£64.00
17 DIVISION Headquarters, Branches and Services Commander Royal Artillery : 1 January 1917 - 30 April 1919 (First World War, War Diary, WO95/1988)	WD1988	9781474523462	£62.00
17 DIVISION Headquarters, Branches and Services Royal Army Medical Corps Assistant Director Medical Services : 10 July 1915 - 2 May 1919 (First World War, War Diary, WO95/1989)	WD1989	9781474523479	£84.00
17 DIVISION Headquarters, Branches and Services Commander Royal Engineers : 1 January 1915 - 1 May 1919 (First World War, War Diary, WO95/1990/1)	WD1990_1	9781474523486	£19.00
17 DIVISION Headquarters, Branches and Services Royal Army Ordnance Corps Deputy Assistant Director Ordnance Services : 14 July 1915 - 12 February 1919 (First World War, War Diary, WO95/1990/2)	WD1990_2	9781474510233	£15.00
17 DIVISION Headquarters, Branches and Services Royal Army Veterinary Corps Assistant Director Veterinary Services : 15 July 1915 - 31 March 1919 (First World War, War Diary, WO95/1990/3)	WD1990_3	9781474510240	£15.00
17 DIVISION Divisional Troops `A' Squadron Yorkshire Dragoons : 28 March 1915 - 15 May 1916 (First World War, War Diary, WO95/1991/1)	WD1991_1	9781474510257	£15.00
17 DIVISION Divisional Troops Divisional Cyclist Company : 13 July 1915 - 31 May 1916 (First World War, War Diary, WO95/1991/2)	WD1991_2	9781474510264	£15.00
17 DIVISION Divisional Troops 78 Brigade Royal Field Artillery : 12 July 1915 - 31 March 1919 (First World War, War Diary, WO95/1991/3)	WD1991_3	9781474510271	£17.00
17 DIVISION Divisional Troops 79 Brigade Royal Field Artillery : 13 July 1915 - 31 March 1919 (First World War, War Diary, WO95/1991/4)	WD1991_4	9781474510288	£19.00
17 DIVISION Divisional Troops 80 Brigade Royal Field Artillery : 14 July 1915 - 31 August 1916 (First World War, War Diary, WO95/1991/5)	WD1991_5	9781474510295	£15.00

Title	Product Code	ISBN	Price
17 DIVISION Divisional Troops 81 Brigade Royal Field Artillery : 1 September 1915 - 27 January 1917 (First World War, War Diary, WO95/1991/6)	WD1991_6	9781474510301	£15.00
17 DIVISION Divisional Troops Divisional Trench Mortar Batteries, 32 Trench Mortar Battery and Divisional Ammunition Column : 13 July 1915 - 31 December 1918 (First World War, War Diary, WO95/1992)	WD1992	9781474510318	£32.00
17 DIVISION Divisional Troops 77 Field Company Royal Engineers : 14 July 1915 - 23 May 1919 (First World War, War Diary, WO95/1993/1)	WD1993_1	9781474510325	£15.00
17 DIVISION Divisional Troops 78 Field Company Royal Engineers : 15 April 1915 - 11 April 1919 (First World War, War Diary, WO95/1993/2)	WD1993_2	9781474510332	£36.00
17 DIVISION Divisional Troops 93 Field Company Royal Engineers : 15 July 1915 - 31 March 1919 (First World War, War Diary, WO95/1993/3)	WD1993_3	9781474510349	£26.00
17 DIVISION Divisional Troops Divisional Signal Company : 1 June 1915 - 28 February 1918 (First World War, War Diary, WO95/1994)	WD1994	9781474510356	£32.00
17 DIVISION Divisional Troops York and Lancaster Regiment 7th (Service) Battalion Pioneers : 13 July 1915 - 17 April 1919 (First World War, War Diary, WO95/1995/1)	WD1995_1	9781474510363	£40.00
17 DIVISION Divisional Troops Machine Gun Corps 17 Battalion : 24 February 1918 - 28 February 1919 (First World War, War Diary, WO95/1995/2)	WD1995_2	9781474510370	£15.00
17 DIVISION Divisional Troops 236 Machine Gun Company : 1 July 1917 - 28 February 1918 (First World War, War Diary, WO95/1995/3)	WD1995_3	9781474510387	£15.00
17 DIVISION Divisional Troops Royal Army Medical Corps 51 Field Ambulance : 12 July 1915 - 6 May 1919 (First World War, War Diary, WO95/1996/1)	WD1996_1	9781474510394	£27.00
17 DIVISION Divisional Troops Royal Army Medical Corps 52 and 53 Field Ambulance : 14 July 1915 - 29 March 1919 (First World War, War Diary, WO95/1996/2-3)	WD1996_2	9781474510400	£56.00
17 DIVISION Divisional Troops Royal Army Medical Corps Divisional Field Ambulance Workshop Unit : 15 June 1915 - 2 April 1916 (First World War, War Diary, WO95/1997/1)	WD1997_1	9781474510417	£15.00
17 DIVISION Divisional Troops 34 Sanitary Sections : 28 June 1915 - 31 March 1917 (First World War, War Diary, WO95/1997/2)	WD1997_2	9781474510424	£15.00
17 DIVISION Divisional Troops Royal Army Veterinary Corps 29 Mobile Veterinary Section : 15 July 1915 - 31 January 1919 (First World War, War Diary, WO95/1997/3)	WD1997_3	9781474510431	£19.00
17 DIVISION Divisional Troops Royal Army Service Corps Divisional Train (146, 147, 148, 149, Companies A.S.C.) : 13 July 1915 - 17 June 1916 (First World War, War Diary, WO95/1997/4)	WD1997_4	9781474523493	£50.00
17 DIVISION 50 Infantry Brigade Headquarters : 6 July 1915 - 31 July 1917 (First World War, War Diary, WO95/1998)	WD1998	9781474523509	£60.00
17 DIVISION 50 Infantry Brigade Headquarters : 1 September 1917 - 31 March 1919 (First World War, War Diary, WO95/1999)	WD1999	9781474523516	£43.00
17 DIVISION 50 Infantry Brigade Dorsetshire Regiment 6th Battalion : 7 July 1915 - 31 December 1917 (First World War, War Diary, WO95/2000)	WD2000	9781474510448	£66.00
17 DIVISION 50 Infantry Brigade Dorsetshire Regiment 6th Battalion : 1 January 1918 - 27 May 1919 (First World War, War Diary, WO95/2001)	WD2001	9781474510455	£54.00

Title	Product Code	ISBN	Price
17 DIVISION 50 Infantry Brigade East Yorkshire Regiment 7th Battalion : 13 July 1915 - 31 December 1916 (First World War, War Diary, WO95/2002)	WD2002	9781474510462	£39.00
17 DIVISION 50 Infantry Brigade East Yorkshire Regiment 7th Battalion : 1 January 1917 - 24 April 1919 (First World War, War Diary, WO95/2003)	WD2003	9781474523523	£77.00
17 DIVISION 50 Infantry Brigade Prince of Wales's Own (West Yorkshire Regiment) 10th Battalion : 1 August 1915 - 22 April 1919 (First World War, War Diary, WO95/2004/1)	WD2004_1	9781474523530	£35.00
17 DIVISION 50 Infantry Brigade Alexandra, Princess of Wales's Own (Yorkshire Regiment) 7th Battalion : 13 July 1915 - 28 February 1918 (First World War, War Diary, WO95/2004/2)	WD2004_2	9781474510479	£23.00
17 DIVISION 50 Infantry Brigade, Brigade Machine Gun Company (9 February 1916 - 23 February 1918) and Brigade Trench Mortar Battery (2 December 1915 - 25 March 1916) :(First World War, War Diary, WO95/2004/3-4)	WD2004_3-4	9781474510486	£24.00
17 DIVISION 51 Infantry Brigade Headquarters : 7 July 1915 - 31 October 1917 (First World War, War Diary, WO95/2005)	WD2005	9781474510493	£54.00
17 DIVISION 51 Infantry Brigade Headquarters : 1 November 1917 - 29 March 1919 (First World War, War Diary, WO95/2006)	WD2006	9781474523547	£70.00
17 DIVISION 51 Infantry Brigade Lincolnshire Regiment 7th Battalion : 10 July 1915 - 31 March 1919 (First World War, War Diary, WO95/2007/1)	WD2007_1	9781474523554	£61.00
17 DIVISION 51 Infantry Brigade South Staffordshire Regiment 8th Service Battalion : 6 July 1915 - 23 February 1918 (First World War, War Diary, WO95/2007/2)	WD2007_2	9781474510509	£19.00
17 DIVISION 51 Infantry Brigade Border Regiment 7th Battalion : 12 July 1915 - 31 March 1919 (First World War, War Diary, WO95/2008/1)	WD2008_1	9781474510516	£36.00
17 DIVISION 51 Infantry Brigade Sherwood Foresters (Nottinghamshire and Derbyshire Regiment) 10th Battalion : 14 July 1915 - 31 March 1919 (First World War, War Diary, WO95/2008/2)	WD2008_2	9781474510523	£24.00
17 DIVISION 51 Infantry Brigade, Brigade Machine Gun Company : 14 February 1916 - 28 February 1918 (First World War, War Diary, WO95/2008/3)	WD2008_3	9781474510530	£15.00
17 DIVISION 51 Infantry Brigade, Brigade Trench Mortar Battery : 10 November 1915 - 31 January 1916 (First World War, War Diary, WO95/2008/4)	WD2008_4	9781474510547	£15.00
17 DIVISION 52 Infantry Brigade Headquarters : 7 July 1915 - 31 January 1917 (First World War, War Diary, WO95/2009)	WD2009	9781474523561	£70.00
17 DIVISION 52 Infantry Brigade Headquarters : 1 January 1917 - 31 December 1917 (First World War, War Diary, WO95/2010)	WD2010	9781474523578	£56.00
17 DIVISION 52 Infantry Brigade Headquarters : 1 January 1918 - 28 April 1919 (First World War, War Diary, WO95/2011)	WD2011	9781474523585	£64.00
17 DIVISION 52 Infantry Brigade Lancashire Fusiliers 10th Battalion : 15 July 1915 - 31 January 1919 (First World War, War Diary, WO95/2012/1)	WD2012_1	9781474523592	£44.00
17 DIVISION 52 Infantry Brigade Manchester Regiment 12th Battalion : 5 July 1915 - 31 March 1919 (First World War, War Diary, WO95/2012/2)	WD2012_2	9781474510554	£21.00
17 DIVISION 52 Infantry Brigade Northumberland Fusiliers 9th Battalion : 6 July 1915 - 31 July 1917 (First World War, War Diary, WO95/2013/1)	WD2013_1	9781474510561	£27.00

Title	Product Code	ISBN	Price
17 DIVISION 52 Infantry Brigade Queen's Own (Royal West Kent Regiment) 3/4th Battalion : 31 May 1917 - 28 February 1918 (First World War, War Diary, WO95/2013/2)	WD2013_2	9781474510578	£32.00
17 DIVISION 52 Infantry Brigade Duke of Wellington's (West Riding Regiment) 9th Battalion and Brigade Machine Gun Company : 15 July 1915 - 23 February 1918 (First World War, War Diary, WO95/2014)	WD2014	9781474510585	£42.00

Title	Product Code	ISBN	Price
18 DIVISION			
18 DIVISION Headquarters, Branches and Services General Staff : 24 July 1915 - 31 December 1916 (First World War, War Diary, WO95/2015)	WD2015	9781474510592	£45.00
18 DIVISION Headquarters, Branches and Services General Staff : 2 January 1917 - 31 December 1917 (First World War, War Diary, WO95/2016)	WD2016	9781474510608	£37.00
18 DIVISION Headquarters, Branches and Services General Staff : 1 January 1918 - 21 March 1919 (First World War, War Diary, WO95/2017)	WD2017	9781474510615	£41.00
18 DIVISION Headquarters, Branches and Services Adjutant and Quarter-Master General : 18 July 1915 - 28 February 1919 (First World War, War Diary, WO95/2018)	WD2018	9781474523608	£66.00
18 DIVISION Headquarters, Branches and Services Commander Royal Artillery : 26 July 1915 - 30 November 1916 (First World War, War Diary, WO95/2019)	WD2019	9781474523615	£71.00
18 DIVISION Headquarters, Branches and Services Commander Royal Artillery : 1 December 1916 - 31 May 1917 (First World War, War Diary, WO95/2020)	WD2020	9781474523622	£49.00
18 DIVISION Headquarters, Branches and Services Commander Royal Artillery : 1 June 1917 - 31 March 1919 (First World War, War Diary, WO95/2021)	WD2021	9781474510622	£38.00
18 DIVISION Headquarters, Branches and Services Royal Army Medical Corps Assistant Director Medical Services : 25 July 1915 - 31 January 1919 (First World War, War Diary, WO95/2022)	WD2022	9781474510639	£76.00
18 DIVISION Headquarters, Branches and Services Commander Royal Engineers : 25 July 1915 - 1 April 1919 (First World War, War Diary, WO95/2023/1)	WD2023_1	9781474510646	£15.00
18 DIVISION Headquarters, Branches and Services Royal Army Ordnance Corps Assistant Director Ordnance Services : 21 July 1915 - 28 February 1919 (First World War, War Diary, WO95/2023/2)	WD2023_2	9781474510653	£15.00
18 DIVISION Headquarters, Branches and Services Royal Army Veterinary Corps Assistant Director Veterinary Services : 26 July 1915 - 31 March 1919 (First World War, War Diary, WO95/2023/3)	WD2023_3	9781474510660	£15.00
18 DIVISION Headquarters, Branches and Services Senior Chaplain (C of E) : 1 August 1916 - 30 November 1916 (First World War, War Diary, WO95/2023/4)	WD2023_4	9781474510677	£15.00
18 DIVISION Divisional Troops C Squadron Westmorland and Cumberland Yeomanry : 20 July 1915 - 30 April 1916 (First World War, War Diary, WO95/2024/1)	WD2024_1	9781474510684	£15.00
18 DIVISION Divisional Troops Divisional Cyclist Company : 1 January 1915 - 21 May 1916 (First World War, War Diary, WO95/2024/2)	WD2024_2	9781474510691	£15.00
18 DIVISION Divisional Troops 82 Brigade Royal Field Artillery : 23 July 1915 - 31 March 1919 (First World War, War Diary, WO95/2024/3)	WD2024_3	9781474510707	£52.00
18 DIVISION Divisional Troops 83 Brigade Royal Field Artillery : 24 July 1915 - 29 July 1919 (First World War, War Diary, WO95/2025/1)	WD2025_1	9781474510714	£18.00
18 DIVISION Divisional Troops 84 Brigade Royal Field Artillery : 20 February 1915 - 28 December 1916 (First World War, War Diary, WO95/2025/2)	WD2025_2	9781474510721	£15.00
18 DIVISION Divisional Troops 85 Brigade Royal Field Artillery : 20 July 1915 - 3 December 1916 (First World War, War Diary, WO95/2025/3)	WD2025_3	9781474510738	£18.00

Title	Product Code	ISBN	Price
18 DIVISION Divisional Troops Divisional Trench Mortar Batteries : 31 December 1915 - 31 January 1918 (First World War, War Diary, WO95/2026/1)	WD2026_1	9781474510745	£23.00
18 DIVISION Divisional Troops Divisional Ammunition Column : 26 June 1915 - 31 March 1919 (First World War, War Diary, WO95/2026/2)	WD2026_2	9781474510752	£15.00
18 DIVISION Divisional Troops 79 Field Company Royal Engineers : 25 July 1915 - 30 April 1919 (First World War, War Diary, WO95/2027/1)	WD2027_1	9781474510769	£15.00
18 DIVISION Divisional Troops 80 Field Company Royal Engineers : 1 January 1916 - 30 April 1919 (First World War, War Diary, WO95/2027/2)	WD2027_2	9781474510776	£15.00
18 DIVISION Divisional Troops 92 Field Company Royal Engineers : 27 July 1915 - 3 August 1919 (First World War, War Diary, WO95/2027/3)	WD2027_3	9781474510783	£15.00
18 DIVISION Divisional Troops Divisional Signal Company : 25 July 1915 - 1 January 1919 (First World War, War Diary, WO95/2028/1)	WD2028_1	9781474510790	£23.00
18 DIVISION Divisional Troops Machine Gun Corps 18 Battalion : 19 February 1918 - 31 March 1919 (First World War, War Diary, WO95/2028/2)	WD2028_2	9781474510806	£27.00
18 DIVISION Divisional Troops 15 Motor Machine Gun Battery : 24 July 1915 - 31 December 1915 (First World War, War Diary, WO95/2028/3)	WD2028_3	9781474510813	£15.00
18 DIVISION Divisional Troops Royal Sussex Regiment 8th Battalion : 3 September 1914 - 25 February 1919 (First World War, War Diary, WO95/2029)	WD2029	9781474523639	£85.00
18 DIVISION Divisional Troops Royal Army Medical Corps 55 Field Ambulance : 26 July 1915 - 30 April 1919 (First World War, War Diary, WO95/2030/1)	WD2030_1	9781474523646	£15.00
18 DIVISION Divisional Troops Royal Army Medical Corps 56 Field Ambulance : 16 June 1915 - 30 April 1919 (First World War, War Diary, WO95/2030/2)	WD2030_2	9781474510820	£55.00
18 DIVISION Divisional Troops Royal Army Medical Corps 54 Field Ambulance, Divisional Field Ambulance Workshop and 35 Sanitary Section : 14 April 1915 - 29 March 1917 (First World War, War Diary, WO95/2031)	WD2031	9781474523653	£57.00
18 DIVISION Divisional Troops 30 Mobile Veterinary Section, Divisional Train (150, 151, 152, 153, Companies A.S.C.), Divisional Salvage Company and Divisional Anti-Gas School: 23 July 1915 - 11 November 1918 (First World War, War Diary, WO95/2032)	WD2032	9781474523660	£34.00
18 DIVISION 53 Infantry Brigade Headquarters : 24 July 1915 - 30 April 1916 (First World War, War Diary, WO95/2033)	WD2033	9781474510837	£62.00
18 DIVISION Headquarters, Branches and Services Headquarters : 1 May 1916 - 31 December 1916 (First World War, War Diary, WO95/2034)	WD2034	9781474510844	£39.00
18 DIVISION Headquarters, Branches and Services Headquarters : 1 January 1917 - 31 December 1917 (First World War, War Diary, WO95/2035)	WD2035	9781474523677	£49.00
18 DIVISION Headquarters, Branches and Services Headquarters : 1 January 1918 - 23 January 1919 (First World War, War Diary, WO95/2036)	WD2036	9781474523684	£63.00
18 DIVISION 53 Infantry Brigade Princess Charlotte of Wales's (Royal Berkshire Regiment) 6th Battalion and 8th Battalion : 24 July 1915 - 30 April 1919 (First World War, War Diary, WO95/2037)	WD2037	9781474523691	£71.00

Title	Product Code	ISBN	Price
18 DIVISION 53 Infantry Brigade Essex Regiment 10th Battalion : 24 July 1915 - 30 April 1919 (First World War, War Diary, WO95/2038)	WD2038	9781474523707	£57.00
18 DIVISION 53 Infantry Brigade Suffolk Regiment 8th Battalion : 23 July 1915 - 24 February 1918 (First World War, War Diary, WO95/2039)	WD2039	9781474510851	£62.00
18 DIVISION 53 Infantry Brigade Norfolk Regiment 8th Battalion : 25 July 1915 - 20 February 1918 (First World War, War Diary, WO95/2040/1)	WD2040_1	9781474510868	£48.00
18 DIVISION 53 Infantry Brigade Queen's Own (Royal West Kent Regiment) 7th Battalion : 1 February 1918 - 30 April 1919 (First World War, War Diary, WO95/2040/2)	WD2040_2	9781474510875	£15.00
18 DIVISION 53 Infantry Brigade, Brigade Machine Gun Company : 9 February 1916 - 31 December 1917 (First World War, War Diary, WO95/2040/3)	WD2040_3	9781474510882	£16.00
18 DIVISION 54 Infantry Brigade Headquarters : 25 July 1915 - 31 August 1915 (First World War, War Diary, WO95/2041)	WD2041	9781474523714	£74.00
18 DIVISION 54 Infantry Brigade Headquarters : 1 June 1917 - 30 April 1919 (First World War, War Diary, WO95/2042/1)	WD2042_1	9781474523721	£51.00
18 DIVISION 54 Infantry Brigade Bedfordshire Regiment 2nd Battalion : 1 November 1915 - 28 February 1919 (First World War, War Diary, WO95/2042/2)	WD2042_2	9781474510899	£15.00
18 DIVISION 54 Infantry Brigade Bedfordshire Regiment 7th Battalion : 25 July 1915 - 30 June 1918 (First World War, War Diary, WO95/2043)	WD2043	9781474523738	£75.00
18 DIVISION 54 Infantry Brigade Duke of Cambridge's Own (Middlesex Regiment) 12th Battalion : 27 April 1915 - 30 April 1919 (First World War, War Diary, WO95/2044/1)	WD2044_1	9781474523745	£25.00
18 DIVISION 54 Infantry Brigade Northamptonshire Regiment 6th Battalion : 21 April 1915 - 28 February 1918 (First World War, War Diary, WO95/2044/2)	WD2044_2	9781474510905	£37.00
18 DIVISION 54 Infantry Brigade Royal Fusiliers (City of London Regiment) 11th Battalion : 26 July 1915 - 30 April 1919 (First World War, War Diary, WO95/2045/1)	WD2045_1	9781474510912	£30.00
18 DIVISION 54 Infantry Brigade, Brigade Machine Gun Company : 8 February 1916 - 31 January 1918 (First World War, War Diary, WO95/2045/2)	WD2045_2	9781474510929	£15.00
18 DIVISION 55 Infantry Brigade Headquarters : 18 July 1915 - 31 December 1916 (First World War, War Diary, WO95/2046)	WD2046	9781474510936	£54.00
18 DIVISION 55 Infantry Brigade Headquarters : 10 October 1915 - 31 December 1917 (First World War, War Diary, WO95/2047)	WD2047	9781474510943	£47.00
18 DIVISION 55 Infantry Brigade Headquarters : 2 January 1918 - 31 March 1919 (First World War, War Diary, WO95/2048)	WD2048	9781474510950	£49.00
18 DIVISION 55 Infantry Brigade Buffs (East Kent Regiment) 7th Battalion : 20 July 1915 - 30 April 1919 (First World War, War Diary, WO95/2049/1)	WD2049_1	9781474510967	£46.00
18 DIVISION 55 Infantry Brigade Queen's Own (Royal West Kent Regiment) 7th Battalion : 20 July 1915 - 31 January 1918 (First World War, War Diary, WO95/2049/2)	WD2049_2	9781474510974	£28.00
18 DIVISION 55 Infantry Brigade East Surrey Regiment 8th Battalion : 12 September 1915 - 15 April 1919 (First World War, War Diary, WO95/2050)	WD2050	9781474510981	£79.00

Title	Product Code	ISBN	Price
18 DIVISION 55 Infantry Brigade Queen's (Royal West Surrey Regiment) 7th Battalion and Brigade Machine Gun Company : 14 July 1915 - 30 June 1919 (First World War, War Diary, WO95/2051)	WD2051	9781474510998	£57.00

Title	Product Code	ISBN	Price
19 DIVISION			
19 DIVISION Headquarters, Branches and Services General Staff : 17 July 1915 - 31 December 1915 (First World War, War Diary, WO95/2052)	WD2052	9781474511001	£49.00
19 DIVISION Headquarters, Branches and Services General Staff : 1 January 1916 - 30 November 1916 (First World War, War Diary, WO95/2053)	WD2053	9781474523752	£83.00
19 DIVISION Headquarters, Branches and Services General Staff : 1 January 1917 - 7 June 1917 (First World War, War Diary, WO95/2054)	WD2054	9781474523769	£53.00
19 DIVISION Headquarters, Branches and Services General Staff : 1 July 1917 - 31 December 1917 (First World War, War Diary, WO95/2055)	WD2055	9781474523776	£69.00
19 DIVISION Headquarters, Branches and Services General Staff : 1 January 1918 - 29 May 1918 (First World War, War Diary, WO95/2056)	WD2056	9781474523783	£67.00
19 DIVISION Headquarters, Branches and Services General Staff : 7 June 1918 - 11 December 1918 (First World War, War Diary, WO95/2057)	WD2057	9781474523790	£50.00
19 DIVISION Headquarters, Branches and Services Adjutant and Quarter-Master General : 11 July 1915 - 31 March 1919 (First World War, War Diary, WO95/2058)	WD2058	9781474523806	£41.00
19 DIVISION Headquarters, Branches and Services Commander Royal Artillery : 10 July 1915 - 30 September 1916 (First World War, War Diary, WO95/2059)	WD2059	9781474511018	£65.00
19 DIVISION Headquarters, Branches and Services Commander Royal Artillery : 1 October 1916 - 31 October 1916 (First World War, War Diary, WO95/2060)	WD2060	9781474511025	£49.00
19 DIVISION Headquarters, Branches and Services Commander Royal Artillery : 1 July 1917 - 31 December 1917 (First World War, War Diary, WO95/2061)	WD2061	9781474511032	£51.00
19 DIVISION Headquarters, Branches and Services Commander Royal Artillery : 1 January 1918 - 31 October 1918 (First World War, War Diary, WO95/2062)	WD2062	9781474511049	£45.00
19 DIVISION Headquarters, Branches and Services Royal Army Medical Corps Assistant Director Medical Services : 17 July 1915 - 31 May 1917 (First World War, War Diary, WO95/2063)	WD2063	9781474523813	£72.00
19 DIVISION Headquarters, Branches and Services Royal Army Medical Corps Assistant Director Medical Services : 20 June 1916 - 31 December 1917 (First World War, War Diary, WO95/2064)	WD2064	9781474523820	£72.00
19 DIVISION Headquarters, Branches and Services Royal Army Medical Corps Assistant Director Medical Services : 3 January 1917 - 31 March 1919 (First World War, War Diary, WO95/2065)	WD2065	9781474523837	£61.00
19 DIVISION Headquarters, Branches and Services Commander Royal Engineers : 17 July 1915 - 7 July 1919 (First World War, War Diary, WO95/2066/1)	WD2066_1	9781474511056	£56.00
19 DIVISION Headquarters, Branches and Services Royal Army Ordnance Corps Deputy Assistant Director Ordnance Services : 2 September 1915 - 27 January 1919 (First World War, War Diary, WO95/2066/2)	WD2066_2	9781474511063	£15.00
19 DIVISION Headquarters, Branches and Services Royal Army Veterinary Corps Assistant Director Veterinary Services : 16 July 1915 - 30 November 1918 (First World War, War Diary, WO95/2066/3)	WD2066_3	9781474511070	£15.00

Title	Product Code	ISBN	Price
19 DIVISION Divisional Troops C Squadron 1/1 Yorkshire Dragoons : 26 June 1915 - 9 May 1916 (First World War, War Diary, WO95/2067/1)	WD2067_1	9781474511087	£15.00
19 DIVISION Divisional Troops Divisional Cyclist Company : 17 July 1915 - 30 April 1916 (First World War, War Diary, WO95/2067/2)	WD2067_2	9781474511094	£15.00
19 DIVISION Divisional Troops 86 Brigade Royal Field Artillery : 15 July 1915 - 30 December 1916 (First World War, War Diary, WO95/2067/3)	WD2067_3	9781474511100	£15.00
19 DIVISION Divisional Troops 87 Brigade Royal Field Artillery : 17 July 1915 - 31 October 1918 (First World War, War Diary, WO95/2067/4)	WD2067_4	9781474511117	£15.00
19 DIVISION Divisional Troops 88 Brigade Royal Field Artillery : 1 July 1915 - 31 December 1918 (First World War, War Diary, WO95/2067/5)	WD2067_5	9781474511124	£15.00
19 DIVISION Divisional Troops 89 Brigade Royal Field Artillery, Divisional Trench Mortar Batteries, Divisional Ammunition Column : 11 January 1915 - 31 October 1918 (First World War, War Diary, WO95/2068)	WD2068	9781474511131	£32.00
19 DIVISION Divisional Troops 81 Field Company Royal Engineers and 82 Field Company Royal Engineers : 15 July 1915 - 15 March 1919 (First World War, War Diary, WO95/2069)	WD2069	9781474511148	£41.00
19 DIVISION Divisional Troops 94 Field Company Royal Engineers : 17 October 1914 - 31 May 1919 (First World War, War Diary, WO95/2070/1)	WD2070_1	9781474523844	£71.00
19 DIVISION Divisional Troops Divisional Signal Company : 16 July 1915 - 31 October 1918 (First World War, War Diary, WO95/2070/2)	WD2070_2	9781474523851	£15.00
19 DIVISION Divisional Troops South Wales Borderers 5th Battalion Pioneers, Machine Gun Corps 19 Battalion and 246 Machine Gun Company : 14 July 1915 - 28 February 1918 (First World War, War Diary, WO95/2071)	WD2071	9781474511155	£36.00
19 DIVISION Divisional Troops Royal Army Medical Corps 57 Field Ambulance : 14 August 1915 - 21 May 1919 (First World War, War Diary, WO95/2072/1)	WD2072_1	9781474511162	£32.00
19 DIVISION Divisional Troops Royal Army Medical Corps 58 Field Ambulance : 12 June 1915 - 29 May 1919 (First World War, War Diary, WO95/2072/2)	WD2072_2	9781474511179	£40.00
19 DIVISION Divisional Troops Royal Army Medical Corps 59 Field Ambulance : 18 July 1915 - 31 March 1919 (First World War, War Diary, WO95/2073/1)	WD2073_1	9781474511186	£53.00
19 DIVISION Divisional Troops Royal Army Medical Corps Divisional Field Ambulance Workshop Unit : 16 July 1915 - 6 April 1916 (First World War, War Diary, WO95/2073/2)	WD2073_2	9781474511193	£15.00
19 DIVISION Divisional Troops 36 Sanitary Section : 19 July 1915 - 31 March 1917 (First World War, War Diary, WO95/2073/3)	WD2073_3	9781474511209	£31.00
19 DIVISION Divisional Troops Royal Army Veterinary Corps 31 Mobile Veterinary Section : 19 July 1915 - 31 January 1919 (First World War, War Diary, WO95/2074/1)	WD2074_1	9781474511216	£15.00
19 DIVISION Divisional Troops Royal Army Service Corps Divisional Train (154, 155, 156, 157 Companies A.S.C) : 16 July 1915 - 25 May 1919 (First World War, War Diary, WO95/2074/2)	WD2074_2	9781474523868	£52.00
19 DIVISION 56 Infantry Brigade Headquarters : 6 July 1915 - 31 July 1917 (First World War, War Diary, WO95/2075)	WD2075	9781474523875	£71.00

Title	Product Code	ISBN	Price
19 DIVISION 56 Infantry Brigade Headquarters : 31 July 1917 - 31 December 1917 (First World War, War Diary, WO95/2076)	WD2076	9781474523882	£78.00
19 DIVISION 56 Infantry Brigade Headquarters : 1 January 1918 - 19 May 1919 (First World War, War Diary, WO95/2077)	WD2077	9781474511223	£59.00
19 DIVISION 56 Infantry Brigade King's Own (Royal Lancaster Regiment) 7th Battalion : 7 July 1915 - 28 February 1918 (First World War, War Diary, WO95/2078/1)	WD2078_1	9781474511230	£54.00
19 DIVISION 56 Infantry Brigade King's (Shropshire Light Infantry) 1/4th Battalion : 5 January 1918 - 18 May 1919 (First World War, War Diary, WO95/2078/2)	WD2078_2	9781474511247	£15.00
19 DIVISION 56 Infantry Brigade Cheshire Regiment 9th Battalion : 10 February 1918 - 28 February 1919 (First World War, War Diary, WO95/2079/1)	WD2079_1	9781474511254	£17.00
19 DIVISION 56 Infantry Brigade East Lancashire Regiment 7th Battalion : 6 July 1915 - 31 January 1918 (First World War, War Diary, WO95/2079/2)	WD2079_2	9781474511261	£18.00
19 DIVISION 56 Infantry Brigade Loyal North Lancashire Regiment 7th Battalion : 6 July 1915 - 31 January 1918 (First World War, War Diary, WO95/2080)	WD2080	9781474511278	£51.00
19 DIVISION 56 Infantry Brigade Prince of Wales's Volunteers (South Lancashire Regiment) 7th Battalion : 7 July 1915 - 22 February 1918 (First World War, War Diary, WO95/2081)	WD2081	9781474523899	£81.00
19 DIVISION 56 Infantry Brigade Prince of Wales's (North Staffordshire Regiment) 8th Battalion : 1 March 1918 - 19 May 1919 (First World War, War Diary, WO95/2082/1)	WD2082_1	9781474523905	£15.00
19 DIVISION 56 Infantry Brigade, Brigade Machine Gun Company : 7 November 1915 - 28 February 1918 (First World War, War Diary, WO95/2082/2)	WD2082_2	9781474511285	£15.00
19 DIVISION 56 Infantry Brigade, Brigade Trench Mortar Battery : 4 February 1916 - 31 December 1918 (First World War, War Diary, WO95/2082/3)	WD2082_3	9781474511292	£15.00
19 DIVISION 57 Infantry Brigade Headquarters : 12 January 1915 - 30 June 1917 (First World War, War Diary, WO95/2083)	WD2083	9781474511308	£49.00
19 DIVISION Headquarters, Branches and Services Headquarters : 1 July 1917 - 1 January 1919 (First World War, War Diary, WO95/2084)	WD2084	9781474523912	£56.00
19 DIVISION 57 Infantry Brigade Gloucestershire Regiment 8th Service Battalion : 17 July 1915 - 31 March 1919 (First World War, War Diary, WO95/2085/1)	WD2085_1	9781474523929	£21.00
19 DIVISION 57 Infantry Brigade Prince of Wales's (North Staffordshire Regiment) 8th Battalion : 1 June 1915 - 31 January 1918 (First World War, War Diary, WO95/2085/2)	WD2085_2	9781474511315	£15.00
19 DIVISION 57 Infantry Brigade Royal Warwickshire Regiment 10th Battalion : 17 July 1915 - 27 March 1918 (First World War, War Diary, WO95/2085/3)	WD2085_3	9781474511322	£40.00
19 DIVISION 57 Infantry Brigade Worcestershire Regiment 3rd Battalion, Worcestershire Regiment 10th Battalion, Brigade Machine Gun Company and Brigade Trench Mortar Battery : 17 July 1915 - 20 October 1918 (First World War, War Diary, WO95/2086)	WD2086	9781474511339	£27.00

Title	Product Code	ISBN	Price
19 DIVISION 58 Infantry Brigade Headquarters : 1 January 1915 - 31 August 1916 (First World War, War Diary, WO95/2087)	WD2087	9781474511346	£43.00
19 DIVISION 58 Infantry Brigade Headquarters : 1 October 1916 - 10 October 1917 (First World War, War Diary, WO95/2088)	WD2088	9781474511353	£52.00
19 DIVISION 58 Infantry Brigade Headquarters : 1 January 1918 - 31 December 1919 (First World War, War Diary, WO95/2089)	WD2089	9781474511360	£32.00
19 DIVISION 58 Infantry Brigade Cheshire Regiment 9th Battalion : 19 July 1915 - 31 May 1917 (First World War, War Diary, WO95/2090)	WD2090	9781474511377	£72.00
19 DIVISION 58 Infantry Brigade Cheshire Regiment 9th Battalion : 1 June 1917 - 31 January 1918 (First World War, War Diary, WO95/2091)	WD2091	9781474511384	£76.00
19 DIVISION 58 Infantry Brigade Royal Welsh Fusiliers 9th Battalion : 18 July 1915 - 31 March 1919 (First World War, War Diary, WO95/2092/1)	WD2092_1	9781474511391	£26.00
19 DIVISION 58 Infantry Brigade Welsh Regiment 9th Battalion : 18 July 1915 - 31 March 1919 (First World War, War Diary, WO95/2092/2)	WD2092_2	9781474511407	£18.00
19 DIVISION 58 Infantry Brigade Duke of Edinburgh's (Wiltshire Regiment) 2nd Battalion : 1 May 1918 - 28 February 1919 (First World War, War Diary, WO95/2093/1)	WD2093_1	9781474511414	£15.00
19 DIVISION 58 Infantry Brigade Duke of Edinburgh's (Wiltshire Regiment) 6th Battalion : 5 January 1915 - 31 May 1918 (First World War, War Diary, WO95/2093/2)	WD2093_2	9781474511421	£16.00
19 DIVISION 58 Infantry Brigade, Brigade Machine Gun Company : 1 March 1916 - 28 February 1918 (First World War, War Diary, WO95/2093/3)	WD2093_3	9781474511438	£15.00
19 DIVISION 58 Infantry Brigade, Brigade Trench Mortar Battery : 1 January 1918 - 29 November 1918 (First World War, War Diary, WO95/2093/4)	WD2093_4	9781474511445	£15.00

Title	Product Code	ISBN	Price
2 CAVALRY DIVISION			
2 CAVALRY DIVISION Headquarters, Branches and Services General Staff : 15 September 1914 - 31 December 1915 (First World War, War Diary, WO95/1117)	WD1117	9781474500319	£67.00
2 CAVALRY DIVISION Headquarters, Branches and Services General Staff : 1 January 1916 - 26 April 1919 (First World War, War Diary, WO95/1118)	WD1118	9781474500326	£73.00
2 CAVALRY DIVISION Headquarters, Branches and Services Adjutant and Quarter-Master General : 4 January 1914 - 31 December 1916 (First World War, War Diary, WO95/1119)	WD1119	9781474500333	£45.00
2 CAVALRY DIVISION Headquarters, Branches and Services Adjutant and Quarter-Master General : 1 January 1917 - 31 March 1919 (First World War, War Diary, WO95/1120)	WD1120	9781474500340	£45.00
2 CAVALRY DIVISION Headquarters, Branches and Services Royal Army Medical Corps Assistant Director Medical Services : 22 September 1914 - 31 March 1919 (First World War, War Diary, WO95/1121)	WD1121	9781474500357	£45.00
2 CAVALRY DIVISION Headquarters, Branches and Services Royal Army Ordnance Corps Assistant Director Ordnance Services and Branches and Services Royal Army Veterinary Corps Assistant Director Veterinary Services : 1 September 1914 - 31 March 1919 (First Wo	WD1122	9781474500364	£48.00
2 CAVALRY DIVISION Divisional Troops 3 Brigade Royal Horse Artillery : 4 August 1914 - 29 September 1914, 15 March 1915 - 1 June 1915, 12 October 1915 - 29 December 1915 and 1 July 1916 - 1 February 1919 (First World War, War Diary, WO95/1123/1-4)	WD1123_1-4	9781474500371	£17.00
2 CAVALRY DIVISION Divisional Troops 3 Brigade Ammunition Column : 13 October 1914 - 26 February 1918 (First World War, War Diary, WO95/1123/5)	WD1123_5	9781474500388	£15.00
2 CAVALRY DIVISION Divisional Troops 2 Field Squadron Royal Engineers : 4 August 1914 - 30 April 1919 (First World War, War Diary, WO95/1123/6)	WD1123_6	9781474500395	£15.00
2 CAVALRY DIVISION Divisional Troops Signal Squadron Royal Engineers : 1 August 1915 - 30 April 1919 (First World War, War Diary, WO95/1123/7)	WD1123_7	9781474500401	£18.00
2 CAVALRY DIVISION Divisional Troops Royal Army Medical Corps 2 and 4 Cavalry Field Ambulance : 4 August 1914 - 20 May 1919 (First World War, War Diary, WO95/1124)	WD1124	9781474500418	£75.00
2 CAVALRY DIVISION Divisional Troops Royal Army Medical Corps 5 Cavalry Field Ambulance and 4A Sanitary Section : 8 August 1914 - 10 March 1919 (First World War, War Diary, WO95/1125)	WD1125	9781474500425	£43.00
2 CAVALRY DIVISION Divisional Troops Royal Army Veterinary Corps 7 Mobile Veterinary Section : 3 August 1914 - 30 April 1919 (First World War, War Diary, WO95/1126/1)	WD1126_1	9781474500432	£36.00
2 CAVALRY DIVISION Divisional Troops Royal Army Veterinary Corps 8 Mobile Veterinary Section : 4 August 1914 - 30 June 1915 (First World War, War Diary, WO95/1126/2)	WD1126_2	9781474500449	£32.00
2 CAVALRY DIVISION Divisional Troops Royal Army Veterinary Corps 9 Mobile Veterinary Section : 1 October 1914 - 28 April 1919 (First World War, War Diary, WO95/1127)	WD1127	9781474500456	£69.00
2 CAVALRY DIVISION Divisional Troops Royal Army Service Corps Headquarters Divisional Army Service Corps (424 Company A.S.C.) : 13 March 1915 - 31 March 1919 (First World War, War Diary, WO95/1128/1)	WD1128_1	9781474500463	£24.00

Title	Product Code	ISBN	Price
2 CAVALRY DIVISION Divisional Troops Royal Army Service Corps 2 Cavalry Division Auxiliary Horse Transport (575 Company A.S.C.) : 9 June 1915 - 23 June 1919 (First World War, War Diary, WO95/1128/2)	WD1128_2	9781474500470	£21.00
2 CAVALRY DIVISION Divisional Troops Royal Army Service Corps 2 Cavalry Division Ammunition Park (56 Company A.S.C.) : 20 August 1914 - 12 June 1916 (First World War, War Diary, WO95/1128/3)	WD1128_3	9781474500487	£31.00
2 CAVALRY DIVISION Divisional Troops Royal Army Service Corps Divisional Supply Column (46 Company A.S.C.) : 1 March 1915 - 13 May 1919 (First World War, War Diary, WO95/1129)	WD1129	9781474500494	£76.00
2 CAVALRY DIVISION 3 Cavalry Brigade Headquarters : 4 August 1914 - 30 September 1914 (First World War, War Diary, WO95/1130)	WD1130	9781474500500	£17.00
2 CAVALRY DIVISION 3 Cavalry Brigade Headquarters : 1 October 1914 - 31 October 1914 (First World War, War Diary, WO95/1131)	WD1131	9781474500517	£70.00
2 CAVALRY DIVISION 3 Cavalry Brigade Headquarters : 31 October 1914 - 31 December 1914 (First World War, War Diary, WO95/1132)	WD1132	9781474500524	£47.00
2 CAVALRY DIVISION 3 Cavalry Brigade Headquarters, `D' Battery Royal Horse Artillery and Brigade Machine Gun Squadron : 4 August 1914 - 31 March 1919 (First World War, War Diary, WO95/1133)	WD1133	9781474500531	£64.00
2 CAVALRY DIVISION 3 Cavalry Brigade 4th (Queen's Own) Hussars, 5 (Royal Irish) Lancers and 16 (The Queens) Lancers : 4 August 1914 - 31 October 1917 (First World War, War Diary, WO95/1134)	WD1134	9781474500548	£50.00
2 CAVALRY DIVISION 4 Cavalry Brigade Headquarters, `J' Battery Royal Horse Artillery and Brigade Machine Gun Squadron : 4 August 1914 - 25 April 1919 (First World War, War Diary, WO95/1135)	WD1135	9781474500555	£66.00
2 CAVALRY DIVISION 4 Cavalry Brigade Corps of Hussars. 3rd (King's Own) Hussars : 4 August 1914 - 31 March 1919 (First World War, War Diary, WO95/1136)	WD1136	9781474500562	£47.00
2 CAVALRY DIVISION 4 Cavalry Brigade 6th Dragoon Guards (Carabineers) and 1/1 (Queen's Own) Oxfordshire Hussars : 1 August 1914 - 31 March 1919 (First World War, War Diary, WO95/1137)	WD1137	9781474500579	£49.00
2 CAVALRY DIVISION 5 Cavalry Brigade Headquarters : 4 August 1914 - 31 March 1919 (First World War, War Diary, WO95/1138)	WD1138	9781474500586	£60.00
2 CAVALRY DIVISION 5 Cavalry Brigade `E' Battery Royal Horse Artillery, Brigade Machine Gun Squadron and 2nd Dragoons (Scots Greys) : 5 August 1914 - 31 December 1918 (First World War, War Diary, WO95/1139)	WD1139	9781474500593	£55.00
2 CAVALRY DIVISION 5 Cavalry Brigade 12 (Prince of Wales) Lancers and 20th Hussars : 16 August 1914 - 28 February 1919 (First World War, War Diary, WO95/1140)	WD1140	9781474500609	£67.00

Title	Product Code	ISBN	Price
2 DIVISION			
2 DIVISION Headquarters, Branches and Services General Staff : 5 August 1914 - 31 December 1914 (First World War, War Diary, WO95/1283)	WD1283	9781474502856	£73.00
2 DIVISION Headquarters, Branches and Services General Staff : 1 January 1915 - 31 March 1915 (First World War, War Diary, WO95/1284)	WD1284	9781474521727	£76.00
2 DIVISION Headquarters, Branches and Services General Staff : 1 April 1915 - 31 May 1915 (First World War, War Diary, WO95/1285)	WD1285	9781474502863	£55.00
2 DIVISION Headquarters, Branches and Services General Staff : 1 June 1915 - 30 June 1915 (First World War, War Diary, WO95/1286)	WD1286	9781474502870	£60.00
2 DIVISION Headquarters, Branches and Services General Staff : 1 September 1915 - 24 October 1915 (First World War, War Diary, WO95/1287)	WD1287	9781474502887	£49.00
2 DIVISION Headquarters, Branches and Services General Staff : 1 November 1915 - 31 December 1915 (First World War, War Diary, WO95/1288)	WD1288	9781474502894	£45.00
2 DIVISION Headquarters, Branches and Services General Staff : 1 January 1916 - 31 March 1916 (First World War, War Diary, WO95/1289)	WD1289	9781474502900	£62.00
2 DIVISION Headquarters, Branches and Services General Staff : 1 April 1916 - 10 July 1916 (First World War, War Diary, WO95/1290)	WD1290	9781474502917	£51.00
2 DIVISION Headquarters, Branches and Services General Staff : 28 June 1916 - 2 July 1916 (First World War, War Diary, WO95/1291)	WD1291	9781474502924	£34.00
2 DIVISION Headquarters, Branches and Services General Staff : 1 August 1916 - 30 September 1916 (First World War, War Diary, WO95/1292)	WD1292	9781474521734	£78.00
2 DIVISION Headquarters, Branches and Services General Staff : 1 October 1916 - 15 November 1916 (First World War, War Diary, WO95/1293)	WD1293	9781474502931	£47.00
2 DIVISION Headquarters, Branches and Services General Staff : 1 November 1916 - 31 January 1917 (First World War, War Diary, WO95/1294)	WD1294	9781474502948	£42.00
2 DIVISION Headquarters, Branches and Services General Staff : 1 February 1917 - 28 February 1917 (First World War, War Diary, WO95/1295)	WD1295	9781474502955	£46.00
2 DIVISION Headquarters, Branches and Services General Staff : 1 March 1917 - 30 April 1917 (First World War, War Diary, WO95/1296)	WD1296	9781474502962	£66.00
2 DIVISION Headquarters, Branches and Services General Staff : 1 May 1917 - 30 September 1917 (First World War, War Diary, WO95/1297)	WD1297	9781474502979	£65.00
2 DIVISION Headquarters, Branches and Services General Staff : 30 September 1917 - 31 December 1917 (First World War, War Diary, WO95/1298)	WD1298	9781474502986	£46.00
2 DIVISION Headquarters, Branches and Services General Staff : 1 January 1918 - 30 June 1918 (First World War, War Diary, WO95/1299)	WD1299	9781474502993	£69.00
2 DIVISION Headquarters, Branches and Services General Staff : 1 July 1918 - 31 July 1918 (First World War, War Diary, WO95/1300)	WD1300	9781474503006	£32.00
2 DIVISION Headquarters, Branches and Services General Staff : 1 August 1918 - 24 August 1918 (First World War, War Diary, WO95/1301)	WD1301	9781474503013	£48.00
2 DIVISION Headquarters, Branches and Services General Staff : 1 September 1918 - 30 September 1918 (First World War, War Diary, WO95/1302)	WD1302	9781474503020	£36.00

Title	Product Code	ISBN	Price
2 DIVISION Headquarters, Branches and Services General Staff : 1 October 1918 - 31 October 1918 (First World War, War Diary, WO95/1303)	WD1303	9781474503037	£20.00
2 DIVISION Headquarters, Branches and Services General Staff : 1 November 1918 - 31 October 1919 (First World War, War Diary, WO95/1304)	WD1304	9781474503044	£63.00
2 DIVISION Headquarters, Branches and Services Adjutant and Quarter-Master General : 5 August 1914 - 30 June 1915 (First World War, War Diary, WO95/1305)	WD1305	9781474503051	£49.00
2 DIVISION Headquarters, Branches and Services Adjutant and Quarter-Master General : 4 July 1915 - 30 December 1915 (First World War, War Diary, WO95/1306)	WD1306	9781474503068	£58.00
2 DIVISION Headquarters, Branches and Services Adjutant and Quarter-Master General : 1 January 1916 - 31 July 1916 (First World War, War Diary, WO95/1307)	WD1307	9781474503075	£44.00
2 DIVISION Headquarters, Branches and Services Adjutant and Quarter-Master General : 1 August 1916 - 31 December 1916 (First World War, War Diary, WO95/1308)	WD1308	9781474503082	£63.00
2 DIVISION Headquarters, Branches and Services Adjutant and Quarter-Master General : 1 January 1917 - 30 June 1917 (First World War, War Diary, WO95/1309)	WD1309	9781474503099	£46.00
2 DIVISION Headquarters, Branches and Services Adjutant and Quarter-Master General : 1 July 1917 - 31 December 1917 (First World War, War Diary, WO95/1310)	WD1310	9781474503105	£49.00
2 DIVISION Headquarters, Branches and Services Adjutant and Quarter-Master General : 29 September 1916 - 31 December 1918 (First World War, War Diary, WO95/1311)	WD1311	9781474521741	£88.00
2 DIVISION Headquarters, Branches and Services Adjutant and Quarter-Master General : 1 January 1919 - 31 August 1919 (First World War, War Diary, WO95/1312)	WD1312	9781474503112	£51.00
2 DIVISION Headquarters, Branches and Services Commander Royal Artillery : 15 August 1914 - 31 January 1915 (First World War, War Diary, WO95/1313A)	WD1313_A	9781474521758	£54.00
2 DIVISION Headquarters, Branches and Services Commander Royal Artillery : 1 February 1915 - 28 February 1915 (First World War, War Diary, WO95/1313B)	WD1313_B	9781474521765	£44.00
2 DIVISION Headquarters, Branches and Services Commander Royal Artillery : 1 March 1915 - 31 May 1915 (First World War, War Diary, WO95/1314A)	WD1314_A	9781474521772	£50.00
2 DIVISION Headquarters, Branches and Services Commander Royal Artillery : 1 June 1915 - 30 June 1915 (First World War, War Diary, WO95/1314B)	WD1314_B	9781474521789	£43.00
2 DIVISION Headquarters, Branches and Services Commander Royal Artillery : 1 July 1915 - 30 September 1915 (First World War, War Diary, WO95/1315)	WD1315	9781474503129	£78.00
2 DIVISION Headquarters, Branches and Services Commander Royal Artillery : 1 October 1915 - 31 October 1915 (First World War, War Diary, WO95/1316/1)	WD1316_1	9781474503136	£25.00

Title	Product Code	ISBN	Price
2 DIVISION Headquarters, Branches and Services Commander Royal Artillery : 1 November 1915 - 30 November 1915 (First World War, War Diary, WO95/1316/2)	WD1316_2	9781474503143	£17.00
2 DIVISION Headquarters, Branches and Services Commander Royal Artillery : 1 December 1915 - 31 December 1915 (First World War, War Diary, WO95/1316/3)	WD1316_3	9781474503150	£21.00
2 DIVISION Headquarters, Branches and Services Commander Royal Artillery : 1 January 1916 - 30 June 1916 (First World War, War Diary, WO95/1317)	WD1317	9781474503167	£68.00
2 DIVISION Headquarters, Branches and Services Commander Royal Artillery : 1 July 1916 - 31 December 1916 (First World War, War Diary, WO95/1318)	WD1318	9781474503174	£43.00
2 DIVISION Headquarters, Branches and Services Commander Royal Artillery : 1 July 1917 - 31 December 1918 (First World War, War Diary, WO95/1319)	WD1319	9781474503181	£49.00
2 DIVISION Headquarters, Branches and Services Royal Army Medical Corps Assistant Director Medical Services : 8 August 1914 - 31 December 1914 (First World War, War Diary, WO95/1320A)	WD1320_A	9781474521796	£45.00
2 DIVISION Headquarters, Branches and Services Royal Army Medical Corps Assistant Director Medical Services : 1 January 1915 - 30 June 1916 (First World War, War Diary, WO95/1320B)	WD1320_B	9781474521802	£71.00
2 DIVISION Headquarters, Branches and Services Royal Army Medical Corps Assistant Director Medical Services : 1 July 1916 - 31 October 1919 (First World War, War Diary, WO95/1321)	WD1321	9781474521819	£83.00
2 DIVISION Headquarters, Branches and Services Commander Royal Engineers and Deputy Assistant Director Ordnance Services : 1 February 1914 - 30 August 1919 (First World War, War Diary, WO95/1322)	WD1322	9781474503198	£42.00
2 DIVISION Headquarters, Branches and Services Royal Army Veterinary Corps Assistant Director Veterinary Services : 6 August 1914 - 31 October 1919 (First World War, War Diary, WO95/1323)	WD1323	9781474503204	£48.00
2 DIVISION Divisional Troops `B' Squadron 15 Hussars, `S' Squadron South Irish Horse, Divisional Cyclist Company and 34 Brigade Royal Field Artillery : 16 August 1914 - 30 April 1917 (First World War, War Diary, WO95/1324)	WD1324	9781474503211	£40.00
2 DIVISION Divisional Troops 36 Brigade Royal Field Artillery : 4 August 1914 - 31 December 1918 (First World War, War Diary, WO95/1325)	WD1325	9781474503228	£39.00
2 DIVISION Divisional Troops 41 Brigade Royal Field Artillery : 4 August 1914 - 31 December 1915 (First World War, War Diary, WO95/1326)	WD1326	9781474503235	£37.00
2 DIVISION Divisional Troops 41 and 44 Brigade Royal Field Artillery : 4 August 1914 - 30 April 1916 (First World War, War Diary, WO95/1327)	WD1327	9781474503242	£34.00
2 DIVISION Divisional Troops Anti-Aircraft Section and Divisional Ammunition Column : 5 August 1914 - 31 December 1918 (First World War, War Diary, WO95/1328)	WD1328	9781474503259	£19.00
2 DIVISION Divisional Troops Divisional Trench Mortar Batteries : 27 May 1916 - 31 December 1918 (First World War, War Diary, WO95/1329)	WD1329	9781474503266	£24.00
2 DIVISION Divisional Troops 5 Field Company Royal Engineers : 4 August 1914 - 31 December 1918 (First World War, War Diary, WO95/1330)	WD1330	9781474503273	£60.00

Title	Product Code	ISBN	Price
2 DIVISION Divisional Troops 11 Field Company Royal Engineers : 15 August 1914 - 30 November 1915 (First World War, War Diary, WO95/1331/1)	WD1331_1	9781474503280	£36.00
2 DIVISION Divisional Troops 226 Field Company Royal Engineers : 17 November 1915 - 30 November 1915 (First World War, War Diary, WO95/1331/2)	WD1331_2	9781474503297	£40.00
2 DIVISION Divisional Troops 483 Field Company Royal Engineers : 23 December 1914 - 31 August 1919 (First World War, War Diary, WO95/1332)	WD1332	9781474503303	£21.00
2 DIVISION Divisional Troops Divisional Signal Company : 7 August 1914 - 31 December 1918 (First World War, War Diary, WO95/1333)	WD1333	9781474503310	£57.00
2 DIVISION Divisional Troops 2 Battalion Machine Gun Corps and 242 Machine Gun Company : 13 July 1917 - 27 February 1918 (First World War, War Diary, WO95/1334)	WD1334	9781474521826	£87.00
2 DIVISION Divisional Troops Duke of Cornwall's Light Infantry 10th Battalion Pioneers and 5th Battalion Pioneers : 16 June 1916 - 4 November 1919 (First World War, War Diary, WO95/1335)	WD1335	9781474503327	£47.00
2 DIVISION Divisional Troops Royal Army Medical Corps 4 Field Ambulance : 12 September 1914 - 31 December 1914 (First World War, War Diary, WO95/1336/1)	WD1336_1	9781474503334	£17.00
2 DIVISION Divisional Troops Royal Army Medical Corps 4 Field Ambulance : 1 January 1915 - 28 February 1915 (First World War, War Diary, WO95/1336/2)	WD1336_2	9781474503341	£15.00
2 DIVISION Divisional Troops Royal Army Medical Corps 4 Field Ambulance : 1 March 1915 - 31 March 1915 (First World War, War Diary, WO95/1336/3)	WD1336_3	9781474503358	£15.00
2 DIVISION Divisional Troops Royal Army Medical Corps 4 Field Ambulance : 1 April 1915 - 30 April 1915 (First World War, War Diary, WO95/1336/4)	WD1336_4	9781474503365	£15.00
2 DIVISION Divisional Troops Royal Army Medical Corps 4 Field Ambulance : 1 May 1915 - 31 May 1915 (First World War, War Diary, WO95/1336/5)	WD1336_5	9781474503372	£15.00
2 DIVISION Divisional Troops Royal Army Medical Corps 4 Field Ambulance : 1 June 1915 - 31 July 1915 (First World War, War Diary, WO95/1336/6)	WD1336_6	9781474503389	£15.00
2 DIVISION Divisional Troops Royal Army Medical Corps 5 Field Ambulance : 1 January 1914 - 31 August 1919 (First World War, War Diary, WO95/1337)	WD1337	9781474503396	£64.00
2 DIVISION Divisional Troops Royal Army Medical Corps 6 Field Ambulance : 5 August 1914 - 31 August 1919 (First World War, War Diary, WO95/1338)	WD1338	9781474503402	£32.00
2 DIVISION Divisional Troops Royal Army Medical Corps 100 Field Ambulance : 16 November 1915 - 22 June 1919 (First World War, War Diary, WO95/1339/1)	WD1339_1	9781474503419	£32.00
2 DIVISION Divisional Troops 11 Sanitary Section : 9 January 1915 - 30 March 1917 (First World War, War Diary, WO95/1339/2)	WD1339_2	9781474503426	£25.00
2 DIVISION Divisional Troops Royal Army Veterinary Corps 3 Mobile Veterinary Section : 4 August 1914 - 28 October 1919 (First World War, War Diary, WO95/1340/1)	WD1340_1	9781474503433	£21.00

Title	Product Code	ISBN	Price
2 DIVISION Divisional Troops Royal Army Service Corps 2 Divisional Train (28, 31, 35, 172 Companies A.S.C.) : 4 August 1914 - 31 August 1919 (First World War, War Diary, WO95/1340/2)	WD1340_2	9781474503440	£45.00
2 DIVISION 4 Guards Brigade Headquarters : 4 August 1914 - 31 July 1915 (First World War, War Diary, WO95/1341)	WD1341	9781474503457	£47.00
2 DIVISION 4 Guards Brigade Grenadier Guards 2nd Battalion, Coldstream Guards 2 Battalion, Coldstream Guards 3 Battalion, Irish Guards 1st Battalion and Hertfordshire Regiment 1/1st Battalion : 30 July 1914 - 31 July 1915 (First World War, War Diary, W	WD1342	9781474503464	£52.00
2 DIVISION 5 Infantry Brigade Headquarters : 4 August 1914 - 31 December 1915 (First World War, War Diary, WO95/1343)	WD1343	9781474503471	£42.00
2 DIVISION 5 Infantry Brigade Headquarters : 1 January 1916 - 31 December 1916 (First World War, War Diary, WO95/1344)	WD1344	9781474503488	£48.00
2 DIVISION 5 Infantry Brigade Headquarters : 1 January 1917 - 31 December 1917 (First World War, War Diary, WO95/1345)	WD1345	9781474503495	£38.00
2 DIVISION 5 Infantry Brigade Headquarters : 1 January 1918 - 31 March 1919 (First World War, War Diary, WO95/1346)	WD1346	9781474503501	£63.00
2 DIVISION 5 Infantry Brigade Connaught Rangers 2nd Battalion, Highland Light Infantry 2nd Battalion and Highland Light Infantry 9th (Glasgow Highland) Battalion (Territorial) : 4 August 1914 - 30 April 1916 (First World War, War Diary, WO95/1347)	WD1347	9781474503518	£44.00
2 DIVISION 5 Infantry Brigade Oxfordshire and Buckinghamshire Light Infantry 2nd Battalion : 4 August 1914 - 30 March 1919 (First World War, War Diary, WO95/1348)	WD1348	9781474503525	£44.00
2 DIVISION 5 Infantry Brigade Royal Fusiliers (City of London Regiment) 24th Battalion : 8 November 1915 - 31 March 1919 (First World War, War Diary, WO95/1349)	WD1349	9781474503532	£71.00
2 DIVISION 5 Infantry Brigade Royal Inniskilling Fusiliers 2nd Battalion : 1 January 1915 - 31 December 1915 (First World War, War Diary, WO95/1350/1)	WD1350_1	9781474503549	£15.00
2 DIVISION 5 Infantry Brigade Royal Fusiliers (City of London Regiment) 17th Battalion : 15 November 1915 - 31 January 1918 (First World War, War Diary, WO95/1350/2)	WD1350_2	9781474503556	£15.00
2 DIVISION 5 Infantry Brigade Queen's (Royal West Surrey Regiment) 1st Battalion : 1 January 1915 - 31 December 1915 (First World War, War Diary, WO95/1350/3)	WD1350_3	9781474503563	£15.00
2 DIVISION 5 Infantry Brigade Worcestershire Regiment 2nd Battalion and Machine Gun Company : 4 August 1914 - 28 February 1918 (First World War, War Diary, WO95/1351)	WD1351	9781474503570	£41.00
2 DIVISION 6 Infantry Brigade Headquarters : 3 February 1914 - 30 September 1915 (First World War, War Diary, WO95/1352)	WD1352	9781474521833	£72.00
2 DIVISION 6 Infantry Brigade Headquarters : 1 October 1915 - 31 March 1916 (First World War, War Diary, WO95/1353)	WD1353	9781474503587	£66.00
2 DIVISION 6 Infantry Brigade Headquarters : 1 April 1916 - 31 July 1916 (First World War, War Diary, WO95/1354)	WD1354	9781474503594	£77.00
2 DIVISION 6 Infantry Brigade Headquarters : 1 August 1916 - 31 December 1916 (First World War, War Diary, WO95/1355)	WD1355	9781474503600	£56.00

Title	Product Code	ISBN	Price
2 DIVISION 6 Infantry Brigade Headquarters : 1 January 1917 - 31 December 1917 (First World War, War Diary, WO95/1356)	WD1356	9781474503617	£62.00
2 DIVISION 6 Infantry Brigade Headquarters : 1 January 1918 - 31 March 1919 (First World War, War Diary, WO95/1357)	WD1357	9781474503624	£46.00
2 DIVISION 6 Infantry Brigade Essex Regiment 13th Battalion : 16 November 1915 - 31 January 1918 (First World War, War Diary, WO95/1358/1)	WD1358_1	9781474503631	£30.00
2 DIVISION 6 Infantry Brigade Herefordshire Regiment 1/1st Battalion : 2 August 1915 - 29 February 1916 (First World War, War Diary, WO95/1358/2)	WD1358_2	9781474503648	£15.00
2 DIVISION 6 Infantry Brigade King's Royal Rifle Corps 1st Battalion : 12 August 1914 - 17 December 1915 (First World War, War Diary, WO95/1358/3)	WD1358_3	9781474503655	£18.00
2 DIVISION 6 Infantry Brigade King's (Liverpool Regiment) 1st Battalion : 12 August 1914 - 31 December 1917 (First World War, War Diary, WO95/1359)	WD1359	9781474503662	£43.00
2 DIVISION 6 Infantry Brigade King's (Liverpool Regiment) 1st Battalion : 1 February 1915 - 31 December 1915 (First World War, War Diary, WO95/1360/1)	WD1360_1	9781474503679	£15.00
2 DIVISION 6 Infantry Brigade King's (Liverpool Regiment) 7th Battalion : 1 March 1915 - 31 December 1915 (First World War, War Diary, WO95/1360/2)	WD1360_2	9781474503686	£15.00
2 DIVISION 6 Infantry Brigade King's (Liverpool Regiment) 5th Battalion : 1 January 1918 - 30 April 1919 (First World War, War Diary, WO95/1360/3)	WD1360_3	9781474503693	£68.00
2 DIVISION 6 Infantry Brigade Princess Charlotte of Wales's (Royal Berkshire Regiment) 1st Battalion and Duke of Cambridge's Own (Middlesex Regiment) 17th Battalion: 8 March 1914 - 22 February 1918 (First World War, War Diary, WO95/1361)	WD1361	9781474503709	£41.00
2 DIVISION 6 Infantry Brigade South Staffordshire Regiment 2nd Battalion : 4 August 1914 - 30 April 1919 (First World War, War Diary, WO95/1362)	WD1362	9781474503716	£37.00
2 DIVISION 6 Infantry Brigade Royal Fusiliers (City of London Regiment) 17th Battalion and Machine Gun Company : 4 January 1916 - 28 February 1918 (First World War, War Diary, WO95/1363)	WD1363	9781474503723	£30.00
2 DIVISION 19 Infantry Brigade Headquarters : 22 August 1914 - 31 July 1915 (First World War, War Diary, WO95/1364)	WD1364	9781474503730	£31.00
2 DIVISION 19 Infantry Brigade Princess Louise's (Argyll & Sutherland Highlanders) 2nd Battalion : 2 February 1914 - 30 November 1915 (First World War, War Diary, WO95/1365/1)	WD1365_1	9781474503747	£17.00
2 DIVISION 19 Infantry Brigade Duke of Cambridge's Own (Middlesex Regiment) 1st Battalion : 23 August 1914 - 30 November 1915 (First World War, War Diary, WO95/1365/2)	WD1365_2	9781474503754	£15.00
2 DIVISION 19 Infantry Brigade Royal Welsh Fusiliers 2nd Battalion : 4 August 1914 - 30 November 1915 (First World War, War Diary, WO95/1365/3)	WD1365_3	9781474503761	£15.00
2 DIVISION 19 Infantry Brigade Cameronians (Scottish Rifles) 1st and 5th Battalions and 19 Field Ambulance : 23 July 1914 - 30 July 1914 (First World War, War Diary, WO95/1366)	WD1366	9781474503778	£43.00

Title	Product Code	ISBN	Price
2 DIVISION 19 Infantry Brigade Royal Army Veterinary Corps Veterinary Officer : 21 August 1914 - 30 September 1914 (First World War, War Diary, WO95/1367/1)	WD1367_1	9781474503785	£15.00
2 DIVISION 19 Infantry Brigade, Brigade Train : 22 August 1914 - 30 November 1914 (First World War, War Diary, WO95/1367/2)	WD1367_2	9781474503792	£15.00
2 DIVISION 19 Infantry Brigade, Brigade Ammunition Column : 21 August 1914 - 24 August 1915 (First World War, War Diary, WO95/1367/3)	WD1367_3	9781474503808	£15.00
2 DIVISION 19 Infantry Brigade, Brigade Supply Column : 20 August 1914 - 20 August 1915 (First World War, War Diary, WO95/1367/4)	WD1367_4	9781474503815	£15.00
2 DIVISION 99 Infantry Brigade Headquarters : 15 November 1915 - 30 September 1916 (First World War, War Diary, WO95/1368)	WD1368	9781474503822	£38.00
2 DIVISION 99 Infantry Brigade Headquarters : 1 January 1917 - 31 December 1917 (First World War, War Diary, WO95/1369)	WD1369	9781474503839	£47.00
2 DIVISION 99 Infantry Brigade Headquarters : 1 January 1918 - 31 March 1919 (First World War, War Diary, WO95/1370)	WD1370	9781474521840	£61.00
2 DIVISION 99 Infantry Brigade Princess Charlotte of Wales's (Royal Berkshire Regiment) 1st Battalion : 11 February 1915 - 31 December 1918 (First World War, War Diary, WO95/1371/1)	WD1371_1	9781474503846	£26.00
2 DIVISION 99 Infantry Brigade King's Royal Rifle Corps 1st Battalion : 29 November 1915 - 1 February 1919 (First World War, War Diary, WO95/1371/2)	WD1371_2	9781474503853	£37.00
2 DIVISION 99 Infantry Brigade Royal Fusiliers (City of London Regiment) 17th, 22nd and 23rd Battalions : 1 December 1915 - 31 December 1915 (First World War, War Diary, WO95/1372/1-2)	WD1372_1-2	9781474503860	£40.00
2 DIVISION 99 Infantry Brigade Machine Gun Company : 26 April 1916 - 31 December 1917 (First World War, War Diary, WO95/1373/1)	WD1373_1	9781474503877	£15.00
2 DIVISION 99 Infantry Brigade Trench Mortar Battery : 1 November 1915 - 31 December 1915 (First World War, War Diary, WO95/1373/2)	WD1373_2	9781474503884	£15.00
2 DIVISION 3 Light Brigade Rifle Brigade (The Prince Consort's Own) 51 Battalion : 28 March 1919 - 2 November 1919 (First World War, War Diary, WO95/1374/10)	WD1374_10	9781474503952	£15.00
2 DIVISION 3 Light Brigade Rifle Brigade (The Prince Consort's Own) 52 Battalion : 1 March 1919 - 21 October 1919 (First World War, War Diary, WO95/1374/11)	WD1374_11	9781474503969	£15.00
2 DIVISION 3 Light Brigade Rifle Brigade (The Prince Consort's Own) 53 Battalion : 21 March 1919 - 21 October 1919 (First World War, War Diary, WO95/1374/12)	WD1374_12	9781474503976	£15.00
2 DIVISION 1 Light Brigade Headquarters, King's Royal Rifle Corps 13th, 18th and 20th Battalions : 3 April 1919 - 31 July 1919 (First World War, War Diary, WO95/1374/1-4)	WD1374_1-4	9781474503891	£15.00
2 DIVISION 2 Light Brigade Headquarters : 6 April 1919 - 25 October 1919 (First World War, War Diary, WO95/1374/5)	WD1374_5	9781474503907	£15.00
2 DIVISION 2 Light Brigade London Regiment 6th (City of London) Battalion (Rifles) : 1 March 1919 - 23 October 1919 (First World War, War Diary, WO95/1374/6)	WD1374_6	9781474503914	£15.00

Title	Product Code	ISBN	Price
2 DIVISION 2 Light Brigade London Regiment 9th (County of London) Battalion (Queen Victoria's Rifles) : 1 March 1919 - 24 October 1919 (First World War, War Diary, WO95/1374/7)	WD1374_7	9781474503921	£15.00
2 DIVISION 2 Light Brigade Royal Irish Rifles 12th Battalion : 1 April 1919 - 31 October 1919 (First World War, War Diary, WO95/1374/8)	WD1374_8	9781474503938	£15.00
2 DIVISION 3 Light Brigade Headquarters : 1 April 1919 - 14 November 1919 (First World War, War Diary, WO95/1374/9)	WD1374_9	9781474503945	£15.00

Title	Product Code	ISBN	Price
2 INDIAN CAVALRY DIVISION			
2 INDIAN CAVALRY DIVISION Headquarters, Branches and Services General Staff, Adjutant and Quarter-Master General and Commander Royal Artillery: 3 September 1914 - 23 May 1915 (First World War, War Diary, WO95/1180)	WD1180	9781474501637	£82.00
2 INDIAN CAVALRY DIVISION Headquarters, Branches and Services Royal Army Medical Corps Assistant Director Medical Services, Royal Army Ordnance Corps Deputy Assistant Director Ordnance Services and Royal Army Veterinary Corps Assistant Director Veterinary	WD1181	9781474501644	£46.00
2 INDIAN CAVALRY DIVISION Divisional Troops 2 Brigade Royal Horse Artillery, Divisional Ammunition Column, 9 Light Armoured Car Battery, 2 Field Squadron Royal Engineers, 1 (K.G.O) Sappers and Miners and Divisional Signal Squadron : 3 January 1914 - 31 De	WD1182	9781474501651	£44.00
2 INDIAN CAVALRY DIVISION Divisional Troops Ambala Field Ambulance, 119 (Meerut) Field Ambulance, 141 (Secunderabad) Field Ambulance, and Divisional Sanitary Section) : 17 August 1914 - 31 December 1916 (First World War, War Diary, WO95/1183)	WD1183	9781474501668	£68.00
2 INDIAN CAVALRY DIVISION Divisional Troops Headquarters (427 Company A.S.C.), Divisional Supply Column (71 & 83 Companies A.S.C.) and 2 Divisional Ammunition Park (72 Company A.S.C. : 19 September 1914 - 31 October 1916 (First World War, War Diary, WO95/	WD1184	9781474501675	£26.00
2 INDIAN CAVALRY DIVISION Ambala Cavalry Brigade Headquarters, 8th (King's Royal Irish) Hussars, 9 Hodson's Horse, 18 Lancers, 30 Lancers, `X' Battery Royal Horse Artillery, Brigade Signal Troop, Brigade Machine Gun Squadron and Brigade Supply Officer :	WD1185	9781474501682	£65.00
2 INDIAN CAVALRY DIVISION Meerut Cavalry Brigade Headquarters, 3 Skinner's Horse, 13th Hussars, 18 Lancers, `V' Battery Royal Horse Artillery, Brigade Signal Troop and Mobile Veterinary Section : 14 October 1914 - 25 May 1916 (First World War, War Diar	WD1186	9781474501699	£46.00
2 INDIAN CAVALRY DIVISION Secunderabad Cavalry Brigade Headquarters, 7th Dragoon Guards (Princess Royal), 20 Deccan Horse and 34 Poona Horse : 9 August 1914 - 24 December 1916 (First World War, War Diary, WO95/1187)	WD1187	9781474501705	£61.00
2 INDIAN CAVALRY DIVISION Secunderabad Cavalry Brigade `N' Battery Royal Horse Artillery, Brigade Signal Troop, Brigade Machine Gun Squadron and Mobile Veterinary Section : 12 March 1914 - 31 December 1916 (First World War, War Diary, WO95/1188)	WD1188	9781474501712	£19.00

Title	Product Code	ISBN	Price
20 DIVISION			
20 DIVISION Headquarters, Branches and Services General Staff : 20 July 1915 - 31 December 1915 (First World War, War Diary, WO95/2094)	WD2094	9781474511452	£58.00
20 DIVISION Headquarters, Branches and Services General Staff : 19 April 1915 - 31 December 1916 (First World War, War Diary, WO95/2095)	WD2095	9781474511469	£73.00
20 DIVISION Headquarters, Branches and Services General Staff : 1 January 1917 - 31 July 1917 (First World War, War Diary, WO95/2096)	WD2096	9781474511476	£50.00
20 DIVISION Headquarters, Branches and Services General Staff : 1 August 1917 - 31 January 1919 (First World War, War Diary, WO95/2097)	WD2097	9781474523936	£75.00
20 DIVISION Headquarters, Branches and Services Adjutant and Quarter-Master General : 21 July 1915 - 31 December 1915 (First World War, War Diary, WO95/2098)	WD2098	9781474523943	£66.00
20 DIVISION Headquarters, Branches and Services Adjutant and Quarter-Master General : 1 January 1916 - 10 May 1919 (First World War, War Diary, WO95/2099)	WD2099	9781474511483	£67.00
20 DIVISION Headquarters, Branches and Services Commander Royal Artillery : 22 January 1915 - 31 December 1916 (First World War, War Diary, WO95/2100)	WD2100	9781474523950	£65.00
20 DIVISION Headquarters, Branches and Services Commander Royal Artillery : 1 January 1917 - 31 December 1917 (First World War, War Diary, WO95/2101)	WD2101	9781474523967	£62.00
20 DIVISION Headquarters, Branches and Services Commander Royal Artillery : 1 May 1917 - 20 April 1919 (First World War, War Diary, WO95/2102)	WD2102	9781474523974	£44.00
20 DIVISION Headquarters, Branches and Services Royal Army Medical Corps Assistant Director Medical Services : 22 July 1915 - 19 March 1919 (First World War, War Diary, WO95/2103)	WD2103	9781474511490	£58.00
20 DIVISION Headquarters, Branches and Services Commander Royal Engineers : 21 July 1915 - 25 April 1919 (First World War, War Diary, WO95/2104/1)	WD2104_1	9781474511506	£16.00
20 DIVISION Headquarters, Branches and Services Royal Army Ordnance Corps Deputy Assistant Director Ordnance Services : 22 July 1915 - 31 March 1919 (First World War, War Diary, WO95/2104/2)	WD2104_2	9781474511513	£15.00
20 DIVISION Headquarters, Branches and Services Royal Army Veterinary Corps Assistant Director Veterinary Services : 20 July 1915 - 18 March 1919 (First World War, War Diary, WO95/2104/3)	WD2104_3	9781474511520	£15.00
20 DIVISION Divisional Troops D Squadron 1/1 Westmorland and Cumberland Yeomanry, Divisional Cyclist Company and 90, 91, 92 and 92 Brigade Royal Field Artillery : 18 July 1915 - 31 May 1916 (First World War, War Diary, WO95/2105)	WD2105	9781474523981	£64.00
20 DIVISION Divisional Troops 93 Brigade Royal Field Artillery : 1 August 1915 - 31 December 1916 (First World War, War Diary, WO95/2106/1)	WD2106_1	9781474523998	£15.00
20 DIVISION Divisional Troops Divisional Trench Mortar Batteries : 24 May 1916 - 30 January 1919 (First World War, War Diary, WO95/2106/2)	WD2106_2	9781474511537	£15.00
20 DIVISION Divisional Troops Divisional Ammunition Column : 28 July 1915 - 21 April 1919 (First World War, War Diary, WO95/2106/3)	WD2106_3	9781474511544	£24.00

Title	Product Code	ISBN	Price
20 DIVISION Divisional Troops 83 Field Company Royal Engineers : 22 July 1915 - 31 May 1919 (First World War, War Diary, WO95/2107/1)	WD2107_1	9781474511551	£15.00
20 DIVISION Divisional Troops 84 Field Company Royal Engineers : 23 July 1915 - 20 June 1919 (First World War, War Diary, WO95/2107/2)	WD2107_2	9781474511568	£15.00
20 DIVISION Divisional Troops 96 Field Company Royal Engineers : 2 August 1915 - 29 May 1919 (First World War, War Diary, WO95/2107/3)	WD2107_3	9781474511575	£22.00
20 DIVISION Divisional Troops Divisional Signal Company : 20 July 1915 - 29 April 1919 (First World War, War Diary, WO95/2108/1)	WD2108_1	9781474511582	£20.00
20 DIVISION Divisional Troops Durham Light Infantry 11th Battalion Pioneers : 21 July 1915 - 24 June 1919 (First World War, War Diary, WO95/2108/2)	WD2108_2	9781474511599	£27.00
20 DIVISION Divisional Troops Machine Gun Corps 20 Battalion : 15 March 1918 - 28 February 1919 (First World War, War Diary, WO95/2108/3)	WD2108_3	9781474511605	£15.00
20 DIVISION Divisional Troops 217 Machine Gun Company : 16 March 1917 - 28 February 1918 (First World War, War Diary, WO95/2108/4)	WD2108_4	9781474511612	£15.00
20 DIVISION Divisional Troops Royal Army Medical Corps 60 Field Ambulance : 23 July 1915 - 1 May 1919 (First World War, War Diary, WO95/2109/1)	WD2109_1	9781474511629	£31.00
20 DIVISION Divisional Troops Royal Army Medical Corps 61 Field Ambulance : 1 November 1915 - 9 June 1919 (First World War, War Diary, WO95/2109/2)	WD2109_2	9781474511636	£23.00
20 DIVISION Divisional Troops Royal Army Medical Corps 62 Field Ambulance : 24 July 1915 - 30 May 1919 (First World War, War Diary, WO95/2109/3)	WD2109_3	9781474511643	£24.00
20 DIVISION Divisional Troops Royal Army Medical Corps Divisional Field Ambulance Workshop Unit : 14 June 1915 - 31 March 1916 (First World War, War Diary, WO95/2110/1)	WD2110_1	9781474511650	£15.00
20 DIVISION Divisional Troops 33 Sanitary Section : 23 July 1915 - 31 March 1917 (First World War, War Diary, WO95/2110/2)	WD2110_2	9781474511667	£29.00
20 DIVISION Divisional Troops Royal Army Veterinary Corps 32 Mobile Veterinary Section : 23 July 1915 - 28 March 1919 (First World War, War Diary, WO95/2110/3)	WD2110_3	9781474511674	£15.00
20 DIVISION Divisional Troops Divisional Salvage Company : 7 August 1915 - 31 March 1916 (First World War, War Diary, WO95/2110/4)	WD2110_4	9781474511681	£15.00
20 DIVISION Divisional Troops Royal Army Service Corps Divisional Train (158, 159, 160, 161 Companies A.S.C.) : 28 July 1915 - 30 April 1919 (First World War, War Diary, WO95/2110/5)	WD2110_5	9781474511698	£29.00
20 DIVISION 59 Infantry Brigade Headquarters : 18 July 1915 - 30 June 1916 (First World War, War Diary, WO95/2111)	WD2111	9781474511704	£50.00
20 DIVISION 59 Infantry Brigade Headquarters : 1 July 1916 - 28 February 1917 (First World War, War Diary, WO95/2112)	WD2112	9781474511711	£46.00
20 DIVISION 59 Infantry Brigade Headquarters : 1 March 1917 - 30 September 1917 (First World War, War Diary, WO95/2113)	WD2113	9781474511728	£51.00
20 DIVISION 59 Infantry Brigade Headquarters : 1 October 1917 - 26 May 1919 (First World War, War Diary, WO95/2114)	WD2114	9781474511735	£57.00

Title	Product Code	ISBN	Price
20 DIVISION 59 Infantry Brigade King's Royal Rifle Corps 10th Battalion and King's Royal Rifle Corps 11th Battalion : 16 July 1915 - 28 March 1919 (First World War, War Diary, WO95/2115)	WD2115	9781474511742	£58.00
20 DIVISION 59 Infantry Brigade Rifle Brigade (The Prince Consort's Own) 11th Battalion : 21 July 1915 - 30 May 1919 (First World War, War Diary, WO95/2116)	WD2116	9781474511759	£73.00
20 DIVISION 59 Infantry Brigade Rifle Brigade (The Prince Consort's Own) 10th Battalion : 20 July 1915 - 21 February 1918 (First World War, War Diary, WO95/2117/1)	WD2117_1	9781474511766	£52.00
20 DIVISION 59 Infantry Brigade Cameronians (Scottish Rifles) 2nd Battalion : 1 February 1918 - 8 April 1919 (First World War, War Diary, WO95/2117/2)	WD2117_2	9781474511773	£15.00
20 DIVISION 59 Infantry Brigade, Brigade Machine Gun Company : 23 February 1916 - 27 February 1918 (First World War, War Diary, WO95/2117/3)	WD2117_3	9781474511780	£15.00
20 DIVISION 60 Infantry Brigade Headquarters : 20 July 1915 - 31 July 1917 (First World War, War Diary, WO95/2118)	WD2118	9781474511797	£53.00
20 DIVISION 60 Infantry Brigade Headquarters : 1 January 1917 - 30 April 1919 (First World War, War Diary, WO95/2119)	WD2119	9781474524001	£57.00
20 DIVISION 60 Infantry Brigade King's Royal Rifle Corps 12th Battalion and Oxfordshire and Buckinghamshire Light Infantry 6th Battalion : 21 July 1915 - 31 January 1918 (First World War, War Diary, WO95/2120)	WD2120	9781474524018	£31.00
20 DIVISION 60 Infantry Brigade Rifle Brigade (The Prince Consort's Own) 12th Battalion : 21 July 1915 - 30 December 1917 (First World War, War Diary, WO95/2121)	WD2121	9781474524025	£80.00
20 DIVISION 60 Infantry Brigade King's (Shropshire Light Infantry) 6th Battalion and Brigade Machine Gun Company : 20 July 1915 - 24 February 1918 (First World War, War Diary, WO95/2122)	WD2122	9781474524032	£39.00
20 DIVISION 61 Infantry Brigade Headquarters : 22 July 1915 - 31 August 1916 (First World War, War Diary, WO95/2123)	WD2123	9781474511803	£58.00
20 DIVISION 61 Infantry Brigade Headquarters : 1 September 1916 - 31 August 1917 (First World War, War Diary, WO95/2124)	WD2124	9781474524049	£71.00
20 DIVISION 61 Infantry Brigade Headquarters : 1 September 1917 - 31 May 1919 (First World War, War Diary, WO95/2125)	WD2125	9781474524056	£80.00
20 DIVISION 61 Infantry Brigade Duke of Cornwall's Light Infantry 7th Battalion and King's (Liverpool Regiment) 12th Battalion : 22 July 1915 - 30 April 1919 (First World War, War Diary, WO95/2126)	WD2126	9781474524063	£62.00
20 DIVISION 61 Infantry Brigade Prince Albert's (Somerset Light Infantry) 7th Battalion, Brigade King's Own (Yorkshire Light Infantry) 7th Battalion and Brigade Machine Gun Company : 22 July 1915 - 31 December 1916 (First World War, War Diary, WO95/2127)	WD2127	9781474524070	£68.00

Title	Product Code	ISBN	Price
21 DIVISION			
21 DIVISION Headquarters, Branches and Services General Staff : 13 September 1915 - 31 December 1915 (First World War, War Diary, WO95/2128)	WD2128	9781474524087	£49.00
21 DIVISION Headquarters, Branches and Services General Staff : 1 January 1916 - 30 April 1916 (First World War, War Diary, WO95/2129)	WD2129	9781474511810	£51.00
21 DIVISION Headquarters, Branches and Services General Staff : 1 May 1916 - 17 June 1916 (First World War, War Diary, WO95/2130)	WD2130	9781474524094	£60.00
21 DIVISION Headquarters, Branches and Services General Staff : 1 August 1916 - 31 March 1917 (First World War, War Diary, WO95/2131)	WD2131	9781474524100	£50.00
21 DIVISION Headquarters, Branches and Services General Staff : 1 April 1917 - 31 December 1917 (First World War, War Diary, WO95/2132)	WD2132	9781474511827	£55.00
21 DIVISION Headquarters, Branches and Services General Staff : 1 January 1918 - 31 August 1918 (First World War, War Diary, WO95/2133)	WD2133	9781474511834	£58.00
21 DIVISION Headquarters, Branches and Services General Staff : 1 September 1918 - 31 March 1919 (First World War, War Diary, WO95/2134)	WD2134	9781474511841	£34.00
21 DIVISION Headquarters, Branches and Services Adjutant and Quarter-Master General : 10 September 1915 - 31 March 1917 (First World War, War Diary, WO95/2135A)	WD2135_A	9781474524117	£46.00
21 DIVISION Headquarters, Branches and Services Adjutant and Quarter-Master General : 1 April 1917 - 19 May 1919 (First World War, War Diary, WO95/2135B)	WD2135_B	9781474524124	£51.00
21 DIVISION Headquarters, Branches and Services Commander Royal Artillery : 7 September 1915 - 31 December 1916 (First World War, War Diary, WO95/2136)	WD2136	9781474511858	£55.00
21 DIVISION Headquarters, Branches and Services Commander Royal Artillery : 1 January 1917 - 30 June 1917 (First World War, War Diary, WO95/2137)	WD2137	9781474511865	£53.00
21 DIVISION Headquarters, Branches and Services Commander Royal Artillery : 3 July 1917 - 30 April 1919 (First World War, War Diary, WO95/2138)	WD2138	9781474511872	£57.00
21 DIVISION Headquarters, Branches and Services Commander Royal Artillery : 9 September 1915 - 29 April 1919 (First World War, War Diary, WO95/2139)	WD2139	9781474524131	£67.00
21 DIVISION Headquarters, Branches and Services Royal Army Medical Corps Assistant Director Medical Services : 28 August 1915 - 29 March 1919 (First World War, War Diary, WO95/2140/1)	WD2140_1	9781474524148	£47.00
21 DIVISION Headquarters, Branches and Services Royal Army Ordnance Corps Deputy Assistant Director Ordnance Services : 23 October 1915 - 31 May 1919 (First World War, War Diary, WO95/2140/2)	WD2140_2	9781474511889	£16.00
21 DIVISION Headquarters, Branches and Services Royal Army Veterinary Corps Assistant Director Veterinary Services : 9 September 1915 - 31 March 1919 (First World War, War Diary, WO95/2140/3)	WD2140_3	9781474511896	£15.00
21 DIVISION Divisional Troops `A' Squadron South Irish Horse : 11 September 1915 - 31 May 1916 (First World War, War Diary, WO95/2141/1)	WD2141_1	9781474511902	£15.00

Title	Product Code	ISBN	Price
21 DIVISION Divisional Troops Divisional Cyclist Company : 9 September 1915 - 30 April 1916 (First World War, War Diary, WO95/2141/2)	WD2141_2	9781474511919	£15.00
21 DIVISION Divisional Troops 94 Brigade Royal Field Artillery : 7 September 1915 - 30 April 1919 (First World War, War Diary, WO95/2141/3)	WD2141_3	9781474511926	£15.00
21 DIVISION Divisional Troops 95 Brigade Royal Field Artillery : 1 September 1915 - 27 February 1919 (First World War, War Diary, WO95/2142)	WD2142	9781474511933	£46.00
21 DIVISION Divisional Troops 96 Brigade Royal Field Artillery : 10 September 1915 - 27 December 1916 (First World War, War Diary, WO95/2143/1)	WD2143_1	9781474511940	£15.00
21 DIVISION Divisional Troops 97 Brigade Royal Field Artillery : 8 September 1915 - 11 September 1916 (First World War, War Diary, WO95/2143/2)	WD2143_2	9781474511957	£15.00
21 DIVISION Divisional Troops Divisional Trench Mortar Batteries : 1 March 1916 - 19 December 1918 (First World War, War Diary, WO95/2143/3)	WD2143_3	9781474511964	£15.00
21 DIVISION Divisional Troops Divisional Ammunition Column : 12 September 1915 - 30 April 1919 (First World War, War Diary, WO95/2143/4)	WD2143_4	9781474511971	£15.00
21 DIVISION Divisional Troops 97 Field Company Royal Engineers : 11 September 1915 - 29 April 1919 (First World War, War Diary, WO95/2144/1)	WD2144_1	9781474511988	£19.00
21 DIVISION Divisional Troops 98 Field Company Royal Engineers : 11 September 1915 - 7 June 1919 (First World War, War Diary, WO95/2144/2)	WD2144_2	9781474511995	£15.00
21 DIVISION Divisional Troops 126 Field Company Royal Engineers : 11 September 1915 - 22 April 1919 (First World War, War Diary, WO95/2144/3)	WD2144_3	9781474512008	£15.00
21 DIVISION Divisional Troops Divisional Signal Company : 8 September 1915 - 22 June 1919 (First World War, War Diary, WO95/2145/1)	WD2145_1	9781474512015	£23.00
21 DIVISION Divisional Troops Machine Gun Corps 21 Battalion : 1 March 1918 - 31 March 1919 (First World War, War Diary, WO95/2145/2)	WD2145_2	9781474512022	£33.00
21 DIVISION Divisional Troops 237 Machine Gun Company : 12 July 1917 - 28 February 1918 (First World War, War Diary, WO95/2145/3)	WD2145_3	9781474512039	£15.00
21 DIVISION Divisional Troops Northumberland Fusiliers 14th Battalion Pioneers : 3 September 1915 - 24 May 1919 (First World War, War Diary, WO95/2146)	WD2146	9781474512046	£65.00
21 DIVISION Divisional Troops Royal Army Medical Corps 63 Field Ambulance : 28 August 1915 - 7 May 1919 (First World War, War Diary, WO95/2147/1)	WD2147_1	9781474512053	£22.00
21 DIVISION Divisional Troops Royal Army Medical Corps 64 Field Ambulance : 29 August 1915 - 19 May 1919 (First World War, War Diary, WO95/2147/2)	WD2147_2	9781474512060	£47.00
21 DIVISION Divisional Troops Royal Army Medical Corps 65 Field Ambulance : 28 August 1915 - 5 June 1919 (First World War, War Diary, WO95/2148/1)	WD2148_1	9781474512077	£23.00

Title	Product Code	ISBN	Price
21 DIVISION Divisional Troops Royal Army Medical Corps Divisional Field Ambulance Workshop Unit : 1 October 1915 - 31 March 1916 (First World War, War Diary, WO95/2148/2)	WD2148_2	9781474512084	£15.00
21 DIVISION Divisional Troops 38 Sanitary Section : 11 September 1915 - 31 March 1917 (First World War, War Diary, WO95/2148/3)	WD2148_3	9781474512091	£15.00
21 DIVISION Divisional Troops Royal Army Veterinary Corps 33 Mobile Veterinary Section : 1 September 1915 - 31 March 1919 (First World War, War Diary, WO95/2148/4)	WD2148_4	9781474512107	£15.00
21 DIVISION Divisional Troops Senior Supply Officer : 15 September 1915 - 28 February 1919 (First World War, War Diary, WO95/2149/1)	WD2149_1	9781474512114	£21.00
21 DIVISION Divisional Troops Royal Army Service Corps Divisional Train (182, 183, 184, 185, Companies A.S.C.) : 8 September 1915 - 31 December 1916 (First World War, War Diary, WO95/2149/2)	WD2149_2	9781474512121	£50.00
21 DIVISION Divisional Troops Royal Army Service Corps Divisional Train (182, 183, 184, 185, Companies A.S.C.) : 1 January 1917 - 21 May 1919 (First World War, War Diary, WO95/2150)	WD2150	9781474524155	£58.00
21 DIVISION 62 Infantry Brigade Headquarters : 8 September 1915 - 31 December 1916 (First World War, War Diary, WO95/2151)	WD2151	9781474524162	£51.00
21 DIVISION 62 Infantry Brigade Headquarters : 1 January 1917 - 31 December 1917 (First World War, War Diary, WO95/2152)	WD2152	9781474512138	£41.00
21 DIVISION 62 Infantry Brigade Headquarters : 1 January 1918 - 24 April 1919 (First World War, War Diary, WO95/2153)	WD2153	9781474512145	£63.00
21 DIVISION 62 Infantry Brigade Lincolnshire Regiment 1st Battalion : 1 November 1915 - 30 March 1919 (First World War, War Diary, WO95/2154/1)	WD2154_1	9781474512152	£50.00
21 DIVISION 62 Infantry Brigade Lincolnshire Regiment 2nd Battalion : 1 February 1918 - 31 March 1919 (First World War, War Diary, WO95/2154/2)	WD2154_2	9781474512169	£15.00
21 DIVISION 62 Infantry Brigade Northumberland Fusiliers 12th Battalion : 1 January 1915 - 31 July 1917 (First World War, War Diary, WO95/2155/1)	WD2155_1	9781474512176	£17.00
21 DIVISION 62 Infantry Brigade Northumberland Fusiliers 13th Battalion : 9 September 1915 - 31 July 1917 (First World War, War Diary, WO95/2155/2)	WD2155_2	9781474512183	£48.00
21 DIVISION 62 Infantry Brigade Northumberland Fusiliers 12/13th Battalion : 1 August 1917 - 24 April 1919 (First World War, War Diary, WO95/2155/3)	WD2155_3	9781474512190	£17.00
21 DIVISION 62 Infantry Brigade Queen's (Royal West Surrey Regiment) 3/4th Battalion : 1 January 1917 - 31 January 1917 (First World War, War Diary, WO95/2156/1)	WD2156_1	9781474512206	£15.00
21 DIVISION 62 Infantry Brigade Alexandra, Princess of Wales's Own (Yorkshire Regiment) 10th Battalion : 1 January 1915 - 27 February 1918 (First World War, War Diary, WO95/2156/2)	WD2156_2	9781474512213	£19.00
21 DIVISION 62 Infantry Brigade, Brigade Machine Gun Company : 23 February 1916 - 28 February 1918 (First World War, War Diary, WO95/2156/3)	WD2156_3	9781474512220	£15.00
21 DIVISION 63 Infantry Brigade Headquarters : 10 September 1915 - 30 June 1916 (First World War, War Diary, WO95/2157)	WD2157	9781474512237	£44.00

Title	Product Code	ISBN	Price
21 DIVISION 63 Infantry Brigade Lincolnshire Regiment 8th Battalion : 10 September 1915 - 31 July 1916 (First World War, War Diary, WO95/2158/1)	WD2158_1	9781474512244	£15.00
21 DIVISION 63 Infantry Brigade Duke of Cambridge's Own (Middlesex Regiment) 4th Battalion : 1 November 1915 - 30 June 1916 (First World War, War Diary, WO95/2158/2)	WD2158_2	9781474512251	£15.00
21 DIVISION 63 Infantry Brigade Prince Albert's (Somerset Light Infantry) 8th Battalion : 9 September 1915 - 31 July 1916 (First World War, War Diary, WO95/2158/3)	WD2158_3	9781474512268	£15.00
21 DIVISION 63 Infantry Brigade York and Lancaster Regiment 10th (Service) Battalion : 10 September 1915 - 1 August 1916 (First World War, War Diary, WO95/2158/4)	WD2158_4	9781474512275	£15.00
21 DIVISION 63 Infantry Brigade, Brigade Machine Gun Company : 1 March 1916 - 31 July 1916 (First World War, War Diary, WO95/2158/5)	WD2158_5	9781474512282	£15.00
21 DIVISION 64 Infantry Brigade Headquarters : 11 September 1915 - 30 April 1917 (First World War, War Diary, WO95/2159)	WD2159	9781474512299	£50.00
21 DIVISION 64 Infantry Brigade Headquarters : 1 June 1917 - 1 February 1919 (First World War, War Diary, WO95/2160)	WD2160	9781474524179	£62.00
21 DIVISION 64 Infantry Brigade Durham Light Infantry 15th Battalion and East Yorkshire Regiment 1st Battalion : 11 September 1915 - 30 April 1919 (First World War, War Diary, WO95/2161)	WD2161	9781474524186	£41.00
21 DIVISION 64 Infantry Brigade King's Own (Yorkshire Light Infantry) 9th Battalion : 10 September 1915 - 31 March 1919 (First World War, War Diary, WO95/2162/1)	WD2162_1	9781474512305	£52.00
21 DIVISION 64 Infantry Brigade King's Own (Yorkshire Light Infantry) 10th Battalion : 11 January 1915 - 31 January 1918 (First World War, War Diary, WO95/2162/2)	WD2162_2	9781474512312	£15.00
21 DIVISION 64 Infantry Brigade, Brigade Machine Gun Company : 31 January 1916 - 31 January 1918 (First World War, War Diary, WO95/2162/3)	WD2162_3	9781474512329	£15.00
21 DIVISION 110 Infantry Brigade Headquarters : 1 July 1916 - 14 June 1919 (First World War, War Diary, WO95/2163)	WD2163	9781474512336	£59.00
21 DIVISION 110 Infantry Brigade Leicestershire Regiment 6th Battalion : 1 July 1916 - 31 March 1919 (First World War, War Diary, WO95/2164/1)	WD2164_1	9781474512343	£15.00
21 DIVISION 110 Infantry Brigade Leicestershire Regiment 7th Battalion : 29 June 1916 - 29 March 1919 (First World War, War Diary, WO95/2164/2)	WD2164_2	9781474512350	£25.00
21 DIVISION 110 Infantry Brigade Leicestershire Regiment 8th Battalion : 1 July 1916 - 31 May 1918 (First World War, War Diary, WO95/2165/1)	WD2165_1	9781474512367	£16.00
21 DIVISION 110 Infantry Brigade Leicestershire Regiment 9th Battalion : 1 July 1916 - 20 February 1918 (First World War, War Diary, WO95/2165/2)	WD2165_2	9781474512374	£15.00
21 DIVISION 110 Infantry Brigade Duke of Edinburgh's (Wiltshire Regiment) 1st Battalion : 1 July 1918 - 29 May 1919 (First World War, War Diary, WO95/2165/3)	WD2165_3	9781474512381	£15.00
21 DIVISION 110 Infantry Brigade, Brigade Machine Gun Company and Brigade Trench Mortar Battery : 28 October 1914 - 28 February 1918 (First World War, War Diary, WO95/2165/4-5)	WD2165_4-5	9781474512398	£15.00

Title	Product Code	ISBN	Price
22 DIVISION			
22 DIVISION Headquarters, Branches and Services General Staff, Adjutant and Quarter-Master General, Commander RA, Assistant Director Medical Services, Commander RE, Assistant Director Veterinary Services, 99,100 and 101 Brigade RFA, Divisional Ammuniti	WD2166	9781474512404	£52.00

Title	Product Code	ISBN	Price
23 DIVISION			
23 DIVISION Headquarters, Branches and Services General Staff : 1 April 1915 - 31 July 1916 (First World War, War Diary, WO95/2167)	WD2167	9781474512411	£50.00
23 DIVISION Headquarters, Branches and Services General Staff : 1 August 1916 - 30 June 1917 (First World War, War Diary, WO95/2168)	WD2168	9781474512428	£54.00
23 DIVISION Headquarters, Branches and Services General Staff : 1 July 1917 - 24 September 1917 (First World War, War Diary, WO95/2169)	WD2169	9781474512435	£45.00
23 DIVISION Headquarters, Branches and Services Adjutant and Quarter-Master General : 8 March 1915 - 24 July 1917 (First World War, War Diary, WO95/2170/1)	WD2170_1	9781474512442	£18.00
23 DIVISION Headquarters, Branches and Services Commander Royal Artillery : 1 June 1915 - 31 August 1916 (First World War, War Diary, WO95/2170/2)	WD2170_2	9781474512459	£33.00
23 DIVISION Headquarters, Branches and Services Commander Royal Artillery : 1 September 1916 - 31 October 1917 (First World War, War Diary, WO95/2171)	WD2171	9781474512466	£42.00
23 DIVISION Headquarters, Branches and Services Royal Army Medical Corps Assistant Director Medical Services : 25 August 1915 - 30 April 1916 (First World War, War Diary, WO95/2172)	WD2172	9781474512473	£52.00
23 DIVISION Headquarters, Branches and Services Royal Army Medical Corps Assistant Director Medical Services : 1 January 1917 - 31 October 1917 (First World War, War Diary, WO95/2173)	WD2173	9781474512480	£56.00
23 DIVISION Headquarters, Branches and Services Commander Royal Engineers, Assistant Director Ordnance Services and Assistant Director Veterinary Services : 20 August 1915 - 31 October 1917 (First World War, War Diary, WO95/2174)	WD2174	9781474512497	£31.00
23 DIVISION Divisional Troops C Squadron 1/1 Duke of Lancaster's Own Yeomanry, Divisional Cyclist Company, 102 and 103 Brigade Royal Field Artillery : 24 August 1915 - 30 April 1916 (First World War, War Diary, WO95/2175)	WD2175	9781474512503	£46.00
23 DIVISION Divisional Troops 104 and 105 Brigade Royal Field Artillery, Divisional Trench Mortar Batteries and Divisional Ammunition Column : 24 September 1914 - 31 October 1917 (First World War, War Diary, WO95/2176)	WD2176	9781474512510	£32.00
23 DIVISION Divisional Troops 101 Field Company Royal Engineers : 25 August 1915 - 31 October 1917 (First World War, War Diary, WO95/2177/1)	WD2177_1	9781474512527	£15.00
23 DIVISION Divisional Troops 102 Field Company Royal Engineers : 25 August 1915 - 31 October 1917 (First World War, War Diary, WO95/2177/2)	WD2177_2	9781474512534	£15.00
23 DIVISION Divisional Troops 128 Field Company Royal Engineers : 31 August 1915 - 31 October 1917 (First World War, War Diary, WO95/2177/3)	WD2177_3	9781474512541	£15.00
23 DIVISION Divisional Troops Divisional Signal Company : 24 August 1915 - 31 October 1917 (First World War, War Diary, WO95/2177/4)	WD2177_4	9781474512558	£15.00
23 DIVISION Divisional Troops 194 Machine Gun Company : 12 December 1916 - 31 October 1917 (First World War, War Diary, WO95/2178/1)	WD2178_1	9781474512565	£15.00

Title	Product Code	ISBN	Price
23 DIVISION Divisional Troops South Staffordshire Regiment 9th Service Battalion (Pioneers) : 20 August 1915 - 31 October 1917 (First World War, War Diary, WO95/2178/2)	WD2178_2	9781474524193	£74.00
23 DIVISION Divisional Troops Royal Army Medical Corps 69, 70 and 71 Field Ambulance : 23 August 1915 - 31 October 1917 (First World War, War Diary, WO95/2179)	WD2179	9781474524209	£54.00
23 DIVISION Divisional Troops Royal Army Medical Corps Divisional Field Ambulance Workshop Unit : 30 July 1915 - 31 March 1916 (First World War, War Diary, WO95/2180/1)	WD2180_1	9781474512572	£15.00
23 DIVISION Divisional Troops 40 Sanitary Section : 20 August 1915 - 1 April 1917 (First World War, War Diary, WO95/2180/2)	WD2180_2	9781474512589	£15.00
23 DIVISION Divisional Troops Royal Army Veterinary Corps 35 Mobile Veterinary Section : 27 August 1915 - 31 October 1917 (First World War, War Diary, WO95/2180/3)	WD2180_3	9781474512596	£15.00
23 DIVISION Divisional Troops Royal Army Service Corps Divisional Train (190, 191, 192, 193 Companies A.S.C.) : 1 September 1915 - 31 October 1917 (First World War, War Diary, WO95/2180/4)	WD2180_4	9781474512602	£33.00
23 DIVISION 68 Infantry Brigade Headquarters : 24 August 1915 - 5 October 1917 (First World War, War Diary, WO95/2181)	WD2181	9781474524216	£67.00
23 DIVISION 68 Infantry Brigade Durham Light Infantry 12th Battalion : 8 February 1915 - 31 October 1917 (First World War, War Diary, WO95/2182/1)	WD2182_1	9781474524223	£15.00
23 DIVISION 68 Infantry Brigade Durham Light Infantry 13th Battalion : 17 September 1914 - 31 October 1917 (First World War, War Diary, WO95/2182/2)	WD2182_2	9781474512619	£17.00
23 DIVISION 68 Infantry Brigade Northumberland Fusiliers 10th Battalion : 25 August 1915 - 31 October 1917 (First World War, War Diary, WO95/2182/3)	WD2182_3	9781474512626	£18.00
23 DIVISION 68 Infantry Brigade Northumberland Fusiliers 11th Battalion : 10 January 1915 - 31 October 1917 (First World War, War Diary, WO95/2182/4)	WD2182_4	9781474512633	£23.00
23 DIVISION 68 Infantry Brigade, Brigade Machine Gun Company : 13 December 1915 - 31 October 1917 (First World War, War Diary, WO95/2182/5)	WD2182_5	9781474512640	£15.00
23 DIVISION 69 Infantry Brigade Headquarters : 20 August 1915 - 31 October 1917 (First World War, War Diary, WO95/2183)	WD2183	9781474512657	£67.00
23 DIVISION 69 Infantry Brigade Duke of Wellington's (West Riding Regiment) 10th Battalion : 23 August 1915 - 31 October 1917 (First World War, War Diary, WO95/2184/1)	WD2184_1	9781474512664	£24.00
23 DIVISION 69 Infantry Brigade Alexandra, Princess of Wales's Own (Yorkshire Regiment) 8th Battalion : 26 August 1915 - 31 December 1917 (First World War, War Diary, WO95/2184/2)	WD2184_2	9781474512671	£15.00
23 DIVISION 69 Infantry Brigade Alexandra, Princess of Wales's Own (Yorkshire Regiment) 9th Battalion : 23 August 1915 - 31 October 1917 (First World War, War Diary, WO95/2184/3)	WD2184_3	9781474512688	£15.00
23 DIVISION 69 Infantry Brigade Prince of Wales's Own (West Yorkshire Regiment) 11th Battalion : 25 August 1915 - 31 October 1917 (First World War, War Diary, WO95/2184/4)	WD2184_4	9781474512695	£15.00

Title	Product Code	ISBN	Price
23 DIVISION 69 Infantry Brigade, Brigade Machine Gun Company : 19 February 1916 - 1 November 1917 (First World War, War Diary, WO95/2184/5)	WD2184_5	9781474512701	£15.00
23 DIVISION 69 Infantry Brigade, Brigade Trench Mortar Battery : 1 July 1916 - 31 October 1917 (First World War, War Diary, WO95/2184/6)	WD2184_6	9781474512718	£15.00
23 DIVISION 70 Infantry Brigade Headquarters : 27 May 1915 - 31 December 1916 (First World War, War Diary, WO95/2185)	WD2185	9781474512725	£56.00
23 DIVISION 70 Infantry Brigade Headquarters : 1 January 1917 - 31 October 1917 (First World War, War Diary, WO95/2186)	WD2186	9781474512732	£50.00
23 DIVISION 70 Infantry Brigade Duke of Cambridge's Own (Middlesex Regiment) 1/8th (T.F.) Battalion, King's Own (Yorkshire Light Infantry) 8th Battalion and Sherwood Foresters (Nottinghamshire and Derbyshire Regiment) 11th Battalion. : 2 August 1915 - 1	WD2187	9781474512749	£31.00
23 DIVISION 70 Infantry Brigade York and Lancaster Regiment 8th (Service) Battalion : 27 August 1915 - 31 October 1917 (First World War, War Diary, WO95/2188/1)	WD2188_1	9781474524230	£36.00
23 DIVISION 70 Infantry Brigade York and Lancaster Regiment 9th (Service) Battalion : 27 August 1915 - 31 October 1917 (First World War, War Diary, WO95/2188/2)	WD2188_2	9781474524247	£16.00
23 DIVISION 70 Infantry Brigade, Brigade Machine Gun Company : 1 April 1916 - 31 October 1917 (First World War, War Diary, WO95/2188/3)	WD2188_3	9781474524254	£15.00

Title	Product Code	ISBN	Price
24 DIVISION			
24 DIVISION Headquarters, Branches and Services General Staff : 21 August 1915 - 31 July 1916 (First World War, War Diary, WO95/2189)	WD2189	9781474512756	£55.00
24 DIVISION Headquarters, Branches and Services General Staff : 2 August 1916 - 4 December 1916 (First World War, War Diary, WO95/2190)	WD2190	9781474524261	£67.00
24 DIVISION Headquarters, Branches and Services General Staff : 1 July 1917 - 31 December 1917 (First World War, War Diary, WO95/2191)	WD2191	9781474524278	£71.00
24 DIVISION Headquarters, Branches and Services General Staff : 1 January 1918 - 26 March 1919 (First World War, War Diary, WO95/2192)	WD2192	9781474524285	£62.00
24 DIVISION Headquarters, Branches and Services Adjutant and Quarter-Master General : 21 August 1915 - 31 October 1916 (First World War, War Diary, WO95/2193)	WD2193	9781474512763	£44.00
24 DIVISION Headquarters, Branches and Services Adjutant and Quarter-Master General : 1 January 1917 - 30 June 1919 (First World War, War Diary, WO95/2194)	WD2194	9781474512770	£56.00
24 DIVISION Headquarters, Branches and Services Commander Royal Artillery : 21 August 1915 - 28 March 1919 (First World War, War Diary, WO95/2195)	WD2195	9781474524292	£71.00
24 DIVISION Headquarters, Branches and Services Royal Army Medical Corps Assistant Director Medical Services : 21 August 1915 - 29 March 1919 (First World War, War Diary, WO95/2196/1)	WD2196_1	9781474524308	£25.00
24 DIVISION Headquarters, Branches and Services Commander Royal Engineers : 25 August 1915 - 25 June 1919 (First World War, War Diary, WO95/2196/2)	WD2196_2	9781474512787	£26.00
24 DIVISION Headquarters, Branches and Services Royal Army Ordnance Corps Assistant Director Ordnance Services : 21 August 1915 - 31 December 1918 (First World War, War Diary, WO95/2196/3)	WD2196_3	9781474512794	£15.00
24 DIVISION Headquarters, Branches and Services Royal Army Veterinary Corps Assistant Director Veterinary Services : 21 August 1915 - 28 February 1919 (First World War, War Diary, WO95/2196/4)	WD2196_4	9781474512800	£24.00
24 DIVISION Divisional Troops A Squadron Glasgow Yeomanry : 31 August 1915 - 30 April 1916 (First World War, War Diary, WO95/2197/1)	WD2197_1	9781474512817	£15.00
24 DIVISION Divisional Troops Divisional Cyclist Company : 21 August 1915 - 18 May 1916 (First World War, War Diary, WO95/2197/2)	WD2197_2	9781474512824	£15.00
24 DIVISION Divisional Troops 106 Brigade Royal Field Artillery : 29 September 1915 - 31 May 1919 (First World War, War Diary, WO95/2197/3)	WD2197_3	9781474512831	£20.00
24 DIVISION Divisional Troops 107 Brigade Royal Field Artillery : 21 August 1915 - 31 March 1919 (First World War, War Diary, WO95/2197/4)	WD2197_4	9781474512848	£35.00
24 DIVISION Divisional Troops 108 Brigade Royal Field Artillery : 28 August 1915 - 28 December 1916 (First World War, War Diary, WO95/2197/5)	WD2197_5	9781474512855	£15.00
24 DIVISION Divisional Troops 109 Brigade Royal Field Artillery : 1 September 1915 - 31 August 1916 (First World War, War Diary, WO95/2198/1)	WD2198_1	9781474512862	£15.00
24 DIVISION Divisional Troops Divisional Trench Mortar Batteries : 6 January 1916 - 24 February 1919 (First World War, War Diary, WO95/2198/2)	WD2198_2	9781474512879	£15.00

Title	Product Code	ISBN	Price
24 DIVISION Divisional Troops Divisional Ammunition Column : 12 September 1915 - 31 March 1919 (First World War, War Diary, WO95/2198/3)	WD2198_3	9781474524315	£55.00
24 DIVISION Divisional Troops 103,104 and 129 Field Company Royal Engineers : 21 August 1915 - 28 June 1919 (First World War, War Diary, WO95/2199)	WD2199	9781474524322	£74.00
24 DIVISION Divisional Troops Divisional Signal Company : 1 March 1915 - 31 December 1916 (First World War, War Diary, WO95/2200A)	WD2200_A	9781474524339	£29.00
24 DIVISION Divisional Troops Divisional Signal Company : 1 January 1917 - 30 May 1919 (First World War, War Diary, WO95/2200B)	WD2200_B	9781474524346	£62.00
24 DIVISION Divisional Troops Sherwood Foresters (Nottinghamshire and Derbyshire Regiment) 15th Battalion : 21 August 1915 - 31 May 1919 (First World War, War Diary, WO95/2201/1)	WD2201_1	9781474524353	£55.00
24 DIVISION Divisional Troops Machine Gun Corps 24 Battalion : 5 March 1918 - 30 May 1919 (First World War, War Diary, WO95/2201/2)	WD2201_2	9781474512886	£15.00
24 DIVISION Divisional Troops 191 Machine Gun Company : 13 December 1916 - 28 February 1918 (First World War, War Diary, WO95/2201/3)	WD2201_3	9781474512893	£15.00
24 DIVISION Divisional Troops Royal Army Medical Corps 72 Field Ambulance : 1 September 1915 - 30 April 1919 (First World War, War Diary, WO95/2202/1)	WD2202_1	9781474512909	£27.00
24 DIVISION Divisional Troops Royal Army Medical Corps 73 Field Ambulance : 21 August 1915 - 30 April 1919 (First World War, War Diary, WO95/2202/2)	WD2202_2	9781474512916	£17.00
24 DIVISION Divisional Troops Royal Army Medical Corps 74 Field Ambulance : 1 June 1915 - 31 May 1919 (First World War, War Diary, WO95/2202/3)	WD2202_3	9781474512923	£19.00
24 DIVISION Divisional Troops Royal Army Medical Corps Divisional Field Ambulance Workshop Unit : 31 August 1915 - 31 March 1916 (First World War, War Diary, WO95/2203/1)	WD2203_1	9781474512930	£15.00
24 DIVISION Divisional Troops 41 Sanitary Section : 2 September 1915 - 31 March 1917 (First World War, War Diary, WO95/2203/2)	WD2203_2	9781474512947	£32.00
24 DIVISION Divisional Troops Royal Army Veterinary Corps 36 Mobile Veterinary Section : 1 September 1915 - 3 April 1919 (First World War, War Diary, WO95/2203/3)	WD2203_3	9781474512954	£15.00
24 DIVISION Divisional Troops Royal Army Service Corps Divisional Train (194,195,196,197 Companies A.S.C.) : 29 August 1915 - 25 June 1919 (First World War, War Diary, WO95/2203/4)	WD2203_4	9781474512961	£35.00
24 DIVISION 17 Infantry Brigade Headquarters : 1 November 1915 - 30 September 1917 (First World War, War Diary, WO95/2204)	WD2204	9781474512978	£61.00
24 DIVISION 17 Infantry Brigade Headquarters : 1 October 1917 - 29 May 1919 (First World War, War Diary, WO95/2205)	WD2205	9781474512985	£64.00
24 DIVISION 17 Infantry Brigade Rifle Brigade (The Prince Consort's Own) 3rd Battalion : 1 November 1915 - 26 April 1919 (First World War, War Diary, WO95/2206)	WD2206	9781474512992	£55.00
24 DIVISION 17 Infantry Brigade Buffs (East Kent Regiment) 8th Battalion : 21 August 1915 - 31 January 1918 (First World War, War Diary, WO95/2207/1)	WD2207_1	9781474513005	£23.00

Title	Product Code	ISBN	Price
24 DIVISION 17 Infantry Brigade Royal Fusiliers (City of London Regiment) 1st Battalion : 1 November 1915 - 30 May 1919 (First World War, War Diary, WO95/2207/2)	WD2207_2	9781474513012	£43.00
24 DIVISION 17 Infantry Brigade Royal Fusiliers (City of London Regiment) 12th Battalion : 21 August 1915 - 13 February 1918 (First World War, War Diary, WO95/2208/1)	WD2208_1	9781474513029	£24.00
24 DIVISION 17 Infantry Brigade Queen's (Royal West Surrey Regiment) 8th Battalion : 1 February 1918 - 30 April 1919 (First World War, War Diary, WO95/2208/2)	WD2208_2	9781474513036	£28.00
24 DIVISION 17 Infantry Brigade, Brigade Machine Gun Company : 29 June 1915 - 28 February 1918 (First World War, War Diary, WO95/2209/1)	WD2209_1	9781474513043	£26.00
24 DIVISION 17 Infantry Brigade, Brigade Trench Mortar Battery : 16 March 1916 - 30 September 1918 (First World War, War Diary, WO95/2209/2)	WD2209_2	9781474513050	£15.00
24 DIVISION 72 Infantry Brigade Headquarters : 21 August 1915 - 31 December 1916 (First World War, War Diary, WO95/2210)	WD2210	9781474513067	£48.00
24 DIVISION 72 Infantry Brigade Headquarters : 1 January 1917 - 31 December 1917 (First World War, War Diary, WO95/2211)	WD2211	9781474513074	£55.00
24 DIVISION 72 Infantry Brigade Headquarters : 1 January 1918 - 30 April 1919 (First World War, War Diary, WO95/2212)	WD2212	9781474513081	£38.00
24 DIVISION 72 Infantry Brigade Prince of Wales's (North Staffordshire Regiment) 1st Battalion : 1 November 1915 - 31 May 1919 (First World War, War Diary, WO95/2213/1)	WD2213_1	9781474513098	£32.00
24 DIVISION 72 Infantry Brigade Queen's Own (Royal West Kent Regiment) 8th Battalion : 29 August 1915 - 30 April 1919 (First World War, War Diary, WO95/2213/2)	WD2213_2	9781474513104	£20.00
24 DIVISION 72 Infantry Brigade Queen's (Royal West Surrey Regiment) 8th Battalion : 21 August 1915 - 31 January 1918 (First World War, War Diary, WO95/2214)	WD2214	9781474524360	£62.00
24 DIVISION 72 Infantry Brigade East Surrey Regiment 9th Battalion : 21 August 1915 - 31 March 1919 (First World War, War Diary, WO95/2215/1)	WD2215_1	9781474524377	£39.00
24 DIVISION 72 Infantry Brigade, Brigade Machine Gun Company : 9 March 1916 - 28 February 1918 (First World War, War Diary, WO95/2215/2)	WD2215_2	9781474513111	£15.00
24 DIVISION 72 Infantry Brigade, Brigade Trench Mortar Battery : 3 February 1918 - 31 January 1919 (First World War, War Diary, WO95/2215/3)	WD2215_3	9781474513128	£15.00
24 DIVISION 73 Infantry Brigade Headquarters : 18 January 1915 - 31 December 1916 (First World War, War Diary, WO95/2216)	WD2216	9781474513135	£41.00
24 DIVISION 73 Infantry Brigade Headquarters : 1 January 1917 - 28 March 1919 (First World War, War Diary, WO95/2217)	WD2217	9781474513142	£59.00
24 DIVISION 73 Infantry Brigade Prince of Wales's Leinster Regiment (Royal Canadians) 2nd Battalion : 1 November 1915 - 31 January 1918 (First World War, War Diary, WO95/2218/1)	WD2218_1	9781474513159	£21.00
24 DIVISION 73 Infantry Brigade Northamptonshire Regiment 7th Battalion : 21 August 1915 - 7 June 1919 (First World War, War Diary, WO95/2218/2)	WD2218_2	9781474513166	£32.00

Title	Product Code	ISBN	Price
24 DIVISION 73 Infantry Brigade Duke of Cambridge's Own (Middlesex Regiment) 13th Battalion : 21 August 1915 - 29 November 1919 (First World War, War Diary, WO95/2219/1)	WD2219_1	9781474513173	£23.00
24 DIVISION 73 Infantry Brigade Royal Sussex Regiment 9th Battalion : 21 August 1915 - 31 May 1919 (First World War, War Diary, WO95/2219/2)	WD2219_2	9781474513180	£21.00
24 DIVISION 73 Infantry Brigade, Brigade Machine Gun Company : 22 February 1916 - 28 February 1918 (First World War, War Diary, WO95/2219/3)	WD2219_3	9781474513197	£20.00
24 DIVISION 73 Infantry Brigade, Brigade Trench Mortar Battery : 5 December 1917 - 22 January 1919 (First World War, War Diary, WO95/2219/4)	WD2219_4	9781474513203	£15.00

Title	Product Code	ISBN	Price
25 DIVISION			
25 DIVISION Headquarters, Branches and Services General Staff : 23 September 1915 - 25 February 1916 (First World War, War Diary, WO95/2220)	WD2220	9781474513210	£59.00
25 DIVISION Headquarters, Branches and Services General Staff : 1 March 1916 - 5 May 1916 (First World War, War Diary, WO95/2221)	WD2221	9781474513227	£69.00
25 DIVISION Headquarters, Branches and Services General Staff Appendices to 2221 : 29 April 1916 - 19 December 1916 (First World War, War Diary, WO95/2222)	WD2222	9781474524384	£72.00
25 DIVISION Headquarters, Branches and Services General Staff Appendices to 2221 : 8 July 1916 - 27 July 1916 (First World War, War Diary, WO95/2223)	WD2223	9781474524391	£41.00
25 DIVISION Headquarters, Branches and Services General Staff : 1 August 1916 - 31 December 1917 (First World War, War Diary, WO95/2224)	WD2224	9781474524407	£87.00
25 DIVISION Headquarters, Branches and Services General Staff : 1 January 1918 - 31 March 1918 (First World War, War Diary, WO95/2225)	WD2225	9781474524414	£49.00
25 DIVISION Headquarters, Branches and Services General Staff : 1 April 1918 - 30 April 1918 (First World War, War Diary, WO95/2226)	WD2226	9781474513234	£41.00
25 DIVISION Headquarters, Branches and Services General Staff : 1 May 1918 - 28 February 1919 (First World War, War Diary, WO95/2227)	WD2227	9781474513241	£39.00
25 DIVISION Headquarters, Branches and Services Adjutant and Quarter-Master General : 25 September 1915 - 31 December 1918 (First World War, War Diary, WO95/2228)	WD2228	9781474513258	£46.00
25 DIVISION Headquarters, Branches and Services Commander Royal Artillery : 20 September 1915 - 31 December 1916 (First World War, War Diary, WO95/2229)	WD2229	9781474513265	£56.00
25 DIVISION Headquarters, Branches and Services Commander Royal Artillery : 1 January 1917 - 25 February 1919 (First World War, War Diary, WO95/2230)	WD2230	9781474513272	£53.00
25 DIVISION Headquarters, Branches and Services Royal Army Medical Corps Assistant Director Medical Services : 25 September 1915 - 28 February 1919 (First World War, War Diary, WO95/2231)	WD2231	9781474524421	£79.00
25 DIVISION Headquarters, Branches and Services Commander Royal Engineers : 27 September 1915 - 28 February 1919 (First World War, War Diary, WO95/2232/1)	WD2232_1	9781474524438	£38.00
25 DIVISION Headquarters, Branches and Services Royal Army Ordnance Corps Deputy Director Ordnance Services : 1 April 1916 - 20 February 1919 (First World War, War Diary, WO95/2232/2)	WD2232_2	9781474513289	£15.00
25 DIVISION Headquarters, Branches and Services Royal Army Veterinary Corps Assistant Director Veterinary Services : 29 September 1915 - 28 February 1919 (First World War, War Diary, WO95/2232/3)	WD2232_3	9781474513296	£16.00
25 DIVISION Divisional Troops `B' Squadron 1/1 Lothian and Border Horse : 28 September 1915 - 30 May 1916 (First World War, War Diary, WO95/2233/1)	WD2233_1	9781474513302	£15.00
25 DIVISION Divisional Troops Divisional Cyclist Company : 25 September 1915 - 18 April 1916 (First World War, War Diary, WO95/2233/2)	WD2233_2	9781474513319	£15.00

Title	Product Code	ISBN	Price
25 DIVISION Divisional Troops 110 Brigade Royal Field Artillery : 23 September 1915 - 15 June 1919 (First World War, War Diary, WO95/2233/3)	WD2233_3	9781474513326	£43.00
25 DIVISION Divisional Troops 111 Brigade Royal Field Artillery : 15 September 1915 - 27 November 1916 (First World War, War Diary, WO95/2233/4)	WD2233_4	9781474513333	£15.00
25 DIVISION Divisional Troops 112 Brigade Royal Field Artillery : 1 September 1915 - 28 February 1919 (First World War, War Diary, WO95/2234/1)	WD2234_1	9781474513340	£15.00
25 DIVISION Divisional Troops 113 Brigade Royal Field Artillery : 25 September 1915 - 28 February 1917 (First World War, War Diary, WO95/2234/2)	WD2234_2	9781474513357	£15.00
25 DIVISION Divisional Troops Divisional Trench Mortar Batteries : 1 March 1917 - 30 April 1918 (First World War, War Diary, WO95/2234/3)	WD2234_3	9781474513364	£15.00
25 DIVISION Divisional Troops Divisional Ammunition Column : 27 September 1915 - 31 March 1919 (First World War, War Diary, WO95/2234/4)	WD2234_4	9781474513371	£15.00
25 DIVISION Divisional Troops Machine Gun Corps 25 Battalion, 195 Machine Gun Company, 105 and 106 Field Company Royal Engineers : 26 September 1915 - 19 April 1919 (First World War, War Diary, WO95/2235)	WD2235	9781474513388	£44.00
25 DIVISION Divisional Troops 130 Field Company Royal Engineers : 27 September 1915 - 31 July 1917 (First World War, War Diary, WO95/2236)	WD2236	9781474513395	£48.00
25 DIVISION Divisional Troops 130 Field Company Royal Engineers : 1 August 1917 - 28 February 1919 (First World War, War Diary, WO95/2237)	WD2237	9781474513401	£56.00
25 DIVISION Divisional Troops Divisional Signal Company : 24 September 1915 - 20 February 1919 (First World War, War Diary, WO95/2238/1)	WD2238_1	9781474513418	£49.00
25 DIVISION Divisional Troops South Wales Borderers 6th Battalion Pioneers : 24 September 1915 - 31 May 1918 (First World War, War Diary, WO95/2238/2)	WD2238_2	9781474513425	£18.00
25 DIVISION Divisional Troops Royal Army Medical Corps 75 Field Ambulance : 25 September 1915 - 15 February 1918 (First World War, War Diary, WO95/2239/1)	WD2239_1	9781474513432	£15.00
25 DIVISION Divisional Troops Royal Army Medical Corps 76 Field Ambulance : 26 September 1915 - 28 February 1919 (First World War, War Diary, WO95/2239/2)	WD2239_2	9781474513449	£38.00
25 DIVISION Divisional Troops Royal Army Medical Corps 77 Field Ambulance : 1 September 1915 - 28 February 1919 (First World War, War Diary, WO95/2239/3)	WD2239_3	9781474513456	£23.00
25 DIVISION Divisional Troops Royal Army Medical Corps Divisional Field Ambulance Workshop Unit, 42 Sanitary Section, 37 Mobile Veterinary Section and Divisional Train (198,199,200 201 Companies A.S.C.) : 24 September 1915 - 31 May 1919 (First World War,	WD2240	9781474513463	£80.00
25 DIVISION 7 Infantry Brigade Headquarters : 1 November 1915 - 31 May 1917 (First World War, War Diary, WO95/2241)	WD2241	9781474513470	£51.00
25 DIVISION 7 Infantry Brigade Headquarters : 1 June 1917 - 28 July 1919 (First World War, War Diary, WO95/2242)	WD2242	9781474513487	£63.00

Title	Product Code	ISBN	Price
25 DIVISION 7 Infantry Brigade Cheshire Regiment 10th Battalion : 27 September 1915 - 30 June 1918 (First World War, War Diary, WO95/2243/1)	WD2243_1	9781474513494	£52.00
25 DIVISION 7 Infantry Brigade Loyal North Lancashire Regiment 8th Battalion : 24 September 1915 - 10 February 1918 (First World War, War Diary, WO95/2243/2)	WD2243_2	9781474513500	£16.00
25 DIVISION 7 Infantry Brigade Duke of Edinburgh's (Wiltshire Regiment) 1st Battalion : 4 November 1915 - 30 June 1918 (First World War, War Diary, WO95/2243/3)	WD2243_3	9781474513517	£26.00
25 DIVISION 7 Infantry Brigade Worcestershire Regiment 3rd Battalion : 1 January 1916 - 31 October 1917 (First World War, War Diary, WO95/2244/1)	WD2244_1	9781474513524	£15.00
25 DIVISION 7 Infantry Brigade South Staffordshire Regiment 4th Special Reserve Battalion : 8 October 1917 - 31 July 1918 (First World War, War Diary, WO95/2244/2)	WD2244_2	9781474513531	£15.00
25 DIVISION 7 Infantry Brigade Devonshire Regiment 9th (Service) Battalion : 1 September 1918 - 29 June 1919 (First World War, War Diary, WO95/2244/3)	WD2244_3	9781474513548	£15.00
25 DIVISION 7 Infantry Brigade Manchester Regiment 20th Battalion : 29 November 1916 - 30 June 1919 (First World War, War Diary, WO95/2244/4)	WD2244_4	9781474513555	£15.00
25 DIVISION 7 Infantry Brigade Manchester Regiment 21st Battalion : 1 September 1918 - 5 July 1919 (First World War, War Diary, WO95/2244/5)	WD2244_5	9781474513562	£15.00
25 DIVISION 7 Infantry Brigade, Brigade Machine Gun Company : 12 January 1916 - 28 February 1918 (First World War, War Diary, WO95/2244/6)	WD2244_6	9781474513579	£15.00
25 DIVISION 7 Infantry Brigade, Brigade Trench Mortar Battery : 1 July 1916 - 28 August 1916 (First World War, War Diary, WO95/2244/7)	WD2244_7	9781474513586	£15.00
25 DIVISION 74 Infantry Brigade Headquarters : 2 November 1915 - 30 June 1919 (First World War, War Diary, WO95/2245)	WD2245	9781474513593	£45.00
25 DIVISION 74 Infantry Brigade Loyal North Lancashire Regiment 9th Battalion, Lancashire Fusiliers 11th Battalion and Cheshire Regiment 13th Battalion : 24 September 1915 - 31 January 1918 (First World War, War Diary, WO95/2246)	WD2246	9781474513609	£44.00
25 DIVISION 74 Infantry Brigade Royal Irish Rifles 2nd Battalion and Worcestershire Regiment 3rd Battalion : 1 November 1915 - 31 May 1918 (First World War, War Diary, WO95/2247/1)	WD2247_1	9781474524445	£18.00
25 DIVISION 74 Infantry Brigade Alexandra, Princess of Wales's Own (Yorkshire Regiment) 9th Battalion : 1 September 1918 - 28 February 1919 (First World War, War Diary, WO95/2247/2)	WD2247_2	9781474524452	£15.00
25 DIVISION 74 Infantry Brigade Durham Light Infantry 13th Battalion : 1 September 1918 - 28 February 1919 (First World War, War Diary, WO95/2247/3)	WD2247_3	9781474524469	£15.00
25 DIVISION 74 Infantry Brigade Sherwood Foresters (Nottinghamshire and Derbyshire Regiment) 1/7th Battalion : 1 September 1918 - 28 February 1919 (First World War, War Diary, WO95/2247/4)	WD2247_4	9781474524476	£15.00

Title	Product Code	ISBN	Price
25 DIVISION 74 Infantry Brigade, Brigade Machine Gun Company : 10 March 1916 - 28 February 1918 (First World War, War Diary, WO95/2247/5)	WD2247_5	9781474524483	£15.00
25 DIVISION 74 Infantry Brigade, Brigade Trench Mortar Battery : 1 July 1916 - 31 August 1916 (First World War, War Diary, WO95/2247/6)	WD2247_6	9781474524490	£15.00
25 DIVISION 75 Infantry Brigade Headquarters : 20 September 1915 - 31 August 1916 (First World War, War Diary, WO95/2248)	WD2248	9781474513616	£37.00
25 DIVISION 75 Infantry Brigade Headquarters : 1 September 1916 - 28 February 1919 (First World War, War Diary, WO95/2249)	WD2249	9781474513623	£56.00
25 DIVISION 75 Infantry Brigade Cheshire Regiment 11th Battalion : 25 September 1915 - 31 July 1918 (First World War, War Diary, WO95/2250/1)	WD2250_1	9781474513630	£15.00
25 DIVISION 75 Infantry Brigade Prince of Wales's Volunteers (South Lancashire Regiment) 2nd Battalion : 1 December 1915 - 30 June 1918 (First World War, War Diary, WO95/2250/2)	WD2250_2	9781474513647	£45.00
25 DIVISION 75 Infantry Brigade Prince of Wales's Volunteers (South Lancashire Regiment) 8th Battalion : 26 September 1915 - 31 January 1918 (First World War, War Diary, WO95/2250/3)	WD2250_3	9781474513654	£15.00
25 DIVISION 75 Infantry Brigade Gloucestershire Regiment 1/5th Battalion (Territorial) : 1 September 1918 - 28 February 1919 (First World War, War Diary, WO95/2251/1)	WD2251_1	9781474513661	£15.00
25 DIVISION 75 Infantry Brigade Worcestershire Regiment 1/8th Battalion : 1 September 1918 - 28 February 1919 (First World War, War Diary, WO95/2251/2)	WD2251_2	9781474513678	£15.00
25 DIVISION 75 Infantry Brigade Border Regiment 8th Battalion : 26 September 1915 - 30 June 1918 (First World War, War Diary, WO95/2251/3)	WD2251_3	9781474513685	£18.00
25 DIVISION 75 Infantry Brigade Royal Warwickshire Regiment 1/8th Territorial Battalion : 1 September 1918 - 28 February 1919 (First World War, War Diary, WO95/2251/4)	WD2251_4	9781474513692	£15.00
25 DIVISION 75 Infantry Brigade, Brigade Machine Gun Company : 19 December 1915 - 1 May 1917 (First World War, War Diary, WO95/2251/5)	WD2251_5	9781474513708	£15.00
25 DIVISION 75 Infantry Brigade, Brigade Trench Mortar Battery : 21 March 1916 - 31 May 1916 (First World War, War Diary, WO95/2251/6)	WD2251_6	9781474513715	£15.00

Title	Product Code	ISBN	Price
26 DIVISION			
26 DIVISION Headquarters, Branches and Services General Staff, Adjutant and Quarter-Master General, Commander Royal Artillery, Assistant Director Medical Services, Commander Royal Engineers, Deputy Assistant Director Ordnance Services, Assistant Director	WD2252	9781474513722	£59.00
26 DIVISION 77 Infantry Brigade Headquarters, Royal Scots Fusiliers 8th Battalion, Black Watch (Royal Highlanders) 10th Battalion, Cameronians (Scottish Rifles) 11th Battalion and Princess Louise's (Argyll & Sutherland Highlanders) 12th Battalion : 1 Sept	WD2253_1	9781474524506	£15.00
26 DIVISION 78 Infantry Brigade Headquarters, Princess Charlotte of Wales's (Royal Berkshire Regiment) 7th Battalion, Oxfordshire and Buckinghamshire Light Infantry 7th Battalion, Gloucestershire Regiment 9th (Service) Battalion and Worcestershire Regimen	WD2253_2	9781474524513	£15.00
26 DIVISION 79 Infantry Brigade Headquarters, Duke of Cornwall's Light Infantry 8th Battalion, Devonshire Regiment 10th (Service) Battalion, Hampshire Regiment 12th (Service) Battalion and Duke of Edinburgh's (Wiltshire Regiment) 7th Battalion : 15 Sept	WD2253_3	9781474524520	£15.00

Title	Product Code	ISBN	Price
27 DIVISION			
27 DIVISION Headquarters, Branches and Services General Staff : 13 November 1914 - 30 June 1915 (First World War, War Diary, WO95/2254)	WD2254	9781474513739	£64.00
27 DIVISION Headquarters, Branches and Services General Staff and Adjutant and Quarter-Master General : 19 December 1914 - 30 November 1915 (First World War, War Diary, WO95/2255)	WD2255	9781474513746	£83.00
27 DIVISION Headquarters, Branches and Services Commander Royal Artillery : 17 November 1914 - 21 November 1915 (First World War, War Diary, WO95/2256/1)	WD2256_1	9781474513753	£15.00
27 DIVISION Headquarters, Branches and Services Royal Army Medical Corps Assistant Director Medical Services : 19 December 1914 - 31 December 1915 (First World War, War Diary, WO95/2256/2)	WD2256_2	9781474513760	£17.00
27 DIVISION Headquarters, Branches and Services Commander Royal Engineers : 21 March 1915 - 31 December 1915 (First World War, War Diary, WO95/2256/3)	WD2256_3	9781474513777	£15.00
27 DIVISION Headquarters, Branches and Services Royal Army Ordnance Corps Deputy Assistant Director Ordnance Services : 1 June 1915 - 30 November 1915 (First World War, War Diary, WO95/2256/4)	WD2256_4	9781474513784	£15.00
27 DIVISION Headquarters, Branches and Services Royal Army Veterinary Corps Assistant Director Veterinary Services : 23 April 1915 - 31 December 1915 (First World War, War Diary, WO95/2256/5)	WD2256_5	9781474513791	£15.00
27 DIVISION Divisional Troops A Squadron Surrey Yeomanry : 21 December 1914 - 28 October 1915 (First World War, War Diary, WO95/2257/1)	WD2257_1	9781474513807	£15.00
27 DIVISION Divisional Troops Divisional Cyclist Company : 1 January 1915 - 1 November 1915 (First World War, War Diary, WO95/2257/2)	WD2257_2	9781474513814	£15.00
27 DIVISION Divisional Troops 1 Brigade Royal Field Artillery : 23 November 1914 - 31 December 1915 (First World War, War Diary, WO95/2257/3)	WD2257_3	9781474513821	£15.00
27 DIVISION Divisional Troops 19 Brigade Royal Field Artillery : 15 October 1914 - 29 April 1915 (First World War, War Diary, WO95/2257/4)	WD2257_4	9781474513838	£15.00
27 DIVISION Divisional Troops 20 Brigade Royal Field Artillery : 28 September 1914 - 30 January 1915 (First World War, War Diary, WO95/2257/5)	WD2257_5	9781474513845	£25.00
27 DIVISION Divisional Troops 129 Brigade Royal Field Artillery : 26 August 1915 - 26 December 1915 (First World War, War Diary, WO95/2257/6)	WD2257_6	9781474513852	£15.00
27 DIVISION Divisional Troops Divisional Ammunition Column : 21 December 1914 - 1 January 1916 (First World War, War Diary, WO95/2257/7)	WD2257_7	9781474513869	£15.00
27 DIVISION Divisional Troops 17 Field Company Royal Engineers : 1 April 1915 - 31 December 1915 (First World War, War Diary, WO95/2258/1)	WD2258_1	9781474513876	£15.00
27 DIVISION Divisional Troops 1/1 Wessex Field Company Royal Engineers : 21 December 1914 - 31 December 1915 (First World War, War Diary, WO95/2258/2)	WD2258_2	9781474513883	£15.00
27 DIVISION Divisional Troops 1/2 Wessex Field Company Royal Engineers : 21 December 1914 - 31 December 1915 (First World War, War Diary, WO95/2258/3)	WD2258_3	9781474513890	£15.00

Title	Product Code	ISBN	Price
27 DIVISION Divisional Troops 1/1 South Midland Field Company Royal Engineers : 21 December 1914 - 30 April 1915 (First World War, War Diary, WO95/2258/4)	WD2258_4	9781474513906	£15.00
27 DIVISION Divisional Troops Divisional Signal Company : 1 September 1915 - 30 November 1915 (First World War, War Diary, WO95/2258/5)	WD2258_5	9781474513913	£15.00
27 DIVISION Divisional Troops Royal Army Medical Corps 81 Field Ambulance : 22 December 1914 - 31 October 1915 (First World War, War Diary, WO95/2259/1)	WD2259_1	9781474513920	£15.00
27 DIVISION Divisional Troops Royal Army Medical Corps 82 Field Ambulance : 21 December 1914 - 30 November 1915 (First World War, War Diary, WO95/2259/2)	WD2259_2	9781474513937	£15.00
27 DIVISION Divisional Troops Royal Army Medical Corps 83 Field Ambulance and 7 Sanitary Section : 27 December 1914 - 30 November 1915 (First World War, War Diary, WO95/2259/3-4)	WD2259_3-4	9781474513944	£15.00
27 DIVISION Divisional Troops Royal Army Veterinary Corps 16 Mobile Veterinary Section : 21 December 1914 - 19 July 1915 (First World War, War Diary, WO95/2259/5)	WD2259_5	9781474513951	£15.00
27 DIVISION Divisional Troops Royal Army Service Corps Divisional Train (95, 96, 97, 98 Companies ASC) : 1 January 1915 - 27 November 1915 (First World War, War Diary, WO95/2259/6)	WD2259_6	9781474513968	£15.00
27 DIVISION 80 Infantry Brigade Headquarters : 17 November 1914 - 31 October 1915 (First World War, War Diary, WO95/2260)	WD2260	9781474524537	£67.00
27 DIVISION 80 Infantry Brigade King's Royal Rifle Corps 3rd Battalion : 20 December 1914 - 31 October 1915 (First World War, War Diary, WO95/2261)	WD2261	9781474524544	£52.00
27 DIVISION 80 Infantry Brigade King's Royal Rifle Corps 4th Battalion : 18 October 1914 - 28 October 1915 (First World War, War Diary, WO95/2262/1)	WD2262_1	9781474513975	£15.00
27 DIVISION 80 Infantry Brigade Rifle Brigade (The Prince Consort's Own) 4th Battalion : 20 December 1914 - 28 October 1915 (First World War, War Diary, WO95/2262/2)	WD2262_2	9781474513982	£15.00
27 DIVISION 80 Infantry Brigade King's (Shropshire Light Infantry) 2nd Battalion : 1 March 1914 - 31 October 1915 (First World War, War Diary, WO95/2262/3)	WD2262_3	9781474513999	£15.00
27 DIVISION 80 Infantry Brigade Princess Patricia's Canadian Light Infantry : 4 November 1914 - 31 October 1915 (First World War, War Diary, WO95/2262/4)	WD2262_4	9781474514002	£15.00
27 DIVISION 81 Infantry Brigade Headquarters : 11 February 1914 - 30 September 1915 (First World War, War Diary, WO95/2263/1)	WD2263_1	9781474514019	£34.00
27 DIVISION 81 Infantry Brigade Princess Louise's (Argyll & Sutherland Highlanders) 1st Battalion : 19 December 1914 - 31 October 1915 (First World War, War Diary, WO95/2263/2)	WD2263_2	9781474514026	£15.00
27 DIVISION 81 Infantry Brigade Princess Louise's (Argyll & Sutherland Highlanders) 1/9th Battalion : 18 February 1915 - 30 April 1915 (First World War, War Diary, WO95/2263/3)	WD2263_3	9781474514033	£15.00
27 DIVISION 81 Infantry Brigade Royal Scots (Lothian Regiment) 1st Battalion : 12 October 1914 - 31 October 1915 (First World War, War Diary, WO95/2264/1)	WD2264_1	9781474514040	£15.00

Title	Product Code	ISBN	Price
27 DIVISION 81 Infantry Brigade Royal Scots (Lothian Regiment) 9th Battalion : 26 February 1915 - 31 December 1915 (First World War, War Diary, WO95/2264/2)	WD2264_2	9781474514057	£15.00
27 DIVISION 81 Infantry Brigade Queen's Own Cameron Highlanders 2nd Battalion : 18 December 1914 - 31 October 1915 (First World War, War Diary, WO95/2264/3)	WD2264_3	9781474514064	£26.00
27 DIVISION 81 Infantry Brigade Gloucestershire Regiment 2nd Battalion : 8 November 1914 - 31 October 1915 (First World War, War Diary, WO95/2264/4)	WD2264_4	9781474514071	£15.00
27 DIVISION 82 Infantry Brigade Headquarters : 17 November 1914 - 31 October 1915 (First World War, War Diary, WO95/2265)	WD2265	9781474514088	£70.00
27 DIVISION 82 Infantry Brigade Cambridgeshire Regiment 1st Battalion, Duke of Cornwall's Light Infantry 2nd Battalion, Prince of Wales's Leinster Regiment (Royal Canadians) 1st Battalion, Royal Irish Regiment 1st Battalion and Princess Victoria's (Royal	WD2266	9781474514095	£54.00

Title	Product Code	ISBN	Price
28 DIVISION			
28 DIVISION Headquarters, Branches and Services General Staff : 15 December 1914 - 30 April 1915 (First World War, War Diary, WO95/2267)	WD2267	9781474514101	£63.00
28 DIVISION Headquarters, Branches and Services General Staff : 1 February 1915 - 26 May 1915 (First World War, War Diary, WO95/2268)	WD2268	9781474524551	£78.00
28 DIVISION Headquarters, Branches and Services Adjutant and Quarter-Master General : 16 November 1914 - 25 October 1915 (First World War, War Diary, WO95/2269/1)	WD2269_1	9781474524568	£27.00
28 DIVISION Headquarters, Branches and Services Commander Royal Artillery : 15 December 1914 - 31 October 1915 (First World War, War Diary, WO95/2269/2)	WD2269_2	9781474524575	£31.00
28 DIVISION Headquarters, Branches and Services Royal Army Medical Corps Assistant Director Medical Services, Commander Royal Engineers, Deputy Assistant Director Ordnance Services, Assistant Director Veterinary Services : 15 December 1914 - 31 October 19	WD2270	9781474514118	£29.00
28 DIVISION Divisional Troops B Squadron Surrey Yeomanry : 1 February 1915 - 31 October 1915 (First World War, War Diary, WO95/2271/1)	WD2271_1	9781474514125	£15.00
28 DIVISION Divisional Troops Divisional Cyclist Company : 28 December 1914 - 31 October 1915 (First World War, War Diary, WO95/2271/2)	WD2271_2	9781474514132	£15.00
28 DIVISION Divisional Troops 3 Brigade Royal Field Artillery : 16 November 1914 - 31 October 1915 (First World War, War Diary, WO95/2271/3)	WD2271_3	9781474514149	£15.00
28 DIVISION Divisional Troops 31 Brigade Royal Field Artillery : 22 December 1914 - 31 October 1915 (First World War, War Diary, WO95/2271/4)	WD2271_4	9781474514156	£24.00
28 DIVISION Divisional Troops 130 Brigade Royal Field Artillery : 13 February 1915 - 2 December 1915 (First World War, War Diary, WO95/2271/5)	WD2271_5	9781474514163	£15.00
28 DIVISION Divisional Troops 146 Brigade Royal Field Artillery : 22 December 1914 - 18 October 1915 (First World War, War Diary, WO95/2271/6)	WD2271_6	9781474514170	£15.00
28 DIVISION Divisional Troops Divisional Ammunition Column : 29 December 1914 - 31 October 1915 (First World War, War Diary, WO95/2271/7)	WD2271_7	9781474514187	£15.00
28 DIVISION Divisional Troops 38 Field Company Royal Engineers : 1 April 1915 - 31 October 1915 (First World War, War Diary, WO95/2272/1)	WD2272_1	9781474524582	£15.00
28 DIVISION Divisional Troops 1/1 Northumbrian Field Company Royal Engineers and 2/1 Northumbrian Field Company Royal Engineers : 18 January 1915 - 31 May 1915 (First World War, War Diary, WO95/2272/2-3)	WD2272_2-3	9781474524599	£15.00
28 DIVISION Divisional Troops Divisional Signal Company : 30 November 1914 - 30 October 1915 (First World War, War Diary, WO95/2272/4)	WD2272_4	9781474524605	£15.00
28 DIVISION Divisional Troops Royal Army Medical Corps 84 Field Ambulance : 2 January 1915 - 31 October 1915 (First World War, War Diary, WO95/2272/5)	WD2272_5	9781474524612	£15.00
28 DIVISION Divisional Troops Royal Army Medical Corps 85 Field Ambulance : 1 January 1915 - 31 October 1915 (First World War, War Diary, WO95/2272/6)	WD2272_6	9781474524629	£15.00

Title	Product Code	ISBN	Price
28 DIVISION Divisional Troops Royal Army Medical Corps 86 Field Ambulance : 14 January 1915 - 30 October 1915 (First World War, War Diary, WO95/2272/7)	WD2272_7	9781474524636	£15.00
28 DIVISION Divisional Troops Royal Army Veterinary Corps 17 Mobile Veterinary Section : 1 March 1915 - 26 September 1915 (First World War, War Diary, WO95/2272/8)	WD2272_8	9781474524643	£15.00
28 DIVISION Divisional Troops Royal Army Service Corps Divisional Train (170, 171, 172, 173 Companies A.S.C.) : 15 January 1915 - 17 November 1915 (First World War, War Diary, WO95/2272/9)	WD2272_9	9781474524650	£15.00
28 DIVISION 83 Infantry Brigade Headquarters : 1 January 1915 - 18 October 1915 (First World War, War Diary, WO95/2273)	WD2273	9781474514194	£60.00
28 DIVISION 83 Infantry Brigade King's Own (Yorkshire Light Infantry) 1st Battalion : 8 November 1914 - 31 October 1915 (First World War, War Diary, WO95/2274/1)	WD2274_1	9781474514200	£15.00
28 DIVISION 83 Infantry Brigade King's Own (Royal Lancaster Regiment) 2nd Battalion : 22 December 1914 - 31 October 1915 (First World War, War Diary, WO95/2274/2)	WD2274_2	9781474514217	£15.00
28 DIVISION 83 Infantry Brigade King's Own (Royal Lancaster Regiment) 1/5th Battalion : 14 February 1915 - 31 October 1915 (First World War, War Diary, WO95/2274/3)	WD2274_3	9781474514224	£15.00
28 DIVISION 83 Infantry Brigade Monmouthshire Regiment (Territorial Force) 3rd Battalion : 4 August 1914 - 31 October 1915 (First World War, War Diary, WO95/2274/4)	WD2274_4	9781474514231	£15.00
28 DIVISION 83 Infantry Brigade East Yorkshire Regiment 2nd Battalion : 15 January 1915 - 31 October 1915 (First World War, War Diary, WO95/2275/1)	WD2275_1	9781474514248	£15.00
28 DIVISION 83 Infantry Brigade York and Lancaster Regiment 1st Battalion : 15 January 1915 - 31 October 1915 (First World War, War Diary, WO95/2275/2)	WD2275_2	9781474514255	£33.00
28 DIVISION 84 Infantry Brigade Headquarters : 23 December 1914 - 29 October 1915 (First World War, War Diary, WO95/2276/1)	WD2276_1	9781474514262	£43.00
28 DIVISION 84 Infantry Brigade Cheshire Regiment 2nd Battalion : 2 February 1915 - 31 October 1915 (First World War, War Diary, WO95/2276/2)	WD2276_2	9781474514279	£15.00
28 DIVISION 84 Infantry Brigade Monmouthshire Regiment (Territorial Force) 1st Battalion : 13 February 1915 - 31 August 1915 (First World War, War Diary, WO95/2277/1)	WD2277_1	9781474514286	£15.00
28 DIVISION 84 Infantry Brigade Northumberland Fusiliers 2nd Battalion : 16 January 1915 - 31 October 1915 (First World War, War Diary, WO95/2277/2)	WD2277_2	9781474514293	£15.00
28 DIVISION 84 Infantry Brigade Suffolk Regiment 1st Battalion : 1 February 1915 - 20 October 1915 (First World War, War Diary, WO95/2277/3)	WD2277_3	9781474514309	£15.00
28 DIVISION 84 Infantry Brigade Welsh Regiment 1st Battalion : 5 July 1915 - 31 July 1915 (First World War, War Diary, WO95/2277/4)	WD2277_4	9781474514316	£15.00
28 DIVISION 84 Infantry Brigade Welsh Regiment 1/6th Battalion. : 23 October 1914 - 31 October 1915 (First World War, War Diary, WO95/2277/5)	WD2277_5	9781474514323	£15.00

Title	Product Code	ISBN	Price
28 DIVISION 85 Infantry Brigade Headquarters : 23 December 1914 - 31 October 1915 (First World War, War Diary, WO95/2278)	WD2278	9781474524667	£85.00
28 DIVISION 85 Infantry Brigade East Surrey Regiment 2nd Battalion, Buffs (East Kent Regiment) 2nd Battalion, Royal Fusiliers (City of London Regiment) 3rd Battalion, Duke of Cambridge's Own (Middlesex Regiment) 3rd Battalion and 1/8th (T.F.) Battalion :	WD2279	9781474524674	£54.00

Title	Product Code	ISBN	Price
29 DIVISION			
29 DIVISION Headquarters, Branches and Services General Staff : 1 March 1916 - 31 March 1916 (First World War, War Diary, WO95/2280/1)	WD2280_1	9781474514330	£19.00
29 DIVISION Headquarters, Branches and Services General Staff : 1 April 1916 - 31 May 1916 (First World War, War Diary, WO95/2280/2)	WD2280_2	9781474514347	£16.00
29 DIVISION Headquarters, Branches and Services General Staff : 1 June 1916 - 30 June 1916 (First World War, War Diary, WO95/2280/3)	WD2280_3	9781474514354	£21.00
29 DIVISION Headquarters, Branches and Services General Staff : 1 July 1916 - 31 July 1916 (First World War, War Diary, WO95/2280/4)	WD2280_4	9781474514361	£20.00
29 DIVISION Headquarters, Branches and Services General Staff : 1 August 1916 - 31 August 1916 (First World War, War Diary, WO95/2280/5)	WD2280_5	9781474514378	£15.00
29 DIVISION Headquarters, Branches and Services General Staff : 1 September 1916 - 31 December 1916 (First World War, War Diary, WO95/2281/1)	WD2281_1	9781474514385	£27.00
29 DIVISION Headquarters, Branches and Services General Staff : 1 January 1917 - 25 April 1917 (First World War, War Diary, WO95/2281/2)	WD2281_2	9781474514392	£52.00
29 DIVISION Headquarters, Branches and Services General Staff : 1 May 1917 - 16 August 1917 (First World War, War Diary, WO95/2282/3)	WD2282	9781474514408	£67.00
29 DIVISION Headquarters, Branches and Services General Staff : 9 October 1915 - 31 December 1917 (First World War, War Diary, WO95/2283)	WD2283	9781474514415	£34.00
29 DIVISION Headquarters, Branches and Services General Staff : 1 January 1918 - 30 June 1918 (First World War, War Diary, WO95/2284)	WD2284	9781474514422	£64.00
29 DIVISION Headquarters, Branches and Services General Staff : 1 July 1918 - 31 October 1919 (First World War, War Diary, WO95/2285)	WD2285	9781474514439	£57.00
29 DIVISION Headquarters, Branches and Services Adjutant and Quarter-Master General : 1 March 1916 - 31 October 1919 (First World War, War Diary, WO95/2286)	WD2286	9781474514446	£55.00
29 DIVISION Headquarters, Branches and Services Commander Royal Artillery : 1 March 1916 - 20 March 1918 (First World War, War Diary, WO95/2287)	WD2287	9781474514453	£51.00
29 DIVISION Headquarters, Branches and Services Commander Royal Artillery : 1 April 1918 - 30 October 1919 (First World War, War Diary, WO95/2288)	WD2288	9781474514460	£67.00
29 DIVISION Headquarters, Branches and Services Royal Army Medical Corps Assistant Director Medical Services : 1 March 1916 - 31 October 1919 (First World War, War Diary, WO95/2289)	WD2289	9781474514477	£37.00
29 DIVISION Headquarters, Branches and Services Commander Royal Engineers : 1 April 1916 - 31 October 1919 (First World War, War Diary, WO95/2290/1)	WD2290_1	9781474514484	£47.00
29 DIVISION Headquarters, Branches and Services Royal Army Ordnance Corps Deputy Assistant Director Ordnance Services : 28 July 1915 - 31 October 1919 (First World War, War Diary, WO95/2290/2)	WD2290_2	9781474514491	£15.00
29 DIVISION Headquarters, Branches and Services Royal Army Veterinary Corps Assistant Director Veterinary Services : 2 March 1916 - 31 October 1919 (First World War, War Diary, WO95/2290/3)	WD2290_3	9781474514507	£15.00

Title	Product Code	ISBN	Price
29 DIVISION Divisional Troops Divisional Cyclist Company : 1 March 1916 - 30 April 1916 (First World War, War Diary, WO95/2291/1)	WD2291_1	9781474514514	£15.00
29 DIVISION Divisional Troops 15 Brigade Royal Horse Artillery : 1 March 1916 - 1 February 1919 (First World War, War Diary, WO95/2291/2)	WD2291_2	9781474514521	£43.00
29 DIVISION Divisional Troops 17 Brigade Royal Field Artillery : 1 March 1916 - 28 February 1919 (First World War, War Diary, WO95/2291/3)	WD2291_3	9781474514538	£29.00
29 DIVISION Divisional Troops 132 Brigade Royal Field Artillery : 1 March 1916 - 12 September 1916 (First World War, War Diary, WO95/2292/1)	WD2292_1	9781474514545	£15.00
29 DIVISION Divisional Troops 147 Brigade Royal Field Artillery : 1 March 1916 - 31 December 1916 (First World War, War Diary, WO95/2292/2)	WD2292_2	9781474514552	£15.00
29 DIVISION Divisional Troops Divisional Trench Mortar Batteries : 1 August 1916 - 31 January 1919 (First World War, War Diary, WO95/2292/3)	WD2292_3	9781474514569	£26.00
29 DIVISION Divisional Troops Divisional Ammunition Column : 1 March 1916 - 31 October 1919 (First World War, War Diary, WO95/2292/4)	WD2292_4	9781474514576	£15.00
29 DIVISION Divisional Troops 455 (1/1 West Riding) Field Company Royal Engineers : 1 March 1916 - 28 October 1919 (First World War, War Diary, WO95/2293/1)	WD2293_1	9781474514583	£27.00
29 DIVISION Divisional Troops 497 (1/3 Kent) Field Company Royal Engineers : 2 October 1915 - 27 October 1919 (First World War, War Diary, WO95/2293/2)	WD2293_2	9781474514590	£19.00
29 DIVISION Divisional Troops 510 (1/2 London) Field Company Royal Engineers : 1 July 1916 - 28 October 1919 (First World War, War Diary, WO95/2293/3)	WD2293_3	9781474514606	£15.00
29 DIVISION Divisional Troops Divisional Signal Company : 1 July 1916 - 7 September 1919 (First World War, War Diary, WO95/2294/1)	WD2294_1	9781474514613	£34.00
29 DIVISION Divisional Troops 227 Machine Gun Company : 12 July 1917 - 31 January 1918 (First World War, War Diary, WO95/2294/2)	WD2294_2	9781474514620	£15.00
29 DIVISION Divisional Troops Machine Gun Corps 29 Battalion : 1 February 1918 - 31 October 1919 (First World War, War Diary, WO95/2294/3)	WD2294_3	9781474514637	£17.00
29 DIVISION Divisional Troops Gloucestershire Regiment 9th (Service) Battalion Pioneers : 1 May 1919 - 31 October 1919 (First World War, War Diary, WO95/2294/4)	WD2294_4	9781474514644	£15.00
29 DIVISION Divisional Troops Monmouthshire Regiment (Territorial Force) 1/2 Battalion Pioneers : 1 March 1916 - 31 May 1919 (First World War, War Diary, WO95/2295)	WD2295	9781474514651	£52.00
29 DIVISION Divisional Troops Royal Army Medical Corps 87 Field Ambulance and 88 Field Ambulance : 12 May 1914 - 31 December 1918 (First World War, War Diary, WO95/2296)	WD2296	9781474514668	£69.00
29 DIVISION Divisional Troops Royal Army Medical Corps 89 Field Ambulance : 2 March 1916 - 25 July 1919 (First World War, War Diary, WO95/2297/1)	WD2297_1	9781474514675	£31.00
29 DIVISION Divisional Troops 16 Sanitary Section : 12 April 1916 - 31 March 1917 (First World War, War Diary, WO95/2297/2)	WD2297_2	9781474514682	£15.00

Title	Product Code	ISBN	Price
29 DIVISION Divisional Troops Royal Army Veterinary Corps 18 Mobile Veterinary Section : 1 February 1916 - 30 October 1919 (First World War, War Diary, WO95/2297/3)	WD2297_3	9781474514699	£15.00
29 DIVISION Divisional Troops Royal Army Service Corps Divisional Train (225, 226, 227, 228 Companies A.S.C.) : 20 March 1916 - 31 October 1919 (First World War, War Diary, WO95/2297/4)	WD2297_4	9781474514705	£15.00
29 DIVISION 86 Infantry Brigade Headquarters : 2 March 1916 - 31 December 1917 (First World War, War Diary, WO95/2298)	WD2298	9781474514712	£49.00
29 DIVISION 86 Infantry Brigade Headquarters : 1 January 1918 - 31 October 1919 (First World War, War Diary, WO95/2299)	WD2299	9781474514729	£54.00
29 DIVISION 86 Infantry Brigade Lancashire Fusiliers 1st Battalion : 1 March 1916 - 28 February 1919 (First World War, War Diary, WO95/2300/1-24)	WD2300_1-24	9781474514736	£61.00
29 DIVISION 86 Infantry Brigade Royal Dublin Fusiliers 1st Battalion : 19 March 1916 - 30 September 1917 (First World War, War Diary, WO95/2301/1)	WD2301_1	9781474514743	£17.00
29 DIVISION 86 Infantry Brigade Royal Dublin Fusiliers 1st Battalion : 1 August 1917 - 31 May 1919 (First World War, War Diary, WO95/2301/2)	WD2301_2	9781474514750	£19.00
29 DIVISION 86 Infantry Brigade Royal Fusiliers (City of London Regiment) 2nd Battalion : 25 February 1916 - 1 April 1919 (First World War, War Diary, WO95/2301/3)	WD2301_3	9781474514767	£28.00
29 DIVISION 86 Infantry Brigade 1 Battalion Royal Guernsey Light Infantry : 26 September 1917 - 30 April 1918 (First World War, War Diary, WO95/2302/1)	WD2302_1	9781474514774	£15.00
29 DIVISION 86 Infantry Brigade Duke of Cambridge's Own (Middlesex Regiment) 16th Battalion : 24 April 1916 - 22 February 1918 (First World War, War Diary, WO95/2302/2)	WD2302_2	9781474514781	£15.00
29 DIVISION 86 Infantry Brigade Royal Warwickshire Regiment 51st Battalion : 1 May 1919 - 31 October 1919 (First World War, War Diary, WO95/2302/3)	WD2302_3	9781474514798	£15.00
29 DIVISION 86 Infantry Brigade Royal Warwickshire Regiment 52 Battalion : 1 May 1919 - 29 October 1919 (First World War, War Diary, WO95/2302/4)	WD2302_4	9781474514804	£15.00
29 DIVISION 86 Infantry Brigade Royal Warwickshire Regiment 53 Battalion : 17 March 1919 - 1 October 1919 (First World War, War Diary, WO95/2302/5)	WD2302_5	9781474514811	£15.00
29 DIVISION 86 Infantry Brigade, Brigade Machine Gun Company : 27 February 1916 - 31 January 1918 (First World War, War Diary, WO95/2302/6)	WD2302_6	9781474514828	£21.00
29 DIVISION 86 Infantry Brigade, Brigade Trench Mortar Battery : 1 July 1916 - 31 July 1916 (First World War, War Diary, WO95/2302/7)	WD2302_7	9781474514835	£15.00
29 DIVISION 86 Infantry Brigade, Brigade Trench Mortar Battery : 5 July 1917 - 31 August 1918 (First World War, War Diary, WO95/2302/8)	WD2302_8	9781474514842	£15.00
29 DIVISION 87 Infantry Brigade Headquarters : 1 March 1916 - 31 October 1919 (First World War, War Diary, WO95/2303)	WD2303	9781474514859	£57.00
29 DIVISION 87 Infantry Brigade King's Own Scottish Borderers 1st Battalion : 1 March 1916 - 2 April 1919 (First World War, War Diary, WO95/2304/1)	WD2304_1	9781474514866	£31.00

Title	Product Code	ISBN	Price
29 DIVISION 87 Infantry Brigade South Wales Borderers 2nd Battalion : 1 March 1916 - 5 April 1919 (First World War, War Diary, WO95/2304/2)	WD2304_2	9781474514873	£34.00
29 DIVISION 87 Infantry Brigade Border Regiment 1st Battalion : 2 April 1916 - 3 April 1919 (First World War, War Diary, WO95/2305/1)	WD2305_1	9781474514880	£27.00
29 DIVISION 87 Infantry Brigade Royal Inniskilling Fusiliers 1st Battalion : 1 March 1916 - 31 January 1918 (First World War, War Diary, WO95/2305/2)	WD2305_2	9781474514897	£25.00
29 DIVISION 87 Infantry Brigade Devonshire Regiment 5th (P.O.W.) Battalion (Territorials). : 1 May 1919 - 31 October 1919 (First World War, War Diary, WO95/2305/3)	WD2305_3	9781474514903	£15.00
29 DIVISION 87 Infantry Brigade Devonshire Regiment 51st (Y.S.) Battalion : 12 March 1919 - 31 October 1919 (First World War, War Diary, WO95/2305/4)	WD2305_4	9781474514910	£15.00
29 DIVISION 87 Infantry Brigade Devonshire Regiment 52nd Battalion : 10 March 1919 - 31 October 1919 (First World War, War Diary, WO95/2305/5)	WD2305_5	9781474514927	£15.00
29 DIVISION 87 Infantry Brigade, Brigade Machine Gun Company : 2 June 1916 - 28 January 1918 (First World War, War Diary, WO95/2305/6)	WD2305_6	9781474514934	£15.00
29 DIVISION 87 Infantry Brigade, Brigade Trench Mortar Battery : 1 July 1916 - 31 August 1916 (First World War, War Diary, WO95/2305/7)	WD2305_7	9781474514941	£15.00
29 DIVISION 88 Infantry Brigade Headquarters : 7 March 1916 - 29 May 1917 (First World War, War Diary, WO95/2306)	WD2306	9781474514958	£43.00
29 DIVISION 88 Infantry Brigade Headquarters : 1 June 1917 - 26 October 1919 (First World War, War Diary, WO95/2307)	WD2307	9781474514965	£75.00
29 DIVISION 88 Infantry Brigade Prince of Wales's Leinster Regiment (Royal Canadians) 2nd Battalion : 1 February 1918 - 23 June 1919 (First World War, War Diary, WO95/2308/1)	WD2308_1	9781474514972	£15.00
29 DIVISION 88 Infantry Brigade Hampshire Regiment 2nd Battalion : 2 March 1916 - 28 February 1919 (First World War, War Diary, WO95/2308/2)	WD2308_2	9781474514989	£46.00
29 DIVISION 88 Infantry Brigade Essex Regiment 1st Battalion : 27 January 1916 - 31 January 1918 (First World War, War Diary, WO95/2309/1)	WD2309_1	9781474524681	£15.00
29 DIVISION 88 Infantry Brigade Worcestershire Regiment 4th Battalion, Royal Scots (Lothian Regiment) 5th Battalion, Hampshire Regiment 2/4th (T.F.) Battalion, 15th (Service) Battalion and 51st (Y.S.) Battalion : 1 March 1916 - 30 April 1919 (First Worl	WD2309_2-6	9781474514996	£28.00
29 DIVISION 88 Infantry Brigade, Brigade Machine Gun Company and Trench Mortar Battery : 25 January 1916 - 31 January 1918 (First World War, War Diary, WO95/2309/7-8)	WD2309_7-8	9781474524698	£30.00

Title	Product Code	ISBN	Price
3 CAVALRY DIVISION			
3 CAVALRY DIVISION Headquarters, Branches and Services General Staff : 2 October 1914 - 31 May 1919 (First World War, War Diary, WO95/1141)	WD1141	9781474500616	£60.00
3 CAVALRY DIVISION Headquarters, Branches and Services General Staff Appendices to 1141 : 11 October 1914 - 30 November 1914 (First World War, War Diary, WO95/1142/1)	WD1142_1	9781474500623	£32.00
3 CAVALRY DIVISION Headquarters, Branches and Services General Staff Appendices to 1141 : 31 July 1916 - 7 November 1918 (First World War, War Diary, WO95/1142/2)	WD1142_2	9781474500630	£15.00
3 CAVALRY DIVISION Headquarters, Branches and Services General Staff Appendices to 1141 : 3 April 1917 - 30 June 1917 (First World War, War Diary, WO95/1142/3)	WD1142_3	9781474500647	£15.00
3 CAVALRY DIVISION Headquarters, Branches and Services General Staff Appendices to 1141 : 1 January 1918 - 22 January 1918 (First World War, War Diary, WO95/1142/4)	WD1142_4	9781474500654	£15.00
3 CAVALRY DIVISION Headquarters, Branches and Services General Staff Appendices to 1141 : 4 May 1918 - 15 October 1918 (First World War, War Diary, WO95/1142/5)	WD1142_5	9781474500661	£15.00
3 CAVALRY DIVISION Headquarters, Branches and Services General Staff Appendices to 1141 : 5 August 1918 - 21 December 1918 (First World War, War Diary, WO95/1142/6)	WD1142_6	9781474500678	£15.00
3 CAVALRY DIVISION Headquarters, Branches and Services Adjutant and Quarter-Master General : 24 September 1914 - 31 December 1917 (First World War, War Diary, WO95/1143)	WD1143	9781474500685	£49.00
3 CAVALRY DIVISION Headquarters, Branches and Services Adjutant and Quarter-Master General : 1 January 1918 - 31 March 1919 (First World War, War Diary, WO95/1144)	WD1144	9781474500692	£76.00
3 CAVALRY DIVISION Headquarters, Branches and Services Royal Army Medical Corps Assistant Director Medical Services : 1 June 1914 - 31 March 1919 (First World War, War Diary, WO95/1145/1)	WD1145_1	9781474500708	£57.00
3 CAVALRY DIVISION Headquarters, Branches and Services Royal Army Ordnance Corps Assistant Director Ordnance Services : 2 September 1914 - 27 February 1919 (First World War, War Diary, WO95/1145/2)	WD1145_2	9781474500715	£15.00
3 CAVALRY DIVISION Headquarters, Branches and Services Royal Army Veterinary Corps Assistant Director Veterinary Services : 23 November 1915 - 30 April 1919 (First World War, War Diary, WO95/1145/3)	WD1145_3	9781474500722	£15.00
3 CAVALRY DIVISION Divisional Troops 4 Brigade Royal Horse Artillery : 1 October 1914 - 10 June 1919 (First World War, War Diary, WO95/1146/1)	WD1146_1	9781474500739	£24.00
3 CAVALRY DIVISION Divisional Troops 7 Light Armoured Battery : 1 July 1916 - 29 June 1917 (First World War, War Diary, WO95/1146/2)	WD1146_2	9781474500746	£15.00
3 CAVALRY DIVISION Divisional Troops 3 Field Squadron Royal Engineers : 16 September 1914 - 22 May 1919 (First World War, War Diary, WO95/1146/3)	WD1146_3	9781474500753	£15.00
3 CAVALRY DIVISION Divisional Troops Signal Squadron : 1 January 1915 - 31 March 1919 (First World War, War Diary, WO95/1146/4)	WD1146_4	9781474500760	£20.00
3 CAVALRY DIVISION Divisional Troops Royal Army Medical Corps 6 Cavalry Field Ambulance : 11 September 1914 - 19 May 1919 (First World War, War Diary, WO95/1147/1)	WD1147_1	9781474500777	£31.00

Title	Product Code	ISBN	Price
3 CAVALRY DIVISION Divisional Troops Royal Army Medical Corps 7 Cavalry Field Ambulance : 3 October 1914 - 14 June 1917 (First World War, War Diary, WO95/1147/2)	WD1147_2	9781474500784	£41.00
3 CAVALRY DIVISION Divisional Troops Royal Army Medical Corps 7 Cavalry Field Ambulance : 1 July 1917 - 25 April 1919 (First World War, War Diary, WO95/1148/1)	WD1148_1	9781474500791	£65.00
3 CAVALRY DIVISION Divisional Troops Royal Army Medical Corps 8 Cavalry Field Ambulance : 4 December 1914 - 11 April 1918 (First World War, War Diary, WO95/1148/2)	WD1148_2	9781474500807	£24.00
3 CAVALRY DIVISION Divisional Troops 12 Sanitary Section : 11 January 1915 - 30 June 1917 (First World War, War Diary, WO95/1149/1)	WD1149_1	9781474500814	£20.00
3 CAVALRY DIVISION Divisional Troops Royal Army Veterinary Corps 13 Mobile Veterinary Section : 4 October 1914 - 30 April 1919 (First World War, War Diary, WO95/1149/2)	WD1149_2	9781474500821	£16.00
3 CAVALRY DIVISION Divisional Troops Royal Army Veterinary Corps 14 Mobile Veterinary Section : 3 October 1914 - 31 May 1919 (First World War, War Diary, WO95/1149/3)	WD1149_3	9781474500838	£15.00
3 CAVALRY DIVISION Divisional Troops Royal Army Veterinary Corps 20 Mobile Veterinary Section : 1 March 1915 - 26 February 1918 (First World War, War Diary, WO95/1149/4)	WD1149_4	9781474500845	£15.00
3 CAVALRY DIVISION Divisional Troops Royal Army Service Corps Headquarters Divisional Army Service Corps (81 Company A.S.C.) : 4 September 1914 - 30 June 1919 (First World War, War Diary, WO95/1150/1)	WD1150_1	9781474500852	£33.00
3 CAVALRY DIVISION Divisional Troops Royal Army Service Corps Divisional Supply Column (73 Company A.S.C.) : 3 October 1914 - 31 March 1919 (First World War, War Diary, WO95/1150/2)	WD1150_2	9781474500869	£33.00
3 CAVALRY DIVISION Divisional Troops Royal Army Service Corps Divisional Auxiliary Horse Transport Company (576 Company A.S.C.) : 24 January 1916 - 16 May 1919 (First World War, War Diary, WO95/1151/1)	WD1151_1	9781474500876	£15.00
3 CAVALRY DIVISION Divisional Troops Royal Army Service Corps Divisional Ammunition Park (76 Company A.S.C.) : 1 February 1915 - 31 October 1917 (First World War, War Diary, WO95/1151/2)	WD1151_2	9781474500883	£28.00
3 CAVALRY DIVISION 6 Cavalry Brigade Headquarters : 19 September 1914 - 27 February 1919 (First World War, War Diary, WO95/1152/1)	WD1152_1	9781474500890	£29.00
3 CAVALRY DIVISION 6 Cavalry Brigade `C' Battery Royal Horse Artillery : 22 March 1915 - 30 November 1918 (First World War, War Diary, WO95/1152/2)	WD1152_2	9781474500906	£15.00
3 CAVALRY DIVISION 6 Cavalry Brigade 6 Machine Gun Squadron : 29 February 1916 - 31 May 1918 (First World War, War Diary, WO95/1152/3)	WD1152_3	9781474500913	£15.00
3 CAVALRY DIVISION 6 Cavalry Brigade 1st Dragoons (Royals) : 19 September 1914 - 31 March 1919 (First World War, War Diary, WO95/1153/1)	WD1153_1	9781474500920	£23.00
3 CAVALRY DIVISION 6 Cavalry Brigade 3rd Dragoon Guards (Prince of Wales' Own) : 30 October 1914 - 31 January 1919 (First World War, War Diary, WO95/1153/2)	WD1153_2	9781474500937	£15.00

Title	Product Code	ISBN	Price
3 CAVALRY DIVISION 6 Cavalry Brigade 10th (Prince of Wales' Own Royal) Hussars : 1 March 1918 - 31 March 1919 (First World War, War Diary, WO95/1153/3)	WD1153_3	9781474500944	£15.00
3 CAVALRY DIVISION 6 Cavalry Brigade 1st/1st North Somerset Yeomanry : 2 November 1914 - 31 March 1918 (First World War, War Diary, WO95/1153/4)	WD1153_4	9781474500951	£15.00
3 CAVALRY DIVISION 7 Cavalry Brigade Headquarters and `K' Battery Royal Horse Artillery : 5 October 1914 - 20 March 1919 (First World War, War Diary, WO95/1154/1-2)	WD1154_1-2	9781474500968	£36.00
3 CAVALRY DIVISION 7 Cavalry Brigade 7 Machine Gun Squadron : 29 February 1916 - 18 June 1919 (First World War, War Diary, WO95/1154/3)	WD1154_3	9781474500975	£15.00
3 CAVALRY DIVISION 7 Cavalry Brigade 1 Life Guards, 2 Life Guards, Royal Horse Guards, 6th Dragoons (Inniskilling), 7th Dragoon Guards (Princess Royal), 17th Lancers (Duke of Cambridge's Own) and Leicestershire Yeomanry : 25 August 1914 - 27 October 1917	WD1155	9781474500982	£53.00
3 CAVALRY DIVISION 8 Cavalry Brigade Headquarters, `G' Battery Royal Horse Artillery, Royal Horse Guards, 10th (Prince of Wales' Own Royal) Hussars, Essex Yeomanry, Leicestershire Yeomanry and Machine Gun Squadron : 6 October 1914 - 29 February 1916 (Fi	WD1156	9781474500999	£57.00

Title	Product Code	ISBN	Price
3 DIVISION			
3 DIVISION Headquarters, Branches and Services General Staff : 5 August 1914 - 30 October 1914 (First World War, War Diary, WO95/1375)	WD1375	9781474503983	£87.00
3 DIVISION Headquarters, Branches and Services General Staff : 1 November 1914 - 31 March 1915 (First World War, War Diary, WO95/1376)	WD1376	9781474521857	£74.00
3 DIVISION Headquarters, Branches and Services General Staff : 1 April 1915 - 31 July 1916 (First World War, War Diary, WO95/1377)	WD1377	9781474503990	£79.00
3 DIVISION Headquarters, Branches and Services General Staff : 1 August 1916 - 31 March 1917 (First World War, War Diary, WO95/1378)	WD1378	9781474504003	£49.00
3 DIVISION Headquarters, Branches and Services General Staff : 1 May 1917 - 31 December 1917 (First World War, War Diary, WO95/1379)	WD1379	9781474504010	£58.00
3 DIVISION Headquarters, Branches and Services General Staff : 1 January 1918 - 30 June 1918 (First World War, War Diary, WO95/1380)	WD1380	9781474504027	£54.00
3 DIVISION Headquarters, Branches and Services General Staff : 1 July 1918 - 31 October 1918 (First World War, War Diary, WO95/1381)	WD1381	9781474504034	£57.00
3 DIVISION Headquarters, Branches and Services General Staff : 1 November 1918 - 30 June 1919 (First World War, War Diary, WO95/1382)	WD1382	9781474504041	£31.00
3 DIVISION Headquarters, Branches and Services Adjutant and Quarter-Master General : 29 July 1914 - 31 December 1915 (First World War, War Diary, WO95/1383)	WD1383	9781474504058	£69.00
3 DIVISION Headquarters, Branches and Services Adjutant and Quarter-Master General : 1 January 1916 - 23 June 1917 (First World War, War Diary, WO95/1384)	WD1384	9781474504065	£74.00
3 DIVISION Headquarters, Branches and Services Adjutant and Quarter-Master General : 1 July 1917 - 30 September 1917 (First World War, War Diary, WO95/1385)	WD1385	9781474504072	£59.00
3 DIVISION Headquarters, Branches and Services Adjutant and Quarter-Master General : 7 December 1916 - 31 December 1917 (First World War, War Diary, WO95/1386)	WD1386	9781474504089	£49.00
3 DIVISION Headquarters, Branches and Services Adjutant and Quarter-Master General : 1 January 1918 - 28 February 1918 (First World War, War Diary, WO95/1387)	WD1387	9781474504096	£62.00
3 DIVISION Headquarters, Branches and Services Adjutant and Quarter-Master General : 19 July 1916 - 31 August 1918 (First World War, War Diary, WO95/1388)	WD1388	9781474504102	£60.00
3 DIVISION Headquarters, Branches and Services Adjutant and Quarter-Master General : 10 January 1918 - 31 December 1918 (First World War, War Diary, WO95/1389)	WD1389	9781474504119	£75.00
3 DIVISION Headquarters, Branches and Services Commander Royal Artillery : 4 August 1914 - 30 June 1915 (First World War, War Diary, WO95/1390)	WD1390	9781474504126	£63.00
3 DIVISION Headquarters, Branches and Services Commander Royal Artillery : 1 July 1915 - 31 March 1916 (First World War, War Diary, WO95/1391)	WD1391	9781474504133	£57.00

Title	Product Code	ISBN	Price
3 DIVISION Headquarters, Branches and Services Commander Royal Artillery : 1 April 1916 - 31 December 1916 (First World War, War Diary, WO95/1392)	WD1392	9781474504140	£50.00
3 DIVISION Headquarters, Branches and Services Commander Royal Artillery : 1 January 1917 - 30 December 1917 (First World War, War Diary, WO95/1393)	WD1393	9781474504157	£38.00
3 DIVISION Headquarters, Branches and Services Commander Royal Artillery : 2 February 1917 - 28 June 1919 (First World War, War Diary, WO95/1394)	WD1394	9781474504164	£37.00
3 DIVISION Headquarters, Branches and Services Royal Army Medical Corps Assistant Director Medical Services : 16 August 1914 - 31 December 1915 (First World War, War Diary, WO95/1395)	WD1395	9781474504171	£57.00
3 DIVISION Headquarters, Branches and Services Royal Army Medical Corps Assistant Director Medical Services : 1 January 1916 - 30 October 1919 (First World War, War Diary, WO95/1396)	WD1396	9781474521864	£63.00
3 DIVISION Headquarters, Branches and Services Commander Royal Engineers : 4 August 1914 - 28 October 1919 (First World War, War Diary, WO95/1397)	WD1397	9781474504188	£34.00
3 DIVISION Headquarters, Branches and Services Royal Army Veterinary Corps Deputy Assistant Director Veterinary Services : 13 May 1915 - 30 June 1919 (First World War, War Diary, WO95/1398/2)	WD1398_2	9781474504195	£24.00
3 DIVISION Headquarters, Branches and Services Royal Army Veterinary Corps Deputy Assistant Director Veterinary Services : 4 August 1914 - 31 October 1919 (First World War, War Diary, WO95/1398/3)	WD1398_3	9781474504201	£47.00
3 DIVISION Divisional Troops `A' Squadron 15 Hussars, `C' Squadron North Irish Horse, Divisional Cyclist Company, 23 Brigade Royal Field Artillery and 30 Brigade Royal Field Artillery : 4 August 1914 - 29 January 1916 (First World War, War Diary, WO95/13	WD1399	9781474504218	£30.00
3 DIVISION Divisional Troops 40 Brigade Royal Field Artillery : 5 August 1914 - 28 February 1919 (First World War, War Diary, WO95/1400)	WD1400	9781474504225	£34.00
3 DIVISION Divisional Troops 42 Brigade Royal Field Artillery, 7 Belgian Field Artillery Brigade, 74 Brigade Royal Field Artillery and 75 Brigade Royal Field Artillery : 4 August 1914 - 1 October 1919 (First World War, War Diary, WO95/1401)	WD1401	9781474504232	£39.00
3 DIVISION Divisional Troops Divisional Ammunition Column and Trench Mortar Batteries : 5 August 1914 - 31 December 1917 (First World War, War Diary, WO95/1402)	WD1402	9781474504249	£20.00
3 DIVISION Divisional Troops 56 Field Company Royal Engineers : 16 August 1914 - 31 May 1919 (First World War, War Diary, WO95/1403/1)	WD1403_1	9781474504256	£20.00
3 DIVISION Divisional Troops 57 Field Company Royal Engineers : 4 August 1914 - 30 June 1915 (First World War, War Diary, WO95/1403/2)	WD1403_2	9781474504263	£15.00
3 DIVISION Divisional Troops 438 (Cheshire) Field Company Royal Engineers : 1 December 1914 - 30 October 1919 (First World War, War Diary, WO95/1403/3)	WD1403_3	9781474504270	£18.00
3 DIVISION Divisional Troops 529 (East Riding) Field Company Royal Engineers, 231 Field Company Royal Engineers and Divisional Signal Company : 13 September 1914 - 31 October 1919 (First World War, War Diary, WO95/1404)	WD1404	9781474504287	£34.00

Title	Product Code	ISBN	Price
3 DIVISION Divisional Troops Machine Gun Corps 3 Battalion : 24 February 1918 - 30 September 1919 (First World War, War Diary, WO95/1405/1)	WD1405_1	9781474504294	£26.00
3 DIVISION Divisional Troops 233 Machine Gun Company : 1 July 1917 - 28 February 1918 (First World War, War Diary, WO95/1405/2)	WD1405_2	9781474504300	£15.00
3 DIVISION Divisional Troops Durham Light Infantry 1/9th Battalion Pioneers : 1 January 1917 - 31 December 1917 (First World War, War Diary, WO95/1405/3)	WD1405_3	9781474504317	£15.00
3 DIVISION Divisional Troops King's Royal Rifle Corps 20th Battalion Pioneers : 27 March 1916 - 31 December 1916 (First World War, War Diary, WO95/1405/4)	WD1405_4	9781474504324	£15.00
3 DIVISION Divisional Troops Royal Army Medical Corps 7 Field Ambulance : 19 August 1914 - 31 October 1919 (First World War, War Diary, WO95/1406)	WD1406	9781474504331	£67.00
3 DIVISION Divisional Troops Royal Army Medical Corps 8 Field Ambulance : 5 August 1914 - 28 May 1919 (First World War, War Diary, WO95/1407/2)	WD1407_2	9781474504348	£34.00
3 DIVISION Divisional Troops Royal Army Medical Corps 9 Field Ambulance : 5 August 1914 - 31 July 1915 (First World War, War Diary, WO95/1407/3)	WD1407_3	9781474504355	£23.00
3 DIVISION Divisional Troops Royal Army Medical Corps 142 Field Ambulance : 12 August 1915 - 31 October 1919 (First World War, War Diary, WO95/1408/1)	WD1408_1	9781474504362	£27.00
3 DIVISION Divisional Troops 5(A) Sanitary Section : 14 January 1916 - 31 March 1917 (First World War, War Diary, WO95/1408/2)	WD1408_2	9781474504379	£15.00
3 DIVISION Divisional Troops Royal Army Veterinary Corps 11 Mobile Veterinary Section : 5 August 1914 - 27 October 1919 (First World War, War Diary, WO95/1408/3)	WD1408_3	9781474504386	£17.00
3 DIVISION Divisional Troops Royal Army Service Corps 3 Divisional Train (15,21,22,29 Companies A.S.C.) : 1 August 1914 - 31 May 1915 (First World War, War Diary, WO95/1409A)	WD1409_A	9781474521871	£51.00
3 DIVISION Divisional Troops Royal Army Service Corps 3 Divisional Train (15,21,22,29 Companies A.S.C.) : 1 November 1914 - 29 December 1915 (First World War, War Diary, WO95/1409B)	WD1409_B	9781474521888	£56.00
3 DIVISION Divisional Troops Royal Army Service Corps 3 Divisional Train (15,21,22,29 Companies A.S.C.) : 30 December 1915 - 31 December 1916 (First World War, War Diary, WO95/1410/1)	WD1410_1	9781474504393	£41.00
3 DIVISION Divisional Troops Royal Army Service Corps 3 Divisional Train (15,21,22,29 Companies A.S.C.) : 1 January 1916 - 31 December 1916 (First World War, War Diary, WO95/1410/2)	WD1410_2	9781474504409	£28.00
3 DIVISION Divisional Troops Royal Army Service Corps 3 Divisional Train (15,21,22,29 Companies A.S.C.) : 31 December 1916 - 31 July 1917 (First World War, War Diary, WO95/1411)	WD1411	9781474504416	£39.00
3 DIVISION Divisional Troops Royal Army Service Corps 3 Divisional Train (15,21,22,29 Companies A.S.C.) : 1 January 1918 - 29 October 1919 (First World War, War Diary, WO95/1412)	WD1412	9781474504423	£61.00
3 DIVISION 7 Infantry Brigade Headquarters : 4 August 1914 - 31 October 1915 (First World War, War Diary, WO95/1413)	WD1413	9781474504430	£52.00

Title	Product Code	ISBN	Price
3 DIVISION 7 Infantry Brigade Prince of Wales's Volunteers (South Lancashire Regiment) 2nd and 1/4th Battalions : 4 August 1914 - 31 December 1915 (First World War, War Diary, WO95/1414)	WD1414	9781474504447	£28.00
3 DIVISION 7 Infantry Brigade Royal Irish Rifles 2nd Battalion : 4 August 1914 - 31 October 1915 (First World War, War Diary, WO95/1415/1)	WD1415_1	9781474504454	£15.00
3 DIVISION 7 Infantry Brigade Duke of Edinburgh's (Wiltshire Regiment) 1st Battalion : 4 August 1914 - 31 October 1915 (First World War, War Diary, WO95/1415/2)	WD1415_2	9781474504461	£15.00
3 DIVISION 7 Infantry Brigade Worcestershire Regiment 3rd Battalion : 4 August 1914 - 31 October 1915 (First World War, War Diary, WO95/1415/3)	WD1415_3	9781474504478	£15.00
3 DIVISION 7 Infantry Brigade Honourable Artillery Company 1 Battalion Honourable Artillery Company : 12 September 1914 - 16 June 1915 (First World War, War Diary, WO95/1415/4)	WD1415_4	9781474504485	£15.00
3 DIVISION 8 Infantry Brigade Headquarters : 4 August 1914 - 31 December 1916 (First World War, War Diary, WO95/1416)	WD1416	9781474504492	£58.00
3 DIVISION 8 Infantry Brigade Headquarters : 1 January 1917 - 31 August 1917 (First World War, War Diary, WO95/1417)	WD1417	9781474504508	£66.00
3 DIVISION 8 Infantry Brigade Headquarters : 1 September 1917 - 31 December 1917 (First World War, War Diary, WO95/1418)	WD1418	9781474504515	£60.00
3 DIVISION 8 Infantry Brigade Headquarters : 1 January 1918 - 18 August 1918 (First World War, War Diary, WO95/1419)	WD1419	9781474504522	£78.00
3 DIVISION 8 Infantry Brigade Headquarters : 1 September 1918 - 31 March 1919 (First World War, War Diary, WO95/1420)	WD1420	9781474504539	£64.00
3 DIVISION 8 Infantry Brigade Gordon Highlanders 1st Battalion : 4 August 1914 - 31 October 1915 (First World War, War Diary, WO95/1421/1)	WD1421_1	9781474504546	£15.00
3 DIVISION 8 Infantry Brigade Gordon Highlanders 4th Battalion : 11 March 1915 - 29 February 1916 (First World War, War Diary,	WD1421_2	9781474504553	£15.00
3 DIVISION 8 Infantry Brigade Royal Irish Regiment 2nd Battalion : 14 August 1914 - 31 January 1915 (First World War, War Diary, WO95/1421/3)	WD1421_3	9781474504560	£15.00
3 DIVISION 8 Infantry Brigade King's (Shropshire Light Infantry) 7th Battalion : 22 August 1914 - 17 October 1915 (First World War, War Diary, WO95/1421/4)	WD1421_4	9781474504577	£46.00
3 DIVISION 8 Infantry Brigade King's (Liverpool Regiment) 13th Battalion, Duke of Cambridge's Own (Middlesex Regiment) 4th Battalion and Royal Scots Fusiliers 1st Battalion : 4 August 1914 - 15 May 1919 (First World War, War Diary, WO95/1422)	WD1422	9781474504584	£39.00
3 DIVISION 8 Infantry Brigade Royal Scots (Lothian Regiment) 2nd Battalion : 4 August 1914 - 11 May 1919 (First World War, War Diary, WO95/1423)	WD1423	9781474521895	£64.00
3 DIVISION 8 Infantry Brigade Suffolk Regiment 2nd Battalion, East Yorkshire Regiment 8th Battalion, 8 Machine Gun Company and 8 Trench Mortar Battery : 4 August 1914 - 31 August 1916 (First World War, War Diary, WO95/1424)	WD1424	9781474504591	£31.00
3 DIVISION 9 Infantry Brigade Headquarters : 4 August 1914 - 31 December 1914 (First World War, War Diary, WO95/1425)	WD1425	9781474504607	£89.00

Title	Product Code	ISBN	Price
3 DIVISION 9 Infantry Brigade Headquarters : 1 January 1915 - 31 July 1916 (First World War, War Diary, WO95/1426)	WD1426	9781474504614	£40.00
3 DIVISION 9 Infantry Brigade Headquarters : 1 August 1916 - 30 June 1917 (First World War, War Diary, WO95/1427)	WD1427	9781474504621	£54.00
3 DIVISION 9 Infantry Brigade Headquarters : 1 July 1917 - 31 December 1918 (First World War, War Diary, WO95/1428)	WD1428	9781474504638	£58.00
3 DIVISION 9 Infantry Brigade King's (Liverpool Regiment) 10th and 13th Battalions and Lincolnshire Regiment 1st Battalion : 4 August 1914 - 31 October 1915 (First World War, War Diary, WO95/1429)	WD1429	9781474504645	£34.00
3 DIVISION 9 Infantry Brigade Northumberland Fusiliers 1st Battalion : 4 August 1914 - 31 May 1919 (First World War, War Diary, WO95/1430)	WD1430	9781474504652	£56.00
3 DIVISION 9 Infantry Brigade Royal Fusiliers (City of London Regiment) 4th Battalion : 4 August 1914 - 13 April 1919 (First World War, War Diary, WO95/1431)	WD1431	9781474504669	£39.00
3 DIVISION 9 Infantry Brigade Royal Scots Fusiliers 1st Battalion, Prince of Wales's Own (West Yorkshire Regiment) 12th Battalion, Brigade Machine Gun Company and Brigade Trench Mortar Battery : 29 July 1914 - 31 August 1916 (First World War, War Diary,	WD1432	9781474504676	£39.00
3 DIVISION 76 Infantry Brigade Headquarters : 26 September 1915 - 31 December 1917 (First World War, War Diary, WO95/1433)	WD1433	9781474504683	£50.00
3 DIVISION 76 Infantry Brigade Headquarters : 1 January 1918 - 31 March 1919 (First World War, War Diary, WO95/1434)	WD1434	9781474504690	£33.00
3 DIVISION 76 Infantry Brigade Gordon Highlanders 1st Battalion : 1 March 1915 - 10 April 1919 (First World War, War Diary, WO95/1435)	WD1435	9781474504706	£29.00
3 DIVISION 76 Infantry Brigade King's Own (Royal Lancaster Regiment) 8th Battalion and Royal Welsh Fusiliers 10th Battalion : 26 September 1915 - 31 January 1918 (First World War, War Diary, WO95/1436)	WD1436	9781474504713	£44.00
3 DIVISION 76 Infantry Brigade Suffolk Regiment 2nd Battalion, Brigade Machine Gun Company and Brigade Trench Mortar Battery : 1 November 1915 - 28 May 1919 (First World War, War Diary, WO95/1437)	WD1437	9781474504720	£41.00
3 DIVISION 1 Northern Brigade Headquarters, Northumberland Fusiliers 51st, 52nd and 53rd Battalions (Y.S.Bns), King's (Liverpool Regiment) 13th Battalion, Prince of Wales's Own (West Yorkshire Regiment) 1/5th and 1/6thBattalions, York and Lancaster Regime	WD1438	9781474504737	£32.00

Title	Product Code	ISBN	Price
3 INDIAN (LAHORE) DIVISION			
3 INDIAN (LAHORE) DIVISION Headquarters, Branches and Services General Staff : 8 August 1914 - 31 December 1914 (First World War, War Diary, WO95/3911)	WD3911	9781474534765	£50.00
3 INDIAN (LAHORE) DIVISION Headquarters, Branches and Services General Staff : 1 January 1915 - 28 February 1915 (First World War, War Diary, WO95/3912)	WD3912	9781474534772	£39.00
3 INDIAN (LAHORE) DIVISION Headquarters, Branches and Services General Staff : 1 March 1915 - 30 June 1915 (First World War, War Diary, WO95/3913)	WD3913	9781474534789	£58.00
3 INDIAN (LAHORE) DIVISION Headquarters, Branches and Services General Staff : 1 July 1915 - 30 December 1915 (First World War, War Diary, WO95/3914)	WD3914	9781474534796	£59.00
3 INDIAN (LAHORE) DIVISION Headquarters, Branches and Services Adjutant and Quarter-Master General : 8 August 1914 - 28 February 1915 (First World War, War Diary, WO95/3915)	WD3915	9781474534802	£46.00
3 INDIAN (LAHORE) DIVISION Headquarters, Branches and Services Commander Royal Artillery : 8 August 1914 - 26 December 1914 (First World War, War Diary, WO95/3916)	WD3916	9781474534819	£66.00
3 INDIAN (LAHORE) DIVISION Headquarters, Branches and Services Royal Army Medical Corps Assistant Director Medical Services, Commander Royal Engineers and Assistant Director Ordnance Services : 8 August 1914 - 31 January 1915 (First World War, War Diary,	WD3917	9781474534826	£81.00
3 INDIAN (LAHORE) DIVISION Divisional Troops 15 Lancers, 5, 11 and 18 Brigade Royal Field Artillery and Divisional Ammunition Column : 3 August 1914 - 31 January 1915 (First World War, War Diary, WO95/3918)	WD3918	9781474534833	£49.00
3 INDIAN (LAHORE) DIVISION Divisional Troops 20 and 21 Field Company Sappers and Miners, Divisional Signal Company and 34 Sikh Pioneers : 11 January 1914 - 31 December 1915 (First World War, War Diary, WO95/3919)	WD3919	9781474534840	£85.00
3 INDIAN (LAHORE) DIVISION Divisional Troops Royal Army Medical Corps 7 British Field Ambulance : 11 August 1914 - 31 December 1915 (First World War, War Diary, WO95/3920/1)	WD3920_1	9781474534857	£31.00
3 INDIAN (LAHORE) DIVISION Divisional Troops Royal Army Medical Corps 8 British Field Ambulance : 11 August 1914 - 30 November 1915 (First World War, War Diary, WO95/3920/2)	WD3920_2	9781474534864	£18.00
3 INDIAN (LAHORE) DIVISION Divisional Troops Royal Army Medical Corps 111 Indian Field Ambulance : 12 August 1914 - 31 December 1915 (First World War, War Diary, WO95/3920/3)	WD3920_3	9781474534871	£15.00
3 INDIAN (LAHORE) DIVISION Divisional Troops Royal Army Medical Corps 112 Indian Field Ambulance : 1 January 1914 - 29 December 1915 (First World War, War Diary, WO95/3920/4)	WD3920_4	9781474534888	£15.00
3 INDIAN (LAHORE) DIVISION Divisional Troops Royal Army Medical Corps 113 Indian Field Ambulance, Divisional Field Ambulance Workshop, Divisional Sanitary Section, Mobile Veterinary Section, Indian Mule Corps, Headquarters and Divisional Train : 14 Aug	WD3921	9781474534895	£62.00

Title	Product Code	ISBN	Price
3 INDIAN (LAHORE) DIVISION 7 (Ferozepore) Infantry Brigade Headquarters : 8 August 1914 - 31 December 1915 (First World War, War Diary, WO95/3922)	WD3922	9781474534901	£59.00
3 INDIAN (LAHORE) DIVISION 7 (Ferozepore) Infantry Brigade Connaught Rangers 1st Battalion, London Regiment 1/4 Battalion (City of London), 9 Battalion Bhopal Infantry and 57 Rifles : 8 August 1914 - 31 January 1916 (First World War, War Diary, WO95/3923)	WD3923	9781474534918	£47.00
3 INDIAN (LAHORE) DIVISION 7 (Ferozepore) Infantry Brigade 89 Punjabis, 125 Napier Rifles and 129 (D.C.O.) Baluchis : 12 July 1914 - 31 August 1915 (First World War, War Diary, WO95/3924)	WD3924	9781474534925	£66.00
3 INDIAN (LAHORE) DIVISION 7 (Ferozepore) Infantry Brigade 129 (D.C.O.) Baluchis : 1 April 1915 - 31 July 1915 (First World War, War Diary, WO95/3925A)	WD3925_A	9781474534932	£57.00
3 INDIAN (LAHORE) DIVISION 8 (Jullundur) Infantry Brigade Headquarters : 8 August 1914 - 4 January 1916 (First World War, War Diary, WO95/3926)	WD3926	9781474534956	£58.00
3 INDIAN (LAHORE) DIVISION 8 (Jullundur) Infantry Brigade Manchester Regiment 1st Battalion, Suffolk Regiment 4th Battalion, 40 Pathans, 47 Sikhs and 59 Scinde Rifles : 1 March 1914 - 31 December 1915 (First World War, War Diary, WO95/3927)	WD3927	9781474534963	£58.00
3 INDIAN (LAHORE) DIVISION 9 (Sirhind) Infantry Brigade Headquarters : 8 August 1914 - 20 November 1914 (First World War, War Diary, WO95/3928)	WD3928	9781474534970	£58.00
3 INDIAN (LAHORE) DIVISION 9 (Sirhind) Infantry Brigade Highland Light Infantry 1st Battalion, King's (Liverpool Regiment) 4th Battalion, 1/1 Battalion Gurkha Rifles, 1/4 Battalion Gurkha Rifles, 15 Sikhs and 27 Punjabis: 8 August 1914 - 30 December 1915	WD3929	9781474534987	£54.00

Title	Product Code	ISBN	Price
3 INDIAN (LAHORE) DIVISION 7			
3 INDIAN (LAHORE) DIVISION 7 (Ferozepore) Infantry Brigade 129 (D.C.O.) Baluchis : 1 August 1915 - 30 November 1915 (First World War, War Diary, WO95/3925B)	WD3925_B	9781474534949	£58.00

Title	Product Code	ISBN	Price
30 DIVISION			
30 DIVISION Headquarters, Branches and Services General Staff : 4 November 1915 - 31 July 1916 (First World War, War Diary, WO95/2310)	WD2310	9781474515009	£59.00
30 DIVISION Headquarters, Branches and Services General Staff : 1 August 1916 - 30 April 1917 (First World War, War Diary, WO95/2311)	WD2311	9781474515016	£56.00
30 DIVISION Headquarters, Branches and Services General Staff : 1 May 1917 - 1 September 1917 (First World War, War Diary, WO95/2312)	WD2312	9781474515023	£73.00
30 DIVISION Headquarters, Branches and Services General Staff : 27 March 1917 - 25 March 1918 (First World War, War Diary, WO95/2313)	WD2313	9781474515030	£66.00
30 DIVISION Headquarters, Branches and Services General Staff : 1 May 1918 - 1 September 1919 (First World War, War Diary, WO95/2314)	WD2314	9781474515047	£50.00
30 DIVISION Headquarters, Branches and Services Adjutant and Quarter-Master General : 31 October 1915 - 26 July 1919 (First World War, War Diary, WO95/2315)	WD2315	9781474524704	£73.00
30 DIVISION Headquarters, Branches and Services Commander Royal Artillery : 28 November 1915 - 31 December 1916 (First World War, War Diary, WO95/2316)	WD2316	9781474515054	£65.00
30 DIVISION Headquarters, Branches and Services Commander Royal Artillery : 1 January 1917 - 31 March 1919 (First World War, War Diary, WO95/2317)	WD2317	9781474515061	£39.00
30 DIVISION Headquarters, Branches and Services Royal Army Medical Corps Assistant Director Medical Services : 6 November 1915 - 30 April 1917 (First World War, War Diary, WO95/2318)	WD2318	9781474515078	£61.00
30 DIVISION Headquarters, Branches and Services Royal Army Medical Corps Assistant Director Medical Services : 1 May 1917 - 8 April 1919 (First World War, War Diary, WO95/2319)	WD2319	9781474515085	£73.00
30 DIVISION Headquarters, Branches and Services Commander Royal Engineers : 11 January 1915 - 24 March 1919 (First World War, War Diary, WO95/2320/1)	WD2320_1	9781474515092	£29.00
30 DIVISION Headquarters, Branches and Services Royal Army Ordnance Corps Deputy Assistant Director Ordnance Services : 7 November 1915 - 31 March 1919 (First World War, War Diary, WO95/2320/2)	WD2320_2	9781474515108	£16.00
30 DIVISION Headquarters, Branches and Services Royal Army Veterinary Corps Assistant Director Veterinary Services : 16 November 1915 - 31 March 1919 (First World War, War Diary, WO95/2320/3)	WD2320_3	9781474515115	£15.00
30 DIVISION Divisional Troops D Squadron 1/1 Lancashire Hussars : 9 November 1915 - 30 April 1916 (First World War, War Diary, WO95/2321/1)	WD2321_1	9781474515122	£15.00
30 DIVISION Divisional Troops Divisional Cyclist Company : 7 November 1915 - 22 May 1916 (First World War, War Diary, WO95/2321/2)	WD2321_2	9781474515139	£15.00
30 DIVISION Divisional Troops 148 Brigade Royal Field Artillery : 29 November 1915 - 28 February 1919 (First World War, War Diary, WO95/2321/3)	WD2321_3	9781474515146	£18.00
30 DIVISION Divisional Troops 149 Brigade Royal Field Artillery : 27 November 1915 - 30 April 1919 (First World War, War Diary, WO95/2321/4)	WD2321_4	9781474515153	£15.00

Title	Product Code	ISBN	Price
30 DIVISION Divisional Troops 150 Brigade Royal Field Artillery : 15 October 1915 - 31 December 1916 (First World War, War Diary, WO95/2321/5)	WD2321_5	9781474515160	£15.00
30 DIVISION Divisional Troops 151 Brigade Royal Field Artillery : 29 November 1915 - 31 August 1916 (First World War, War Diary, WO95/2321/6)	WD2321_6	9781474515177	£15.00
30 DIVISION Divisional Troops Divisional Trench Mortar Batteries : 1 July 1916 - 1 October 1918 (First World War, War Diary, WO95/2321/7)	WD2321_7	9781474515184	£15.00
30 DIVISION Divisional Troops Divisional Ammunition Column : 20 January 1914 - 11 December 1918 (First World War, War Diary, WO95/2321/8)	WD2321_8	9781474515191	£15.00
30 DIVISION Divisional Troops 200 Field Company Royal Engineers : 3 November 1915 - 17 May 1919 (First World War, War Diary, WO95/2322/1)	WD2322_1	9781474515207	£27.00
30 DIVISION Divisional Troops 201 Field Company Royal Engineers : 3 November 1915 - 16 May 1919 (First World War, War Diary, WO95/2322/2)	WD2322_2	9781474515214	£55.00
30 DIVISION Divisional Troops 202 Field Company Royal Engineers : 9 November 1915 - 20 March 1919 (First World War, War Diary, WO95/2323/1)	WD2323_1	9781474515221	£21.00
30 DIVISION Divisional Troops Divisional Signal Company : 6 November 1915 - 31 May 1919 (First World War, War Diary, WO95/2323/2)	WD2323_2	9781474515238	£15.00
30 DIVISION Divisional Troops Prince of Wales's Volunteers (South Lancashire Regiment) 11th Battalion Pioneers : 6 November 1915 - 27 May 1918 (First World War, War Diary, WO95/2323/3)	WD2323_3	9781474515245	£15.00
30 DIVISION Divisional Troops South Wales Borderers 6th Battalion : 1 June 1918 - 30 June 1919 (First World War, War Diary, WO95/2323/4)	WD2323_4	9781474515252	£15.00
30 DIVISION Divisional Troops Machine Gun Corps 30 Battalion : 1 March 1918 - 18 September 1919 (First World War, War Diary, WO95/2323/5)	WD2323_5	9781474515269	£16.00
30 DIVISION Divisional Troops 226 Machine Gun Company : 11 July 1917 - 28 February 1918 (First World War, War Diary, WO95/2323/6)	WD2323_6	9781474515276	£15.00
30 DIVISION Divisional Troops Royal Army Medical Corps 96 Field Ambulance : 10 November 1915 - 13 August 1919 (First World War, War Diary, WO95/2324/1)	WD2324_1	9781474515283	£63.00
30 DIVISION Divisional Troops Royal Army Medical Corps 97 Field Ambulance : 2 November 1915 - 2 July 1919 (First World War, War Diary, WO95/2324/2)	WD2324_2	9781474515290	£32.00
30 DIVISION 30 Division Royal Army Medical Corps 98 Field Ambulance, Divisional Field Ambulance Workshop Unit and 70 Sanitary Section: 6 November 1915 - 24 March 1917 (First World War, War Diary, WO95/2325/1-3)	WD2325	9781474515306	£70.00
30 DIVISION Divisional Troops Royal Army Veterinary Corps 40 Mobile Veterinary Section, Divisional Train (186,187,188,189, Companies A.S.C.) : 4 September 1915 - 27 May 1919 (First World War, War Diary, WO95/2326/1-2)	WD2326	9781474515313	£32.00
30 DIVISION 21 Infantry Brigade Headquarters : 1 January 1916 - 31 July 1917 (First World War, War Diary, WO95/2327)	WD2327	9781474515320	£47.00
30 DIVISION 21 Infantry Brigade Headquarters : 2 August 1917 - 31 August 1919 (First World War, War Diary, WO95/2328)	WD2328	9781474515337	£42.00

Title	Product Code	ISBN	Price
30 DIVISION 21 Infantry Brigade Duke of Edinburgh's (Wiltshire Regiment) 2nd Battalion, Alexandra, Princess of Wales's Own (Yorkshire Regiment) 2nd Battalion and 6th Battalion and Manchester Regiment 19th Battalion: 7 November 1915 - 28 February 1918 (Fir	WD2329	9781474515344	£52.00
30 DIVISION 21 Infantry Brigade King's (Liverpool Regiment) 18th Battalion, Cheshire Regiment 6 Battalion Cheshire Regiment, Royal Irish Regiment 7th Battalion, London Regiment 2/23 Battalion, Brigade Machine Gun Company and Brigade Trench Mortar Batter	WD2330	9781474515351	£52.00
30 DIVISION 89 Infantry Brigade Headquarters : 8 November 1915 - 31 March 1917 (First World War, War Diary, WO95/2331)	WD2331	9781474515368	£54.00
30 DIVISION 89 Infantry Brigade Headquarters : 1 April 1917 - 25 October 1919 (First World War, War Diary, WO95/2332)	WD2332	9781474515375	£57.00
30 DIVISION 89 Infantry Brigade Bedfordshire Regiment 2nd Battalion : 1 January 1916 - 30 April 1918 (First World War, War Diary, WO95/2333)	WD2333	9781474515382	£51.00
30 DIVISION 89 Infantry Brigade King's (Liverpool Regiment) 17th Battalion : 6 November 1915 - 31 July 1918 (First World War, War Diary, WO95/2334/1)	WD2334_1	9781474515399	£36.00
30 DIVISION 89 Infantry Brigade King's (Liverpool Regiment) 19th Battalion : 6 November 1915 - 30 June 1918 (First World War, War Diary, WO95/2334/2)	WD2334_2	9781474515405	£16.00
30 DIVISION 89 Infantry Brigade King's (Liverpool Regiment) 20th Battalion : 30 October 1915 - 6 February 1918 (First World War, War Diary, WO95/2335)	WD2335	9781474515412	£52.00
30 DIVISION 89 Infantry Brigade Royal Inniskilling Fusiliers 7/8th Battalion, Prince of Wales's Volunteers (South Lancashire Regiment) 2nd Battalion, London Regiment 2/17 Battalion, Brigade Machine Gun Company, Brigade Trench Mortar Battery : 17 Septembe	WD2336	9781474515429	£32.00
30 DIVISION 90 Infantry Brigade Headquarters : 3 November 1915 - 30 August 1917 (First World War, War Diary, WO95/2337)	WD2337	9781474515436	£55.00
30 DIVISION 90 Infantry Brigade Headquarters : 1 October 1917 - 31 August 1919 (First World War, War Diary, WO95/2338)	WD2338	9781474515443	£49.00
30 DIVISION 90 Infantry Brigade Manchester Regiment 16th Battalion : 7 November 1915 - 17 June 1918 (First World War, War Diary, WO95/2339/1)	WD2339_1	9781474515450	£16.00
30 DIVISION 90 Infantry Brigade Manchester Regiment 17th Battalion : 7 November 1915 - 30 July 1918 (First World War, War Diary, WO95/2339/2)	WD2339_2	9781474515467	£43.00
30 DIVISION 90 Infantry Brigade Manchester Regiment 18th Battalion : 8 November 1915 - 20 February 1918 (First World War, War Diary, WO95/2339/3)	WD2339_3	9781474515474	£29.00
30 DIVISION 90 Infantry Brigade Royal Scots Fusiliers 2nd Battalion : 1 January 1916 - 31 March 1918 (First World War, War Diary, WO95/2340/1)	WD2340_1	9781474515481	£15.00
30 DIVISION 90 Infantry Brigade London Regiment 2/14 Battalion (London Scottish) : 1 June 1918 - 31 August 1919 (First World War, War Diary, WO95/2340/2)	WD2340_2	9781474515498	£15.00
30 DIVISION 90 Infantry Brigade London Regiment 2/15 Battalion (Civil Service Rifles) : 1 June 1918 - 19 October 1919 (First World War, War Diary, WO95/2340/3)	WD2340_3	9781474515504	£15.00

Title	Product Code	ISBN	Price
30 DIVISION 90 Infantry Brigade London Regiment 2/16 Battalion (Queen's Westminster Rifles) : 1 June 1918 - 31 October 1919 (First World War, War Diary, WO95/2340/4)	WD2340_4	9781474515511	£15.00
30 DIVISION 90 Infantry Brigade, Brigade Machine Gun Company : 11 March 1916 - 28 February 1918 (First World War, War Diary, WO95/2340/5)	WD2340_5	9781474515528	£15.00

Title	Product Code	ISBN	Price
31 DIVISION			
31 DIVISION Headquarters, Branches and Services General Staff : 1 March 1916 - 31 December 1916 (First World War, War Diary, WO95/2341)	WD2341	9781474524711	£61.00
31 DIVISION Headquarters, Branches and Services General Staff : 1 January 1917 - 31 December 1917 (First World War, War Diary, WO95/2342)	WD2342	9781474524728	£59.00
31 DIVISION Headquarters, Branches and Services General Staff : 1 January 1918 - 28 February 1919 (First World War, War Diary, WO95/2343)	WD2343	9781474515535	£54.00
31 DIVISION Headquarters, Branches and Services Adjutant and Quarter-Master General : 29 March 1916 - 20 May 1919 (First World War, War Diary, WO95/2344)	WD2344	9781474524735	£77.00
31 DIVISION Headquarters, Branches and Services Commander Royal Artillery : 1 March 1916 - 31 December 1916 (First World War, War Diary, WO95/2345)	WD2345	9781474515542	£58.00
31 DIVISION Headquarters, Branches and Services Commander Royal Artillery : 1 January 1917 - 30 September 1917 (First World War, War Diary, WO95/2346)	WD2346	9781474515559	£59.00
31 DIVISION Headquarters, Branches and Services Commander Royal Artillery : 1 October 1917 - 26 May 1919 (First World War, War Diary, WO95/2347)	WD2347	9781474524742	£69.00
31 DIVISION Headquarters, Branches and Services Royal Army Medical Corps Assistant Director Medical Services : 1 March 1916 - 31 March 1919 (First World War, War Diary, WO95/2348/1)	WD2348_1	9781474515566	£37.00
31 DIVISION Headquarters, Branches and Services Commander Royal Engineers : 1 March 1916 - 23 March 1919 (First World War, War Diary, WO95/2348/2)	WD2348_2	9781474515573	£23.00
31 DIVISION Headquarters, Branches and Services Royal Army Ordnance Corps Deputy Assistant Director Ordnance Services : 6 March 1916 - 31 December 1918 (First World War, War Diary, WO95/2348/3)	WD2348_3	9781474515580	£15.00
31 DIVISION Headquarters, Branches and Services Royal Army Veterinary Corps Assistant Director Veterinary Services : 1 March 1916 - 27 April 1919 (First World War, War Diary, WO95/2348/4)	WD2348_4	9781474515597	£15.00
31 DIVISION Divisional Troops B Squadron 1/1 Lancashire Hussars, Divisional Cyclist Company, 165, 169 and 171 Brigade Royal Field Artillery : 28 February 1916 - 26 March 1916 (First World War, War Diary, WO95/2349/1-5)	WD2349_1-5	9781474524759	£31.00
31 DIVISION Divisional Troops 170 Brigade Royal Field Artillery : 28 February 1916 - 17 May 1919 (First World War, War Diary, WO95/2350)	WD2350	9781474524766	£88.00
31 DIVISION Divisional Troops Divisional Ammunition Column : 3 April 1916 - 30 April 1919 (First World War, War Diary, WO95/2351/1)	WD2351_1	9781474515603	£15.00
31 DIVISION Divisional Troops Divisional Trench Mortar Batteries : 7 April 1916 - 28 February 1919 (First World War, War Diary, WO95/2351/2)	WD2351_2	9781474515610	£25.00
31 DIVISION Divisional Troops 210 Field Company Royal Engineers : 8 March 1916 - 30 April 1919 (First World War, War Diary, WO95/2352/1)	WD2352_1	9781474515627	£15.00
31 DIVISION Divisional Troops 211 Field Company Royal Engineers : 28 February 1916 - 30 April 1919 (First World War, War Diary, WO95/2352/2)	WD2352_2	9781474515634	£15.00
31 DIVISION Divisional Troops 223 Field Company Royal Engineers : 5 January 1916 - 14 April 1919 (First World War, War Diary, WO95/2352/3)	WD2352_3	9781474515641	£15.00

Title	Product Code	ISBN	Price
31 DIVISION Divisional Troops Divisional Signal Company : 1 April 1916 - 26 February 1919 (First World War, War Diary, WO95/2352/4)	WD2352_4	9781474515658	£17.00
31 DIVISION Divisional Troops King's Own (Yorkshire Light Infantry) 12th Battalion, Machine Gun Corps 31 Battalion, 243 Machine Gun Company : 1 March 1916 - 17 February 1918 (First World War, War Diary, WO95/2353)	WD2353	9781474515665	£57.00
31 DIVISION Divisional Troops Royal Army Medical Corps 93 Field Ambulance : 1 March 1916 - 24 May 1919 (First World War, War Diary, WO95/2354/1)	WD2354_1	9781474515672	£35.00
31 DIVISION Divisional Troops Royal Army Medical Corps 94 Field Ambulance : 1 March 1916 - 30 April 1919 (First World War, War Diary, WO95/2354/2)	WD2354_2	9781474515689	£31.00
31 DIVISION Divisional Troops Royal Army Medical Corps 95 Field Ambulance : 2 March 1916 - 31 May 1919 (First World War, War Diary, WO95/2354/3)	WD2354_3	9781474515696	£15.00
31 DIVISION Divisional Troops 71 Sanitary Section : 1 March 1916 - 31 March 1917 (First World War, War Diary, WO95/2355/1)	WD2355_1	9781474515702	£15.00
31 DIVISION Divisional Troops Royal Army Veterinary Corps 41 Mobile Veterinary Section : 15 March 1916 - 30 April 1919 (First World War, War Diary, WO95/2355/2)	WD2355_2	9781474515719	£15.00
31 DIVISION Divisional Troops Royal Army Service Corps Divisional Train (221, 222, 223, 279 Companies A.S.C.) : 8 March 1916 - 2 June 1919 (First World War, War Diary, WO95/2355/3)	WD2355_3	9781474515726	£44.00
31 DIVISION 92 Infantry Brigade Headquarters : 29 February 1916 - 31 March 1919 (First World War, War Diary, WO95/2356)	WD2356	9781474524773	£59.00
31 DIVISION 92 Infantry Brigade East Yorkshire Regiment 10th, 11th, 12th and 13th Battalion : 6 May 1915 - 31 January 1918 (First World War, War Diary, WO95/2357)	WD2357	9781474524780	£66.00
31 DIVISION 92 Infantry Brigade East Lancashire Regiment 11th Battalion, Brigade Machine Gun Company and Brigade Trench Mortar Battery : 1 January 1916 - 31 August 1916 (First World War, War Diary, WO95/2358)	WD2358	9781474515733	£28.00
31 DIVISION 93 Infantry Brigade Headquarters : 29 February 1916 - 31 May 1917 (First World War, War Diary, WO95/2359)	WD2359	9781474515740	£53.00
31 DIVISION 93 Infantry Brigade Headquarters : 23 January 1917 - 28 February 1919 (First World War, War Diary, WO95/2360)	WD2360	9781474515757	£53.00
31 DIVISION 93 Infantry Brigade Durham Light Infantry 18th Battalion, York and Lancaster Regiment 13th (Service) (1st Barnsley) Battalion, Prince of Wales's Own (West Yorkshire Regiment) 15th Battalion and 15/17th Battalion : 2 March 1916 - 28 February 1	WD2361	9781474515764	£72.00
31 DIVISION 93 Infantry Brigade Prince of Wales's Own (West Yorkshire Regiment) 16th and 18th Battalion, Brigade Machine Gun Company and Brigade Trench Mortar Battery : 29 February 1916 - 28 February 1918 (First World War, War Diary, WO95/2362)	WD2362	9781474515771	£84.00
31 DIVISION 94 Infantry Brigade Headquarters : 2 March 1916 - 30 June 1917 (First World War, War Diary, WO95/2363)	WD2363	9781474515788	£47.00
31 DIVISION 94 Infantry Brigade Headquarters : 1 July 1917 - 31 July 1917 (First World War, War Diary, WO95/2364)	WD2364	9781474515795	£61.00

Title	Product Code	ISBN	Price
31 DIVISION 94 Infantry Brigade York and Lancaster Regiment 12th (Service) (Sheffield) Battalion : 1 March 1916 - 28 February 1918 (First World War, War Diary, WO95/2365/1)	WD2365_1	9781474515801	£27.00
31 DIVISION 94 Infantry Brigade York and Lancaster Regiment 13th (Service) (1st Barnsley) Battalion : 1 March 1916 - 28 February 1918 (First World War, War Diary, WO95/2365/2)	WD2365_2	9781474515818	£15.00
31 DIVISION 94 Infantry Brigade York and Lancaster Regiment 14th (Service) (2nd Barnsley) Battalion : 1 March 1916 - 16 February 1918 (First World War, War Diary, WO95/2365/3)	WD2365_3	9781474515825	£41.00
31 DIVISION 94 Infantry Brigade East Lancashire Regiment 11th Battalion : 2 March 1916 - 31 January 1918 (First World War, War Diary, WO95/2366/1)	WD2366_1	9781474515832	£15.00
31 DIVISION 94 Infantry Brigade Norfolk Regiment 12th Battalion : 1 May 1918 - 24 May 1919 (First World War, War Diary, WO95/2366/2)	WD2366_2	9781474515849	£15.00
31 DIVISION 94 Infantry Brigade Royal Scots Fusiliers 12th Battalion : 1 May 1918 - 21 May 1919 (First World War, War Diary, WO95/2366/3)	WD2366_3	9781474515856	£15.00
31 DIVISION 94 Infantry Brigade Royal Welsh Fusiliers 24th Battalion : 2 May 1918 - 30 April 1919 (First World War, War Diary, WO95/2366/4)	WD2366_4	9781474515863	£15.00
31 DIVISION 94 Infantry Brigade, Brigade Machine Gun Company : 15 May 1916 - 28 February 1918 (First World War, War Diary, WO95/2366/5)	WD2366_5	9781474515870	£25.00
31 DIVISION 94 Infantry Brigade, Brigade Trench Mortar Battery : 28 April 1916 - 1 September 1916 (First World War, War Diary, WO95/2366/6)	WD2366_6	9781474515887	£15.00

Title	Product Code	ISBN	Price
32 DIVISION			
32 DIVISION Headquarters, Branches and Services General Staff : 12 November 1915 - 30 June 1916 (First World War, War Diary, WO95/2367)	WD2367	9781474515894	£53.00
32 DIVISION Headquarters, Branches and Services General Staff : 1 July 1916 - 28 February 1917 (First World War, War Diary, WO95/2368)	WD2368	9781474515900	£69.00
32 DIVISION Headquarters, Branches and Services General Staff : 1 March 1917 - 31 July 1917 (First World War, War Diary, WO95/2369)	WD2369	9781474515917	£54.00
32 DIVISION Headquarters, Branches and Services General Staff : 1 August 1917 - 31 December 1917 (First World War, War Diary, WO95/2370)	WD2370	9781474515924	£55.00
32 DIVISION Headquarters, Branches and Services General Staff : 1 January 1918 - 31 January 1918 (First World War, War Diary, WO95/2371)	WD2371	9781474524797	£60.00
32 DIVISION Headquarters, Branches and Services General Staff : 1 June 1918 - 31 October 1919 (First World War, War Diary, WO95/2372)	WD2372	9781474524803	£66.00
32 DIVISION Headquarters, Branches and Services Adjutant and Quarter-Master General : 11 November 1915 - 31 December 1917 (First World War, War Diary, WO95/2373)	WD2373	9781474515931	£54.00
32 DIVISION Headquarters, Branches and Services Adjutant and Quarter-Master General. : 1 January 1918 - 16 December 1919 (First World War, War Diary, WO95/2374)	WD2374	9781474515948	£50.00
32 DIVISION Headquarters, Branches and Services Commander Royal Artillery : 1 January 1916 - 30 June 1917 (First World War, War Diary, WO95/2375)	WD2375	9781474515955	£38.00
32 DIVISION Headquarters, Branches and Services Commander Royal Artillery : 1 July 1916 - 28 October 1919 (First World War, War Diary, WO95/2376)	WD2376	9781474515962	£55.00
32 DIVISION Headquarters, Branches and Services Royal Army Medical Corps Assistant Director Medical Services : 23 November 1915 - 31 December 1916 (First World War, War Diary, WO95/2377)	WD2377	9781474515979	£63.00
32 DIVISION Headquarters, Branches and Services Royal Army Medical Corps Assistant Director Medical Services : 1 January 1917 - 15 December 1919 (First World War, War Diary, WO95/2378)	WD2378	9781474524810	£78.00
32 DIVISION Headquarters, Branches and Services Commander Royal Engineers : 22 November 1915 - 31 October 1919 (First World War, War Diary, WO95/2379/1)	WD2379_1	9781474515986	£47.00
32 DIVISION Headquarters, Branches and Services Royal Army Ordnance Corps Deputy Assistant Director Ordnance Services : 1 April 1916 - 31 December 1918 (First World War, War Diary, WO95/2379/2)	WD2379_2	9781474515993	£15.00
32 DIVISION Headquarters, Branches and Services Royal Army Ordnance Corps Deputy Assistant Director Ordnance Services : 1 January 1919 - 30 November 1919 (First World War, War Diary, WO95/2379/3)	WD2379_3	9781474516006	£15.00
32 DIVISION Headquarters, Branches and Services Royal Army Veterinary Corps Assistant Director Veterinary Services : 21 November 1915 - 7 December 1919 (First World War, War Diary, WO95/2379/4)	WD2379_4	9781474516013	£15.00
32 DIVISION Divisional Troops B Squadron South Irish Horse : 5 August 1914 - 31 May 1916 (First World War, War Diary, WO95/2380/1)	WD2380_1	9781474516020	£15.00
32 DIVISION Divisional Troops Divisional Cyclist Company : 10 August 1915 - 31 May 1916 (First World War, War Diary, WO95/2380/2)	WD2380_2	9781474516037	£15.00

Title	Product Code	ISBN	Price
32 DIVISION Divisional Troops 155 Brigade Royal Field Artillery : 29 December 1915 - 27 February 1917 (First World War, War Diary, WO95/2380/3)	WD2380_3	9781474516044	£15.00
32 DIVISION Divisional Troops 161 Brigade Royal Field Artillery : 30 December 1915 - 24 September 1918 (First World War, War Diary, WO95/2380/4)	WD2380_4	9781474516051	£33.00
32 DIVISION Divisional Troops 164 Brigade Royal Field Artillery : 29 December 1915 - 1 September 1916 (First World War, War Diary, WO95/2380/5)	WD2380_5	9781474516068	£15.00
32 DIVISION Divisional Troops 168 Brigade Royal Field Artillery : 3 January 1915 - 31 October 1919 (First World War, War Diary, WO95/2381/1)	WD2381_1	9781474516075	£30.00
32 DIVISION Divisional Troops Divisional Ammunition Column : 28 December 1915 - 28 October 1919 (First World War, War Diary, WO95/2381/2)	WD2381_2	9781474516082	£15.00
32 DIVISION Divisional Troops Divisional Trench Mortar Batteries : 1 September 1916 - 24 April 1919 (First World War, War Diary, WO95/2382)	WD2382	9781474516099	£41.00
32 DIVISION Divisional Troops 206 Field Company Royal Engineers : 22 November 1915 - 31 October 1919 (First World War, War Diary, WO95/2383/1)	WD2383_1	9781474516105	£51.00
32 DIVISION Divisional Troops 218 Field Company Royal Engineers : 23 November 1915 - 31 October 1919 (First World War, War Diary, WO95/2383/2)	WD2383_2	9781474516112	£38.00
32 DIVISION Divisional Troops 219 Field Company Royal Engineers : 20 November 1915 - 27 October 1919 (First World War, War Diary, WO95/2384/1)	WD2384_1	9781474516129	£22.00
32 DIVISION Divisional Troops Divisional Signal Company : 23 November 1915 - 31 October 1919 (First World War, War Diary, WO95/2384/2)	WD2384_2	9781474516136	£37.00
32 DIVISION Divisional Troops Northumberland Fusiliers 23 Battalion (First World War, War Diary, WO95/2385/1)	WD2385_1	9781474516143	£15.00
32 DIVISION Divisional Troops Northumberland Fusiliers 17th Battalion (N.E.R. Pioneers) : 20 November 1915 - 31 May 1918 (First World War, War Diary, WO95/2385/2)	WD2385_2	9781474516150	£15.00
32 DIVISION Divisional Troops Highland Light Infantry 16th (Service) Battalion (2nd Glasgow) Pioneers : 1 March 1918 - 28 February 1919 (First World War, War Diary, WO95/2385/3)	WD2385_3	9781474516167	£15.00
32 DIVISION Divisional Troops Loyal North Lancashire Regiment 12th Battalion Pioneers : 1 March 1919 - 31 October 1919 (First World War, War Diary, WO95/2385/4)	WD2385_4	9781474516174	£15.00
32 DIVISION Divisional Troops Machine Gun Corps 32 Battalion : 21 February 1918 - 31 October 1919 (First World War, War Diary, WO95/2385/5)	WD2385_5	9781474516181	£28.00
32 DIVISION Divisional Troops 219 Machine Gun Company : 16 March 1917 - 28 February 1918 (First World War, War Diary, WO95/2385/6)	WD2385_6	9781474516198	£15.00
32 DIVISION Divisional Troops Royal Army Medical Corps 90 and 91 Field Ambulance : 20 November 1915 - 30 October 1919 (First World War, War Diary, WO95/2386)	WD2386	9781474524827	£60.00

Title	Product Code	ISBN	Price
32 DIVISION Divisional Troops Royal 92 Field Ambulance, Divisional Field Ambulance Workshop Unit, 72 Sanitary Section and 42 Mobile Veterinary Section : 1 November 1915 - 31 October 1919 (First World War, War Diary, WO95/2387)	WD2387	9781474516204	£47.00
32 DIVISION Divisional Troops Royal Army Service Corps Divisional Train (202, 203, 204, 205 Companies A.S.C) : 4 January 1915 - 30 November 1919 (First World War, War Diary, WO95/2388)	WD2388	9781474524834	£87.00
32 DIVISION 14 Infantry Brigade Headquarters : 1 January 1916 - 31 May 1916 (First World War, War Diary, WO95/2389)	WD2389	9781474516211	£58.00
32 DIVISION 14 Infantry Brigade Headquarters : 1 April 1916 - 31 July 1917 (First World War, War Diary, WO95/2390)	WD2390	9781474516228	£52.00
32 DIVISION 14 Infantry Brigade Headquarters : 1 August 1917 - 25 October 1919 (First World War, War Diary, WO95/2391)	WD2391	9781474516235	£62.00
32 DIVISION 14 Infantry Brigade Dorsetshire Regiment 1st Battalion : 1 January 1916 - 31 March 1919 (First World War, War Diary, WO95/2392/1)	WD2392_1	9781474516242	£33.00
32 DIVISION 14 Infantry Brigade Manchester Regiment 2nd Battalion : 1 January 1916 - 31 January 1918 (First World War, War Diary, WO95/2392/2)	WD2392_2	9781474516259	£23.00
32 DIVISION 14 Infantry Brigade Royal Scots (Lothian Regiment) 5/6th Battalion : 10 June 1916 - 28 February 1919 (First World War, War Diary, WO95/2392/3)	WD2392_3	9781474516266	£36.00
32 DIVISION 14 Infantry Brigade Highland Light Infantry 15th (Service) Battalion (1st Glasgow) : 22 November 1915 - 30 September 1917 (First World War, War Diary, WO95/2393A)	WD2393_A	9781474524841	£65.00
32 DIVISION 14 Infantry Brigade Highland Light Infantry 15th (Service) Battalion (1st Glasgow) : 1 October 1917 - 31 March 1919 (First World War, War Diary, WO95/2393B)	WD2393_B	9781474524858	£30.00
32 DIVISION 14 Infantry Brigade Lancashire Fusiliers 19th Battalion : 21 November 1915 - 30 June 1916 (First World War, War Diary, WO95/2394/1)	WD2394_1	9781474524865	£28.00
32 DIVISION 14 Infantry Brigade King's (Liverpool Regiment) 51st Graduated Battalion : 14 March 1919 - 31 October 1919 (First World War, War Diary, WO95/2394/2)	WD2394_2	9781474524872	£15.00
32 DIVISION 14 Infantry Brigade King's (Liverpool Regiment) 52nd Graduated Battalion : 15 March 1919 - 31 October 1919 (First World War, War Diary, WO95/2394/3)	WD2394_3	9781474524889	£15.00
32 DIVISION 14 Infantry Brigade, Brigade Machine Gun Company : 1 February 1916 - 28 February 1918 (First World War, War Diary, WO95/2394/4)	WD2394_4	9781474524896	£18.00
32 DIVISION 14 Infantry Brigade, Brigade Trench Mortar Battery : 8 August 1915 - 31 August 1916 (First World War, War Diary, WO95/2394/5)	WD2394_5	9781474524902	£15.00
32 DIVISION 96 Infantry Brigade Headquarters : 21 November 1915 - 30 April 1917 (First World War, War Diary, WO95/2395)	WD2395	9781474516273	£46.00
32 DIVISION 96 Infantry Brigade Headquarters : 11 November 1915 - 7 November 1919 (First World War, War Diary, WO95/2396)	WD2396	9781474516280	£59.00
32 DIVISION 96 Infantry Brigade Royal Inniskilling Fusiliers 2nd Battalion and Manchester Regiment 2nd Battalion : 1 January 1916 - 31 January 1918 (First World War, War Diary, WO95/2397/1)	WD2397_1	9781474524919	£15.00

Title	Product Code	ISBN	Price
32 DIVISION 96 Infantry Brigade Lancashire Fusiliers 15th and 16th Battalion : 13 September 1914 - 31 October 1919 (First World War, War Diary, WO95/2397/2)	WD2397_2	9781474524926	£35.00
32 DIVISION 96 Infantry Brigade Northumberland Fusiliers 16th Battalion : 22 November 1915 - 7 February 1918 (First World War, War Diary, WO95/2398/1)	WD2398_1	9781474524933	£15.00
32 DIVISION 96 Infantry Brigade, Brigade Machine Gun Company : 24 January 1916 - 21 February 1918 (First World War, War Diary, WO95/2398/2)	WD2398_2	9781474524940	£15.00
32 DIVISION 96 Infantry Brigade, Brigade Trench Mortar Battery : 1 August 1916 - 31 August 1916 (First World War, War Diary, WO95/2398/3)	WD2398_3	9781474524957	£15.00
32 DIVISION 97 Infantry Brigade Headquarters : 23 November 1915 - 30 April 1917 (First World War, War Diary, WO95/2399)	WD2399	9781474516297	£44.00
32 DIVISION 97 Infantry Brigade Headquarters : 1 April 1917 - 30 April 1918 (First World War, War Diary, WO95/2400)	WD2400	9781474516303	£46.00
32 DIVISION 97 Infantry Brigade Headquarters : 1 May 1918 - 31 October 1919 (First World War, War Diary, WO95/2401)	WD2401	9781474516310	£67.00
32 DIVISION 97 Infantry Brigade King's Own (Yorkshire Light Infantry) 2nd Battalion, Border Regiment 5th Battalion and Princess Louise's (Argyll & Sutherland Highlanders) 10th Battalion : 1 January 1916 - 27 February 1919 (First World War, War Diary, WO	WD2402	9781474516327	£49.00
32 DIVISION 97 Infantry Brigade Border Regiment 11th Battalion : 22 November 1915 - 16 July 1918 (First World War, War Diary, WO95/2403/1)	WD2403_1	9781474516334	£17.00
32 DIVISION 97 Infantry Brigade Highland Light Infantry 16th (Service) Battalion (2nd Glasgow) : 23 November 1915 - 30 April 1918 (First World War, War Diary, WO95/2403/2)	WD2403_2	9781474516341	£19.00
32 DIVISION 97 Infantry Brigade Highland Light Infantry 17th (Service) Battalion (3rd Glasgow) : 21 November 1915 - 31 January 1918 (First World War, War Diary, WO95/2403/3)	WD2403_3	9781474516358	£20.00
32 DIVISION 97 Infantry Brigade Manchester Regiment 51st (G) Battalion : 15 March 1919 - 31 October 1919 (First World War, War Diary, WO95/2404/1)	WD2404_1	9781474516365	£15.00
32 DIVISION 97 Infantry Brigade Manchester Regiment 52nd Battalion : 16 March 1919 - 31 October 1919 (First World War, War Diary, WO95/2404/2)	WD2404_2	9781474516372	£15.00
32 DIVISION 97 Infantry Brigade Manchester Regiment 53rd Battalion : 1 March 1919 - 4 November 1919 (First World War, War Diary, WO95/2404/3)	WD2404_3	9781474516389	£15.00
32 DIVISION 97 Infantry Brigade, Brigade Machine Gun Company : 4 March 1916 - 21 February 1918 (First World War, War Diary, WO95/2404/4)	WD2404_4	9781474516396	£17.00
32 DIVISION 97 Infantry Brigade, Brigade Trench Mortar Battery : 1 July 1916 - 31 August 1916 (First World War, War Diary, WO95/2404/5)	WD2404_5	9781474516402	£15.00

Title	Product Code	ISBN	Price
33 DIVISION			
33 DIVISION Headquarters, Branches and Services General Staff : 1 July 1915 - 31 December 1916 (First World War, War Diary, WO95/2405)	WD2405	9781474516419	£63.00
33 DIVISION Headquarters, Branches and Services General Staff : 1 January 1917 - 31 March 1918 (First World War, War Diary, WO95/2406)	WD2406	9781474516426	£56.00
33 DIVISION Headquarters, Branches and Services General Staff : 1 April 1918 - 31 May 1919 (First World War, War Diary, WO95/2407)	WD2407	9781474516433	£76.00
33 DIVISION Headquarters, Branches and Services Adjutant and Quarter-Master General : 4 November 1915 - 30 April 1917 (First World War, War Diary, WO95/2408)	WD2408	9781474524964	£77.00
33 DIVISION Headquarters, Branches and Services Adjutant and Quarter-Master General : 1 May 1917 - 30 June 1919 (First World War, War Diary, WO95/2409)	WD2409	9781474524971	£69.00
33 DIVISION Headquarters, Branches and Services Commander Royal Artillery and Assistant Director Medical Services : 8 November 1915 - 28 March 1919 (First World War, War Diary, WO95/2410)	WD2410	9781474516440	£76.00
33 DIVISION Headquarters, Branches and Services Commander Royal Engineers : 12 November 1915 - 12 May 1919 (First World War, War Diary, WO95/2411)	WD2411	9781474524988	£88.00
33 DIVISION Headquarters, Branches and Services Royal Army Ordnance Corps Deputy Assistant Director Ordnance Services : 7 November 1915 - 30 April 1919 (First World War, War Diary, WO95/2412/1)	WD2412_1	9781474516457	£28.00
33 DIVISION Headquarters, Branches and Services Royal Army Veterinary Corps Assistant Director Veterinary Services : 12 November 1915 - 31 March 1919 (First World War, War Diary, WO95/2412/2)	WD2412_2	9781474516464	£15.00
33 DIVISION Divisional Troops F Squadron North Irish Horse : 16 November 1915 - 31 May 1916 (First World War, War Diary, WO95/2413/1)	WD2413_1	9781474516471	£15.00
33 DIVISION Divisional Troops Divisional Cyclist Company : 27 July 1915 - 27 April 1916 (First World War, War Diary, WO95/2413/2)	WD2413_2	9781474516488	£15.00
33 DIVISION Divisional Troops 156 Brigade Royal Field Artillery : 3 February 1915 - 13 June 1919 (First World War, War Diary, WO95/2413/3)	WD2413_3	9781474516495	£15.00
33 DIVISION Divisional Troops 162 Brigade Royal Field Artillery : 10 December 1915 - 11 June 1919 (First World War, War Diary, WO95/2413/4)	WD2413_4	9781474516501	£15.00
33 DIVISION Divisional Troops 166 Brigade Royal Field Artillery : 1 October 1915 - 31 January 1917 (First World War, War Diary, WO95/2413/5)	WD2413_5	9781474516518	£15.00
33 DIVISION Divisional Troops 167 Brigade Royal Field Artillery : 20 April 1915 - 11 September 1916 (First World War, War Diary, WO95/2413/6)	WD2413_6	9781474516525	£15.00
33 DIVISION Divisional Troops Divisional Trench Mortar Batteries : 29 May 1916 - 31 January 1919 (First World War, War Diary, WO95/2413/7)	WD2413_7	9781474516532	£15.00
33 DIVISION Divisional Troops Divisional Ammunition Column : 11 December 1915 - 14 June 1919 (First World War, War Diary, WO95/2413/8)	WD2413_8	9781474516549	£15.00
33 DIVISION Divisional Troops 11 Field Company Royal Engineers : 9 January 1915 - 30 May 1919 (First World War, War Diary, WO95/2414/1)	WD2414_1	9781474516556	£29.00

Title	Product Code	ISBN	Price
33 DIVISION Divisional Troops 212 Field Company Royal Engineers. : 16 November 1915 - 31 May 1919 (First World War, War Diary, WO95/2414/2)	WD2414_2	9781474516563	£77.00
33 DIVISION Divisional Troops 222 Field Company Royal Engineers : 16 November 1915 - 31 May 1919 (First World War, War Diary, WO95/2415)	WD2415	9781474516570	£54.00
33 DIVISION Divisional Troops Divisional Signal Company : 20 May 1915 - 30 June 1918 (First World War, War Diary, WO95/2416)	WD2416	9781474524995	£69.00
33 DIVISION Divisional Troops Divisional Signal Company, Machine Gun Corps 33 Battalion, 9 Machine Gun Squadron, 248 Machine Gun Company, Duke of Cambridge's Own (Middlesex Regiment) 18th Battalion Pioneers : 10 November 1915 - 31 October 1919 (First Wor	WD2417	9781474516587	£67.00
33 DIVISION Divisional Troops Royal Army Medical Corps 19 Field Ambulance : 1 August 1915 - 19 May 1919 (First World War, War Diary, WO95/2418/1)	WD2418_1	9781474525008	£82.00
33 DIVISION Divisional Troops Royal Army Medical Corps 99 and 101 Field Ambulance and 33 Field Ambulance Workshop Unit : 17 November 1915 - 31 March 1916 (First World War, War Diary, WO95/2418/2-5)	WD2418_2	9781474516594	£15.00
33 DIVISION Divisional Troops 73 Sanitary Section, 43 Mobile Veterinary Section and Divisional Train (170, 171, 172, 173 Companies A.S.C.) : 1 November 1915 - 7 May 1919 (First World War, War Diary, WO95/2419)	WD2419	9781474525015	£83.00
33 DIVISION 19 Infantry Brigade Headquarters : 1 December 1915 - 28 February 1917 (First World War, War Diary, WO95/2420)	WD2420	9781474516600	£51.00
33 DIVISION 19 Infantry Brigade Headquarters : 1 March 1917 - 31 August 1919 (First World War, War Diary, WO95/2421)	WD2421	9781474516617	£59.00
33 DIVISION 19 Infantry Brigade Queen's (Royal West Surrey Regiment) 1st Battalion : 1 February 1918 - 15 May 1919 (First World War, War Diary, WO95/2422/1)	WD2422_1	9781474525022	£15.00
33 DIVISION 19 Infantry Brigade Cameronians (Scottish Rifles) 1st Battalion : 1 December 1915 - 24 May 1919 (First World War, War Diary, WO95/2422/2)	WD2422_2	9781474525039	£24.00
33 DIVISION 19 Infantry Brigade Cameronians (Scottish Rifles) 5th Battalion : 1 December 1915 - 30 September 1918 (First World War, War Diary, WO95/2422/3)	WD2422_3	9781474525046	£17.00
33 DIVISION 19 Infantry Brigade Cameronians (Scottish Rifles) 6th Battalion : 1 June 1916 - 10 August 1916 (First World War, War Diary, WO95/2422/4)	WD2422_4	9781474525053	£15.00
33 DIVISION 19 Infantry Brigade Cameronians (Scottish Rifles) 5/6th Battalion : 1 October 1918 - 31 October 1919 (First World War, War Diary, WO95/2422/5)	WD2422_5	9781474525060	£15.00
33 DIVISION 19 Infantry Brigade Royal Welsh Fusiliers 2nd Battalion, Royal Fusiliers (City of London Regiment) 18th and 20th Battalion, Brigade Trench Mortar Battery and Brigade Machine Gun Company : 1 November 1915 - 31 January 1918 (First World War, War	WD2423	9781474516624	£29.00
33 DIVISION 98 Infantry Brigade Headquarters : 14 November 1915 - 31 December 1916 (First World War, War Diary, WO95/2424)	WD2424	9781474516631	£39.00
33 DIVISION 98 Infantry Brigade Headquarters : 1 January 1917 - 30 July 1919 (First World War, War Diary, WO95/2425)	WD2425	9781474516648	£43.00

Title	Product Code	ISBN	Price
33 DIVISION 98 Infantry Brigade Duke of Cambridge's Own (Middlesex Regiment) 1st Battalion and Princess Louise's (Argyll & Sutherland Highlanders) 2nd Battalion : 11 January 1915 - 14 May 1919 (First World War, War Diary, WO95/2426)	WD2426	9781474525077	£66.00
33 DIVISION 98 Infantry Brigade King's (Liverpool Regiment) 4th Battalion : 1 November 1915 - 23 November 1919 (First World War, War Diary, WO95/2427/1)	WD2427_1	9781474516655	£29.00
33 DIVISION 98 Infantry Brigade Suffolk Regiment 4th Battalion : 1 November 1915 - 30 January 1918 (First World War, War Diary, WO95/2427/2)	WD2427_2	9781474516662	£15.00
33 DIVISION 98 Infantry Brigade Royal Fusiliers (City of London Regiment) 19th Battalion : 14 November 1915 - 29 February 1916 (First World War, War Diary, WO95/2427/3)	WD2427_3	9781474516679	£15.00
33 DIVISION 98 Infantry Brigade Royal Fusiliers (City of London Regiment) 21st Battalion : 26 April 1916 - 31 January 1917 (First World War, War Diary, WO95/2427/4)	WD2427_4	9781474516686	£15.00
33 DIVISION 98 Infantry Brigade, Brigade Machine Gun Company and Brigade Trench Mortar Battery : 16 October 1915 - 5 July 1916 (First World War, War Diary, WO95/2427/5-6)	WD2427_5	9781474516693	£15.00
33 DIVISION 100 Infantry Brigade Headquarters : 5 November 1915 - 30 June 1917 (First World War, War Diary, WO95/2428)	WD2428	9781474516709	£61.00
33 DIVISION 100 Infantry Brigade Headquarters : 1 March 1917 - 30 September 1919 (First World War, War Diary, WO95/2429)	WD2429	9781474516716	£65.00
33 DIVISION 100 Infantry Brigade Queen's (Royal West Surrey Regiment) 1st Battalion : 1 January 1916 - 31 January 1918 (First World War, War Diary, WO95/2430/1)	WD2430_1	9781474516723	£25.00
33 DIVISION 100 Infantry Brigade Worcestershire Regiment 2nd Battalion : 1 January 1916 - 31 May 1919 (First World War, War Diary, WO95/2430/2)	WD2430_2	9781474516730	£22.00
33 DIVISION 100 Infantry Brigade King's Royal Rifle Corps 16th Battalion : 16 November 1915 - 30 November 1919 (First World War, War Diary, WO95/2430/3)	WD2430_3	9781474516747	£25.00
33 DIVISION 100 Infantry Brigade Highland Light Infantry 9th (Glasgow Highland) Battalion (Territorial), Duke of Cambridge's Own (Middlesex Regiment) 16th Battalion, Brigade Machine Gun Company, Brigade Trench Mortar Battery : 16 November 1915 - 31 July 1	WD2431	9781474516754	£58.00

Title	Product Code	ISBN	Price
34 DIVISION			
34 DIVISION Headquarters, Branches and Services General Staff : 8 January 1916 - 31 August 1916 (First World War, War Diary, WO95/2432)	WD2432	9781474525084	£80.00
34 DIVISION Headquarters, Branches and Services General Staff : 1 September 1916 - 30 April 1917 (First World War, War Diary, WO95/2433)	WD2433	9781474516761	£57.00
34 DIVISION Headquarters, Branches and Services General Staff : 1 May 1917 - 31 August 1917 (First World War, War Diary, WO95/2434)	WD2434	9781474525091	£58.00
34 DIVISION Headquarters, Branches and Services General Staff : 1 September 1917 - 31 December 1917 (First World War, War Diary, WO95/2435)	WD2435	9781474516778	£65.00
34 DIVISION Headquarters, Branches and Services General Staff : 1 January 1918 - 29 July 1918 (First World War, War Diary, WO95/2436)	WD2436	9781474525107	£62.00
34 DIVISION Headquarters, Branches and Services General Staff : 1 September 1918 - 30 June 1919 (First World War, War Diary, WO95/2437)	WD2437	9781474516785	£45.00
34 DIVISION Headquarters, Branches and Services Adjutant and Quarter-Master General : 25 June 1915 - 30 April 1917 (First World War, War Diary, WO95/2438)	WD2438	9781474516792	£53.00
34 DIVISION Headquarters, Branches and Services Adjutant and Quarter-Master General : 1 May 1917 - 31 July 1919 (First World War, War Diary, WO95/2439)	WD2439	9781474516808	£50.00
34 DIVISION Headquarters, Branches and Services Commander Royal Artillery : 7 January 1916 - 31 March 1917 (First World War, War Diary, WO95/2440)	WD2440	9781474516815	£47.00
34 DIVISION Headquarters, Branches and Services Commander Royal Artillery : 1 April 1917 - 28 December 1917 (First World War, War Diary, WO95/2441)	WD2441	9781474516822	£36.00
34 DIVISION Headquarters, Branches and Services Commander Royal Artillery : 6 January 1918 - 18 July 1919 (First World War, War Diary, WO95/2442)	WD2442	9781474516839	£35.00
34 DIVISION Headquarters, Branches and Services Royal Army Medical Corps Assistant Director Medical Services : 8 January 1916 - 31 July 1919 (First World War, War Diary, WO95/2443)	WD2443	9781474525114	£89.00
34 DIVISION Headquarters, Branches and Services Commander Royal Engineers, Assistant Director Ordnance Services and Assistant Director Veterinary Services : 5 February 1915 - 30 July 1919 (First World War, War Diary, WO95/2444)	WD2444	9781474516846	£78.00
34 DIVISION Divisional Troops `E' Squadron North Irish Horse : 11 January 1916 - 29 April 1916 (First World War, War Diary, WO95/2445/1)	WD2445_1	9781474516853	£15.00
34 DIVISION Divisional Troops Divisional Cyclist Company : 10 January 1916 - 31 May 1916 (First World War, War Diary, WO95/2445/2)	WD2445_2	9781474516860	£15.00
34 DIVISION Divisional Troops 152 Brigade Royal Field Artillery : 1 February 1916 - 31 July 1919 (First World War, War Diary, WO95/2445/3)	WD2445_3	9781474516877	£35.00
34 DIVISION Divisional Troops 160 Brigade Royal Field Artillery : 1 February 1915 - 31 August 1917 (First World War, War Diary, WO95/2446)	WD2446	9781474516884	£57.00
34 DIVISION Divisional Troops 160 Brigade Royal Field Artillery : 1 September 1917 - 9 July 1919 (First World War, War Diary, WO95/2447)	WD2447	9781474516891	£47.00

Title	Product Code	ISBN	Price
34 DIVISION Divisional Troops 175 Brigade Royal Field Artillery : 30 August 1915 - 31 December 1916 (First World War, War Diary, WO95/2448/1)	WD2448_1	9781474516907	£15.00
34 DIVISION Divisional Troops 176 Brigade Royal Field Artillery : 28 May 1915 - 28 August 1916 (First World War, War Diary, WO95/2448/2)	WD2448_2	9781474516914	£15.00
34 DIVISION Divisional Troops Divisional Trench Mortar Batteries and Divisional Ammunition Column : 11 January 1916 - 31 July 1919 (First World War, War Diary, WO95/2448/3)	WD2448_3	9781474516921	£33.00
34 DIVISION Divisional Troops 207 Field Company Royal Engineers : 4 January 1916 - 27 July 1919 (First World War, War Diary, WO95/2449/1)	WD2449_1	9781474516938	£64.00
34 DIVISION Divisional Troops 208 Field Company Royal Engineers : 9 January 1916 - 31 July 1919 (First World War, War Diary, WO95/2449/2)	WD2449_2	9781474516945	£27.00
34 DIVISION Divisional Troops 209 Field Company Royal Engineers and Divisional Signal Company : 5 February 1915 - 31 July 1919 (First World War, War Diary, WO95/2450)	WD2450	9781474516952	£43.00
34 DIVISION Divisional Troops Northumberland Fusiliers 18th Battalion (Tyneside Pioneers), Prince Albert's (Somerset Light Infantry) 2/4th Battalion Pioneers, Machine Gun Corps 34 Battalion and 240 Machine Gun Company : 1 February 1916 - 26 February 1918	WD2451	9781474516969	£45.00
34 DIVISION Divisional Troops Royal Army Medical Corps 102 Field Ambulance : 4 January 1916 - 31 July 1919 (First World War, War Diary, WO95/2452)	WD2452	9781474516976	£66.00
34 DIVISION Divisional Troops Royal Army Medical Corps 103 and 104 Field Ambulance : 2 January 1916 - 31 May 1919 (First World War, War Diary, WO95/2453)	WD2453	9781474525121	£83.00
34 DIVISION Divisional Troops Royal Army Medical Corps Divisional Field Ambulance Workshop Unit : 8 January 1916 - 31 March 1916 (First World War, War Diary, WO95/2454/1)	WD2454_1	9781474525138	£15.00
34 DIVISION Divisional Troops 74 Sanitary Section : 9 January 1916 - 31 March 1917 (First World War, War Diary, WO95/2454/2)	WD2454_2	9781474525145	£15.00
34 DIVISION Divisional Troops Royal Army Veterinary Corps 44 Mobile Veterinary Section : 1 October 1915 - 31 July 1919 (First World War, War Diary, WO95/2454/3)	WD2454_3	9781474525152	£19.00
34 DIVISION Divisional Troops Royal Army Service Corps Divisional Train (229,230,231,232 Companies) (A.S.C.) : 12 January 1915 - 31 July 1919 (First World War, War Diary, WO95/2454/4)	WD2454_4	9781474525169	£15.00
34 DIVISION 101 Infantry Brigade Headquarters : 13 December 1915 - 30 June 1917 (First World War, War Diary, WO95/2455)	WD2455	9781474516983	£53.00
34 DIVISION 101 Infantry Brigade Headquarters : 1 July 1917 - 31 July 1919 (First World War, War Diary, WO95/2456)	WD2456	9781474516990	£58.00
34 DIVISION 101 Infantry Brigade Lincolnshire Regiment 10th Battalion, Loyal North Lancashire Regiment 2nd Battalion, Queen's Own (Royal West Kent Regiment) 10th Battalion and 2/4th Battalion and Royal Scots (Lothian Regiment) 15th Battalion : 9 September	WD2457	9781474525176	£58.00
34 DIVISION 101 Infantry Brigade Royal Scots (Lothian Regiment) 16th Battalion, Royal Sussex Regiment 4th Battalion, Suffolk Regiment 11th Battalion, Brigade Machine Gun Company and Brigade Trench Mortar Battery : 13 December 1915 - 31 July 1916 (First	WD2458	9781474517003	£76.00

Title	Product Code	ISBN	Price
34 DIVISION 102 Infantry Brigade Headquarters : 4 January 1916 - 31 March 1917 (First World War, War Diary, WO95/2459)	WD2459	9781474517010	£45.00
34 DIVISION 102 Infantry Brigade Headquarters : 1 April 1917 - 21 October 1917 (First World War, War Diary, WO95/2460)	WD2460	9781474517027	£69.00
34 DIVISION 102 Infantry Brigade Headquarters : 1 January 1918 - 28 February 1918 (First World War, War Diary, WO95/2461/1)	WD2461_1	9781474517034	£15.00
34 DIVISION 102 Infantry Brigade Headquarters : 1 March 1918 - 28 June 1918 (First World War, War Diary, WO95/2461/2)	WD2461_2	9781474517041	£15.00
34 DIVISION 102 Infantry Brigade Headquarters : 1 July 1918 - 31 August 1918 (First World War, War Diary, WO95/2461/3)	WD2461_3	9781474517058	£15.00
34 DIVISION 102 Infantry Brigade Headquarters : 1 September 1918 - 31 July 1919 (First World War, War Diary, WO95/2461/4)	WD2461_4	9781474517065	£17.00
34 DIVISION 102 Infantry Brigade Cheshire Regiment 1/4th Battalion. : 20 January 1918 - 22 March 1919 (First World War, War Diary, WO95/2462/1)	WD2462_1	9781474517072	£15.00
34 DIVISION 102 Infantry Brigade Cheshire Regiment 1/7th Battalion. : 1 June 1918 - 29 July 1919 (First World War, War Diary, WO95/2462/2)	WD2462_2	9781474517089	£15.00
34 DIVISION 102 Infantry Brigade Herefordshire Regiment 1/1st Battalion : 1 June 1918 - 30 April 1919 (First World War, War Diary, WO95/2462/3)	WD2462_3	9781474517096	£15.00
34 DIVISION 102 Infantry Brigade Northumberland Fusiliers 20th and 21st Battalion (Tyneside Scottish) : 10 January 1916 - 31 January 1918 (First World War, War Diary, WO95/2462/4)	WD2462_4	9781474525183	£66.00
34 DIVISION 102 Infantry Brigade Northumberland Fusiliers 22nd Battalion (Tyneside Scottish) : 10 January 1916 - 31 May 1918 (First World War, War Diary, WO95/2463/1)	WD2463_1	9781474525190	£15.00
34 DIVISION 102 Infantry Brigade Northumberland Fusiliers 23rd Battalion (Tyneside Scottish) : 19 December 1915 - 20 March 1919 (First World War, War Diary, WO95/2463/2)	WD2463_2	9781474525206	£35.00
34 DIVISION 102 Infantry Brigade Northumberland Fusiliers 25th Battalion (Tyneside Irish) : 1 February 1918 - 30 April 1919 (First World War, War Diary, WO95/2463/3)	WD2463_3	9781474525213	£15.00
34 DIVISION 102 Infantry Brigade Bedfordshire Regiment 51st, 52nd and 53rd Battalion : 23 March 1919 - 12 July 1919 (First World War, War Diary, WO95/2463/4-6)	WD2463_4-6	9781474525220	£15.00
34 DIVISION 102 Infantry Brigade, Brigade Machine Gun Company : 25 April 1916 - 31 January 1918 (First World War, War Diary, WO95/2463/7)	WD2463_7	9781474525237	£15.00
34 DIVISION 103 Infantry Brigade Headquarters : 9 January 1916 - 31 August 1917 (First World War, War Diary, WO95/2464)	WD2464	9781474517102	£59.00
34 DIVISION 103 Infantry Brigade Headquarters : 1 September 1917 - 5 August 1919 (First World War, War Diary, WO95/2465)	WD2465	9781474517119	£59.00
34 DIVISION 103 Infantry Brigade Princess Louise's (Argyll & Sutherland Highlanders) 1/5th Battalion and King's Own Scottish Borderers 5th Battalion : 1 April 1918 - 31 March 1919 (First World War, War Diary, WO95/2466/1)	WD2466_1	9781474525244	£19.00
34 DIVISION 103 Infantry Brigade Northumberland Fusiliers 9th and 24th Battalion : 4 January 1916 - 31 July 1917 (First World War, War Diary, WO95/2466/2)	WD2466_2	9781474525251	£34.00

Title	Product Code	ISBN	Price
34 DIVISION 103 Infantry Brigade Northumberland Fusiliers 25th, 26th, 27th and 24/27th Battalion (Tyneside Irish), Cameronians (Scottish Rifles) 8th Battalion, Royal Sussex Regiment 51st, 52nd and 53rd T.R. Battalion, Brigade Machine Gun Company and Briga	WD2467	9781474517126	£72.00

Title	Product Code	ISBN	Price
35 DIVISION			
35 DIVISION Headquarters, Branches and Services General Staff : 29 January 1916 - 31 May 1917 (First World War, War Diary, WO95/2468)	WD2468	9781474525268	£69.00
35 DIVISION Headquarters, Branches and Services General Staff : 1 June 1917 - 30 June 1918 (First World War, War Diary, WO95/2469)	WD2469	9781474517133	£68.00
35 DIVISION Headquarters, Branches and Services General Staff : 1 July 1918 - 31 March 1919 (First World War, War Diary, WO95/2470/1)	WD2470_1	9781474517140	£25.00
35 DIVISION Headquarters, Branches and Services Register of Messages : 14 October 1918 - 1 November 1918 (First World War, War Diary, WO95/2470/2)	WD2470_2	9781474517157	£37.00
35 DIVISION Headquarters, Branches and Services Adjutant and Quarter-Master General : 21 June 1915 - 18 March 1919 (First World War, War Diary, WO95/2470/3)	WD2470_3	9781474517164	£15.00
35 DIVISION Headquarters, Branches and Services Commander Royal Artillery : 1 February 1916 - 31 March 1919 (First World War, War Diary, WO95/2471)	WD2471	9781474525275	£64.00
35 DIVISION Headquarters, Branches and Services Royal Army Medical Corps Assistant Director Medical Services : 1 February 1916 - 30 September 1916 (First World War, War Diary, WO95/2472)	WD2472	9781474517171	£69.00
35 DIVISION Headquarters, Branches and Services Commander Royal Engineers : 28 January 1916 - 31 March 1919 (First World War, War Diary, WO95/2473/1)	WD2473_1	9781474517188	£41.00
35 DIVISION Headquarters, Branches and Services Royal Army Ordnance Corps Deputy Assistant Director Ordnance Services : 2 March 1916 - 31 March 1919 (First World War, War Diary, WO95/2473/2)	WD2473_2	9781474517195	£15.00
35 DIVISION Headquarters, Branches and Services Royal Army Veterinary Corps Assistant Director Veterinary Services : 1 February 1916 - 17 April 1919 (First World War, War Diary, WO95/2473/3)	WD2473_3	9781474517201	£21.00
35 DIVISION Divisional Troops C Squadron 1/1 Lancashire Hussars Yeomanry, Divisional Cyclist Company, 157, 158 and 159 Brigade Royal Field Artillery : 26 January 1916 - 31 March 1919 (First World War, War Diary, WO95/2474)	WD2474	9781474517218	£51.00
35 DIVISION Divisional Troops 163 Brigade Royal Field Artillery : 30 January 1916 - 8 September 1916 (First World War, War Diary, WO95/2475/1)	WD2475_1	9781474517225	£15.00
35 DIVISION Divisional Troops Divisional Trench Mortar Batteries : 1 July 1916 - 31 January 1919 (First World War, War Diary, WO95/2475/2)	WD2475_2	9781474517232	£21.00
35 DIVISION Divisional Troops Divisional Ammunition Column : 28 January 1916 - 31 March 1918 (First World War, War Diary, WO95/2475/3)	WD2475_3	9781474517249	£20.00
35 DIVISION Divisional Troops 203, 204 and 205 Field Company Royal Engineers, Divisional Signal Company, Machine Gun Corps 35 Battalion and 241 Machine Gun Company : 2 February 1915 - 31 January 1918 (First World War, War Diary, WO95/2476)	WD2476	9781474525282	£68.00
35 DIVISION Divisional Troops Northumberland Fusiliers 19th Battalion (Tyneside Pioneers) : 29 January 1916 - 27 April 1919 (First World War, War Diary, WO95/2477)	WD2477	9781474517256	£77.00
35 DIVISION Divisional Troops Royal Army Medical Corps 105 Field Ambulance : 28 January 1916 - 24 April 1919 (First World War, War Diary, WO95/2478/1)	WD2478_1	9781474517263	£19.00

Title	Product Code	ISBN	Price
35 DIVISION Divisional Troops Royal Army Medical Corps 106 Field Ambulance : 29 January 1916 - 30 April 1919 (First World War, War Diary, WO95/2478/2)	WD2478_2	9781474517270	£37.00
35 DIVISION Divisional Troops Royal Army Medical Corps 107 Field Ambulance, Divisional Field Ambulance Workshop Unit, 75 Sanitary Section and 45 Mobile Veterinary Section : 28 January 1916 - 25 February 1919 (First World War, War Diary, WO95/2479)	WD2479	9781474517287	£45.00
35 DIVISION Divisional Troops Royal Army Service Corps Divisional Train (233, 234, 235, 236, Companies A.S.C.) : 25 October 1915 - 30 June 1917 (First World War, War Diary, WO95/2480)	WD2480	9781474525299	£84.00
35 DIVISION Divisional Troops Royal Army Service Corps Divisional Train (233, 234, 235, 236 Companies A.S.C.) : 1 July 1917 - 31 May 1919 (First World War, War Diary, WO95/2481)	WD2481	9781474517294	£83.00
35 DIVISION 104 Infantry Brigade Headquarters : 22 January 1916 - 31 December 1917 (First World War, War Diary, WO95/2482)	WD2482	9781474517300	£54.00
35 DIVISION 104 Infantry Brigade Headquarters : 1 January 1918 - 30 March 1919 (First World War, War Diary, WO95/2483)	WD2483	9781474517317	£50.00
35 DIVISION 104 Infantry Brigade Lancashire Fusiliers 17th Battalion : 28 January 1916 - 31 March 1919 (First World War, War Diary, WO95/2484/1)	WD2484_1	9781474525305	£21.00
35 DIVISION 104 Infantry Brigade Lancashire Fusiliers 18th and 20th Battalion, Durham Light Infantry 19th Battalion, Manchester Regiment 23rd Battalion and Brigade Machine Gun Company : 23 January 1916 - 31 January 1918 (First World War, War Diary, WO95/2	WD2484_2	9781474525312	£66.00
35 DIVISION 104 Infantry Brigade Headquarters : 29 January 1916 - 31 December 1916 (First World War, War Diary, WO95/2485/1-3)	WD2485_1-3	9781474517324	£45.00
35 DIVISION 105 Infantry Brigade Headquarters : 13 September 1916 - 30 April 1919 (First World War, War Diary, WO95/2486)	WD2486	9781474517331	£36.00
35 DIVISION 105 Infantry Brigade Cheshire Regiment 15th Battalion : 29 January 1916 - 19 April 1919 (First World War, War Diary, WO95/2487/1)	WD2487_1	9781474517348	£40.00
35 DIVISION 105 Infantry Brigade Cheshire Regiment 16th Battalion : 30 January 1916 - 8 February 1918 (First World War, War Diary, WO95/2487/2)	WD2487_2	9781474517355	£15.00
35 DIVISION 105 Infantry Brigade Gloucestershire Regiment 14th (Service) Battalion (West of England) : 31 January 1916 - 14 February 1918 (First World War, War Diary, WO95/2488/1)	WD2488_1	9781474517362	£15.00
35 DIVISION 105 Infantry Brigade Sherwood Foresters (Nottinghamshire and Derbyshire Regiment) 16th Battalion : 28 January 1916 - 22 April 1919 (First World War, War Diary, WO95/2488/2)	WD2488_2	9781474517379	£17.00
35 DIVISION 105 Infantry Brigade Prince of Wales's (North Staffordshire Regiment) 4th Battalion : 6 October 1917 - 24 April 1919 (First World War, War Diary, WO95/2488/3)	WD2488_3	9781474517386	£15.00
35 DIVISION 105 Infantry Brigade, Brigade Machine Gun Company : 11 May 1916 - 31 January 1918 (First World War, War Diary, WO95/2488/4)	WD2488_4	9781474517393	£15.00
35 DIVISION 106 Infantry Brigade Headquarters : 31 January 1916 - 28 February 1919 (First World War, War Diary, WO95/2489)	WD2489	9781474517409	£42.00
35 DIVISION 106 Infantry Brigade Highland Light Infantry 12th (Service) Battn : 1 February 1918 - 29 April 1919 (First World War, War Diary, WO95/2490/1)	WD2490_1	9781474517416	£15.00

Title	Product Code	ISBN	Price
35 DIVISION 106 Infantry Brigade Highland Light Infantry 18th Battalion (4th Glasgow) : 31 January 1916 - 28 February 1919 (First World War, War Diary, WO95/2490/2)	WD2490_2	9781474517423	£31.00
35 DIVISION 106 Infantry Brigade Royal Scots (Lothian Regiment) 17th Battalion : 31 January 1916 - 22 April 1919 (First World War, War Diary, WO95/2490/3)	WD2490_3	9781474517430	£15.00
35 DIVISION 106 Infantry Brigade Prince of Wales's Own (West Yorkshire Regiment) 17th Battalion : 22 August 1915 - 8 December 1917 (First World War, War Diary, WO95/2490/4)	WD2490_4	9781474517447	£15.00
35 DIVISION 106 Infantry Brigade Durham Light Infantry 19th Battalion : 31 January 1916 - 31 January 1918 (First World War, War Diary, WO95/2490/5)	WD2490_5	9781474517454	£15.00
35 DIVISION 106 Infantry Brigade, Brigade Machine Gun Company : 24 April 1916 - 30 January 1918 (First World War, War Diary, WO95/2490/6)	WD2490_6	9781474525329	£20.00
35 DIVISION 106 Infantry Brigade, Brigade Trench Mortar Battery: 1 July 1916 - 31 July 1916 (First World War, War Diary, WO95/2490/7)	WD2490_7	9781474525336	£15.00

Title	Product Code	ISBN	Price
36 DIVISION			
36 DIVISION Headquarters, Branches and Services General Staff : 1 November 1915 - 31 July 1917 (First World War, War Diary, WO95/2491)	WD2491	9781474517461	£69.00
36 DIVISION Headquarters, Branches and Services General Staff : 1 August 1917 - 26 December 1918 (First World War, War Diary, WO95/2492)	WD2492	9781474517478	£41.00
36 DIVISION Headquarters, Branches and Services Adjutant and Quarter-Master General : 26 September 1915 - 29 June 1919 (First World War, War Diary, WO95/2493)	WD2493	9781474517485	£43.00
36 DIVISION Headquarters, Branches and Services Commander Royal Artillery : 27 November 1915 - 28 February 1919 (First World War, War Diary, WO95/2494/1)	WD2494_1	9781474517492	£25.00
36 DIVISION Headquarters, Branches and Services Royal Army Medical Corps Assistant Director Medical Services : 23 August 1915 - 24 March 1919 (First World War, War Diary, WO95/2494/2)	WD2494_2	9781474517508	£64.00
36 DIVISION Headquarters, Branches and Services Commander Royal Engineers : 6 October 1915 - 14 February 1919 (First World War, War Diary, WO95/2495/1)	WD2495_1	9781474517515	£31.00
36 DIVISION Headquarters, Branches and Services Royal Army Ordnance Corps Deputy Assistant Director Ordnance Services : 30 September 1915 - 30 May 1919 (First World War, War Diary, WO95/2495/2)	WD2495_2	9781474517522	£19.00
36 DIVISION Headquarters, Branches and Services Royal Army Veterinary Corps Assistant Director Veterinary Services : 1 October 1915 - 24 March 1919 (First World War, War Diary, WO95/2495/3)	WD2495_3	9781474517539	£18.00
36 DIVISION Divisional Troops Service Squadron 6 Inniskilling Dragoons : 5 October 1915 - 30 May 1916 (First World War, War Diary, WO95/2496/1)	WD2496_1	9781474517546	£15.00
36 DIVISION Divisional Troops Divisional Cyclist Company : 4 October 1915 - 28 June 1916 (First World War, War Diary, WO95/2496/2)	WD2496_2	9781474517553	£15.00
36 DIVISION Divisional Troops 153 Brigade Royal Field Artillery : 21 January 1916 - 31 December 1918 (First World War, War Diary, WO95/2496/3)	WD2496_3	9781474525343	£15.00
36 DIVISION Divisional Troops 154 Brigade Royal Field Artillery : 26 November 1915 - 31 August 1916 (First World War, War Diary, WO95/2496/4)	WD2496_4	9781474517560	£15.00
36 DIVISION Divisional Troops 172 Brigade Royal Field Artillery : 1 December 1915 - 31 January 1917 (First World War, War Diary, WO95/2496/5)	WD2496_5	9781474517577	£15.00
36 DIVISION Divisional Troops 173 Brigade Royal Field Artillery. : 27 November 1915 - 20 February 1919 (First World War, War Diary, WO95/2496/6)	WD2496_6	9781474517584	£20.00
36 DIVISION Divisional Troops Divisional Trench Mortar Batteries : 1 August 1916 - 28 February 1919 (First World War, War Diary, WO95/2496/7)	WD2496_7	9781474517591	£15.00
36 DIVISION Divisional Troops Divisional Ammunition Column : 21 September 1915 - 28 February 1919 (First World War, War Diary, WO95/2496/8)	WD2496_8	9781474517607	£15.00
36 DIVISION Divisional Troops 121 Field Company Royal Engineers : 3 October 1915 - 28 February 1919 (First World War, War Diary, WO95/2497/1)	WD2497_1	9781474517614	£19.00

Title	Product Code	ISBN	Price
36 DIVISION Divisional Troops 122 Field Company Royal Engineers : 4 October 1915 - 28 February 1919 (First World War, War Diary, WO95/2497/2)	WD2497_2	9781474517621	£15.00
36 DIVISION Divisional Troops 150 Field Company Royal Engineers : 5 October 1915 - 28 February 1919 (First World War, War Diary, WO95/2497/3)	WD2497_3	9781474517638	£29.00
36 DIVISION Divisional Troops Divisional Signal Company : 2 October 1915 - 31 January 1919 (First World War, War Diary, WO95/2498/1)	WD2498_1	9781474517645	£15.00
36 DIVISION Divisional Troops Royal Irish Rifles 16th Battalion Pioneers : 1 October 1915 - 31 March 1919 (First World War, War Diary, WO95/2498/2)	WD2498_2	9781474517652	£15.00
36 DIVISION Divisional Troops Machine Gun Corps 36 Battalion : 12 January 1918 - 28 February 1919 (First World War, War Diary, WO95/2498/3)	WD2498_3	9781474517669	£15.00
36 DIVISION Divisional Troops Royal Army Medical Corps 108 Field Ambulance : 9 September 1915 - 28 June 1919 (First World War, War Diary, WO95/2499/1)	WD2499_1	9781474517676	£32.00
36 DIVISION Divisional Troops Royal Army Medical Corps 109 Field Ambulance : 5 October 1915 - 14 June 1919 (First World War, War Diary, WO95/2499/2)	WD2499_2	9781474517683	£25.00
36 DIVISION Divisional Troops Royal Army Medical Corps 110 Field Ambulance : 4 October 1915 - 17 June 1919 (First World War, War Diary, WO95/2500/1)	WD2500_1	9781474517690	£20.00
36 DIVISION Divisional Troops Royal Army Medical Corps Divisional Field Ambulance Workshop Unit : 15 September 1915 - 9 April 1916 (First World War, War Diary, WO95/2500/2)	WD2500_2	9781474517706	£15.00
36 DIVISION Divisional Troops 76 Sanitary Section : 25 June 1915 - 31 March 1917 (First World War, War Diary, WO95/2500/3)	WD2500_3	9781474517713	£18.00
36 DIVISION Divisional Troops Royal Army Veterinary Corps 48 Mobile Veterinary Section : 1 October 1915 - 10 November 1919 (First World War, War Diary, WO95/2500/4)	WD2500_4	9781474517720	£15.00
36 DIVISION Divisional Troops Royal Army Service Corps Divisional Train (251, 252, 253, 254 Companies ASC) : 2 October 1915 - 14 June 1919 (First World War, War Diary, WO95/2501)	WD2501	9781474517737	£62.00
36 DIVISION 107 Infantry Brigade Headquarters : 20 October 1915 - 31 March 1919 (First World War, War Diary, WO95/2502/1)	WD2502_1	9781474517744	£24.00
36 DIVISION 107 Infantry Brigade Princess Victoria's (Royal Irish Fusiliers) 1st Battalion : 1 August 1917 - 31 December 1917 (First World War, War Diary, WO95/2502/2)	WD2502_2	9781474517751	£15.00
36 DIVISION 107 Infantry Brigade Royal Irish Rifles 1st Battalion : 1 February 1918 - 29 May 1919 (First World War, War Diary, WO95/2502/3)	WD2502_3	9781474517768	£15.00
36 DIVISION 107 Infantry Brigade Royal Irish Rifles 2nd Battalion : 1 November 1917 - 28 February 1918 (First World War, War Diary, WO95/2502/4)	WD2502_4	9781474517775	£15.00
36 DIVISION 107 Infantry Brigade Royal Irish Rifles 8th Battalion : 3 October 1915 - 31 August 1917 (First World War, War Diary, WO95/2503/1)	WD2503_1	9781474517782	£15.00

Title	Product Code	ISBN	Price
36 DIVISION 107 Infantry Brigade Royal Irish Rifles 9th Battalion : 1 March 1915 - 30 August 1917 (First World War, War Diary, WO95/2503/2)	WD2503_2	9781474517799	£15.00
36 DIVISION 107 Infantry Brigade Royal Irish Rifles 8/9th Battalion : 1 September 1917 - 31 January 1918 (First World War, War Diary, WO95/2503/3)	WD2503_3	9781474517805	£15.00
36 DIVISION 107 Infantry Brigade Royal Irish Rifles 10th Battalion : 3 October 1915 - 19 January 1918 (First World War, War Diary, WO95/2503/4)	WD2503_4	9781474517812	£15.00
36 DIVISION 107 Infantry Brigade Royal Irish Rifles 15th Battalion : 3 October 1915 - 31 May 1919 (First World War, War Diary, WO95/2503/5)	WD2503_5	9781474517829	£15.00
36 DIVISION 107 Infantry Brigade, Brigade Machine Gun Company : 18 December 1915 - 31 January 1918 (First World War, War Diary, WO95/2503/6)	WD2503_6	9781474517836	£15.00
36 DIVISION 107 Infantry Brigade, Brigade Trench Mortar Battery : 26 September 1915 - 31 August 1916 (First World War, War Diary, WO95/2503/7)	WD2503_7	9781474517843	£15.00
36 DIVISION 108 Infantry Brigade Headquarters : 4 October 1915 - 28 February 1919 (First World War, War Diary, WO95/2504)	WD2504	9781474517850	£41.00
36 DIVISION 108 Infantry Brigade Princess Victoria's (Royal Irish Fusiliers) 1st and 9th Battalion : 4 October 1915 - 9 June 1919 (First World War, War Diary, WO95/2505)	WD2505	9781474517867	£48.00
36 DIVISION 108 Infantry Brigade Royal Irish Rifles 11th, 12th, 13th and 11/13th Battalion, Brigade Machine Gun Company and Brigade Trench Mortar Battery : 15 March 1915 - 31 August 1916 (First World War, War Diary, WO95/2506)	WD2506	9781474517874	£63.00
36 DIVISION 109 Infantry Brigade Headquarters : 5 October 1915 - 31 December 1916 (First World War, War Diary, WO95/2507)	WD2507	9781474517881	£51.00
36 DIVISION 109 Infantry Brigade Headquarters : 1 January 1917 - 30 June 1917 (First World War, War Diary, WO95/2508)	WD2508	9781474517898	£38.00
36 DIVISION 109 Infantry Brigade Headquarters : 1 July 1917 - 28 February 1919 (First World War, War Diary, WO95/2509)	WD2509	9781474517904	£50.00
36 DIVISION 109 Infantry Brigade Royal Inniskilling Fusiliers 1st Battalion : 1 February 1918 - 28 March 1919 (First World War, War Diary, WO95/2510/1)	WD2510_1	9781474517911	£15.00
36 DIVISION 109 Infantry Brigade Royal Inniskilling Fusiliers 2nd Battalion : 1 February 1918 - 30 April 1919 (First World War, War Diary, WO95/2510/2)	WD2510_2	9781474517928	£15.00
36 DIVISION 109 Infantry Brigade Royal Inniskilling Fusiliers 9th Battalion : 4 October 1915 - 4 April 1919 (First World War, War Diary, WO95/2510/3)	WD2510_3	9781474517935	£20.00
36 DIVISION 109 Infantry Brigade Royal Inniskilling Fusiliers 10th Battalion : 4 October 1915 - 31 January 1918 (First World War, War Diary, WO95/2510/4)	WD2510_4	9781474517942	£19.00
36 DIVISION 109 Infantry Brigade Royal Inniskilling Fusiliers 11th Battalion : 4 October 1915 - 21 February 1918 (First World War, War Diary, WO95/2510/5)	WD2510_5	9781474517959	£17.00
36 DIVISION 109 Infantry Brigade Royal Irish Rifles 14th Battalion : 3 October 1915 - 28 February 1918 (First World War, War Diary, WO95/2511/1)	WD2511_1	9781474517966	£37.00

Title	Product Code	ISBN	Price
36 DIVISION 109 Infantry Brigade, Brigade Machine Gun Company : 23 January 1916 - 31 January 1918 (First World War, War Diary, WO95/2511/2)	WD2511_2	9781474517973	£22.00

Title	Product Code	ISBN	Price
37 DIVISION			
37 DIVISION Headquarters, Branches and Services General Staff : 4 July 1915 - 14 June 1916 (First World War, War Diary, WO95/2512)	WD2512	9781474517980	£56.00
37 DIVISION Headquarters, Branches and Services General Staff : 1 July 1916 - 31 July 1917 (First World War, War Diary, WO95/2513)	WD2513	9781474517997	£61.00
37 DIVISION Headquarters, Branches and Services General Staff : 1 August 1917 - 31 March 1918 (First World War, War Diary, WO95/2514)	WD2514	9781474525350	£67.00
37 DIVISION Headquarters, Branches and Services General Staff : 1 June 1918 - 31 March 1919 (First World War, War Diary, WO95/2515)	WD2515	9781474525367	£79.00
37 DIVISION Headquarters, Branches and Services Adjutant and Quarter-Master General : 1 August 1915 - 30 June 1918 (First World War, War Diary, WO95/2516/1)	WD2516_1	9781474518000	£19.00
37 DIVISION Headquarters, Branches and Services Commander Royal Artillery : 4 August 1915 - 31 December 1916 (First World War, War Diary, WO95/2516/2)	WD2516_2	9781474518017	£39.00
37 DIVISION Headquarters, Branches and Services Commander Royal Artillery : 1 January 1917 - 30 May 1917 (First World War, War Diary, WO95/2517/1)	WD2517_1	9781474518024	£15.00
37 DIVISION Headquarters, Branches and Services Commander Royal Artillery : 2 June 1917 - 31 January 1919 (First World War, War Diary, WO95/2517/2)	WD2517_2	9781474518031	£41.00
37 DIVISION Headquarters, Branches and Services Royal Army Medical Corps Assistant Director Medical Services : 20 July 1915 - 31 March 1919 (First World War, War Diary, WO95/2518)	WD2518	9781474518048	£57.00
37 DIVISION Headquarters, Branches and Services Commander Royal Engineers : 29 July 1915 - 25 March 1919 (First World War, War Diary, WO95/2519)	WD2519	9781474518055	£71.00
37 DIVISION Headquarters, Branches and Services Royal Army Ordnance Corps Deputy Assistant Director Ordnance Services : 1 October 1915 - 30 April 1919 (First World War, War Diary, WO95/2520/1)	WD2520_1	9781474518062	£23.00
37 DIVISION Headquarters, Branches and Services Royal Army Veterinary Corps Assistant Director Veterinary Services : 5 May 1915 - 21 April 1919 (First World War, War Diary, WO95/2520/2)	WD2520_2	9781474518079	£15.00
37 DIVISION Divisional Troops B Squadron 1/1 Yorkshire Dragoons, Divisional Cyclist Company, 123, 124, 125 and 126 Brigade Royal Field Artillery, Divisional Trench Mortar Batteries and Divisional Ammunition Column : 15 April 1915 - 30 March 1919 (First Wo	WD2521	9781474525374	£65.00
37 DIVISION Divisional Troops 152 and 153 Field Company Royal Engineers : 29 July 1915 - 31 March 1919 (First World War, War Diary, WO95/2522)	WD2522	9781474518086	£66.00
37 DIVISION Divisional Troops 154 Field Company Royal Engineers and Divisional Signal Company : 28 July 1915 - 31 March 1919 (First World War, War Diary, WO95/2523)	WD2523	9781474518093	£56.00
37 DIVISION Divisional Troops Prince of Wales's (North Staffordshire Regiment) 9th Battalion Pioneers : 28 July 1915 - 30 April 1918 (First World War, War Diary, WO95/2524/1)	WD2524_1	9781474518109	£43.00
37 DIVISION Divisional Troops Prince of Wales's (North Staffordshire Regiment) 9 Battalion (Maps) (First World War, War Diary, WO95/2524/2)	WD2524_2	9781474518116	£15.00

Title	Product Code	ISBN	Price
37 DIVISION Divisional Troops Machine Gun Corps 37 Battalion : 4 March 1918 - 31 May 1919 (First World War, War Diary, WO95/2524/3)	WD2524_3	9781474518123	£15.00
37 DIVISION Divisional Troops 247 Machine Gun Company : 16 July 1917 - 28 February 1918 (First World War, War Diary, WO95/2524/4)	WD2524_4	9781474518130	£15.00
37 DIVISION Divisional Troops Royal Army Medical Corps 48 Field Ambulance : 28 July 1915 - 17 April 1919 (First World War, War Diary, WO95/2525/1)	WD2525_1	9781474518147	£28.00
37 DIVISION Divisional Troops Royal Army Medical Corps 49 Field Ambulance : 14 June 1915 - 25 April 1919 (First World War, War Diary, WO95/2525/2)	WD2525_2	9781474518154	£34.00
37 DIVISION Divisional Troops Royal Army Medical Corps 50 Field Ambulance : 10 June 1915 - 30 April 1919 (First World War, War Diary, WO95/2526/1)	WD2526_1	9781474518161	£21.00
37 DIVISION Divisional Troops Royal Army Medical Corps Divisional Field Ambulance Workshop Unit : 1 August 1915 - 31 March 1916 (First World War, War Diary, WO95/2526/2)	WD2526_2	9781474518178	£15.00
37 DIVISION Divisional Troops 37 Sanitary Section : 31 July 1915 - 31 March 1917 (First World War, War Diary, WO95/2526/3)	WD2526_3	9781474518185	£15.00
37 DIVISION Divisional Troops Royal Army Veterinary Corps 28 Mobile Veterinary Section : 28 April 1915 - 31 March 1919 (First World War, War Diary, WO95/2526/4)	WD2526_4	9781474518192	£15.00
37 DIVISION Divisional Troops Royal Army Service Corps Divisional Train (288, 289, 290, 291 Companies A.S.C.) : 6 March 1915 - 31 March 1917 (First World War, War Diary, WO95/2527A)	WD2527_A	9781474525381	£51.00
37 DIVISION Divisional Troops Royal Army Service Corps Divisional Train (288, 289, 290, 291 Companies A.S.C.) : 1 April 1917 - 22 April 1919 (First World War, War Diary, WO95/2527B)	WD2527_B	9781474525398	£48.00
37 DIVISION 63 Infantry Brigade Headquarters : 1 July 1916 - 31 January 1919 (First World War, War Diary, WO95/2528/1)	WD2528_1	9781474525404	£35.00
37 DIVISION 63 Infantry Brigade Duke of Cambridge's Own (Middlesex Regiment) 4th Battalion : 1 July 1916 - 28 February 1919 (First World War, War Diary, WO95/2528/2)	WD2528_2	9781474525411	£22.00
37 DIVISION 63 Infantry Brigade Lincolnshire Regiment 8th Battalion : 1 March 1916 - 31 March 1919 (First World War, War Diary, WO95/2529/1)	WD2529_1	9781474525428	£15.00
37 DIVISION 63 Infantry Brigade Prince Albert's (Somerset Light Infantry) 8th Battalion : 28 July 1916 - 24 April 1919 (First World War, War Diary, WO95/2529/2)	WD2529_2	9781474525435	£15.00
37 DIVISION 63 Infantry Brigade York and Lancaster Regiment 10th (Service) Battalion : 1 August 1916 - 28 January 1918 (First World War, War Diary, WO95/2529/3)	WD2529_3	9781474525442	£18.00
37 DIVISION 63 Infantry Brigade, Brigade Machine Gun Company : 1 August 1916 - 28 February 1918 (First World War, War Diary, WO95/2529/4)	WD2529_4	9781474525459	£16.00
37 DIVISION 63 Infantry Brigade, Brigade Trench Mortar Battery : 1 July 1916 - 30 September 1916 (First World War, War Diary, WO95/2529/5)	WD2529_5	9781474525466	£15.00

Title	Product Code	ISBN	Price
37 DIVISION 110 Infantry Brigade Headquarters, Leicestershire Regiment 6th, 7th, 8th and 9th Battalion, Brigade Machine Gun Company and Brigade Trench Mortar Battery : 24 September 1914 - 29 June 1916 (First World War, War Diary, WO95/2530)	WD2530	9781474518208	£41.00
37 DIVISION 111 Infantry Brigade Headquarters : 29 July 1915 - 22 April 1919 (First World War, War Diary, WO95/2531)	WD2531	9781474518215	£55.00
37 DIVISION 111 Infantry Brigade Royal Fusiliers (City of London Regiment) 10th and 13th Battalion : 28 July 1915 - 31 January 1918 (First World War, War Diary, WO95/2532)	WD2532	9781474525473	£63.00
37 DIVISION 111 Infantry Brigade King's Royal Rifle Corps 13th Battalion : 29 July 1915 - 8 March 1919 (First World War, War Diary, WO95/2533)	WD2533	9781474518222	£48.00
37 DIVISION 111 Infantry Brigade Rifle Brigade (The Prince Consort's Own) 13th Battalion : 29 July 1915 - 31 July 1918 (First World War, War Diary, WO95/2534/1)	WD2534_1	9781474518239	£30.00
37 DIVISION 111 Infantry Brigade, Brigade Machine Gun Company and Brigade Trench Mortar Battery : 24 February 1916 - 28 February 1918 (First World War, War Diary, WO95/2534/2-3)	WD2534_2-3	9781474518246	£15.00
37 DIVISION 112 Infantry Brigade Headquarters : 13 July 1915 - 31 March 1917 (First World War, War Diary, WO95/2535)	WD2535	9781474518253	£47.00
37 DIVISION 112 Infantry Brigade Headquarters : 1 April 1917 - 20 April 1919 (First World War, War Diary, WO95/2536)	WD2536	9781474518260	£38.00
37 DIVISION 112 Infantry Brigade Essex Regiment 1st Battalion : 21 January 1918 - 31 March 1919 (First World War, War Diary, WO95/2537/1)	WD2537_1	9781474518277	£15.00
37 DIVISION 112 Infantry Brigade Hertfordshire Regiment 1 Battalion : 1 May 1918 - 31 March 1919 (First World War, War Diary, WO95/2537/2)	WD2537_2	9781474518284	£15.00
37 DIVISION 112 Infantry Brigade Bedfordshire Regiment 6th Battalion : 30 July 1915 - 30 June 1918 (First World War, War Diary, WO95/2537/3)	WD2537_3	9781474518291	£15.00
37 DIVISION 112 Infantry Brigade East Lancashire Regiment 8th Battalion : 30 July 1915 - 21 February 1918 (First World War, War Diary, WO95/2537/4)	WD2537_4	9781474518307	£15.00
37 DIVISION 112 Infantry Brigade Loyal North Lancashire Regiment 10th Battalion : 30 July 1915 - 21 February 1918 (First World War, War Diary, WO95/2538/1)	WD2538_1	9781474518314	£21.00
37 DIVISION 112 Infantry Brigade Royal Warwickshire Regiment 11th Battalion : 30 July 1915 - 21 February 1918 (First World War, War Diary, WO95/2538/2)	WD2538_2	9781474518321	£23.00
37 DIVISION 112 Infantry Brigade Royal Fusiliers (City of London Regiment) 13th Battalion : 1 February 1918 - 31 March 1919 (First World War, War Diary, WO95/2538/3)	WD2538_3	9781474518338	£15.00
37 DIVISION 112 Infantry Brigade, Brigade Machine Gun Company : 24 February 1916 - 28 February 1918 (First World War, War Diary, WO95/2538/4)	WD2538_4	9781474518345	£15.00

Title	Product Code	ISBN	Price
38 DIVISION			
38 DIVISION Headquarters, Branches and Services General Staff : 6 December 1915 - 31 July 1916 (First World War, War Diary, WO95/2539)	WD2539	9781474518352	£44.00
38 DIVISION Headquarters, Branches and Services General Staff : 1 August 1916 - 30 June 1917 (First World War, War Diary, WO95/2540/1)	WD2540_1	9781474518369	£15.00
38 DIVISION Headquarters, Branches and Services General Staff : 1 July 1917 - 20 February 1919 (First World War, War Diary, WO95/2540/2)	WD2540_2	9781474518376	£33.00
38 DIVISION Headquarters, Branches and Services Adjutant and Quarter-Master General : 1 December 1915 - 17 June 1919 (First World War, War Diary, WO95/2541)	WD2541	9781474518383	£51.00
38 DIVISION Headquarters, Branches and Services Commander Royal Artillery : 18 December 1915 - 30 April 1919 (First World War, War Diary, WO95/2542)	WD2542	9781474518390	£44.00
38 DIVISION Headquarters, Branches and Services Royal Army Medical Corps Assistant Director Medical Services : 1 December 1915 - 31 May 1919 (First World War, War Diary, WO95/2543)	WD2543	9781474518406	£41.00
38 DIVISION Headquarters, Branches and Services Commander Royal Engineers : 2 December 1915 - 7 June 1919 (First World War, War Diary, WO95/2544/1)	WD2544_1	9781474518413	£17.00
38 DIVISION Headquarters, Branches and Services Royal Army Ordnance Corps Deputy Assistant Director Ordnance Services : 1 March 1915 - 30 April 1919 (First World War, War Diary, WO95/2544/2)	WD2544_2	9781474518420	£15.00
38 DIVISION Headquarters, Branches and Services Royal Army Veterinary Corps Assistant Director Veterinary Services : 22 April 1914 - 5 April 1919 (First World War, War Diary, WO95/2544/3)	WD2544_3	9781474518437	£26.00
38 DIVISION Divisional Troops D Squadron 1/1 Wiltshire Yeomanry : 4 December 1915 - 21 April 1916 (First World War, War Diary, WO95/2545/1)	WD2545_1	9781474518444	£15.00
38 DIVISION Divisional Troops Divisional Cyclist Company : 2 December 1915 - 10 May 1916 (First World War, War Diary, WO95/2545/2)	WD2545_2	9781474518451	£15.00
38 DIVISION Divisional Troops 122 Brigade Royal Field Artillery : 26 August 1915 - 18 May 1919 (First World War, War Diary, WO95/2545/3)	WD2545_3	9781474525480	£69.00
38 DIVISION Divisional Troops 119 Brigade Royal Field Artillery : 22 December 1915 - 28 February 1917 (First World War, War Diary, WO95/2546/1)	WD2546_1	9781474518468	£15.00
38 DIVISION Divisional Troops 120 Brigade Royal Field Artillery : 24 December 1915 - 29 August 1916 (First World War, War Diary, WO95/2546/2)	WD2546_2	9781474518475	£15.00
38 DIVISION Divisional Troops 121 Brigade Royal Field Artillery : 1 January 1916 - 1 April 1919 (First World War, War Diary, WO95/2546/3)	WD2546_3	9781474518482	£20.00
38 DIVISION Divisional Troops Divisional Trench Mortar Batteries : 5 April 1916 - 31 January 1919 (First World War, War Diary, WO95/2546/4)	WD2546_4	9781474518499	£17.00
38 DIVISION Divisional Troops Divisional Ammunition Column : 19 December 1915 - 27 May 1919 (First World War, War Diary, WO95/2546/5)	WD2546_5	9781474518505	£15.00
38 DIVISION Divisional Troops 123 Field Company Royal Engineers : 1 December 1915 - 7 June 1919 (First World War, War Diary, WO95/2547/1)	WD2547_1	9781474518512	£23.00

Title	Product Code	ISBN	Price
38 DIVISION Divisional Troops 124 Field Company Royal Engineers : 3 December 1915 - 7 June 1919 (First World War, War Diary, WO95/2547/2)	WD2547_2	9781474518529	£15.00
38 DIVISION Divisional Troops 151 Field Company Royal Engineers : 3 December 1915 - 31 December 1918 (First World War, War Diary, WO95/2547/3)	WD2547_3	9781474518536	£22.00
38 DIVISION Divisional Troops Divisional Signal Company : 8 December 1914 - 7 April 1919 (First World War, War Diary, WO95/2548/1)	WD2548_1	9781474518543	£15.00
38 DIVISION Divisional Troops Welsh Regiment 19th Battalion Pioneers : 5 December 1915 - 30 April 1919 (First World War, War Diary, WO95/2548/2)	WD2548_2	9781474518550	£15.00
38 DIVISION Divisional Troops Machine Gun Corps 38 Battalion : 2 March 1918 - 31 March 1919 (First World War, War Diary, WO95/2548/3)	WD2548_3	9781474518567	£22.00
38 DIVISION Divisional Troops 176 Machine Gun Company : 19 March 1917 - 28 February 1918 (First World War, War Diary, WO95/2548/4)	WD2548_4	9781474518574	£15.00
38 DIVISION Divisional Troops Royal Army Medical Corps 129 Field Ambulance : 1 December 1915 - 22 May 1919 (First World War, War Diary, WO95/2549/1)	WD2549_1	9781474518581	£23.00
38 DIVISION Divisional Troops Royal Army Medical Corps 130 Field Ambulance : 3 December 1915 - 10 June 1919 (First World War, War Diary, WO95/2549/2)	WD2549_2	9781474518598	£28.00
38 DIVISION Divisional Troops Royal Army Medical Corps 131 Field Ambulance : 4 December 1915 - 27 May 1919 (First World War, War Diary, WO95/2550/1)	WD2550_1	9781474518604	£35.00
38 DIVISION Divisional Troops Royal Army Medical Corps Divisional Field Ambulance Workshop Unit : 1 December 1915 - 31 March 1916 (First World War, War Diary, WO95/2550/2)	WD2550_2	9781474518611	£15.00
38 DIVISION Divisional Troops 77 Sanitary Section : 4 December 1915 - 30 April 1917 (First World War, War Diary, WO95/2550/3)	WD2550_3	9781474518628	£15.00
38 DIVISION Divisional Troops Royal Army Veterinary Corps 49 Mobile Veterinary Section : 4 December 1915 - 31 July 1919 (First World War, War Diary, WO95/2550/4)	WD2550_4	9781474518635	£15.00
38 DIVISION Divisional Troops Royal Army Service Corps Divisional Train (330, 331, 332, 333 Companies A.S.C.) : 5 November 1915 - 16 June 1919 (First World War, War Diary, WO95/2550/5)	WD2550_5	9781474518642	£28.00
38 DIVISION 113 Infantry Brigade Headquarters : 24 November 1915 - 1 June 1916 (First World War, War Diary, WO95/2551)	WD2551	9781474518659	£49.00
38 DIVISION 113 Infantry Brigade Headquarters : 1 July 1916 - 28 February 1917 (First World War, War Diary, WO95/2552)	WD2552	9781474518666	£68.00
38 DIVISION 113 Infantry Brigade Headquarters : 1 March 1917 - 31 December 1917 (First World War, War Diary, WO95/2553)	WD2553	9781474518673	£49.00
38 DIVISION 113 Infantry Brigade Headquarters : 1 January 1918 - 30 April 1919 (First World War, War Diary, WO95/2554)	WD2554	9781474518680	£54.00
38 DIVISION 113 Infantry Brigade Royal Welsh Fusiliers 13th Battalion : 1 December 1915 - 30 April 1919 (First World War, War Diary, WO95/2555/1)	WD2555_1	9781474518697	£18.00

Title	Product Code	ISBN	Price
38 DIVISION 113 Infantry Brigade Royal Welsh Fusiliers 14th Battalion : 1 December 1915 - 30 April 1919 (First World War, War Diary, WO95/2555/2)	WD2555_2	9781474518703	£30.00
38 DIVISION 113 Infantry Brigade Royal Welsh Fusiliers 15th Battalion : 1 December 1915 - 28 February 1918 (First World War, War Diary, WO95/2556/1)	WD2556_1	9781474518710	£16.00
38 DIVISION 113 Infantry Brigade Royal Welsh Fusiliers 16th Battalion : 2 December 1915 - 27 April 1919 (First World War, War Diary, WO95/2556/2)	WD2556_2	9781474518727	£20.00
38 DIVISION 113 Infantry Brigade, Brigade Machine Gun Company : 17 May 1916 - 27 February 1918 (First World War, War Diary, WO95/2556/3)	WD2556_3	9781474518734	£15.00
38 DIVISION 113 Infantry Brigade, Brigade Trench Mortar Battery : 1 January 1916 - 30 April 1916 (First World War, War Diary, WO95/2556/4)	WD2556_4	9781474518741	£15.00
38 DIVISION 114 Infantry Brigade Headquarters : 5 December 1915 - 31 December 1916 (First World War, War Diary, WO95/2557)	WD2557	9781474518758	£57.00
38 DIVISION 114 Infantry Brigade Headquarters : 1 January 1917 - 4 June 1919 (First World War, War Diary, WO95/2558)	WD2558	9781474525497	£80.00
38 DIVISION 114 Infantry Brigade Welsh Regiment 10th, 13t, 14th and 15th Battalion, Brigade Machine Gun Company and Brigade Trench Mortar Battery : 16 September 1915 - 31 January 1916 (First World War, War Diary, WO95/2559)	WD2559	9781474525503	£77.00
38 DIVISION 115 Infantry Brigade Headquarters : 3 December 1915 - 25 January 1919 (First World War, War Diary, WO95/2560)	WD2560	9781474518765	£72.00
38 DIVISION 115 Infantry Brigade Royal Welsh Fusiliers 2nd Battalion : 1 February 1918 - 30 April 1919 (First World War, War Diary, WO95/2561/1)	WD2561_1	9781474518772	£15.00
38 DIVISION 115 Infantry Brigade Royal Welsh Fusiliers 17th Battalion : 4 December 1915 - 30 April 1919 (First World War, War Diary, WO95/2561/2)	WD2561_2	9781474518789	£21.00
38 DIVISION 115 Infantry Brigade Welsh Regiment 16th Battalion : 4 December 1915 - 27 February 1918 (First World War, War Diary, WO95/2561/3)	WD2561_3	9781474518796	£15.00
38 DIVISION 115 Infantry Brigade South Wales Borderers 10th Battalion : 4 December 1915 - 21 May 1919 (First World War, War Diary, WO95/2562/1)	WD2562_1	9781474518802	£34.00
38 DIVISION 115 Infantry Brigade South Wales Borderers 11th Battalion : 3 December 1915 - 31 January 1918 (First World War, War Diary, WO95/2562/2)	WD2562_2	9781474518819	£15.00
38 DIVISION 115 Infantry Brigade, Brigade Machine Gun Company : 2 March 1916 - 28 February 1918 (First World War, War Diary, WO95/2562/3)	WD2562_3	9781474518826	£16.00
38 DIVISION 115 Infantry Brigade, Brigade Trench Mortar Battery : 1 July 1916 - 29 August 1916 (First World War, War Diary, WO95/2562/4)	WD2562_4	9781474518833	£15.00

Title	Product Code	ISBN	Price
39 DIVISION			
39 DIVISION Headquarters, Branches and Services General Staff : 5 March 1916 - 30 June 1916 (First World War, War Diary, WO95/2563)	WD2563	9781474518840	£42.00
39 DIVISION Headquarters, Branches and Services General Staff : 1 July 1916 - 30 September 1916 (First World War, War Diary, WO95/2564)	WD2564	9781474518857	£65.00
39 DIVISION Headquarters, Branches and Services General Staff : 1 October 1916 - 31 December 1916 (First World War, War Diary, WO95/2565)	WD2565	9781474518864	£54.00
39 DIVISION Headquarters, Branches and Services General Staff : 1 January 1917 - 16 September 1917 (First World War, War Diary, WO95/2566)	WD2566	9781474518871	£54.00
39 DIVISION Headquarters, Branches and Services General Staff : 1 October 1917 - 10 July 1919 (First World War, War Diary, WO95/2567)	WD2567	9781474518888	£43.00
39 DIVISION Headquarters, Branches and Services Adjutant and Quarter-Master General : 1 March 1916 - 10 July 1919 (First World War, War Diary, WO95/2568)	WD2568	9781474518895	£31.00
39 DIVISION Headquarters, Branches and Services Commander Royal Artillery : 2 March 1916 - 5 December 1916 (First World War, War Diary, WO95/2569)	WD2569	9781474518901	£54.00
39 DIVISION Headquarters, Branches and Services Commander Royal Artillery : 15 January 1917 - 29 December 1918 (First World War, War Diary, WO95/2570)	WD2570	9781474518918	£70.00
39 DIVISION Headquarters, Branches and Services Royal Army Medical Corps Assistant Director Medical Services : 27 February 1916 - 31 March 1917 (First World War, War Diary, WO95/2571)	WD2571	9781474518925	£55.00
39 DIVISION Headquarters, Branches and Services Royal Army Medical Corps Assistant Director Medical Services : 28 February 1917 - 13 November 1918 (First World War, War Diary, WO95/2572)	WD2572	9781474525510	£78.00
39 DIVISION Headquarters, Branches and Services Commander Royal Engineers : 5 March 1916 - 31 December 1918 (First World War, War Diary, WO95/2573/1)	WD2573_1	9781474518932	£22.00
39 DIVISION Headquarters, Branches and Services Royal Army Ordnance Corps Deputy Assistant Director Ordnance Services : 26 February 1916 - 28 February 1919 (First World War, War Diary, WO95/2573/2)	WD2573_2	9781474518949	£15.00
39 DIVISION Headquarters, Branches and Services Royal Army Veterinary Corps Assistant Director Veterinary Services : 5 March 1916 - 31 January 1919 (First World War, War Diary, WO95/2573/3)	WD2573_3	9781474518956	£15.00
39 DIVISION Divisional Troops E Squadron South Irish Horse : 16 March 1916 - 30 April 1916 (First World War, War Diary, WO95/2574/1)	WD2574_1	9781474518963	£15.00
39 DIVISION Divisional Troops Divisional Cyclist Company : 3 March 1916 - 30 April 1916 (First World War, War Diary, WO95/2574/2)	WD2574_2	9781474518970	£15.00
39 DIVISION Divisional Troops 174 and 179 Brigade Royal Field Artillery : 19 May 1915 - 18 January 1917 (First World War, War Diary, WO95/2574/3)	WD2574_3	9781474518987	£15.00
39 DIVISION Divisional Troops 184 Brigade Royal Field Artillery : 4 February 1916 - 30 November 1916 (First World War, War Diary, WO95/2574/4)	WD2574_4	9781474518994	£15.00
39 DIVISION Divisional Troops 186 Brigade Royal Field Artillery : 5 March 1916 - 17 December 1918 (First World War, War Diary, WO95/2574/5)	WD2574_5	9781474519007	£15.00

Title	Product Code	ISBN	Price
39 DIVISION Divisional Troops Divisional Trench Mortar Batteries : 3 July 1916 - 20 July 1918 (First World War, War Diary, WO95/2574/6)	WD2574_6	9781474519014	£15.00
39 DIVISION Divisional Troops Divisional Ammunition Column : 1 March 1916 - 30 March 1919 (First World War, War Diary, WO95/2574/7)	WD2574_7	9781474519021	£15.00
39 DIVISION Divisional Troops 234 Field Company Royal Engineers : 6 March 1916 - 16 December 1918 (First World War, War Diary, WO95/2575)	WD2575	9781474519038	£60.00
39 DIVISION Divisional Troops 225 and 227 Field Company Royal Engineers and Divisional Signal Company : 20 May 1915 - 8 March 1919 (First World War, War Diary, WO95/2576)	WD2576	9781474525527	£57.00
39 DIVISION Divisional Troops Gloucestershire Regiment 13th (Service) Battalion (Forest of Dean) (Pioneers) : 3 March 1916 - 31 May 1919 (First World War, War Diary, WO95/2577/1)	WD2577_1	9781474519045	£15.00
39 DIVISION Divisional Troops East Lancashire Regiment 1/4th Battalion : 1 February 1917 - 7 June 1919 (First World War, War Diary, WO95/2577/2)	WD2577_2	9781474519052	£15.00
39 DIVISION Divisional Troops Sherwood Foresters (Nottinghamshire and Derbyshire Regiment) 1/7th Battalion : 1 August 1918 - 7 June 1919 (First World War, War Diary, WO95/2577/3)	WD2577_3	9781474519069	£15.00
39 DIVISION Divisional Troops Machine Gun Corps 39 Battalion : 1 March 1918 - 19 March 1918 (First World War, War Diary, WO95/2577/4)	WD2577_4	9781474519076	£15.00
39 DIVISION Divisional Troops 228 Machine Gun Company : 2 September 1914 - 28 February 1918 (First World War, War Diary, WO95/2577/5)	WD2577_5	9781474519083	£26.00
39 DIVISION Divisional Troops Royal Army Medical Corps 132 Field Ambulance : 3 March 1916 - 11 December 1918 (First World War, War Diary, WO95/2578/1)	WD2578_1	9781474519090	£27.00
39 DIVISION Divisional Troops Royal Army Medical Corps 133 Field Ambulance : 5 March 1916 - 12 December 1918 (First World War, War Diary, WO95/2578/2)	WD2578_2	9781474519106	£28.00
39 DIVISION Divisional Troops Royal Army Medical Corps 134 Field Ambulance : 6 March 1916 - 12 December 1918 (First World War, War Diary, WO95/2579/1)	WD2579_1	9781474525534	£21.00
39 DIVISION Divisional Troops Royal Army Medical Corps Divisional Field Ambulance Workshop Unit, 82 Sanitary Section, 50 Mobile Veterinary Section : 4 March 1916 - 30 March 1916 (First World War, War Diary, WO95/2579/2-4)	WD2579_2-4	9781474519113	£15.00
39 DIVISION Divisional Troops Royal Army Service Corps Divisional Train (284, 285, 286, 287 Companies A.S.C.) : 1 March 1916 - 31 August 1917 (First World War, War Diary, WO95/2580A)	WD2580_A	9781474525541	£54.00
39 DIVISION Divisional Troops Royal Army Service Corps Divisional Train (284, 285, 286, 287 Companies A.S.C.) : 1 September 1917 - 31 January 1919 (First World War, War Diary, WO95/2580B)	WD2580_B	9781474525558	£52.00
39 DIVISION 116 Infantry Brigade Headquarters : 4 March 1916 - 27 December 1918 (First World War, War Diary, WO95/2581)	WD2581	9781474519120	£48.00
39 DIVISION 116 Infantry Brigade Royal Sussex Regiment 11th Battalion : 4 March 1916 - 30 June 1918 (First World War, War Diary, WO95/2582/1)	WD2582_1	9781474519137	£21.00
39 DIVISION 116 Infantry Brigade Royal Sussex Regiment 12th Battalion : 4 March 1916 - 28 February 1918 (First World War, War Diary, WO95/2582/2)	WD2582_2	9781474519144	£15.00

Title	Product Code	ISBN	Price
39 DIVISION 116 Infantry Brigade Royal Sussex Regiment 13th Battalion : 5 March 1916 - 14 August 1918 (First World War, War Diary, WO95/2582/3)	WD2582_3	9781474519151	£16.00
39 DIVISION 116 Infantry Brigade East Yorkshire Regiment 1/4th Battalion, Alexandra, Princess of Wales's Own (Yorkshire Regiment) 4th and 5th Battalion, South Staffordshire Regiment 4th Special Reserve Battalion, Prince of Wales's (North Staffordshire Re	WD2583	9781474519168	£30.00
39 DIVISION 117 Infantry Brigade Headquarters : 10 March 1916 - 31 December 1916 (First World War, War Diary, WO95/2584)	WD2584	9781474519175	£35.00
39 DIVISION 117 Infantry Brigade Headquarters : 1 January 1917 - 28 January 1919 (First World War, War Diary, WO95/2585)	WD2585	9781474519182	£51.00
39 DIVISION 117 Infantry Brigade Rifle Brigade (The Prince Consort's Own) 16th Battalion : 16 April 1915 - 30 April 1916 (First World War, War Diary, WO95/2586A)	WD2586_A	9781474525565	£48.00
39 DIVISION 117 Infantry Brigade Rifle Brigade (The Prince Consort's Own) 16th Battalion : 1 May 1916 - 30 June 1919 (First World War, War Diary, WO95/2586B)	WD2586_B	9781474525572	£46.00
39 DIVISION 117 Infantry Brigade Sherwood Foresters (Nottinghamshire and Derbyshire Regiment) 16th Battalion : 6 March 1916 - 22 May 1919 (First World War, War Diary, WO95/2587/1)	WD2587_1	9781474525589	£20.00
39 DIVISION 117 Infantry Brigade Sherwood Foresters (Nottinghamshire and Derbyshire Regiment) 17th Battalion : 5 March 1916 - 23 February 1918 (First World War, War Diary, WO95/2587/2)	WD2587_2	9781474525596	£22.00
39 DIVISION Composite Brigade 3 Composite Battalion : 1 April 1918 - 30 April 1918 (First World War, War Diary, WO95/2587/3)	WD2587_3	9781474525602	£15.00
39 DIVISION 117 Infantry Brigade, Brigade Machine Gun Company and Brigade Trench Mortar Battery : 16 May 1916 - 28 February 1918 (First World War, War Diary, WO95/2587/4-5)	WD2587_4-5	9781474525619	£18.00
39 DIVISION 117 Infantry Brigade Sherwood Foresters (Nottinghamshire and Derbyshire Regiment) 9th Battalion : 1 March 1916 - 30 September 1918 (First World War, War Diary, WO95/2587/6)	WD2587_6	9781474525626	£15.00
39 DIVISION 118 Infantry Brigade Headquarters : 8 July 1915 - 31 July 1917 (First World War, War Diary, WO95/2588)	WD2588	9781474519199	£45.00
39 DIVISION 118 Infantry Brigade Headquarters : 28 March 1917 - 4 December 1918 (First World War, War Diary, WO95/2589)	WD2589	9781474519205	£39.00
39 DIVISION 118 Infantry Brigade Cambridgeshire Regiment 1/1 Battalion Cambridgeshire Regiment, Hertfordshire Regiment 1 Battalion, Cheshire Regiment 6 Battalion, Lincolnshire Regiment 4th Battalion, Northumberland Fusiliers 1/4th, 1/5th and 1/6th Battali	WD2590	9781474519212	£53.00
39 DIVISION 118 Infantry Brigade Black Watch (Royal Highlanders) 4th Battalion : 1 November 1915 - 15 March 1916 (First World War, War Diary, WO95/2591/1)	WD2591_1	9781474519229	£15.00
39 DIVISION 118 Infantry Brigade Black Watch (Royal Highlanders) 5th Battalion : 1 January 1916 - 15 March 1916 (First World War, War Diary, WO95/2591/2)	WD2591_2	9781474519236	£15.00
39 DIVISION 118 Infantry Brigade Black Watch (Royal Highlanders) 4/5th (Angus and Dundee) Battalion (Territorial) : 13 March 1916 - 31 March 1918 (First World War, War Diary, WO95/2591/3)	WD2591_3	9781474519243	£28.00

Title	Product Code	ISBN	Price
39 DIVISION 118 Infantry Brigade, Brigade Machine Gun Company and Brigade Trench Mortar Battery : 27 August 1914 - 28 February 1918 (First World War, War Diary, WO95/2591/4-5)	WD2591_4-5	9781474519250	£17.00

Title	Product Code	ISBN	Price
4 CAVALRY DIVISION			
4 CAVALRY DIVISION Headquarters, Branches and Services General Staff, Adjutant and Quarter-Master General, Royal Army Medical Corps Assistant Director Medical Services, Royal Army Ordnance Corps Deputy Director Ordnance Services and Royal Army Veterinary	WD1157	9781474501002	£52.00
4 CAVALRY DIVISION Divisional Troops Jodhpur Imperial Service Lancers : 1 January 1917 - 28 February 1918 (First World War, War Diary, WO95/1158/1)	WD1158_1	9781474501019	£15.00
4 CAVALRY DIVISION Divisional Troops Royal Army Service Corps Auxiliary Horse Transport Company (577 Company A.S.C.) : 1 January 1917 - 31 May 1917 (First World War, War Diary, WO95/1158/10)	WD1158_10	9781474501101	£15.00
4 CAVALRY DIVISION Divisional Troops Royal Army Service Corps Divisional Supply Column (89 Company A.S.C.) : 1 January 1917 - 31 March 1918 (First World War, War Diary, WO95/1158/11)	WD1158_11	9781474501118	£15.00
4 CAVALRY DIVISION Divisional Troops Royal Army Service Corps Divisional Ammunition Park (79 Company A.S.C.) : 14 March 1916 - 12 December 1917 (First World War, War Diary, WO95/1158/12)	WD1158_12	9781474501125	£15.00
4 CAVALRY DIVISION Divisional Troops 16 Brigade Royal Horse Artillery : 1 January 1917 - 24 February 1918 (First World War, War Diary, WO95/1158/2)	WD1158_2	9781474501026	£15.00
4 CAVALRY DIVISION Divisional Troops Brigade Ammunition Column : 1 January 1917 - 31 December 1917 (First World War, War Diary, WO95/1158/3)	WD1158_3	9781474501033	£15.00
4 CAVALRY DIVISION Divisional Troops 4 Field Squadron Royal Engineers : 1 January 1917 - 20 April 1918 (First World War, War Diary, WO95/1158/4)	WD1158_4	9781474501040	£15.00
4 CAVALRY DIVISION Divisional Troops Divisional Signal Squadron : 1 March 1917 - 28 February 1918 (First World War, War Diary, WO95/1158/5)	WD1158_5	9781474501057	£15.00
4 CAVALRY DIVISION Divisional Troops Royal Army Medical Corps Combined Cavalry Field Ambulance Sialkot, Mhow and Lucknow : 1 January 1917 - 31 March 1918 (First World War, War Diary, WO95/1158/6)	WD1158_6	9781474501064	£24.00
4 CAVALRY DIVISION Divisional Troops Royal Army Medical Corps Jodhpur Cavalry Field Ambulance : 1 January 1917 - 28 February 1918 (First World War, War Diary, WO95/1158/7)	WD1158_7	9781474501071	£15.00
4 CAVALRY DIVISION Divisional Troops Divisional Sanitary Section : 1 January 1917 - 21 March 1918 (First World War, War Diary, WO95/1158/8)	WD1158_8	9781474501088	£15.00
4 CAVALRY DIVISION Divisional Troops Royal Army Service Corps Headquarters Divisional Army Service Corps (426 Company A.S.C.) : 1 January 1917 - 31 January 1918 (First World War, War Diary, WO95/1158/9)	WD1158_9	9781474501095	£15.00
4 CAVALRY DIVISION Sialkot Cavalry Brigade Headquarters, `Q' Battery Royal Horse Artillery, 6 (King Edward's Own) Cavalry, 17th Lancers (Duke of Cambridge's Own), 19 Lancers, Divisional Signal Troop, 10 Cavalry Machine Gun Squadron and Royal Army Veter	WD1159	9781474501132	£39.00
4 CAVALRY DIVISION Mhow Cavalry Brigade Headquarters, `A' Battery Royal Horse Artillery, 2 Lancers (Gardner's Horse), 6th Dragoons (Inniskilling), 38 Central Indian Horse, Brigade Signal Troop, 11 Cavalry Machine Gun Squadron and Royal Army Veterinary Co	WD1160	9781474501149	£31.00

Title	Product Code	ISBN	Price
4 CAVALRY DIVISION Lucknow Cavalry Brigade Headquarters, `U' Battery Royal Horse Artillery, 1st King's Dragoon Guards, 29 Lancers, 36 Jacobs Horse, Brigade Signal Troop, 12 Cavalry Machine Gun Squadron and Royal Army Veterinary Corps Mobile Veterinary Se	WD1161	9781474501156	£52.00

Title	Product Code	ISBN	Price
4 DIVISION			
4 DIVISION Headquarters, Branches and Services General Staff : 5 August 1914 - 30 September 1914 (First World War, War Diary, WO95/1439)	WD1439	9781474504744	£49.00
4 DIVISION Headquarters, Branches and Services General Staff : 1 October 1914 - 28 December 1914 (First World War, War Diary, WO95/1440)	WD1440	9781474504751	£47.00
4 DIVISION Headquarters, Branches and Services General Staff : 1 January 1915 - 30 April 1915 (First World War, War Diary, WO95/1441)	WD1441	9781474504768	£28.00
4 DIVISION Headquarters, Branches and Services General Staff : 1 May 1915 - 31 July 1915 (First World War, War Diary, WO95/1442)	WD1442	9781474521901	£51.00
4 DIVISION Headquarters, Branches and Services General Staff : 1 August 1915 - 31 December 1915 (First World War, War Diary, WO95/1443)	WD1443	9781474504775	£62.00
4 DIVISION Headquarters, Branches and Services General Staff : 1 January 1916 - 30 May 1916 (First World War, War Diary, WO95/1444)	WD1444	9781474504782	£54.00
4 DIVISION Headquarters, Branches and Services General Staff : 1 July 1916 - 31 July 1916 (First World War, War Diary, WO95/1445)	WD1445	9781474504799	£31.00
4 DIVISION Headquarters, Branches and Services General Staff : 1 January 1917 - 31 July 1917 (First World War, War Diary, WO95/1446)	WD1446	9781474504805	£52.00
4 DIVISION Headquarters, Branches and Services General Staff : 1 August 1917 - 31 December 1917 (First World War, War Diary, WO95/1447)	WD1447	9781474504812	£33.00
4 DIVISION Headquarters, Branches and Services General Staff : 1 January 1918 - 20 January 1919 (First World War, War Diary, WO95/1448)	WD1448	9781474504829	£70.00
4 DIVISION Headquarters, Branches and Services Adjutant and Quarter-Master General : 1 January 1914 - 31 December 1915 (First World War, War Diary, WO95/1449)	WD1449	9781474504836	£59.00
4 DIVISION Headquarters, Branches and Services Adjutant and Quarter-Master General : 1 January 1916 - 30 March 1917 (First World War, War Diary, WO95/1450)	WD1450	9781474504843	£52.00
4 DIVISION Headquarters, Branches and Services Adjutant and Quarter-Master General : 1 April 1917 - 31 December 1917 (First World War, War Diary, WO95/1451)	WD1451	9781474521918	£73.00
4 DIVISION Headquarters, Branches and Services Adjutant and Quarter-Master General : 1 January 1918 - 28 February 1919 (First World War, War Diary, WO95/1452)	WD1452	9781474504850	£56.00
4 DIVISION Headquarters, Branches and Services Commander Royal Artillery : 15 August 1914 - 30 September 1914 (First World War, War Diary, WO95/1453)	WD1453	9781474504867	£53.00
4 DIVISION Headquarters, Branches and Services Commander Royal Artillery : 1 October 1914 - 31 December 1914 (First World War, War Diary, WO95/1454)	WD1454	9781474504874	£68.00
4 DIVISION Headquarters, Branches and Services Commander Royal Artillery : 1 January 1915 - 31 July 1915 (First World War, War Diary, WO95/1455)	WD1455	9781474504881	£55.00
4 DIVISION Headquarters, Branches and Services Commander Royal Artillery : 1 August 1915 - 31 October 1915 (First World War, War Diary, WO95/1456A)	WD1456_A	9781474521925	£52.00

Title	Product Code	ISBN	Price
4 DIVISION Headquarters, Branches and Services Commander Royal Artillery : 1 November 1915 - 31 December 1915 (First World War, War Diary, WO95/1456B)	WD1456_B	9781474521932	£45.00
4 DIVISION Headquarters, Branches and Services Commander Royal Artillery : 1 January 1916 - 31 May 1916 (First World War, War Diary, WO95/1457)	WD1457	9781474521949	£89.00
4 DIVISION Headquarters, Branches and Services Commander Royal Artillery : 1 June 1916 - 30 September 1916 (First World War, War Diary, WO95/1458)	WD1458	9781474504898	£63.00
4 DIVISION Headquarters, Branches and Services Commander Royal Artillery : 1 October 1916 - 31 October 1917 (First World War, War Diary, WO95/1459)	WD1459	9781474504904	£54.00
4 DIVISION Headquarters, Branches and Services Commander Royal Artillery : 1 November 1917 - 29 January 1919 (First World War, War Diary, WO95/1460)	WD1460	9781474504911	£47.00
4 DIVISION Headquarters, Branches and Services Royal Army Medical Corps Assistant Director Medical Services : 22 August 1914 - 30 June 1916 (First World War, War Diary, WO95/1461)	WD1461	9781474521956	£70.00
4 DIVISION Headquarters, Branches and Services Royal Army Medical Corps Assistant Director Medical Services : 19 July 1917 - 29 January 1919 (First World War, War Diary, WO95/1462)	WD1462	9781474504928	£34.00
4 DIVISION Headquarters, Branches and Services Commander Royal Engineers : 10 August 1914 - 31 December 1916 (First World War, War Diary, WO95/1463)	WD1463	9781474504935	£53.00
4 DIVISION Headquarters, Branches and Services Commander Royal Engineers : 1 January 1917 - 28 February 1919 (First World War, War Diary, WO95/1464)	WD1464	9781474504942	£45.00
4 DIVISION Headquarters, Branches and Services Royal Army Ordnance Corps Deputy Assistant Director Ordnance Services and Royal Army Veterinary Corps Assistant Director Veterinary Services : 4 August 1914 - 31 March 1919 (First World War, War Diary, WO95/	WD1465	9781474504959	£83.00
4 DIVISION Divisional Troops `B' Squadron 19 Hussars, `A' Squadron Northants Yeomanry, Divisional Cyclist Company, 14 Brigade Royal Field Artillery and 29 Brigade Royal Field Artillery : 22 August 1914 - 14 April 1915 (First World War, War Diary, WO95/1	WD1466	9781474504966	£44.00
4 DIVISION Divisional Troops 32, 37 and 127 Brigades Royal Field Artillery : 3 August 1914 - 21 May 1916 (First World War, War Diary, WO95/1467)	WD1467	9781474504973	£28.00
4 DIVISION Divisional Troops Divisional Ammunition Column and Divisional Trench Mortar Batteries: 4 August 1914 - 31 December 1917 (First World War, War Diary, WO95/1468)	WD1468	9781474504980	£37.00
4 DIVISION Divisional Troops 7 and 9 Field Company Royal Engineers, 1/1 West Lancashire, Field Company Royal Engineers : 5 August 1914 - 29 February 1916 (First World War, War Diary, WO95/1469)	WD1469	9781474504997	£38.00
4 DIVISION Divisional Troops 406 Field Company Royal Engineers (formerly 1/1 Renfrew) : 24 June 1914 - 21 June 1919 (First World War, War Diary, WO95/1470/1)	WD1470_1	9781474505000	£20.00

Title	Product Code	ISBN	Price
4 DIVISION Divisional Troops 526 Field Company Royal Engineers : 18 September 1915 - 28 February 1919 (First World War, War Diary, WO95/1470/2)	WD1470_2	9781474505017	£19.00
4 DIVISION Divisional Troops Divisional Signal Company : 4 August 1914 - 28 February 1919 (First World War, War Diary, WO95/1471)	WD1471	9781474505024	£50.00
4 DIVISION Divisional Troops Machine Gun Corps 4 Battalion : 3 March 1918 - 28 February 1919 (First World War, War Diary, WO95/1472/1)	WD1472_1	9781474505031	£15.00
4 DIVISION Divisional Troops 234 Machine Gun Company : 13 July 1917 - 28 February 1918 (First World War, War Diary, WO95/1472/2)	WD1472_2	9781474505048	£15.00
4 DIVISION Divisional Troops Prince of Wales's Own (West Yorkshire Regiment) 21st Battalion Pioneers : 14 June 1916 - 28 February 1919 (First World War, War Diary, WO95/1472/3)	WD1472_3	9781474505055	£15.00
4 DIVISION Divisional Troops Royal Army Medical Corps 10 Field Ambulance : 7 August 1914 - 28 February 1919 (First World War, War Diary, WO95/1473)	WD1473	9781474505062	£62.00
4 DIVISION Divisional Troops Royal Army Medical Corps 12 Field Ambulance : 1 January 1914 - 19 June 1919 (First World War, War Diary, WO95/1474)	WD1474	9781474505079	£64.00
4 DIVISION Divisional Troops Royal Army Medical Corps 11 Field Ambulance and 3 `A' Sanitary Section : 23 August 1914 - 31 March 1917 (First World War, War Diary, WO95/1475)	WD1475	9781474505086	£46.00
4 DIVISION Divisional Troops Royal Army Veterinary Corps 4 Mobile Veterinary Section and Divisional Train (18, 25, 32, 38 Companies A.S.C.) : 4 August 1914 - 31 December 1915 (First World War, War Diary, WO95/1476)	WD1476	9781474505093	£45.00
4 DIVISION 10 Infantry Brigade Headquarters : 31 July 1914 - 31 December 1914 (First World War, War Diary, WO95/1477)	WD1477	9781474505109	£56.00
4 DIVISION 10 Infantry Brigade Headquarters : 1 January 1915 - 30 June 1916 (First World War, War Diary, WO95/1478)	WD1478	9781474505116	£56.00
4 DIVISION 10 Infantry Brigade Headquarters : 1 July 1916 - 30 September 1917 (First World War, War Diary, WO95/1479)	WD1479	9781474505123	£53.00
4 DIVISION 10 Infantry Brigade Headquarters : 1 October 1917 - 14 June 1919 (First World War, War Diary, WO95/1480)	WD1480	9781474505130	£56.00
4 DIVISION 10 Infantry Brigade Household Battalion : 6 November 1916 - 15 February 1918 (First World War, War Diary, WO95/1481/1)	WD1481_1	9781474505147	£19.00
4 DIVISION 10 Infantry Brigade Princess Louise's (Argyll & Sutherland Highlanders) 1/7th Battalion : 1 December 1914 - 30 June 1915 (First World War, War Diary, WO95/1481/2)	WD1481_2	9781474505154	£15.00
4 DIVISION 10 Infantry Brigade Duke of Wellington's (West Riding Regiment) 2nd Battalion : 1 January 1918 - 6 June 1919 (First World War, War Diary, WO95/1481/3)	WD1481_3	9781474505161	£18.00
4 DIVISION 10 Infantry Brigade Royal Dublin Fusiliers 2nd Battalion : 22 August 1914 - 31 October 1916 (First World War, War Diary, WO95/1481/4)	WD1481_4	9781474505178	£22.00
4 DIVISION 10 Infantry Brigade Royal Irish Rifles 1st Battalion : 8 August 1914 - 31 July 1917 (First World War, War Diary, WO95/1482/1)	WD1482_1	9781474505185	£37.00

Title	Product Code	ISBN	Price
4 DIVISION 10 Infantry Brigade Duke of Cambridge's Own (Middlesex Regiment) 3/10th (T.F.) Battalion : 16 June 1917 - 22 February 1918 (First World War, War Diary, WO95/1482/2)	WD1482_2	9781474505192	£15.00
4 DIVISION 10 Infantry Brigade Seaforth Highlanders (Ross-shire Buffs, the Duke of Albany's) 2nd Battalion : 4 August 1914 - 23 April 1919 (First World War, War Diary, WO95/1483)	WD1483	9781474505208	£67.00
4 DIVISION 10 Infantry Brigade Royal Warwickshire Regiment 1st Battalion : 30 July 1914 - 10 June 1919 (First World War, War Diary, WO95/1484)	WD1484	9781474505215	£60.00
4 DIVISION 10 Infantry Brigade, Brigade Machine Gun Company and Brigade Trench Mortar Battery : 17 January 1916 - 31 January 1919 (First World War, War Diary, WO95/1485)	WD1485	9781474505222	£25.00
4 DIVISION 11 Infantry Brigade Headquarters : 18 August 1914 - 31 December 1914 (First World War, War Diary, WO95/1486)	WD1486	9781474505239	£46.00
4 DIVISION 11 Infantry Brigade Headquarters - Appendices to 1486 : 1 October 1914 - 19 October 1914 (First World War, War Diary, WO95/1487A)	WD1487_A	9781474521963	£46.00
4 DIVISION 11 Infantry Brigade Headquarters - Appendices to 1486 : 19 October 1914 - 31 October 1914 (First World War, War Diary, WO95/1487B)	WD1487_B	9781474521970	£51.00
4 DIVISION 11 Infantry Brigade Headquarters - Appendices to 1486 : 31 October 1914 - 10 November 1914 (First World War, War Diary, WO95/1488A)	WD1488_A	9781474521987	£67.00
4 DIVISION 11 Infantry Brigade Headquarters - Appendices to 1486 : 15 November 1914 - 5 December 1914 (First World War, War Diary, WO95/1488B)	WD1488_B	9781474521994	£57.00
4 DIVISION 11 Infantry Brigade Headquarters - Appendices to 1486 : 10 December 1914 - 26 December 1914 (First World War, War Diary, WO95/1488C)	WD1488_C	9781474522007	£66.00
4 DIVISION 11 Infantry Brigade Headquarters : 1 January 1915 - 12 December 1915 (First World War, War Diary, WO95/1489)	WD1489	9781474505246	£53.00
4 DIVISION 11 Infantry Brigade Headquarters : 1 January 1916 - 31 December 1916 (First World War, War Diary, WO95/1490)	WD1490	9781474505253	£65.00
4 DIVISION 11 Infantry Brigade Headquarters : 1 January 1917 - 31 July 1917 (First World War, War Diary, WO95/1491)	WD1491	9781474505260	£48.00
4 DIVISION 11 Infantry Brigade Headquarters : 1 August 1917 - 31 March 1918 (First World War, War Diary, WO95/1492)	WD1492	9781474505277	£53.00
4 DIVISION 11 Infantry Brigade Headquarters : 1 April 1918 - 10 August 1918 (First World War, War Diary, WO95/1493)	WD1493	9781474505284	£59.00
4 DIVISION 11 Infantry Brigade Headquarters : 1 September 1918 - 20 June 1919 (First World War, War Diary, WO95/1494)	WD1494	9781474505291	£48.00
4 DIVISION 11 Infantry Brigade Hampshire Regiment 1st Battalion : 22 August 1914 - 20 June 1919 (First World War, War Diary, WO95/1495)	WD1495	9781474505307	£49.00
4 DIVISION 11 Infantry Brigade Rifle Brigade (The Prince Consort's Own) 1st Battalion : 5 August 1914 - 31 December 1917 (First World War, War Diary, WO95/1496)	WD1496	9781474505314	£56.00

Title	Product Code	ISBN	Price
4 DIVISION 11 Infantry Brigade Rifle Brigade (The Prince Consort's Own) 1st Battalion : 1 January 1918 - 23 April 1919 (First World War, War Diary, WO95/1497/1)	WD1497_1	9781474505321	£32.00
4 DIVISION 11 Infantry Brigade Royal Irish Regiment 2nd Battalion : 1 March 1915 - 31 May 1916 (First World War, War Diary, WO95/1497/2)	WD1497_2	9781474505338	£15.00
4 DIVISION 11 Infantry Brigade East Lancashire Regiment 1st Battalion : 5 August 1914 - 28 February 1918 (First World War, War Diary, WO95/1498/1)	WD1498_1	9781474505345	£42.00
4 DIVISION 11 Infantry Brigade London Regiment 5th (City of London) Battalion (London Rifle Brigade) : 4 November 1914 - 31 January 1916 (First World War, War Diary, WO95/1498/2)	WD1498_2	9781474505352	£15.00
4 DIVISION 11 Infantry Brigade Prince Albert's (Somerset Light Infantry) 1st Battalion : 4 August 1914 - 28 February 1919 (First World War, War Diary, WO95/1499)	WD1499	9781474505369	£55.00
4 DIVISION 11 Infantry Brigade, Brigade Machine Gun Company : 23 December 1915 - 28 February 1918 (First World War, War Diary, WO95/1500/1)	WD1500_1	9781474505376	£44.00
4 DIVISION 11 Infantry Brigade, Brigade Trench Mortar Battery : 1 August 1916 - 31 August 1916 (First World War, War Diary, WO95/1500/2)	WD1500_2	9781474505383	£15.00
4 DIVISION 12 Infantry Brigade Headquarters : 7 August 1914 - 31 December 1915 (First World War, War Diary, WO95/1501)	WD1501	9781474505390	£52.00
4 DIVISION 12 Infantry Brigade Headquarters : 1 January 1916 - 30 April 1917 (First World War, War Diary, WO95/1502)	WD1502	9781474505406	£56.00
4 DIVISION 12 Infantry Brigade Headquarters : 1 May 1917 - 31 December 1917 (First World War, War Diary, WO95/1503)	WD1503	9781474505413	£60.00
4 DIVISION 12 Infantry Brigade Headquarters : 1 January 1918 - 28 February 1919 (First World War, War Diary, WO95/1504)	WD1504	9781474505420	£51.00
4 DIVISION 12 Infantry Brigade Essex Regiment 2nd Battalion : 4 August 1914 - 28 February 1919 (First World War, War Diary, WO95/1505/1)	WD1505_1	9781474505437	£41.00
4 DIVISION 12 Infantry Brigade Royal Inniskilling Fusiliers 2nd Battalion : 25 August 1914 - 31 December 1914 (First World War, War Diary, WO95/1505/2)	WD1505_2	9781474505444	£15.00
4 DIVISION 12 Infantry Brigade King's Own (Royal Lancaster Regiment) 1st Battalion and Monmouthshire Regiment (Territorial Force) 2nd Battalion : 4 August 1914 - 31 January 1916 (First World War, War Diary, WO95/1506)	WD1506	9781474505451	£35.00
4 DIVISION 12 Infantry Brigade Lancashire Fusiliers 2nd Battalion : 23 August 1914 - 28 February 1919 (First World War, War Diary, WO95/1507)	WD1507	9781474505468	£32.00
4 DIVISION 12 Infantry Brigade Duke of Wellington's (West Riding Regiment) 2nd Battalion and Prince of Wales's Volunteers (South Lancashire Regiment) 1/5th Battalion : 13 February 1915 - 27 November 1915 (First World War, War Diary, WO95/1508)	WD1508	9781474505475	£41.00
4 DIVISION 12 Infantry Brigade, Brigade Machine Gun Company : 24 January 1916 - 11 January 1918 (First World War, War Diary, WO95/1509/1)	WD1509_1	9781474505482	£20.00
4 DIVISION 12 Infantry Brigade, Brigade Trench Mortar Battery : 11 June 1916 - 30 April 1918 (First World War, War Diary, WO95/1509/2)	WD1509_2	9781474505499	£15.00

Title	Product Code	ISBN	Price
40 DIVISION			
40 DIVISION Headquarters, Branches and Services General Staff : 5 June 1916 - 30 June 1917 (First World War, War Diary, WO95/2592)	WD2592	9781474519267	£57.00
40 DIVISION Headquarters, Branches and Services General Staff : 1 July 1917 - 31 May 1918 (First World War, War Diary, WO95/2593)	WD2593	9781474525633	£75.00
40 DIVISION Headquarters, Branches and Services General Staff : 1 June 1918 - 25 March 1919 (First World War, War Diary, WO95/2594/1)	WD2594_1	9781474519274	£26.00
40 DIVISION Headquarters, Branches and Services Adjutant and Quarter-Master General : 4 June 1916 - 28 February 1919 (First World War, War Diary, WO95/2594/2)	WD2594_2	9781474519281	£28.00
40 DIVISION Headquarters, Branches and Services Commander Royal Artillery : 1 January 1915 - 31 October 1917 (First World War, War Diary, WO95/2595)	WD2595	9781474525640	£72.00
40 DIVISION Headquarters, Branches and Services Commander Royal Artillery : 1 November 1917 - 28 February 1918 (First World War, War Diary, WO95/2596)	WD2596	9781474519298	£57.00
40 DIVISION Headquarters, Branches and Services Royal Army Medical Corps Assistant Director Medical Services : 2 June 1916 - 31 March 1919 (First World War, War Diary, WO95/2597/1)	WD2597_1	9781474519304	£23.00
40 DIVISION Headquarters, Branches and Services Commander Royal Engineers : 3 June 1916 - 28 February 1919 (First World War, War Diary, WO95/2597/2)	WD2597_2	9781474519311	£15.00
40 DIVISION Headquarters, Branches and Services Royal Army Ordnance Corps Deputy Assistant Director Ordnance Services : 3 January 1916 - 30 April 1919 (First World War, War Diary, WO95/2597/3)	WD2597_3	9781474519328	£16.00
40 DIVISION Headquarters, Branches and Services Royal Army Veterinary Corps Assistant Director Veterinary Services : 3 June 1916 - 16 March 1919 (First World War, War Diary, WO95/2597/4)	WD2597_4	9781474519335	£15.00
40 DIVISION Divisional Troops 178 Brigade Royal Field Artillery : 2 June 1916 - 31 March 1919 (First World War, War Diary, WO95/2598/1)	WD2598_1	9781474519342	£15.00
40 DIVISION Divisional Troops 181 Brigade Royal Field Artillery : 1 June 1916 - 31 December 1918 (First World War, War Diary, WO95/2598/2)	WD2598_2	9781474519359	£47.00
40 DIVISION Divisional Troops 185 Brigade Royal Field Artillery : 4 June 1916 - 31 August 1916 (First World War, War Diary, WO95/2599/1)	WD2599_1	9781474519366	£15.00
40 DIVISION Divisional Troops 188 Brigade Royal Field Artillery : 4 June 1916 - 1 January 1917 (First World War, War Diary, WO95/2599/2)	WD2599_2	9781474519373	£15.00
40 DIVISION Divisional Troops Divisional Trench Mortar Batteries : 6 June 1916 - 27 April 1918 (First World War, War Diary, WO95/2599/3)	WD2599_3	9781474519380	£15.00
40 DIVISION Divisional Troops Divisional Ammunition Column : 8 March 1915 - 31 January 1919 (First World War, War Diary, WO95/2599/4)	WD2599_4	9781474519397	£25.00
40 DIVISION Divisional Troops 224 Field Company Royal Engineers : 1 June 1916 - 30 April 1919 (First World War, War Diary, WO95/2600/1)	WD2600_1	9781474519403	£19.00
40 DIVISION Divisional Troops 229 Field Company Royal Engineers : 2 June 1916 - 11 June 1919 (First World War, War Diary, WO95/2600/2)	WD2600_2	9781474519410	£15.00
40 DIVISION Divisional Troops 231 Field Company Royal Engineers : 3 June 1916 - 31 March 1918 (First World War, War Diary, WO95/2601/1)	WD2601_1	9781474519427	£15.00

Title	Product Code	ISBN	Price
40 DIVISION Divisional Troops Divisional Signal Company : 1 June 1916 - 31 March 1919 (First World War, War Diary, WO95/2601/2)	WD2601_2	9781474519434	£15.00
40 DIVISION Divisional Troops Alexandra, Princess of Wales's Own (Yorkshire Regiment) 12th Battalion Pioneers : 27 May 1916 - 28 June 1918 (First World War, War Diary, WO95/2601/3)	WD2601_3	9781474519441	£15.00
40 DIVISION Divisional Troops Worcestershire Regiment 17th Battalion Pioneers : 1 May 1918 - 8 October 1919 (First World War, War Diary, WO95/2601/4)	WD2601_4	9781474519458	£15.00
40 DIVISION Divisional Troops Machine Gun Corps 40 Battalion : 25 February 1918 - 10 May 1918 (First World War, War Diary, WO95/2601/5)	WD2601_5	9781474519465	£15.00
40 DIVISION Divisional Troops 244 Machine Gun Company : 15 July 1917 - 28 February 1918 (First World War, War Diary, WO95/2601/6)	WD2601_6	9781474519472	£15.00
40 DIVISION Divisional Troops Royal Army Medical Corps 135 Field Ambulance : 1 June 1916 - 28 May 1919 (First World War, War Diary, WO95/2602/1)	WD2602_1	9781474519489	£17.00
40 DIVISION Divisional Troops Royal Army Medical Corps 136 Field Ambulance : 1 June 1916 - 29 May 1919 (First World War, War Diary, WO95/2602/2)	WD2602_2	9781474519496	£15.00
40 DIVISION Divisional Troops Royal Army Medical Corps 137 Field Ambulance : 2 June 1916 - 31 May 1919 (First World War, War Diary, WO95/2602/3)	WD2602_3	9781474519502	£18.00
40 DIVISION Divisional Troops 83 Sanitary Section : 7 June 1916 - 31 March 1917 (First World War, War Diary, WO95/2603/1)	WD2603_1	9781474519519	£15.00
40 DIVISION Divisional Troops Royal Army Veterinary Corps 51 Mobile Veterinary Section : 4 June 1916 - 31 March 1919 (First World War, War Diary, WO95/2603/2)	WD2603_2	9781474519526	£15.00
40 DIVISION Divisional Troops Royal Army Service Corps Divisional Train (292, 293, 294, 295 Companies A.S.C.) : 1 June 1916 - 16 June 1919 (First World War, War Diary, WO95/2603/3)	WD2603_3	9781474519533	£29.00
40 DIVISION 119 Infantry Brigade Headquarters : 5 June 1916 - 28 June 1917 (First World War, War Diary, WO95/2604)	WD2604	9781474519540	£69.00
40 DIVISION 119 Infantry Brigade Headquarters : 1 July 1917 - 30 April 1919 (First World War, War Diary, WO95/2605)	WD2605	9781474519557	£54.00
40 DIVISION 119 Infantry Brigade Royal Inniskilling Fusiliers 13th Battalion : 10 June 1918 - 30 April 1919 (First World War, War Diary, WO95/2606/1)	WD2606_1	9781474519564	£15.00
40 DIVISION 119 Infantry Brigade East Lancashire Regiment 13th Battalion : 10 June 1918 - 30 April 1919 (First World War, War Diary, WO95/2606/2)	WD2606_2	9781474519571	£15.00
40 DIVISION 119 Infantry Brigade Duke of Cambridge's Own (Middlesex Regiment) 21st Battalion : 1 February 1918 - 30 June 1918 (First World War, War Diary, WO95/2606/3)	WD2606_3	9781474519588	£15.00
40 DIVISION 119 Infantry Brigade East Surrey Regiment 13th Battalion : 1 February 1918 - 31 July 1918 (First World War, War Diary, WO95/2606/4)	WD2606_4	9781474519595	£15.00
40 DIVISION 119 Infantry Brigade Prince of Wales's (North Staffordshire Regiment) 12th Battalion : 10 June 1918 - 4 June 1919 (First World War, War Diary, WO95/2606/5)	WD2606_5	9781474519601	£15.00
40 DIVISION 119 Infantry Brigade South Wales Borderers 12th Battalion : 1 June 1916 - 16 February 1918 (First World War, War Diary, WO95/2606/6)	WD2606_6	9781474519618	£15.00

Title	Product Code	ISBN	Price
40 DIVISION 119 Infantry Brigade Welsh Regiment 17th Battalion : 10 December 1915 - 2 November 1917 (First World War, War Diary, WO95/2607/1)	WD2607_1	9781474519625	£18.00
40 DIVISION 119 Infantry Brigade Welsh Regiment 18th Battalion. : 13 June 1915 - 17 June 1918 (First World War, War Diary, WO95/2607/2)	WD2607_2	9781474519632	£15.00
40 DIVISION 119 Infantry Brigade Royal Welsh Fusiliers 19th Battalion : 2 June 1916 - 15 February 1918 (First World War, War Diary, WO95/2607/3)	WD2607_3	9781474519649	£32.00
40 DIVISION 119 Infantry Brigade, Brigade Machine Gun Company : 16 June 1916 - 28 February 1918 (First World War, War Diary, WO95/2607/4)	WD2607_4	9781474519656	£15.00
40 DIVISION 119 Infantry Brigade, Brigade Trench Mortar Battery : 25 June 1916 - 31 August 1916 (First World War, War Diary, WO95/2607/5)	WD2607_5	9781474519663	£15.00
40 DIVISION 120 Infantry Brigade Headquarters : 1 January 1916 - 30 April 1917 (First World War, War Diary, WO95/2608)	WD2608	9781474519670	£53.00
40 DIVISION 120 Infantry Brigade Headquarters : 1 May 1917 - 28 February 1918 (First World War, War Diary, WO95/2609)	WD2609	9781474519687	£66.00
40 DIVISION 120 Infantry Brigade Headquarters : 1 March 1918 - 28 February 1919 (First World War, War Diary, WO95/2610/1)	WD2610_1	9781474519694	£35.00
40 DIVISION 120 Infantry Brigade Headquarters : 13 April 1918 - 15 March 1919 (First World War, War Diary, WO95/2610/2)	WD2610_2	9781474519700	£21.00
40 DIVISION 120 Infantry Brigade Princess Louise's (Argyll & Sutherland Highlanders) 14th Battalion : 27 May 1916 - 31 March 1918 (First World War, War Diary, WO95/2611/1)	WD2611_1	9781474519717	£23.00
40 DIVISION 120 Infantry Brigade Queen's Own Cameron Highlanders 11th Battalion : 9 June 1918 - 1 May 1919 (First World War, War Diary, WO95/2611/2)	WD2611_2	9781474519724	£15.00
40 DIVISION 120 Infantry Brigade King's Own (Royal Lancaster Regiment) 11th Battalion : 2 June 1916 - 17 February 1918 (First World War, War Diary, WO95/2611/3)	WD2611_3	9781474519731	£40.00
40 DIVISION 120 Infantry Brigade King's Own Scottish Borderers 10th Battalion : 10 June 1918 - 28 February 1919 (First World War, War Diary, WO95/2611/4)	WD2611_4	9781474519748	£15.00
40 DIVISION 120 Infantry Brigade Highland Light Infantry 14th (Service) Battalion : 3 June 1916 - 30 April 1919 (First World War, War Diary, WO95/2612/1)	WD2612_1	9781474519755	£15.00
40 DIVISION 120 Infantry Brigade King's Own (Yorkshire Light Infantry) 15th Battalion : 1 March 1918 - 6 June 1919 (First World War, War Diary, WO95/2612/2)	WD2612_2	9781474519762	£17.00
40 DIVISION 120 Infantry Brigade East Surrey Regiment 13th Battalion : 3 June 1916 - 30 January 1918 (First World War, War Diary, WO95/2612/3)	WD2612_3	9781474519779	£21.00
40 DIVISION 120 Infantry Brigade, Brigade Machine Gun Company : 15 June 1916 - 28 February 1918 (First World War, War Diary, WO95/2612/4)	WD2612_4	9781474519786	£15.00
40 DIVISION 120 Infantry Brigade, Brigade Trench Mortar Battery : 26 June 1916 - 31 August 1916 (First World War, War Diary, WO95/2612/5)	WD2612_5	9781474519793	£15.00
40 DIVISION 121 Infantry Brigade Headquarters : 27 May 1916 - 16 October 1916 (First World War, War Diary, WO95/2613)	WD2613	9781474519809	£45.00
40 DIVISION 121 Infantry Brigade Headquarters : 1 August 1917 - 24 March 1919 (First World War, War Diary, WO95/2614)	WD2614	9781474519816	£51.00

Title	Product Code	ISBN	Price
40 DIVISION 121 Infantry Brigade Cheshire Regiment 23rd Battalion, Lancashire Fusiliers 23rd Battalion, Royal Irish Regiment 8th Battalion, Duke of Cambridge's Own (Middlesex Regiment) 20th and 21st Battalion : 27 May 1916 - 31 August 1918 (First World Wa	WD2615	9781474519823	£70.00
40 DIVISION 121 Infantry Brigade Suffolk Regiment 12th Battalion : 27 May 1916 - 31 May 1918 (First World War, War Diary, WO95/2616/1)	WD2616_1	9781474519830	£16.00
40 DIVISION 121 Infantry Brigade Alexandra, Princess of Wales's Own (Yorkshire Regiment) 13th Battalion : 27 May 1916 - 31 July 1918 (First World War, War Diary, WO95/2616/2)	WD2616_2	9781474519847	£17.00
40 DIVISION 121 Infantry Brigade, Brigade Machine Gun Company : 15 June 1916 - 28 February 1918 (First World War, War Diary, WO95/2616/3)	WD2616_3	9781474519854	£18.00
40 DIVISION 121 Infantry Brigade, Brigade Trench Mortar Battery : 15 June 1916 - 31 August 1916 (First World War, War Diary, WO95/2616/4)	WD2616_4	9781474519861	£15.00

Title	Product Code	ISBN	Price
41 DIVISION			
41 DIVISION Headquarters, Branches and Services General Staff : 1 May 1916 - 31 May 1918 (First World War, War Diary, WO95/2617)	WD2617	9781474525657	£65.00
41 DIVISION Headquarters, Branches and Services General Staff : 1 June 1918 - 31 October 1919 (First World War, War Diary, WO95/2618)	WD2618	9781474519878	£73.00
41 DIVISION Headquarters, Branches and Services Appendices to 2617 : 15 September 1915 - 18 September 1918 (First World War, War Diary, WO95/2619)	WD2619	9781474519885	£44.00
41 DIVISION Headquarters, Branches and Services Adjutant and Quarter-Master General : 17 August 1916 - 31 October 1917 (First World War, War Diary, WO95/2620/1)	WD2620_1	9781474519892	£26.00
41 DIVISION Headquarters, Branches and Services Adjutant and Quarter-Master General : 1 May 1916 - 30 August 1918 (First World War, War Diary, WO95/2620/2)	WD2620_2	9781474519908	£15.00
41 DIVISION Headquarters, Branches and Services Commander Royal Artillery : 1 May 1916 - 31 December 1916 (First World War, War Diary, WO95/2620/3)	WD2620_3	9781474519915	£25.00
41 DIVISION Headquarters, Branches and Services Commander Royal Artillery : 1 January 1917 - 31 October 1917 (First World War, War Diary, WO95/2621/1)	WD2621_1	9781474519922	£37.00
41 DIVISION Headquarters, Branches and Services Commander Royal Artillery : 1 March 1918 - 31 March 1919 (First World War, War Diary, WO95/2621/2)	WD2621_2	9781474519939	£28.00
41 DIVISION Headquarters, Branches and Services Royal Army Medical Corps Assistant Director Medical Services : 2 May 1916 - 30 September 1918 (First World War, War Diary, WO95/2622)	WD2622	9781474525664	£52.00
41 DIVISION Headquarters, Branches and Services Royal Army Medical Corps Assistant Director Medical Services : 1 October 1918 - 31 October 1919 (First World War, War Diary, WO95/2623)	WD2623	9781474519946	£60.00
41 DIVISION Headquarters, Branches and Services Commander Royal Engineers : 4 May 1916 - 31 October 1917 (First World War, War Diary, WO95/2624/1)	WD2624_1	9781474519953	£15.00
41 DIVISION Headquarters, Branches and Services Commander Royal Engineers : 1 March 1918 - 31 October 1919 (First World War, War Diary, WO95/2624/2)	WD2624_2	9781474519960	£15.00
41 DIVISION Headquarters, Branches and Services Royal Army Ordnance Corps Deputy Assistant Director Ordnance Services : 27 April 1916 - 31 October 1917 (First World War, War Diary, WO95/2624/3)	WD2624_3	9781474519977	£15.00
41 DIVISION Headquarters, Branches and Services Royal Army Ordnance Corps Deputy Assistant Director Ordnance Services : 1 March 1918 - 30 November 1919 (First World War, War Diary, WO95/2624/4)	WD2624_4	9781474519984	£15.00
41 DIVISION Headquarters, Branches and Services Royal Army Veterinary Corps Assistant Director Veterinary Services : 2 May 1916 - 31 October 1917 (First World War, War Diary, WO95/2624/5)	WD2624_5	9781474519991	£15.00
41 DIVISION Headquarters, Branches and Services Royal Army Veterinary Corps Assistant Director Veterinary Services : 1 March 1918 - 30 September 1919 (First World War, War Diary, WO95/2624/6)	WD2624_6	9781474520003	£15.00

Title	Product Code	ISBN	Price
41 DIVISION Divisional Troops 183 Brigade Royal Field Artillery : 1 May 1916 - 18 November 1916 (First World War, War Diary, WO95/2625/1)	WD2625_1	9781474520010	£15.00
41 DIVISION Divisional Troops 187 Brigade Royal Field Artillery : 1 May 1916 - 25 October 1919 (First World War, War Diary, WO95/2625/2)	WD2625_2	9781474520027	£15.00
41 DIVISION Divisional Troops 189 and 190 Brigade Royal Field Artillery : 3 May 1916 - 30 April 1917 (First World War, War Diary, WO95/2625/3)	WD2625_3	9781474520034	£15.00
41 DIVISION Divisional Troops 190 Brigade Royal Field Artillery : 5 May 1916 - 29 October 1919 (First World War, War Diary, WO95/2625/4)	WD2625_4	9781474520041	£15.00
41 DIVISION Divisional Troops Divisional Trench Mortar Batteries : 17 May 1916 - 29 October 1917 (First World War, War Diary, WO95/2625/5)	WD2625_5	9781474520058	£15.00
41 DIVISION Divisional Troops Divisional Trench Mortar Batteries : 1 March 1918 - 29 October 1918 (First World War, War Diary, WO95/2625/6)	WD2625_6	9781474520065	£15.00
41 DIVISION Divisional Troops 13 Belgium Field Artillery : 1 January 1917 - 17 May 1917 (First World War, War Diary, WO95/2625/7)	WD2625_7	9781474520072	£15.00
41 DIVISION Divisional Troops Divisional Ammunition Column : 5 May 1916 - 29 October 1917 (First World War, War Diary, WO95/2625/8)	WD2625_8	9781474520089	£15.00
41 DIVISION Divisional Troops Divisional Ammunition Column : 6 March 1918 - 30 September 1919 (First World War, War Diary, WO95/2625/9)	WD2625_9	9781474520096	£15.00
41 DIVISION Divisional Troops 228, 233 and 237 Field Company Royal Engineers : 21 April 1916 - 30 September 1919 (First World War, War Diary, WO95/2626)	WD2626	9781474520102	£57.00
41 DIVISION Divisional Troops Divisional Signal Company : 1 May 1916 - 29 November 1917 (First World War, War Diary, WO95/2627/1)	WD2627_1	9781474520119	£15.00
41 DIVISION Divisional Troops Divisional Signal Company : 1 March 1918 - 27 September 1919 (First World War, War Diary, WO95/2627/2)	WD2627_2	9781474520126	£15.00
41 DIVISION Divisional Troops Duke of Cambridge's Own (Middlesex Regiment) 19th Battalion Pioneers : 15 May 1916 - 31 October 1919 (First World War, War Diary, WO95/2627/3)	WD2627_3	9781474520133	£15.00
41 DIVISION Divisional Troops Machine Gun Corps 41 Battalion : 1 March 1918 - 31 October 1919 (First World War, War Diary, WO95/2627/4)	WD2627_4	9781474520140	£20.00
41 DIVISION Divisional Troops 238 Machine Gun Company : 18 February 1917 - 30 September 1917 (First World War, War Diary, WO95/2627/5)	WD2627_5	9781474520157	£15.00
41 DIVISION Divisional Troops Royal Army Medical Corps 138 Field Ambulance : 3 May 1916 - 31 October 1917 (First World War, War Diary, WO95/2628/1)	WD2628_1	9781474520164	£15.00
41 DIVISION Divisional Troops Royal Army Medical Corps 138 Field Ambulance : 1 March 1918 - 31 May 1919 (First World War, War Diary, WO95/2628/2)	WD2628_2	9781474520171	£22.00
41 DIVISION Divisional Troops Royal Army Medical Corps 139 Field Ambulance : 21 April 1916 - 31 October 1917 (First World War, War Diary, WO95/2629/1)	WD2629_1	9781474520188	£22.00
41 DIVISION Divisional Troops Royal Army Medical Corps 139 Field Ambulance : 21 April 1917 - 31 October 1919 (First World War, War Diary, WO95/2629/2)	WD2629_2	9781474520195	£56.00

Title	Product Code	ISBN	Price
41 DIVISION Divisional Troops Royal Army Medical Corps 140 Field Ambulance : 5 May 1916 - 31 October 1917 (First World War, War Diary, WO95/2630/1)	WD2630_1	9781474520201	£15.00
41 DIVISION Divisional Troops Royal Army Medical Corps 140 Field Ambulance : 1 March 1918 - 31 October 1919 (First World War, War Diary, WO95/2630/2)	WD2630_2	9781474520218	£49.00
41 DIVISION Divisional Troops 84 Sanitary Section : 29 March 1916 - 31 March 1917 (First World War, War Diary, WO95/2630/3)	WD2630_3	9781474520225	£28.00
41 DIVISION Divisional Troops Royal Army Veterinary Corps 52 Mobile Veterinary Section : 31 May 1916 - 30 October 1917 (First World War, War Diary, WO95/2630/4)	WD2630_4	9781474520232	£15.00
41 DIVISION Divisional Troops Royal Army Veterinary Corps 52 Mobile Veterinary Section : 2 March 1918 - 29 October 1919 (First World War, War Diary, WO95/2630/5)	WD2630_5	9781474520249	£15.00
41 DIVISION Divisional Troops Royal Army Service Corps Divisional Train (296, 297, 298, 299 Companies ASC) : 28 April 1916 - 31 October 1919 (First World War, War Diary, WO95/2631/1)	WD2631_1	9781474520256	£16.00
41 DIVISION Divisional Troops Royal Army Service Corps Divisional Train (296, 297, 298, 299 Companies ASC) : 1 July 1916 - 30 April 1919 (First World War, War Diary, WO95/2631/2)	WD2631_2	9781474520263	£15.00
41 DIVISION Divisional Troops Royal Army Service Corps 296 Company ASC : 1 May 1916 - 30 September 1919 (First World War, War Diary, WO95/2631/3)	WD2631_3	9781474520270	£18.00
41 DIVISION Divisional Troops Royal Army Service Corps 297 Company ASC : 8 May 1916 - 31 October 1919 (First World War, War Diary, WO95/2631/4)	WD2631_4	9781474520287	£15.00
41 DIVISION Divisional Troops Royal Army Service Corps 298 Company ASC : 3 May 1916 - 31 October 1919 (First World War, War Diary, WO95/2631/5)	WD2631_5	9781474520294	£18.00
41 DIVISION Divisional Troops Royal Army Service Corps 299 Company ASC : 4 May 1916 - 30 September 1919 (First World War, War Diary, WO95/2631/6)	WD2631_6	9781474520300	£15.00
41 DIVISION 122 Infantry Brigade Headquarters : 3 May 1916 - 30 June 1917 (First World War, War Diary, WO95/2632)	WD2632	9781474520317	£78.00
41 DIVISION 122 Infantry Brigade Headquarters : 1 July 1917 - 31 July 1917 (First World War, War Diary, WO95/2633/1)	WD2633_1	9781474525671	£15.00
41 DIVISION 122 Infantry Brigade Headquarters : 1 March 1918 - 31 October 1919 (First World War, War Diary, WO95/2633/2)	WD2633_2	9781474525688	£60.00
41 DIVISION 122 Infantry Brigade East Surrey Regiment 9th and 12th Battalion : 1 April 1919 - 31 October 1919 (First World War, War Diary, WO95/2634/1)	WD2634_1	9781474520324	£15.00
41 DIVISION 122 Infantry Brigade East Surrey Regiment 12th Battalion : 1 May 1916 - 31 March 1919 (First World War, War Diary, WO95/2634/2)	WD2634_2	9781474520331	£34.00
41 DIVISION 122 Infantry Brigade Queen's Own (Royal West Kent Regiment) 11th Battalion : 3 May 1916 - 31 October 1917 (First World War, War Diary, WO95/2634/3)	WD2634_3	9781474520348	£21.00

Title	Product Code	ISBN	Price
41 DIVISION 122 Infantry Brigade Hampshire Regiment 15th (Service) Battalion : 2 May 1916 - 31 October 1917 (First World War, War Diary, WO95/2634/4)	WD2634_4	9781474520355	£15.00
41 DIVISION 122 Infantry Brigade Hampshire Regiment 15th (Service) Battalion : 1 March 1918 - 31 March 1919 (First World War, War Diary, WO95/2634/5)	WD2634_5	9781474520362	£15.00
41 DIVISION 122 Infantry Brigade Duke of Cambridge's Own (Middlesex Regiment) 1/7th and 23rd Battalion, King's Royal Rifle Corps 18th Battalion and Brigade Machine Gun Company : 2 May 1916 - 31 October 1917 (First World War, War Diary, WO95/2635)	WD2635	9781474525695	£77.00
41 DIVISION 123 Infantry Brigade Headquarters : 27 April 1916 - 30 June 1917 (First World War, War Diary, WO95/2636)	WD2636	9781474520379	£46.00
41 DIVISION 123 Infantry Brigade Headquarters : 1 July 1917 - 22 October 1919 (First World War, War Diary, WO95/2637)	WD2637	9781474520386	£36.00
41 DIVISION 123 Infantry Brigade Queen's Own (Royal West Kent Regiment) 10th Battalion : 25 April 1916 - 28 February 1919 (First World War, War Diary, WO95/2638/1)	WD2638_1	9781474520393	£29.00
41 DIVISION 123 Infantry Brigade Queen's (Royal West Surrey Regiment) 2/4th Battalion : 1 March 1919 - 30 September 1919 (First World War, War Diary, WO95/2638/2)	WD2638_2	9781474520409	£15.00
41 DIVISION 123 Infantry Brigade Queen's (Royal West Surrey Regiment) 10th Battalion : 1 March 1919 - 30 September 1919 (First World War, War Diary, WO95/2638/3)	WD2638_3	9781474520416	£15.00
41 DIVISION 123 Infantry Brigade Queen's (Royal West Surrey Regiment) 11th Battalion : 3 May 1916 - 31 October 1917 (First World War, War Diary, WO95/2638/4)	WD2638_4	9781474520423	£15.00
41 DIVISION 123 Infantry Brigade Queen's (Royal West Surrey Regiment) 11th Battalion : 1 March 1918 - 30 September 1919 (First World War, War Diary, WO95/2638/5)	WD2638_5	9781474520430	£17.00
41 DIVISION 123 Infantry Brigade Durham Light Infantry 20th Battalion : 4 May 1916 - 31 October 1917 (First World War, War Diary, WO95/2639/1)	WD2639_1	9781474520447	£16.00
41 DIVISION 123 Infantry Brigade Duke of Cambridge's Own (Middlesex Regiment) 23rd Battalion : 3 May 1916 - 31 October 1917 (First World War, War Diary, WO95/2639/2)	WD2639_2	9781474520454	£15.00
41 DIVISION 123 Infantry Brigade Duke of Cambridge's Own (Middlesex Regiment) 23rd Battalion : 1 March 1918 - 28 February 1919 (First World War, War Diary, WO95/2639/3)	WD2639_3	9781474520461	£15.00
41 DIVISION 123 Infantry Brigade, Brigade Machine Gun Company : 17 June 1916 - 31 October 1917 (First World War, War Diary, WO95/2639/4)	WD2639_4	9781474520478	£15.00
41 DIVISION 124 Infantry Brigade Headquarters : 4 May 1916 - 31 December 1916 (First World War, War Diary, WO95/2640)	WD2640	9781474520485	£39.00
41 DIVISION 124 Infantry Brigade Headquarters : 1 January 1917 - 31 October 1917 (First World War, War Diary, WO95/2641)	WD2641	9781474520492	£58.00
41 DIVISION 124 Infantry Brigade Headquarters : 1 March 1918 - 29 September 1919 (First World War, War Diary, WO95/2642)	WD2642	9781474520508	£58.00
41 DIVISION 124 Infantry Brigade Queen's (Royal West Surrey Regiment) 10th Battalion : 5 May 1916 - 31 October 1917 (First World War, War Diary, WO95/2643/1)	WD2643_1	9781474520515	£15.00

Title	Product Code	ISBN	Price
41 DIVISION 124 Infantry Brigade Queen's (Royal West Surrey Regiment) 10th Battalion : 1 March 1918 - 31 January 1919 (First World War, War Diary, WO95/2643/2)	WD2643_2	9781474520522	£15.00
41 DIVISION 124 Infantry Brigade Durham Light Infantry 20th Battalion : 1 March 1918 - 28 February 1919 (First World War, War Diary, WO95/2643/3)	WD2643_3	9781474520539	£15.00
41 DIVISION 124 Infantry Brigade King's Royal Rifle Corps 21st Battalion : 5 May 1916 - 31 October 1917 (First World War, War Diary, WO95/2643/4)	WD2643_4	9781474520546	£15.00
41 DIVISION 124 Infantry Brigade Royal Fusiliers (City of London Regiment) 17th Battalion : 1 April 1919 - 30 September 1919 (First World War, War Diary, WO95/2643/5)	WD2643_5	9781474520553	£15.00
41 DIVISION 124 Infantry Brigade Royal Fusiliers (City of London Regiment) 23rd Battalion : 1 March 1919 - 30 September 1919 (First World War, War Diary, WO95/2643/6)	WD2643_6	9781474520560	£15.00
41 DIVISION 124 Infantry Brigade Royal Fusiliers (City of London Regiment) 26th Battalion : 4 May 1916 - 30 September 1919 (First World War, War Diary, WO95/2644/1)	WD2644_1	9781474520577	£20.00
41 DIVISION 124 Infantry Brigade Royal Fusiliers (City of London Regiment) 32nd Battalion : 1 May 1916 - 31 October 1917 (First World War, War Diary, WO95/2644/2)	WD2644_2	9781474520584	£15.00
41 DIVISION 124 Infantry Brigade, Brigade Machine Gun Company and Brigade Trench Mortar Battery : 16 June 1916 - 31 August 1916 (First World War, War Diary, WO95/2644/3)	WD2644_3	9781474525701	£26.00

Title	Product Code	ISBN	Price
42 DIVISION			
42 DIVISION Headquarters, Branches and Services General Staff : 1 March 1917 - 31 December 1917 (First World War, War Diary, WO95/2645)	WD2645	9781474520591	£55.00
42 DIVISION Headquarters, Branches and Services General Staff : 1 January 1918 - 15 March 1919 (First World War, War Diary, WO95/2646)	WD2646	9781474520607	£57.00
42 DIVISION Headquarters, Branches and Services Adjutant and Quarter-Master General : 1 March 1917 - 31 January 1919 (First World War, War Diary, WO95/2647/1)	WD2647_1	9781474520614	£40.00
42 DIVISION Headquarters, Branches and Services Commander Royal Artillery : 1 March 1917 - 31 March 1919 (First World War, War Diary, WO95/2647/2)	WD2647_2	9781474520621	£25.00
42 DIVISION Headquarters, Branches and Services Royal Army Medical Corps Assistant Director Medical Services : 5 March 1917 - 28 February 1919 (First World War, War Diary, WO95/2648/1)	WD2648_1	9781474520638	£36.00
42 DIVISION Headquarters, Branches and Services Commander Royal Engineers : 1 March 1917 - 31 March 1919 (First World War, War Diary, WO95/2648/2)	WD2648_2	9781474520645	£15.00
42 DIVISION Headquarters, Branches and Services Royal Army Ordnance Corps Deputy Assistant Director Ordnance Services : 1 March 1917 - 28 February 1919 (First World War, War Diary, WO95/2648/3)	WD2648_3	9781474520652	£15.00
42 DIVISION Headquarters, Branches and Services Royal Army Veterinary Corps Deputy Assistant Director Veterinary Services : 2 March 1917 - 31 March 1919 (First World War, War Diary, WO95/2648/4)	WD2648_4	9781474520669	£15.00
42 DIVISION Divisional Troops 210 Brigade Royal Field Artillery : 1 March 1917 - 11 April 1919 (First World War, War Diary, WO95/2649/1)	WD2649_1	9781474520676	£25.00
42 DIVISION Divisional Troops 211 Brigade Royal Field Artillery : 1 March 1917 - 24 March 1919 (First World War, War Diary, WO95/2649/2)	WD2649_2	9781474520683	£15.00
42 DIVISION Divisional Troops Divisional Ammunition Column : 19 March 1917 - 29 March 1919 (First World War, War Diary, WO95/2649/3)	WD2649_3	9781474520690	£15.00
42 DIVISION Divisional Troops Divisional Trench Mortar Batteries : 1 April 1917 - 31 January 1919 (First World War, War Diary, WO95/2649/4)	WD2649_4	9781474520706	£15.00
42 DIVISION Divisional Troops 427 Field Company Royal Engineers : 1 March 1917 - 31 March 1919 (First World War, War Diary, WO95/2650/1)	WD2650_1	9781474520713	£15.00
42 DIVISION Divisional Troops 428 Field Company Royal Engineers : 26 February 1917 - 31 March 1919 (First World War, War Diary, WO95/2650/2)	WD2650_2	9781474520720	£15.00
42 DIVISION Divisional Troops 429 Field Company Royal Engineers : 1 March 1917 - 29 March 1919 (First World War, War Diary, WO95/2650/3)	WD2650_3	9781474520737	£15.00
42 DIVISION Divisional Troops Northumberland Fusiliers 1/7th Battalion (Territorials) Pioneers : 1 February 1918 - 14 April 1919 (First World War, War Diary, WO95/2650/4)	WD2650_4	9781474520744	£48.00
42 DIVISION Divisional Troops Machine Gun Corps 42 Battalion : 13 January 1918 - 30 June 1919 (First World War, War Diary, WO95/2650/5)	WD2650_5	9781474520751	£16.00
42 DIVISION Divisional Troops Divisional Signal Company : 1 March 1917 - 31 March 1919 (First World War, War Diary, WO95/2651)	WD2651	9781474520768	£31.00

Title	Product Code	ISBN	Price
42 DIVISION Divisional Troops Royal Army Medical Corps 1/1 East Lancashire Field Ambulance : 1 March 1917 - 28 February 1919 (First World War, War Diary, WO95/2652/1)	WD2652_1	9781474520775	£38.00
42 DIVISION Divisional Troops Royal Army Medical Corps 1/2 East Lancashire Field Ambulance : 6 March 1917 - 28 February 1919 (First World War, War Diary, WO95/2652/2)	WD2652_2	9781474520782	£17.00
42 DIVISION Divisional Troops Royal Army Medical Corps 1/3 East Lancashire Field Ambulance : 13 March 1917 - 2 April 1919 (First World War, War Diary, WO95/2652/3)	WD2652_3	9781474520799	£24.00
42 DIVISION Divisional Troops Royal Army Veterinary Corps 19 Mobile Veterinary Section : 1 March 1917 - 31 March 1919 (First World War, War Diary, WO95/2653/1)	WD2653_1	9781474520805	£15.00
42 DIVISION Divisional Troops Royal Army Service Corps Divisional Train (428-429-430-431 Companies A.S.C.) : 9 April 1916 - 14 April 1919 (First World War, War Diary, WO95/2653/2)	WD2653_2	9781474520812	£29.00
42 DIVISION 125 Infantry Brigade Headquarters : 1 March 1917 - 11 April 1919 (First World War, War Diary, WO95/2654/1)	WD2654_1	9781474520829	£32.00
42 DIVISION 125 Infantry Brigade Lancashire Fusiliers 1/5 Battalion (T.F.) : 1 March 1917 - 31 March 1919 (First World War, War Diary, WO95/2654/2)	WD2654_2	9781474520836	£17.00
42 DIVISION 125 Infantry Brigade Lancashire Fusiliers 1/6th Battalion : 1 March 1917 - 11 January 1918 (First World War, War Diary, WO95/2654/3)	WD2654_3	9781474520843	£15.00
42 DIVISION 125 Infantry Brigade Lancashire Fusiliers 1/7th Battalion : 16 June 1916 - 11 April 1919 (First World War, War Diary, WO95/2655/1)	WD2655_1	9781474520850	£15.00
42 DIVISION 125 Infantry Brigade Lancashire Fusiliers 1/8th Battalion : 1 March 1917 - 29 March 1919 (First World War, War Diary, WO95/2655/2)	WD2655_2	9781474520867	£15.00
42 DIVISION 125 Infantry Brigade, Brigade Machine Gun Company : 1 March 1917 - 28 February 1918 (First World War, War Diary, WO95/2655/3)	WD2655_3	9781474520874	£16.00
42 DIVISION 125 Infantry Brigade, Brigade Trench Mortar Battery : 1 July 1917 - 31 December 1918 (First World War, War Diary, WO95/2655/4)	WD2655_4	9781474525718	£15.00
42 DIVISION 126 Infantry Brigade Headquarters and East Lancashire Regiment 1/4th Battalion : 1 March 1917 - 24 September 1917 (First World War, War Diary, WO95/2656)	WD2656	9781474520881	£45.00
42 DIVISION 126 Infantry Brigade East Lancashire Regiment 1/5th Battalion and Manchester Regiment 1/8 Battalion : 1 March 1917 - 4 April 1919 (First World War, War Diary, WO95/2657)	WD2657	9781474520898	£59.00
42 DIVISION 126 Infantry Brigade Manchester Regiment 1/9th Battalion : 1 March 1917 - 19 February 1918 (First World War, War Diary, WO95/2658/1)	WD2658_1	9781474520904	£22.00
42 DIVISION 126 Infantry Brigade Manchester Regiment 1/10th Battalion : 1 March 1917 - 4 April 1919 (First World War, War Diary, WO95/2658/2)	WD2658_2	9781474520911	£27.00
42 DIVISION 126 Infantry Brigade, Brigade Machine Gun Company : 1 March 1917 - 28 February 1918 (First World War, War Diary, WO95/2658/3)	WD2658_3	9781474520928	£15.00
42 DIVISION 126 Infantry Brigade, Brigade Trench Mortar Battery : 26 March 1917 - 31 December 1918 (First World War, War Diary, WO95/2658/4)	WD2658_4	9781474520935	£17.00

Title	Product Code	ISBN	Price
42 DIVISION 127 Infantry Brigade Headquarters : 30 April 1916 - 28 March 1919 (First World War, War Diary, WO95/2659)	WD2659	9781474520942	£66.00
42 DIVISION 127 Infantry Brigade Manchester Regiment 1/5th Battalion : 1 March 1917 - 28 March 1919 (First World War, War Diary, WO95/2660/1)	WD2660_1	9781474520959	£47.00
42 DIVISION 127 Infantry Brigade Manchester Regiment 1/6th Battalion : 1 March 1917 - 28 March 1919 (First World War, War Diary, WO95/2660/2)	WD2660_2	9781474520966	£54.00
42 DIVISION 127 Infantry Brigade Manchester Regiment 1/7th Battalion : 24 February 1917 - 28 March 1919 (First World War, War Diary, WO95/2661/1)	WD2661_1	9781474520973	£23.00
42 DIVISION 127 Infantry Brigade Manchester Regiment 1/8 Battalion : 1 March 1917 - 31 January 1918 (First World War, War Diary, WO95/2661/2)	WD2661_2	9781474520980	£40.00
42 DIVISION 127 Infantry Brigade, Brigade Machine Gun Company : 1 March 1917 - 28 February 1918 (First World War, War Diary, WO95/2661/3)	WD2661_3	9781474520997	£15.00
42 DIVISION 127 Infantry Brigade, Brigade Trench Mortar Battery : 1 April 1917 - 31 December 1918 (First World War, War Diary, WO95/2661/4)	WD2661_4	9781474521000	£15.00

Title	Product Code	ISBN	Price
46 DIVISION			
46 DIVISION Headquarters, Branches and Services General Staff : 26 February 1915 - 31 December 1915 (First World War, War Diary, WO95/2662)	WD2662	9781474521017	£54.00
46 DIVISION Headquarters, Branches and Services General Staff : 1 January 1916 - 31 May 1917 (First World War, War Diary, WO95/2663)	WD2663	9781474521024	£67.00
46 DIVISION Headquarters, Branches and Services General Staff : 1 June 1917 - 31 October 1917 (First World War, War Diary, WO95/2664)	WD2664	9781474521031	£70.00
46 DIVISION Headquarters, Branches and Services General Staff : 1 November 1917 - 31 August 1918 (First World War, War Diary, WO95/2665)	WD2665	9781474521048	£64.00
46 DIVISION Headquarters, Branches and Services General Staff : 3 September 1916 - 21 March 1919 (First World War, War Diary, WO95/2666/1)	WD2666_1	9781474521055	£35.00
46 DIVISION Headquarters, Branches and Services Adjutant and Quarter-Master General : 23 February 1915 - 3 June 1915 (First World War, War Diary, WO95/2666/2)	WD2666_2	9781474521062	£15.00
46 DIVISION Headquarters, Branches and Services Commander Royal Artillery : 1 February 1915 - 30 June 1916 (First World War, War Diary, WO95/2667)	WD2667	9781474521079	£52.00
46 DIVISION Headquarters, Branches and Services Commander Royal Artillery : 1 July 1916 - 31 July 1917 (First World War, War Diary, WO95/2668)	WD2668	9781474521086	£51.00
46 DIVISION Headquarters, Branches and Services Commander Royal Artillery : 1 August 1917 - 31 March 1919 (First World War, War Diary, WO95/2669)	WD2669	9781474521093	£40.00
46 DIVISION Headquarters, Branches and Services Royal Army Medical Corps Assistant Director Medical Services : 1 March 1915 - 31 December 1916 (First World War, War Diary, WO95/2670)	WD2670	9781474521109	£56.00
46 DIVISION Headquarters, Branches and Services Royal Army Medical Corps Assistant Director Medical Services : 1 January 1917 - 31 March 1919 (First World War, War Diary, WO95/2671)	WD2671	9781474521116	£47.00
46 DIVISION Headquarters, Branches and Services Commander Royal Engineers : 19 August 1916 - 14 June 1919 (First World War, War Diary, WO95/2672/1)	WD2672_1	9781474521123	£25.00
46 DIVISION Headquarters, Branches and Services Royal Army Ordnance Corps Deputy Assistant Director Ordnance Services : 1 March 1915 - 28 February 1919 (First World War, War Diary, WO95/2672/2)	WD2672_2	9781474521130	£15.00
46 DIVISION Headquarters, Branches and Services Royal Army Veterinary Corps Assistant Director Veterinary Services : 3 September 1914 - 31 March 1919 (First World War, War Diary, WO95/2672/3)	WD2672_3	9781474521147	£18.00
46 DIVISION Divisional Troops B Squadron Yorkshire Hussars : 26 February 1915 - 31 May 1916 (First World War, War Diary, WO95/2673/1)	WD2673_1	9781474521154	£15.00
46 DIVISION Divisional Troops Divisional Cyclist Company : 1 February 1915 - 9 May 1916 (First World War, War Diary, WO95/2673/2)	WD2673_2	9781474521161	£15.00
46 DIVISION Divisional Troops 230 Brigade Royal Field Artillery : 4 February 1915 - 23 July 1919 (First World War, War Diary, WO95/2673/3)	WD2673_3	9781474521178	£37.00

Title	Product Code	ISBN	Price
46 DIVISION Divisional Troops 231 Brigade Royal Field Artillery : 1 February 1915 - 27 June 1919 (First World War, War Diary, WO95/2674/1)	WD2674_1	9781474521185	£46.00
46 DIVISION Divisional Troops 232 Brigade Royal Field Artillery : 1 January 1915 - 28 February 1917 (First World War, War Diary, WO95/2674/2)	WD2674_2	9781474521192	£16.00
46 DIVISION Divisional Troops 233 Brigade Royal Field Artillery : 1 February 1915 - 29 August 1916 (First World War, War Diary, WO95/2674/3)	WD2674_3	9781474521208	£17.00
46 DIVISION Divisional Troops 7 Belgium Artillery Regiment : 1 August 1915 - 30 December 1916 (First World War, War Diary, WO95/2675/1)	WD2675_1	9781474521215	£15.00
46 DIVISION Divisional Troops Divisional Trench Mortar Batteries : 17 March 1916 - 30 January 1919 (First World War, War Diary, WO95/2675/2)	WD2675_2	9781474521222	£18.00
46 DIVISION Divisional Troops Divisional Ammunition Column : 1 February 1915 - 30 June 1919 (First World War, War Diary, WO95/2675/3)	WD2675_3	9781474521239	£18.00
46 DIVISION Divisional Troops 465 Field Company Royal Engineers : 1 January 1915 - 22 June 1919 (First World War, War Diary, WO95/2676)	WD2676	9781474521246	£44.00
46 DIVISION Divisional Troops 466 Field Company Royal Engineers : 1 April 1915 - 12 July 1919 (First World War, War Diary, WO95/2677)	WD2677	9781474521253	£62.00
46 DIVISION Divisional Troops 468 Field Company Royal Engineers : 1 February 1915 - 23 June 1919 (First World War, War Diary, WO95/2678/1)	WD2678_1	9781474521260	£49.00
46 DIVISION Divisional Troops Divisional Signal Company : 1 March 1915 - 30 June 1919 (First World War, War Diary, WO95/2678/2)	WD2678_2	9781474521277	£28.00
46 DIVISION Divisional Troops Monmouthshire Regiment (Territorial Force) 1st Battalion Pioneers : 1 September 1915 - 22 July 1919 (First World War, War Diary, WO95/2679/1)	WD2679_1	9781474521284	£32.00
46 DIVISION Divisional Troops Machine Gun Corps 46 Battalion : 28 February 1918 - 31 May 1919 (First World War, War Diary, WO95/2679/2)	WD2679_2	9781474521291	£24.00
46 DIVISION Divisional Troops 178 Machine Gun Company : 8 February 1917 - 28 February 1918 (First World War, War Diary, WO95/2679/3)	WD2679_3	9781474521307	£15.00
46 DIVISION Divisional Troops Royal Army Medical Corps 1/1 North Midland Field Ambulance : 1 March 1915 - 31 May 1919 (First World War, War Diary, WO95/2680/1)	WD2680_1	9781474521314	£50.00
46 DIVISION Divisional Troops Royal Army Medical Corps 1/2 North Midland Field Ambulance : 1 December 1915 - 31 May 1919 (First World War, War Diary, WO95/2680/2)	WD2680_2	9781474521321	£30.00
46 DIVISION Divisional Troops Royal Army Medical Corps 1/3 North Midland Field Ambulance : 19 February 1915 - 31 January 1917 (First World War, War Diary, WO95/2681/1)	WD2681_1	9781474521338	£34.00
46 DIVISION Divisional Troops Royal Army Medical Corps Divisional Field Ambulance Workshop Unit : 16 February 1915 - 31 January 1916 (First World War, War Diary, WO95/2681/2)	WD2681_2	9781474521345	£15.00
46 DIVISION Divisional Troops 17 Sanitary Section : 21 August 1916 - 7 December 1916 (First World War, War Diary, WO95/2681/3)	WD2681_3	9781474521352	£15.00
46 DIVISION Divisional Troops Royal Army Veterinary Corps 1/1 North Midland Veterinary Section : 6 April 1915 - 28 February 1916 (First World War, War Diary, WO95/2681/4)	WD2681_4	9781474521369	£15.00
46 DIVISION Divisional Troops Senior Supply Officer : 25 February 1915 - 31 May 1919 (First World War, War Diary, WO95/2682/1)	WD2682_1	9781474521376	£16.00

Title	Product Code	ISBN	Price
46 DIVISION Divisional Troops Royal Army Service Corps Divisional Train (451, 452, 453, 454 Companies A.S.C.) : 25 February 1915 - 30 May 1919 (First World War, War Diary, WO95/2682/2)	WD2682_2	9781474521383	£59.00
46 DIVISION 137 Infantry Brigade Headquarters : 1 February 1915 - 31 December 1916 (First World War, War Diary, WO95/2683)	WD2683	9781474521390	£41.00
46 DIVISION 137 Infantry Brigade Headquarters : 1 January 1917 - 30 June 1919 (First World War, War Diary, WO95/2684)	WD2684	9781474521406	£39.00
46 DIVISION 137 Infantry Brigade Prince of Wales's (North Staffordshire Regiment) 1/5 Battalion : 1 February 1915 - 15 January 1918 (First World War, War Diary, WO95/2685/1)	WD2685_1	9781474521413	£28.00
46 DIVISION 137 Infantry Brigade Prince of Wales's (North Staffordshire Regiment) 1/6th Battalion : 1 February 1915 - 30 June 1919 (First World War, War Diary, WO95/2685/2)	WD2685_2	9781474521420	£41.00
46 DIVISION 137 Infantry Brigade South Staffordshire Regiment 1/5th Battalion (Territorial Force) : 1 February 1915 - 28 February 1919 (First World War, War Diary, WO95/2686)	WD2686	9781474521437	£66.00
46 DIVISION 137 Infantry Brigade South Staffordshire Regiment 1/6th Battalion (Territorial Force) : 1 February 1915 - 31 May 1919 (First World War, War Diary, WO95/2687/1)	WD2687_1	9781474521444	£35.00
46 DIVISION 137 Infantry Brigade, Brigade Machine Gun Company : 25 February 1916 - 14 February 1918 (First World War, War Diary, WO95/2687/2)	WD2687_2	9781474521451	£15.00
46 DIVISION 138 Infantry Brigade Headquarters : 15 January 1915 - 29 December 1916 (First World War, War Diary, WO95/2688)	WD2688	9781474521468	£38.00
46 DIVISION 138 Infantry Brigade Headquarters : 3 January 1917 - 31 May 1919 (First World War, War Diary, WO95/2689)	WD2689	9781474521475	£62.00
46 DIVISION 138 Infantry Brigade Leicestershire Regiment 1/4th Battalion : 1 February 1915 - 30 June 1919 (First World War, War Diary, WO95/2690/1)	WD2690_1	9781474521482	£35.00
46 DIVISION 138 Infantry Brigade Leicestershire Regiment 1/5th Battalion : 1 March 1915 - 31 May 1919 (First World War, War Diary, WO95/2690/2)	WD2690_2	9781474521499	£40.00
46 DIVISION 138 Infantry Brigade Lincolnshire Regiment 4th Battalion. : 1 March 1915 - 30 January 1918 (First World War, War Diary, WO95/2691/1)	WD2691_1	9781474521505	£26.00
46 DIVISION 138 Infantry Brigade Lincolnshire Regiment 5th Battalion, Brigade Machine Gun Company and Brigade Trench Mortar Battery : 1 March 1915 - 31 August 1916 (First World War, War Diary, WO95/2691/2)	WD2691_2	9781474521512	£45.00
46 DIVISION 139 Infantry Brigade Headquarters : 2 September 1914 - 31 December 1916 (First World War, War Diary, WO95/2692)	WD2692	9781474521529	£68.00
46 DIVISION 139 Infantry Brigade Headquarters : 1 January 1917 - 31 December 1918 (First World War, War Diary, WO95/2693)	WD2693	9781474525725	£65.00
46 DIVISION 139 Infantry Brigade Sherwood Foresters (Nottinghamshire and Derbyshire Regiment) 1/6th Battalion : 4 February 1915 - 29 June 1919 (First World War, War Diary, WO95/2694/1)	WD2694_1	9781474525732	£26.00
46 DIVISION 139 Infantry Brigade Sherwood Foresters (Nottinghamshire and Derbyshire Regiment) 1/7th Battalion : 4 February 1915 - 31 January 1918 (First World War, War Diary, WO95/2694/2)	WD2694_2	9781474525749	£42.00

Title	Product Code	ISBN	Price
46 DIVISION 139 Infantry Brigade Sherwood Foresters (Nottinghamshire and Derbyshire Regiment) 1/5 Battalion : 1 March 1915 - 31 May 1919 (First World War, War Diary, WO95/2695/1)	WD2695_1	9781474525756	£15.00
46 DIVISION 139 Infantry Brigade Sherwood Foresters (Nottinghamshire and Derbyshire Regiment) 1/8th Battalion : 31 October 1914 - 30 April 1919 (First World War, War Diary, WO95/2695/2)	WD2695_2	9781474525763	£32.00
46 DIVISION 139 Infantry Brigade, Brigade Machine Gun Company : 16 February 1916 - 28 February 1918 (First World War, War Diary, WO95/2695/3)	WD2695_3	9781474525770	£15.00
46 DIVISION 139 Infantry Brigade, Brigade Trench Mortar Battery : 2 March 1916 - 28 February 1919 (First World War, War Diary, WO95/2695/4)	WD2695_4	9781474525787	£15.00

Title	Product Code	ISBN	Price
47 DIVISION			
47 DIVISION Headquarters, Branches and Services General Staff : 1 February 1915 - 30 April 1915 (First World War, War Diary, WO95/2696)	WD2696	9781474525794	£27.00
47 DIVISION Headquarters, Branches and Services General Staff : 1 May 1915 - 31 May 1915 (First World War, War Diary, WO95/2697A)	WD2697_A	9781474525800	£73.00
47 DIVISION Headquarters, Branches and Services General Staff : 1 June 1915 - 16 May 1916 (First World War, War Diary, WO95/2697B)	WD2697_B	9781474525817	£22.00
47 DIVISION Headquarters, Branches and Services General Staff : 1 July 1915 - 25 October 1915 (First World War, War Diary, WO95/2698)	WD2698	9781474525824	£60.00
47 DIVISION Headquarters, Branches and Services General Staff : 1 October 1915 - 31 December 1915 (First World War, War Diary, WO95/2699)	WD2699	9781474525831	£61.00
47 DIVISION Headquarters, Branches and Services General Staff : 1 January 1916 - 30 June 1916 (First World War, War Diary, WO95/2700)	WD2700	9781474525848	£59.00
47 DIVISION Headquarters, Branches and Services General Staff : 1 July 1916 - 31 December 1916 (First World War, War Diary, WO95/2701)	WD2701	9781474525855	£68.00
47 DIVISION Headquarters, Branches and Services General Staff : 31 December 1916 - 31 May 1917 (First World War, War Diary, WO95/2702)	WD2702	9781474525862	£73.00
47 DIVISION Headquarters, Branches and Services General Staff : 1 June 1917 - 31 December 1917 (First World War, War Diary, WO95/2703)	WD2703	9781474525879	£65.00
47 DIVISION Headquarters, Branches and Services General Staff : 1 January 1918 - 31 May 1918 (First World War, War Diary, WO95/2704)	WD2704	9781474525886	£67.00
47 DIVISION Headquarters, Branches and Services General Staff : 1 June 1918 - 24 March 1919 (First World War, War Diary, WO95/2705)	WD2705	9781474525893	£60.00
47 DIVISION Headquarters, Branches and Services Adjutant and Quarter-Master General. : 1 March 1915 - 31 December 1915 (First World War, War Diary, WO95/2706)	WD2706	9781474525909	£59.00
47 DIVISION Headquarters, Branches and Services Adjutant and Quarter-Master General : 1 January 1916 - 29 March 1919 (First World War, War Diary, WO95/2707)	WD2707	9781474525916	£48.00
47 DIVISION Headquarters, Branches and Services Commander Royal Artillery : 1 March 1915 - 30 September 1915 (First World War, War Diary, WO95/2708)	WD2708	9781474525923	£64.00
47 DIVISION Headquarters, Branches and Services Commander Royal Artillery : 1 October 1915 - 31 December 1915 (First World War, War Diary, WO95/2709)	WD2709	9781474525930	£72.00
47 DIVISION Headquarters, Branches and Services Commander Royal Artillery : 1 January 1916 - 30 June 1916 (First World War, War Diary, WO95/2710A)	WD2710_A	9781474525947	£49.00
47 DIVISION Headquarters, Branches and Services Commander Royal Artillery : 1 July 1916 - 30 December 1916 (First World War, War Diary, WO95/2710B)	WD2710_B	9781474525954	£45.00
47 DIVISION Headquarters, Branches and Services Commander Royal Artillery : 1 January 1917 - 31 December 1917 (First World War, War Diary, WO95/2711)	WD2711	9781474525961	£73.00

Title	Product Code	ISBN	Price
47 DIVISION Headquarters, Branches and Services Commander Royal Artillery : 1 January 1918 - 4 February 1919 (First World War, War Diary, WO95/2712)	WD2712	9781474525978	£60.00
47 DIVISION Headquarters, Branches and Services Royal Army Medical Corps Assistant Director Medical Services : 1 March 1915 - 31 December 1916 (First World War, War Diary, WO95/2713)	WD2713	9781474525985	£41.00
47 DIVISION Headquarters, Branches and Services Royal Army Medical Corps Assistant Director Medical Services : 1 January 1917 - 30 April 1919 (First World War, War Diary, WO95/2714)	WD2714	9781474525992	£61.00
47 DIVISION Headquarters, Branches and Services Commander Royal Engineers : 1 March 1915 - 28 February 1919 (First World War, War Diary, WO95/2715)	WD2715	9781474526005	£56.00
47 DIVISION Headquarters, Branches and Services Royal Army Ordnance Corps Deputy Assistant Director Ordnance Services : 16 March 1915 - 28 February 1919 (First World War, War Diary, WO95/2716/1)	WD2716_1	9781474526012	£18.00
47 DIVISION Headquarters, Branches and Services Royal Army Veterinary Corps Deputy Assistant Director Veterinary Services : 16 March 1915 - 31 March 1919 (First World War, War Diary, WO95/2716/2)	WD2716_2	9781474526029	£28.00
47 DIVISION Divisional Troops C Squadron King Edward's Horse : 21 April 1915 - 31 May 1916 (First World War, War Diary, WO95/2717/1)	WD2717_1	9781474526036	£15.00
47 DIVISION Divisional Troops Divisional Cyclist Company : 15 March 1915 - 31 July 1916 (First World War, War Diary, WO95/2717/2)	WD2717_2	9781474526043	£15.00
47 DIVISION Divisional Troops 235 Brigade Royal Field Artillery : 14 March 1915 - 28 March 1919 (First World War, War Diary, WO95/2717/3)	WD2717_3	9781474526050	£18.00
47 DIVISION Divisional Troops 236 Brigade Royal Field Artillery : 1 March 1915 - 1 May 1919 (First World War, War Diary, WO95/2717/4)	WD2717_4	9781474526067	£29.00
47 DIVISION Divisional Troops 237 Brigade Royal Field Artillery : 1 March 1915 - 29 November 1916 (First World War, War Diary, WO95/2717/5)	WD2717_5	9781474526074	£15.00
47 DIVISION Divisional Troops 238 Brigade Royal Field Artillery : 1 March 1915 - 21 January 1917 (First World War, War Diary, WO95/2718/1)	WD2718_1	9781474526081	£15.00
47 DIVISION Divisional Troops Eley Group Royal Artillery Headquarters : 1 October 1915 - 31 October 1915 (First World War, War Diary, WO95/2718/2)	WD2718_2	9781474526098	£15.00
47 DIVISION Divisional Troops Divisional Trench Mortar Batteries : 1 September 1916 - 31 January 1919 (First World War, War Diary, WO95/2718/3)	WD2718_3	9781474526104	£15.00
47 DIVISION Divisional Troops Divisional Ammunition Column : 20 March 1915 - 30 March 1919 (First World War, War Diary, WO95/2718/4)	WD2718_4	9781474526111	£15.00
47 DIVISION Divisional Troops 517 and 518 Field Company Royal Engineers and Divisional Signal Company : 13 March 1915 - 27 April 1919 (First World War, War Diary, WO95/2719)	WD2719	9781474526128	£73.00
47 DIVISION Divisional Troops 520 Field Company Royal Engineers : 1 February 1915 - 28 February 1919 (First World War, War Diary, WO95/2720)	WD2720	9781474526135	£70.00
47 DIVISION Divisional Troops Royal Welsh Fusiliers 4th Battalion Pioneers : 1 September 1915 - 15 May 1919 (First World War, War Diary, WO95/2721/1)	WD2721_1	9781474526142	£49.00

Title	Product Code	ISBN	Price
47 DIVISION Divisional Troops 239 Machine Gun Company : 13 July 1917 - 31 October 1917 (First World War, War Diary, WO95/2721/2)	WD2721_2	9781474526159	£15.00
47 DIVISION Divisional Troops 255 Machine Gun Company : 12 November 1917 - 28 February 1918 (First World War, War Diary, WO95/2721/3)	WD2721_3	9781474526166	£15.00
47 DIVISION Divisional Troops Machine Gun Corps 47 Battalion : 1 March 1918 - 31 July 1918 (First World War, War Diary, WO95/2722)	WD2722	9781474526173	£60.00
47 DIVISION Divisional Troops Machine Gun Corps 47 Battalion : 1 August 1918 - 30 April 1919 (First World War, War Diary, WO95/2723)	WD2723	9781474526180	£78.00
47 DIVISION Divisional Troops Royal Army Medical Corps 1/5 London Field Ambulance : 1 April 1915 - 2 May 1919 (First World War, War Diary, WO95/2724)	WD2724	9781474526197	£90.00
47 DIVISION Divisional Troops Royal Army Medical Corps 1/4 London Field Ambulance and 1/6 London Field Ambulance and 47 Sanitary Section : 1 March 1915 - 30 April 1917 (First World War, War Diary, WO95/2725)	WD2725	9781474526203	£64.00
47 DIVISION Divisional Troops Royal Army Veterinary Corps 47 Mobile Veterinary Section : 1 September 1915 - 9 May 1919 (First World War, War Diary, WO95/2726/1)	WD2726_1	9781474526210	£22.00
47 DIVISION Divisional Troops Royal Army Service Corps Divisional Train (455-456-457 & 458 Companies ASC) : 4 August 1914 - 18 May 1919 (First World War, War Diary, WO95/2726/2)	WD2726_2	9781474526227	£71.00
47 DIVISION 140 Infantry Brigade Headquarters : 16 March 1915 - 31 December 1916 (First World War, War Diary, WO95/2727)	WD2727	9781474526234	£46.00
47 DIVISION 140 Infantry Brigade Headquarters : 1 January 1917 - 5 May 1919 (First World War, War Diary, WO95/2728)	WD2728	9781474526241	£53.00
47 DIVISION 140 Infantry Brigade London Regiment 6th (City of London) Battalion (Rifles) : 6 March 1915 - 2 February 1918 (First World War, War Diary, WO95/2729)	WD2729	9781474526258	£76.00
47 DIVISION 140 Infantry Brigade London Regiment 7th (City of London) Battalion : 1 March 1915 - 3 February 1918 (First World War, War Diary, WO95/2730)	WD2730	9781474526265	£55.00
47 DIVISION 140 Infantry Brigade London Regiment 8th (City of London) Battalion (Post Office Rifles) : 5 July 1915 - 1 November 1915 (First World War, War Diary, WO95/2731/1)	WD2731_1	9781474526272	£15.00
47 DIVISION 140 Infantry Brigade London Regiment 8th (City of London) Battalion (Post Office Rifles) : 1 December 1915 - 31 December 1915 (First World War, War Diary, WO95/2731/2)	WD2731_2	9781474526289	£15.00
47 DIVISION 140 Infantry Brigade London Regiment 8th (City of London) Battalion (Post Office Rifles) : 1 January 1916 - 31 July 1916 (First World War, War Diary, WO95/2731/3)	WD2731_3	9781474526296	£17.00
47 DIVISION 140 Infantry Brigade London Regiment 8th (City of London) Battalion (Post Office Rifles) : 1 August 1916 - 31 January 1919 (First World War, War Diary, WO95/2731/4)	WD2731_4	9781474526302	£15.00
47 DIVISION 140 Infantry Brigade London Regiment 15th (County of London) Battalion (P.W.O. Civil Service Rifles) and London Regiment 17th (County of London) Battalion (Poplar and Stepney Rifles) : 17 March 1915 - 5 May 1919 (First World War, War Diary, WO	WD2732_1	9781474526319	£35.00

Title	Product Code	ISBN	Price
47 DIVISION 140 Infantry Brigade London Regiment 21st (County of London) Battalion (1st Surrey Rifles) : 1 February 1918 - 5 May 1919 (First World War, War Diary, WO95/2732/2)	WD2732_2	9781474526326	£39.00
47 DIVISION 140 Infantry Brigade, Brigade Machine Gun Company : 1 January 1916 - 28 February 1918 (First World War, War Diary, WO95/2732/3)	WD2732_3	9781474526333	£15.00
47 DIVISION 142 Infantry Brigade London Regiment 21st (County of London) Battalion (1st Surrey Rifles) : 15 March 1915 - 31 January 1918 (First World War, War Diary, WO95/2732/4)	WD2732_4	9781474526340	£15.00
47 DIVISION 142 Infantry Brigade London Regiment 22nd (County of London) Battalion (The Queen's) : 1 September 1918 - 2 May 1919 (First World War, War Diary, WO95/2732/5)	WD2732_5	9781474526357	£15.00
47 DIVISION 141 Infantry Brigade Headquarters : 1 March 1915 - 25 September 1915 (First World War, War Diary, WO95/2733)	WD2733	9781474526364	£77.00
47 DIVISION 141 Infantry Brigade Headquarters : 1 January 1916 - 30 June 1916 (First World War, War Diary, WO95/2734)	WD2734	9781474526371	£63.00
47 DIVISION 141 Infantry Brigade Headquarters : 1 July 1916 - 31 October 1917 (First World War, War Diary, WO95/2735)	WD2735	9781474526388	£61.00
47 DIVISION 141 Infantry Brigade Headquarters : 1 November 1917 - 11 May 1919 (First World War, War Diary, WO95/2736)	WD2736	9781474526395	£63.00
47 DIVISION 141 Infantry Brigade London Regiment 17th (County of London) Battalion (Poplar and Stepney Rifles) : 9 March 1915 - 16 October 1916 (First World War, War Diary, WO95/2737/1)	WD2737_1	9781474526401	£15.00
47 DIVISION 141 Infantry Brigade London Regiment 17th (County of London) Battalion (Poplar and Stepney Rifles) : 9 March 1915 - 31 January 1918 (First World War, War Diary, WO95/2737/2)	WD2737_2	9781474526418	£40.00
47 DIVISION 141 Infantry Brigade London Regiment 18th (County of London) Battalion (London Irish Rifles) : 9 March 1915 - 31 March 1919 (First World War, War Diary, WO95/2737/3)	WD2737_3	9781474526425	£31.00
47 DIVISION 141 Infantry Brigade London Regiment 19th (County of London) Battalion (St. Pancras) and London Regiment 20th (County of London) Battalion (Blackheath and Woolwich) : 2 March 1915 - 9 April 1919 (First World War, War Diary, WO95/2738)	WD2738	9781474526432	£85.00
47 DIVISION 141 Infantry Brigade, Brigade Machine Gun Company : 1 January 1916 - 28 February 1918 (First World War, War Diary, WO95/2739/1)	WD2739_1	9781474526449	£61.00
47 DIVISION 141 Infantry Brigade, Brigade Trench Mortar Battery : 12 June 1916 - 31 August 1916 (First World War, War Diary, WO95/2739/2)	WD2739_2	9781474526456	£15.00
47 DIVISION 142 Infantry Brigade Headquarters : 1 March 1915 - 31 December 1916 (First World War, War Diary, WO95/2740)	WD2740	9781474526463	£57.00
47 DIVISION 142 Infantry Brigade Headquarters : 1 January 1917 - 31 October 1917 (First World War, War Diary, WO95/2741)	WD2741	9781474526470	£37.00
47 DIVISION 142 Infantry Brigade Headquarters : 1 November 1917 - 4 May 1919 (First World War, War Diary, WO95/2742)	WD2742	9781474526487	£63.00
47 DIVISION 142 Infantry Brigade London Regiment 22nd (County of London) Battalion (The Queen's) : 1 March 1915 - 31 August 1918 (First World War, War Diary, WO95/2743)	WD2743	9781474526494	£63.00

Title	Product Code	ISBN	Price
47 DIVISION 142 Infantry Brigade London Regiment 23rd (County of London) Battalion : 14 March 1915 - 3 May 1919 (First World War, War Diary, WO95/2744/1)	WD2744_1	9781474526500	£15.00
47 DIVISION 142 Infantry Brigade London Regiment 23rd (County of London) Battalion : 1 March 1915 - 9 May 1919 (First World War, War Diary, WO95/2744/2)	WD2744_2	9781474526517	£31.00
47 DIVISION 142 Infantry Brigade, Brigade Machine Gun Company : 10 December 1915 - 28 February 1918 (First World War, War Diary, WO95/2744/3)	WD2744_3	9781474526524	£15.00
47 DIVISION 142 Infantry Brigade, Brigade Trench Mortar Battery : 20 March 1916 - 31 December 1918 (First World War, War Diary, WO95/2744/4)	WD2744_4	9781474526531	£15.00

Title	Product Code	ISBN	Price
48 DIVISION			
48 DIVISION Headquarters, Branches and Services General Staff : 30 March 1915 - 31 December 1916 (First World War, War Diary, WO95/2745)	WD2745	9781474526548	£64.00
48 DIVISION Headquarters, Branches and Services General Staff : 1 January 1917 - 31 October 1917 (First World War, War Diary, WO95/2746)	WD2746	9781474526555	£58.00
48 DIVISION Headquarters, Branches and Services Adjutant and Quarter-Master General : 30 March 1915 - 31 October 1917 (First World War, War Diary, WO95/2747/1)	WD2747_1	9781474526562	£25.00
48 DIVISION Headquarters, Branches and Services Commander Royal Artillery : 1 March 1915 - 31 October 1917 (First World War, War Diary, WO95/2747/2)	WD2747_2	9781474526579	£23.00
48 DIVISION Headquarters, Branches and Services Royal Army Medical Corps Assistant Director Medical Services : 29 March 1915 - 31 October 1917 (First World War, War Diary, WO95/2748/1)	WD2748_1	9781474526586	£32.00
48 DIVISION Headquarters, Branches and Services Commander Royal Engineers : 29 March 1915 - 31 October 1917 (First World War, War Diary, WO95/2748/2)	WD2748_2	9781474526593	£17.00
48 DIVISION Headquarters, Branches and Services Royal Army Ordnance Corps Deputy Assistant Director Ordnance Services : 2 April 1915 - 31 October 1917 (First World War, War Diary, WO95/2748/3)	WD2748_3	9781474526609	£15.00
48 DIVISION Headquarters, Branches and Services Royal Army Veterinary Corps Assistant Director Veterinary Services : 3 April 1915 - 29 October 1917 (First World War, War Diary, WO95/2748/4)	WD2748_4	9781474526616	£15.00
48 DIVISION Divisional Troops B Squadron King Edward's Horse : 21 April 1915 - 31 May 1916 (First World War, War Diary, WO95/2749/1)	WD2749_1	9781474526623	£15.00
48 DIVISION Divisional Troops Divisional Cyclist Company : 3 December 1914 - 14 May 1916 (First World War, War Diary, WO95/2749/2)	WD2749_2	9781474526630	£15.00
48 DIVISION Divisional Troops 240 South Midland Brigade Royal Field Artillery : 1 March 1915 - 31 October 1917 (First World War, War Diary, WO95/2749/3)	WD2749_3	9781474526647	£15.00
48 DIVISION Divisional Troops 241 South Midland Brigade Royal Field Artillery : 1 March 1915 - 31 October 1917 (First World War, War Diary, WO95/2749/4)	WD2749_4	9781474526654	£27.00
48 DIVISION Divisional Troops 242 South Midland Brigade Royal Field Artillery : 30 March 1915 - 31 December 1916 (First World War, War Diary, WO95/2750/1)	WD2750_1	9781474526661	£56.00
48 DIVISION Divisional Troops 243 South Midland Brigade Royal Field Artillery : 31 March 1915 - 18 October 1916 (First World War, War Diary, WO95/2750/2)	WD2750_2	9781474526678	£15.00
48 DIVISION Divisional Troops Divisional Trench Mortar Batteries : 21 April 1916 - 30 October 1917 (First World War, War Diary, WO95/2750/3)	WD2750_3	9781474526685	£15.00
48 DIVISION Divisional Troops Divisional Ammunition Column : 1 April 1915 - 31 October 1917 (First World War, War Diary, WO95/2750/4)	WD2750_4	9781474526692	£15.00
48 DIVISION Divisional Troops 474 South Midland Field Company Royal Engineers : 1 May 1915 - 28 October 1917 (First World War, War Diary, WO95/2751/1)	WD2751_1	9781474526708	£15.00

Title	Product Code	ISBN	Price
48 DIVISION Divisional Troops 475 South Midland Field Company Royal Engineers : 29 March 1915 - 31 October 1917 (First World War, War Diary, WO95/2751/2)	WD2751_2	9781474526715	£15.00
48 DIVISION Divisional Troops 477 South Midland Field Company Royal Engineers : 5 June 1915 - 31 October 1917 (First World War, War Diary, WO95/2751/3)	WD2751_3	9781474526722	£15.00
48 DIVISION Divisional Troops Divisional Signal Company : 30 March 1915 - 31 October 1917 (First World War, War Diary, WO95/2751/4)	WD2751_4	9781474526739	£16.00
48 DIVISION Divisional Troops Royal Sussex Regiment 1/5 Battalion : 1 September 1915 - 28 September 1917 (First World War, War Diary, WO95/2751/5)	WD2751_5	9781474526746	£15.00
48 DIVISION Divisional Troops Royal Army Medical Corps 1/1 South Midland Field Ambulance : 30 March 1915 - 31 October 1917 (First World War, War Diary, WO95/2752/1)	WD2752_1	9781474526753	£20.00
48 DIVISION Divisional Troops Royal Army Medical Corps 1/2 South Midland Field Ambulance : 23 March 1915 - 31 October 1917 (First World War, War Diary, WO95/2752/2)	WD2752_2	9781474526760	£28.00
48 DIVISION Divisional Troops Royal Army Medical Corps 1/3 South Midland Field Ambulance : 1 March 1915 - 31 October 1917 (First World War, War Diary, WO95/2752/3)	WD2752_3	9781474526777	£21.00
48 DIVISION Divisional Troops 48 Sanitary Section : 1 June 1915 - 31 March 1917 (First World War, War Diary, WO95/2753/1)	WD2753_1	9781474526784	£15.00
48 DIVISION Divisional Troops Royal Army Veterinary Corps 1/1 South Midland Mobile Veterinary Section and Divisional Train (459-460-461-462 Companies A.S.C.) : 1 December 1914 - 31 October 1917 (First World War, War Diary, WO95/2753/2)	WD2753_2	9781474526791	£43.00
48 DIVISION 143 Infantry Brigade Headquarters : 1 March 1915 - 31 October 1917 (First World War, War Diary, WO95/2754)	WD2754	9781474526807	£51.00
48 DIVISION 143 Infantry Brigade Royal Warwickshire Regiment 1/5th Battalion-Territorial : 22 March 1915 - 9 November 1917 (First World War, War Diary, WO95/2755/1)	WD2755_1	9781474526814	£27.00
48 DIVISION 143 Infantry Brigade Royal Warwickshire Regiment 1/6th Battalion-Territorial : 1 March 1915 - 31 October 1917 (First World War, War Diary, WO95/2755/2)	WD2755_2	9781474526821	£17.00
48 DIVISION 143 Infantry Brigade Royal Warwickshire Regiment 1/7th Battalion and Royal Warwickshire Regiment 1/8th Territorial Battalion : 1 March 1915 - 31 October 1917 (First World War, War Diary, WO95/2756/1)	WD2756_1	9781474526838	£49.00
48 DIVISION 143 Infantry Brigade, Brigade Machine Gun Company : 2 February 1916 - 31 October 1917 (First World War, War Diary, WO95/2756/2)	WD2756_2	9781474526845	£15.00
48 DIVISION 144 Infantry Brigade Headquarters : 2 September 1914 - 31 October 1917 (First World War, War Diary, WO95/2757)	WD2757	9781474526852	£63.00
48 DIVISION 144 Infantry Brigade Gloucestershire Regiment 1/4th (City of Bristol) Battalion (T.F.) : 30 March 1915 - 31 October 1917 (First World War, War Diary, WO95/2758/1)	WD2758_1	9781474526869	£21.00

Title	Product Code	ISBN	Price
48 DIVISION 144 Infantry Brigade Gloucestershire Regiment 1/6th Battalion : 29 March 1915 - 31 October 1917 (First World War, War Diary, WO95/2758/2)	WD2758_2	9781474526876	£17.00
48 DIVISION 144 Infantry Brigade Worcestershire Regiment 1/7th Battalion : 1 January 1916 - 31 October 1917 (First World War, War Diary, WO95/2759/1)	WD2759_1	9781474526883	£15.00
48 DIVISION 144 Infantry Brigade Worcestershire Regiment 1/8th Battalion : 1 April 1915 - 31 October 1917 (First World War, War Diary, WO95/2759/2)	WD2759_2	9781474526890	£15.00
48 DIVISION 144 Infantry Brigade, Brigade Machine Gun Company : 23 January 1915 - 24 April 1916 (First World War, War Diary, WO95/2759/3)	WD2759_3	9781474526906	£18.00
48 DIVISION 145 Infantry Brigade Headquarters : 1 March 1915 - 31 October 1916 (First World War, War Diary, WO95/2760)	WD2760	9781474526913	£47.00
48 DIVISION 145 Infantry Brigade Headquarters : 1 November 1916 - 31 October 1917 (First World War, War Diary, WO95/2761)	WD2761	9781474526920	£42.00
48 DIVISION 145 Infantry Brigade Princess Charlotte of Wales's (Royal Berkshire Regiment) 1/4th Battalion : 30 March 1915 - 31 October 1917 (First World War, War Diary, WO95/2762)	WD2762	9781474526937	£52.00
48 DIVISION 145 Infantry Brigade Gloucestershire Regiment 1/5th Battalion (Territorial) : 1 March 1915 - 31 October 1917 (First World War, War Diary, WO95/2763/1)	WD2763_1	9781474526944	£23.00
48 DIVISION 145 Infantry Brigade Oxfordshire and Buckinghamshire Light Infantry 1st Battalion : 30 March 1915 - 31 October 1917 (First World War, War Diary, WO95/2763/2)	WD2763_2	9781474526951	£22.00
48 DIVISION 145 Infantry Brigade Oxfordshire and Buckinghamshire Light Infantry 1/4 Battalion : 27 March 1915 - 31 October 1917 (First World War, War Diary, WO95/2764/1)	WD2764_1	9781474526968	£29.00
48 DIVISION 145 Infantry Brigade, Brigade Machine Gun Company : 11 January 1916 - 31 October 1917 (First World War, War Diary, WO95/2764/2)	WD2764_2	9781474526975	£18.00

Title	Product Code	ISBN	Price
49 DIVISION			
49 DIVISION Headquarters, Branches and Services General Staff : 31 March 1915 - 31 July 1916 (First World War, War Diary, WO95/2765)	WD2765	9781474526982	£77.00
49 DIVISION Headquarters, Branches and Services General Staff : 1 August 1916 - 28 January 1917 (First World War, War Diary, WO95/2766)	WD2766	9781474526999	£78.00
49 DIVISION Headquarters, Branches and Services General Staff : 1 March 1917 - 30 September 1917 (First World War, War Diary, WO95/2767)	WD2767	9781474527002	£58.00
49 DIVISION Headquarters, Branches and Services General Staff : 1 October 1917 - 28 February 1919 (First World War, War Diary, WO95/2768)	WD2768	9781474527019	£65.00
49 DIVISION Headquarters, Branches and Services Adjutant and Quarter-Master General : 12 April 1915 - 31 October 1916 (First World War, War Diary, WO95/2769)	WD2769	9781474527026	£50.00
49 DIVISION Headquarters, Branches and Services Adjutant and Quarter-Master General : 1 January 1916 - 31 July 1917 (First World War, War Diary, WO95/2770)	WD2770	9781474527033	£57.00
49 DIVISION Headquarters, Branches and Services Adjutant and Quarter-Master General : 1 August 1917 - 30 April 1919 (First World War, War Diary, WO95/2771)	WD2771	9781474527040	£44.00
49 DIVISION Headquarters, Branches and Services Commander Royal Artillery : 31 March 1915 - 30 June 1915 (First World War, War Diary, WO95/2772A)	WD2772_A	9781474527057	£30.00
49 DIVISION Headquarters, Branches and Services Commander Royal Artillery : 12 July 1915 - 31 December 1915 (First World War, War Diary, WO95/2772B)	WD2772_B	9781474527064	£58.00
49 DIVISION Headquarters, Branches and Services Commander Royal Artillery : 1 January 1916 - 28 February 1917 (First World War, War Diary, WO95/2773)	WD2773	9781474527071	£75.00
49 DIVISION Headquarters, Branches and Services Commander Royal Artillery : 1 January 1917 - 31 May 1917 (First World War, War Diary, WO95/2774)	WD2774	9781474527088	£54.00
49 DIVISION Headquarters, Branches and Services Commander Royal Artillery : 1 June 1917 - 31 December 1917 (First World War, War Diary, WO95/2775)	WD2775	9781474527095	£48.00
49 DIVISION Headquarters, Branches and Services Commander Royal Artillery : 1 January 1918 - 31 May 1919 (First World War, War Diary, WO95/2776)	WD2776	9781474527101	£66.00
49 DIVISION Headquarters, Branches and Services Royal Army Medical Corps Assistant Director Medical Services : 13 April 1915 - 31 December 1916 (First World War, War Diary, WO95/2777)	WD2777	9781474527118	£39.00
49 DIVISION Headquarters, Branches and Services Royal Army Medical Corps Assistant Director Medical Services : 1 January 1917 - 31 May 1919 (First World War, War Diary, WO95/2778)	WD2778	9781474527125	£58.00
49 DIVISION Headquarters, Branches and Services Commander Royal Engineers : 31 March 1915 - 31 May 1919 (First World War, War Diary, WO95/2779)	WD2779	9781474527132	£64.00

Title	Product Code	ISBN	Price
49 DIVISION Headquarters, Branches and Services Royal Army Ordnance Corps Deputy Assistant Director Ordnance Services and Royal Army Veterinary Corps Assistant Director Veterinary Services : 13 April 1915 - 31 January 1919 (First World War, War Diary, WO9	WD2780	9781474527149	£66.00
49 DIVISION Divisional Troops C Squadron Yorkshire Hussars, Divisional Cyclist Company and 245 and 246 Brigade Royal Field Artillery : 31 March 1915 - 25 May 1916 (First World War, War Diary, WO95/2781)	WD2781	9781474527156	£64.00
49 DIVISION Divisional Troops 247 Brigade Royal Field Artillery : 1 May 1915 - 30 June 1916 (First World War, War Diary, WO95/2782/1)	WD2782_1	9781474527163	£20.00
49 DIVISION Divisional Troops 248 Brigade Royal Field Artillery : 9 May 1915 - 31 July 1915 (First World War, War Diary, WO95/2782/2)	WD2782_2	9781474527170	£15.00
49 DIVISION Divisional Troops Divisional Trench Mortar Batteries : 9 July 1915 - 30 November 1918 (First World War, War Diary, WO95/2782/3)	WD2782_3	9781474527187	£15.00
49 DIVISION Divisional Troops Divisional Ammunition Column : 9 April 1915 - 22 June 1919 (First World War, War Diary, WO95/2782/4)	WD2782_4	9781474527194	£39.00
49 DIVISION Divisional Troops 456 and 458 Field Company Royal Engineers : 1 March 1915 - 31 May 1919 (First World War, War Diary, WO95/2783)	WD2783	9781474527200	£54.00
49 DIVISION Divisional Troops 57 Field Company Royal Engineers and Divisional Signal Company : 1 August 1915 - 2 May 1919 (First World War, War Diary, WO95/2784)	WD2784	9781474527217	£45.00
49 DIVISION Divisional Troops Lancashire Fusiliers 19th Battalion Pioneers : 1 August 1916 - 14 July 1917 (First World War, War Diary, WO95/2785)	WD2785	9781474527224	£45.00
49 DIVISION Divisional Troops Lancashire Fusiliers 19th Battalion Pioneers : 1 August 1917 - 23 June 1919 (First World War, War Diary, WO95/2786)	WD2786	9781474527231	£59.00
49 DIVISION Divisional Troops Monmouthshire Regiment (Territorial Force) 3rd Battalion and Machine Gun Corps 49 Battalion : 1 November 1915 - 31 August 1916 (First World War, War Diary, WO95/2787/1)	WD2787_1	9781474527248	£23.00
49 DIVISION Divisional Troops 199 Machine Gun Company : 13 December 1916 - 31 October 1917 (First World War, War Diary, WO95/2787/2)	WD2787_2	9781474527255	£15.00
49 DIVISION Divisional Troops 254 Machine Gun Company : 15 November 1917 - 23 February 1918 (First World War, War Diary, WO95/2787/3)	WD2787_3	9781474527262	£15.00
49 DIVISION Divisional Troops Royal Army Medical Corps 1/1st West Riding Field Ambulance : 13 April 1915 - 26 June 1919 (First World War, War Diary, WO95/2788)	WD2788	9781474527279	£45.00
49 DIVISION Divisional Troops Royal Army Medical Corps 1/2 West Riding Field Ambulance : 14 April 1915 - 29 June 1919 (First World War, War Diary, WO95/2789)	WD2789	9781474527286	£43.00
49 DIVISION Divisional Troops Royal Army Medical Corps 1/3 West Riding Field Ambulance : 18 April 1915 - 25 June 1919 (First World War, War Diary, WO95/2790/1)	WD2790_1	9781474527293	£40.00
49 DIVISION Divisional Troops 49 Sanitary Section : 7 April 1915 - 31 March 1917 (First World War, War Diary, WO95/2790/2)	WD2790_2	9781474527309	£15.00
49 DIVISION Divisional Troops Royal Army Veterinary Corps 1/1 West Riding Veterinary Section : 16 April 1915 - 28 March 1919 (First World War, War Diary, WO95/2791/1)	WD2791_1	9781474527316	£20.00

Title	Product Code	ISBN	Price
49 DIVISION Divisional Troops Royal Army Service Corps Divisional Train (463-464-465 & 466 Companies A.S.C.) : 12 April 1915 - 31 May 1919 (First World War, War Diary, WO95/2791/2)	WD2791_2	9781474527323	£31.00
49 DIVISION 146 Infantry Brigade Headquarters : 15 April 1915 - 31 March 1917 (First World War, War Diary, WO95/2792)	WD2792	9781474527330	£39.00
49 DIVISION 146 Infantry Brigade Headquarters : 1 April 1917 - 31 May 1919 (First World War, War Diary, WO95/2793)	WD2793	9781474527347	£52.00
49 DIVISION 146 Infantry Brigade Prince of Wales's Own (West Yorkshire Regiment) 1/5th Battalion : 16 April 1915 - 27 February 1919 (First World War, War Diary, WO95/2794/1)	WD2794_1	9781474527354	£36.00
49 DIVISION 146 Infantry Brigade Prince of Wales's Own (West Yorkshire Regiment) 1/6th Battalion : 4 August 1914 - 28 February 1919 (First World War, War Diary, WO95/2794/2)	WD2794_2	9781474527361	£41.00
49 DIVISION 146 Infantry Brigade Prince of Wales's Own (West Yorkshire Regiment) 1/7th Battalion : 16 April 1915 - 31 May 1919 (First World War, War Diary, WO95/2795/1)	WD2795_1	9781474527378	£15.00
49 DIVISION 146 Infantry Brigade Prince of Wales's Own (West Yorkshire Regiment) 1/8th Battalion : 14 April 1915 - 31 December 1917 (First World War, War Diary, WO95/2795/2)	WD2795_2	9781474527385	£16.00
49 DIVISION 146 Infantry Brigade, Brigade Machine Gun Company : 27 January 1916 - 28 February 1918 (First World War, War Diary, WO95/2795/3)	WD2795_3	9781474527392	£15.00
49 DIVISION 147 Infantry Brigade Headquarters : 12 April 1915 - 31 August 1916 (First World War, War Diary, WO95/2796)	WD2796	9781474527408	£47.00
49 DIVISION 147 Infantry Brigade Headquarters : 1 October 1916 - 30 September 1917 (First World War, War Diary, WO95/2797)	WD2797	9781474527415	£50.00
49 DIVISION 147 Infantry Brigade Headquarters : 1 October 1917 - 22 June 1919 (First World War, War Diary, WO95/2798)	WD2798	9781474527422	£53.00
49 DIVISION 147 Infantry Brigade Duke of Wellington's (West Riding Regiment) 1/4th Battalion : 14 April 1915 - 19 June 1917 (First World War, War Diary, WO95/2799)	WD2799	9781474527439	£46.00
49 DIVISION 147 Infantry Brigade Duke of Wellington's (West Riding Regiment) 1/5th Battalion : 14 April 1915 - 30 January 1918 (First World War, War Diary, WO95/2800)	WD2800	9781474527446	£46.00
49 DIVISION 147 Infantry Brigade Duke of Wellington's (West Riding Regiment) 1/6th Battalion : 1 May 1915 - 16 June 1919 (First World War, War Diary, WO95/2801)	WD2801	9781474527453	£52.00
49 DIVISION 147 Infantry Brigade Duke of Wellington's (West Riding Regiment) 1/7th Battalion : 14 April 1915 - 31 May 1919 (First World War, War Diary, WO95/2802/1)	WD2802_1	9781474527460	£45.00
49 DIVISION 147 Infantry Brigade, Brigade Machine Gun Company : 26 January 1916 - 27 February 1918 (First World War, War Diary, WO95/2802/2)	WD2802_2	9781474527477	£15.00
49 DIVISION 147 Infantry Brigade, Brigade Trench Mortar Battery : 1 April 1916 - 31 August 1916 (First World War, War Diary, WO95/2802/3)	WD2802_3	9781474527484	£15.00
49 DIVISION 148 Infantry Brigade Headquarters : 30 May 1915 - 28 September 1917 (First World War, War Diary, WO95/2803)	WD2803	9781474527491	£64.00

Title	Product Code	ISBN	Price
49 DIVISION 148 Infantry Brigade Headquarters : 1 October 1917 - 30 April 1919 (First World War, War Diary, WO95/2804)	WD2804	9781474527507	£65.00
49 DIVISION 148 Infantry Brigade York and Lancaster Regiment 1/4th (Hallamshire) (T.F.) Battalion and 1/5th (T.F.) Battalion : 4 August 1914 - 31 May 1919 (First World War, War Diary, WO95/2805)	WD2805	9781474527514	£50.00
49 DIVISION 148 Infantry Brigade King's Own (Yorkshire Light Infantry) 4th Battalion and 1/5th Battalion and Brigade Machine Gun Company : 4 August 1914 - 28 February 1918 (First World War, War Diary, WO95/2806)	WD2806	9781474527521	£45.00

Title	Product Code	ISBN	Price
5 CAVALRY DIVISION			
5 CAVALRY DIVISION Headquarters, Branches and Services General Staff : 2 January 1917 - 21 February 1918 (First World War, War Diary, WO95/1162/1)	WD1162_1	9781474501163	£26.00
5 CAVALRY DIVISION Headquarters, Branches and Services Adjutant and Quarter-Master General : 1 January 1917 - 29 April 1918 (First World War, War Diary, WO95/1162/2)	WD1162_2	9781474501170	£18.00
5 CAVALRY DIVISION Headquarters, Branches and Services Royal Army Medical Corps Assistant Director Medical Services : 1 January 1917 - 31 January 1918 (First World War, War Diary, WO95/1162/3)	WD1162_3	9781474501187	£15.00
5 CAVALRY DIVISION Headquarters, Branches and Services Royal Army Ordnance Corps Assistant Director Ordnance Services : 1 January 1917 - 31 August 1917 (First World War, War Diary, WO95/1162/4)	WD1162_4	9781474501194	£15.00
5 CAVALRY DIVISION Headquarters, Branches and Services Royal Army Veterinary Corps Assistant Director Veterinary Services : 1 January 1917 - 30 January 1918 (First World War, War Diary, WO95/1162/5)	WD1162_5	9781474501200	£15.00
5 CAVALRY DIVISION Divisional Troops 17 Brigade Royal Horse Artillery : 1 January 1917 - 31 March 1918 (First World War, War Diary, WO95/1163/1)	WD1163_1	9781474501217	£15.00
5 CAVALRY DIVISION Divisional Troops Royal Army Service Corps Divisional Supply Column (71 Company A.S.C.) : 1 November 1916 - 28 February 1918 (First World War, War Diary, WO95/1163/10)	WD1163_10	9781474501293	£15.00
5 CAVALRY DIVISION Divisional Troops Royal Army Service Corps Divisional Ammunition Park (72 Company A.S.C.) : 1 October 1916 - 16 November 1917 (First World War, War Diary, WO95/1163/11)	WD1163_11	9781474501309	£15.00
5 CAVALRY DIVISION Divisional Troops 9 Light Armoured Battery : 1 January 1917 - 30 October 1917 (First World War, War Diary, WO95/1163/2)	WD1163_2	9781474501224	£15.00
5 CAVALRY DIVISION Divisional Troops 5 Field Squadron Royal Engineers : 1 January 1917 - 20 April 1918 (First World War, War Diary, WO95/1163/3)	WD1163_3	9781474501231	£15.00
5 CAVALRY DIVISION Divisional Troops 5 Signal Squadron : 1 January 1917 - 30 March 1918 (First World War, War Diary, WO95/1163/4)	WD1163_4	9781474501248	£15.00
5 CAVALRY DIVISION Divisional Troops Royal Army Medical Corps Ambala Cavalry Field Ambulance : 1 January 1917 - 31 March 1918 (First World War, War Diary, WO95/1163/5)	WD1163_5	9781474501255	£15.00
5 CAVALRY DIVISION Divisional Troops Royal Army Medical Corps Secunderabad Cavalry Field Ambulance : 1 January 1917 - 30 April 1918 (First World War, War Diary, WO95/1163/6)	WD1163_6	9781474501262	£15.00
5 CAVALRY DIVISION Divisional Troops 5 (Cavalry) Sanitary Section : 1 January 1917 - 30 April 1918 (First World War, War Diary, WO95/1163/7)	WD1163_7	9781474501279	£15.00
5 CAVALRY DIVISION Divisional Troops Royal Army Service Corps Headquarters Army Service Corps (427 Company A.S.C.) and Auxiliary Horse Transport Company (578 Company A.S.C.) : 1 January 1917 - 26 December 1917 (First World War, War Diary, WO95/1163/8-9)	WD1163_8-9	9781474501286	£15.00
5 CAVALRY DIVISION Ambala Cavalry Brigade Headquarters, 8th (King's Royal Irish) Hussars, 9 Hodson's Horse, 18 Lancers and 14 Cavalry Machine Gun Squadron : 1 January 1917 - 27 February 1918 (First World War, War Diary, WO95/1164)	WD1164	9781474501316	£24.00

Title	Product Code	ISBN	Price
5 CAVALRY DIVISION Secunderabad Cavalry Brigade Headquarters, `N' Battery Royal Horse Artillery, 7th Dragoon Guards (Princess Royal), 20 Deccan Horse, 34 Poona Horse, Brigade Signal Troop, 13 Cavalry Machine Gun Squadron and Royal Army Veterinary Corps	WD1165	9781474501323	£34.00

Title	Product Code	ISBN	Price
5 DIVISION			
5 DIVISION Headquarters, Branches and Services General Staff : 7 August 1914 - 31 December 1914 (First World War, War Diary, WO95/1510)	WD1510	9781474505505	£43.00
5 DIVISION Headquarters, Branches and Services General Staff : 1 January 1915 - 31 March 1915 (First World War, War Diary, WO95/1511)	WD1511	9781474522014	£73.00
5 DIVISION Headquarters, Branches and Services General Staff : 1 April 1915 - 31 October 1915 (First World War, War Diary, WO95/1512)	WD1512	9781474522021	£67.00
5 DIVISION Headquarters, Branches and Services General Staff : 1 November 1915 - 30 September 1916 (First World War, War Diary, WO95/1513)	WD1513	9781474505512	£43.00
5 DIVISION Headquarters, Branches and Services General Staff : 1 October 1916 - 30 June 1917 (First World War, War Diary, WO95/1514)	WD1514	9781474505529	£51.00
5 DIVISION Headquarters, Branches and Services General Staff : 1 July 1917 - 30 November 1917 (First World War, War Diary, WO95/1515)	WD1515	9781474505536	£36.00
5 DIVISION Headquarters, Branches and Services General Staff : 1 April 1918 - 28 February 1919 (First World War, War Diary, WO95/1516)	WD1516	9781474522038	£56.00
5 DIVISION Headquarters, Branches and Services Adjutant and Quarter-Master General : 4 August 1914 - 31 December 1915 (First World War, War Diary, WO95/1517)	WD1517	9781474522045	£65.00
5 DIVISION Headquarters, Branches and Services Adjutant and Quarter-Master General : 1 January 1916 - 31 December 1916 (First World War, War Diary, WO95/1518)	WD1518	9781474505543	£50.00
5 DIVISION Headquarters, Branches and Services Adjutant and Quarter-Master General : 1 January 1917 - 30 November 1917 (First World War, War Diary, WO95/1519)	WD1519	9781474505550	£52.00
5 DIVISION Headquarters, Branches and Services Adjutant and Quarter-Master General : 1 January 1918 - 9 May 1919 (First World War, War Diary, WO95/1520)	WD1520	9781474505567	£52.00
5 DIVISION Headquarters, Branches and Services Commander Royal Artillery : 26 August 1914 - 30 September 1915 (First World War, War Diary, WO95/1521)	WD1521	9781474522052	£90.00
5 DIVISION Headquarters, Branches and Services Commander Royal Artillery : 1 October 1915 - 30 April 1917 (First World War, War Diary, WO95/1522)	WD1522	9781474505574	£56.00
5 DIVISION Headquarters, Branches and Services Commander Royal Artillery : 1 May 1917 - 30 November 1917 (First World War, War Diary, WO95/1523)	WD1523	9781474505581	£51.00
5 DIVISION Headquarters, Branches and Services Commander Royal Artillery : 1 April 1918 - 11 April 1919 (First World War, War Diary, WO95/1524)	WD1524	9781474505598	£43.00
5 DIVISION Headquarters, Branches and Services Royal Army Medical Corps Assistant Director Medical Services : 10 August 1914 - 17 March 1919 (First World War, War Diary, WO95/1525)	WD1525	9781474522069	£67.00
5 DIVISION Headquarters, Branches and Services Assistant Provost Marshal, Commander Royal Engineers, Deputy Assistant Director Ordnance Services and Assistant Director Veterinary Services : 2 August 1914 - 30 April 1919 (First World War, War Diary, WO95/1	WD1526	9781474522076	£55.00

Title	Product Code	ISBN	Price
5 DIVISION Divisional Troops `A' Squadron 19 Hussars, `C' Squadron Northamptonshire Yeomanry, Divisional Cyclist Company, 8 Brigade Royal Field Artillery : 4 August 1914 - 19 May 1916 (First World War, War Diary, WO95/1527)	WD1527	9781474522083	£65.00
5 DIVISION Divisional Troops 15 Brigade Royal Field Artillery : 4 August 1914 - 31 March 1919 (First World War, War Diary, WO95/1528)	WD1528	9781474505604	£45.00
5 DIVISION Divisional Troops 27 Brigade Royal Field Artillery : 1 December 1915 - 26 September 1916 (First World War, War Diary, WO95/1529)	WD1529	9781474522090	£65.00
5 DIVISION Divisional Troops 27 Brigade Royal Field Artillery : 1 November 1916 - 30 April 1917 (First World War, War Diary, WO95/1530)	WD1530	9781474505611	£67.00
5 DIVISION Divisional Troops 27 Brigade Royal Field Artillery : 1 May 1917 - 30 November 1917 (First World War, War Diary, WO95/1531/1)	WD1531_1	9781474505628	£67.00
5 DIVISION Divisional Troops 27 Brigade Royal Field Artillery : 1 January 1916 - 31 March 1919 (First World War, War Diary, WO95/1531/2)	WD1531_2	9781474505635	£18.00
5 DIVISION Divisional Troops 28 Brigade Royal Field Artillery and Belgian Artillery Regiment : 1 August 1914 - 9 July 1915 (First World War, War Diary, WO95/1532)	WD1532	9781474505642	£32.00
5 DIVISION Divisional Troops Divisional Trench Mortar Batteries and Divisional Ammunition Column : 5 August 1914 - 30 April 1919 (First World War, War Diary, WO95/1533)	WD1533	9781474522106	£52.00
5 DIVISION Divisional Troops 491 (Home Counties) Field Company Royal Engineers and 527 (Durham) Field Company Royal Engineers : 21 December 1914 - 17 April 1919 (First World War, War Diary, WO95/1534)	WD1534	9781474522113	£84.00
5 DIVISION Divisional Troops 17 and 59 Field Company Royal Engineers : 4 August 1914 - 31 March 1919 (First World War, War Diary, WO95/1535)	WD1535	9781474505659	£42.00
5 DIVISION Divisional Troops Divisional Signal Company : 5 August 1914 - 30 June 1916 (First World War, War Diary, WO95/1536)	WD1536	9781474505666	£52.00
5 DIVISION Divisional Troops Divisional Signal Company : 7 January 1916 - 9 May 1919 (First World War, War Diary, WO95/1537)	WD1537	9781474505673	£45.00
5 DIVISION Divisional Troops Princess Louise's (Argyll & Sutherland Highlanders) 1/6th Battalion Pioneers and Royal Warwickshire Regiment 14th Battalion : 1 July 1916 - 17 April 1919 (First World War, War Diary, WO95/1538)	WD1538	9781474505680	£43.00
5 DIVISION Divisional Troops Machine Gun Corps 5 Battalion : 1 April 1918 - 31 May 1919 (First World War, War Diary, WO95/1539/1)	WD1539_1	9781474505697	£29.00
5 DIVISION Divisional Troops 205 Machine Gun Company : 24 October 1916 - 30 November 1917 (First World War, War Diary, WO95/1539/2)	WD1539_2	9781474505703	£15.00
5 DIVISION Divisional Troops Divisional Anti-Gas School : 1 October 1917 - 30 November 1917 (First World War, War Diary, WO95/1539/3)	WD1539_3	9781474505710	£15.00
5 DIVISION Divisional Troops Divisional Anti-Gas School : 1 April 1918 - 31 March 1919 (First World War, War Diary, WO95/1539/4)	WD1539_4	9781474505727	£15.00
5 DIVISION Divisional Troops Royal Army Medical Corps 13 and 14 Field Ambulance : 5 August 1914 - 31 December 1918 (First World War, War Diary, WO95/1540)	WD1540	9781474522120	£62.00
5 DIVISION Divisional Troops Royal Army Medical Corps 15 Field Ambulance, 6 Sanitary Section and 5 Mobile Veterinary Section : 27 March 1914 - 6 April 1919 (First World War, War Diary, WO95/1541)	WD1541	9781474522137	£60.00

Title	Product Code	ISBN	Price
5 DIVISION Divisional Troops Royal Army Service Corps Divisional Train (4, 6, 33, 37 Companies A.S.C.) : 4 August 1914 - 31 August 1915 (First World War, War Diary, WO95/1542)	WD1542	9781474522144	£85.00
5 DIVISION Divisional Troops Royal Army Service Corps Divisional Train (4, 6, 33, 37 Companies A.S.C.) : 1 September 1915 - 31 December 1916 (First World War, War Diary, WO95/1543)	WD1543	9781474522151	£83.00
5 DIVISION Divisional Troops Royal Army Service Corps Divisional Train (4, 6, 33, 37 Companies A.S.C.) : 1 January 1917 - 31 March 1917 (First World War, War Diary, WO95/1544A)	WD1544_A	9781474522168	£42.00
5 DIVISION Divisional Troops Royal Army Service Corps Divisional Train (4, 6, 33, 37 Companies A.S.C.) : 1 April 1917 - 30 June 1917 (First World War, War Diary, WO95/1544B)	WD1544_B	9781474522175	£56.00
5 DIVISION Divisional Troops Royal Army Service Corps Divisional Train (4, 6, 33, 37 Companies A.S.C.) : 1 July 1917 - 31 August 1917 (First World War, War Diary, WO95/1545A)	WD1545_A	9781474522182	£39.00
5 DIVISION Divisional Troops Royal Army Service Corps Divisional Train (4, 6, 33, 37 Companies A.S.C.) : 1 September 1917 - 31 October 1917 (First World War, War Diary, WO95/1545B)	WD1545_B	9781474522199	£56.00
5 DIVISION Divisional Troops Royal Army Service Corps Divisional Train (4, 6, 33, 37 Companies A.S.C.) : 1 April 1918 - 31 August 1918 (First World War, War Diary, WO95/1546)	WD1546	9781474522205	£56.00
5 DIVISION Divisional Troops Royal Army Service Corps Divisional Train (4, 6, 33, 37 Companies A.S.C.) : 29 August 1918 - 30 April 1919 (First World War, War Diary, WO95/1547)	WD1547	9781474522212	£70.00
5 DIVISION 13 Infantry Brigade Headquarters : 5 August 1914 - 31 December 1915 (First World War, War Diary, WO95/1548)	WD1548	9781474522229	£84.00
5 DIVISION 13 Infantry Brigade Headquarters : 1 January 1916 - 31 March 1917 (First World War, War Diary, WO95/1549)	WD1549	9781474505734	£47.00
5 DIVISION 13 Infantry Brigade Headquarters : 1 April 1917 - 30 November 1917 (First World War, War Diary, WO95/1550)	WD1550	9781474505741	£48.00
5 DIVISION 13 Infantry Brigade Headquarters : 1 April 1918 - 14 May 1919 (First World War, War Diary, WO95/1551)	WD1551	9781474522236	£77.00
5 DIVISION 13 Infantry Brigade Duke of Wellington's (West Riding Regiment) 2nd Battalion and King's Own Scottish Borderers 2nd Battalion : 5 August 1914 - 15 May 1919 (First World War, War Diary, WO95/1552)	WD1552	9781474505758	£45.00
5 DIVISION 13 Infantry Brigade Queen's Own (Royal West Kent Regiment) 1st Battalion : 3 February 1914 - 30 April 1916 (First World War, War Diary, WO95/1553)	WD1553	9781474522243	£69.00
5 DIVISION 13 Infantry Brigade Queen's Own (Royal West Kent Regiment) 1st Battalion : 1 May 1916 - 30 June 1917 (First World War, War Diary, WO95/1554)	WD1554	9781474505765	£45.00
5 DIVISION 13 Infantry Brigade Queen's Own (Royal West Kent Regiment) 1st Battalion : 1 August 1916 - 22 April 1919 (First World War, War Diary, WO95/1555)	WD1555	9781474505772	£54.00
5 DIVISION 13 Infantry Brigade Royal Warwickshire Regiment 14th Battalion : 26 October 1914 - 30 September 1918 (First World War, War Diary, WO95/1556)	WD1556	9781474505789	£44.00

Title	Product Code	ISBN	Price
5 DIVISION 13 Infantry Brigade Royal Warwickshire Regiment 15th and 16th Battalion : 20 November 1915 - 14 April 1919 (First World War, War Diary, WO95/1557)	WD1557	9781474505796	£72.00
5 DIVISION 13 Infantry Brigade King's Own Scottish Borderers 2nd Battalion and London Regiment 9th (County of London) Battalion (Queen Victoria's Rifles) : 4 August 1914 - 31 January 1916 (First World War, War Diary, WO95/1558)	WD1558	9781474505802	£18.00
5 DIVISION 13 Infantry Brigade, Brigade Machine Gun Company and Brigade Trench Mortar Battery : 24 December 1915 - 31 July 1916 (First World War, War Diary, WO95/1559)	WD1559	9781474505819	£50.00
5 DIVISION 14 Infantry Brigade Headquarters : 4 August 1914 - 31 December 1914 (First World War, War Diary, WO95/1560)	WD1560	9781474505826	£49.00
5 DIVISION 14 Infantry Brigade Headquarters : 28 June 1914 - 31 January 1915 (First World War, War Diary, WO95/1561)	WD1561	9781474522250	£90.00
5 DIVISION 14 Infantry Brigade Headquarters : 1 June 1915 - 12 December 1915 (First World War, War Diary, WO95/1562)	WD1562	9781474505833	£76.00
5 DIVISION 14 Infantry Brigade East Surrey Regiment 1st Battalion : 4 August 1914 - 31 December 1915 (First World War, War Diary, WO95/1563)	WD1563	9781474522267	£48.00
5 DIVISION 14 Infantry Brigade Duke of Cornwall's Light Infantry 1st Battalion and Manchester Regiment 2nd Battalion: 4 August 1914 - 31 December 1915 (First World War, War Diary, WO95/1564)	WD1564	9781474505840	£37.00
5 DIVISION 14 Infantry Brigade Devonshire Regiment 1st Battalion and Cheshire Regiment 5th (Reserve) Battalion : 21 August 1914 - 31 December 1915 (First World War, War Diary, WO95/1565)	WD1565	9781474505857	£20.00
5 DIVISION 15 Infantry Brigade Headquarters : 14 August 1914 - 31 December 1915 (First World War, War Diary, WO95/1566)	WD1566	9781474505864	£62.00
5 DIVISION 15 Infantry Brigade Headquarters : 1 January 1916 - 29 December 1916 (First World War, War Diary, WO95/1567)	WD1567	9781474505871	£51.00
5 DIVISION 15 Infantry Brigade Headquarters : 1 January 1917 - 30 November 1917 (First World War, War Diary, WO95/1568)	WD1568	9781474505888	£51.00
5 DIVISION 15 Infantry Brigade Headquarters : 1 February 1918 - 9 May 1919 (First World War, War Diary, WO95/1569)	WD1569	9781474505895	£36.00
5 DIVISION 15 Infantry Brigade Bedfordshire Regiment 1st Battalion : 5 August 1914 - 30 November 1917 (First World War, War Diary, WO95/1570/1-2)	WD1570_1-2	9781474505901	£58.00
5 DIVISION 15 Infantry Brigade Bedfordshire Regiment 1st Battalion : 1 April 1918 - 20 April 1919 (First World War, War Diary, WO95/1570/3)	WD1570_3	9781474505918	£15.00
5 DIVISION 15 Infantry Brigade Cheshire Regiment 1st Battalion : 4 August 1914 - 20 April 1919 (First World War, War Diary, WO95/1571)	WD1571	9781474522274	£65.00
5 DIVISION 15 Infantry Brigade Cheshire Regiment 1/6th Battalion, Dorsetshire Regiment 1st Battalion and King's (Liverpool Regiment) 6th Battalion. : 4 August 1914 - 31 December 1915 (First World War, War Diary, WO95/1572)	WD1572	9781474505925	£33.00
5 DIVISION 15 Infantry Brigade Norfolk Regiment 1st Battalion : 1 October 1914 - 20 April 1919 (First World War, War Diary, WO95/1573)	WD1573	9781474505932	£38.00

Title	Product Code	ISBN	Price
5 DIVISION 15 Infantry Brigade Royal Warwickshire Regiment 16th Battalion, Brigade Machine Gun Company and Brigade Trench Mortar Battery : 20 November 1915 - 1 August 1916 (First World War, War Diary, WO95/1574)	WD1574	9781474505949	£46.00
5 DIVISION 95 Infantry Brigade Headquarters : 4 August 1915 - 30 July 1917 (First World War, War Diary, WO95/1575)	WD1575	9781474522281	£64.00
5 DIVISION 95 Infantry Brigade Headquarters : 4 August 1916 - 27 April 1919 (First World War, War Diary, WO95/1576)	WD1576	9781474522298	£65.00
5 DIVISION 95 Infantry Brigade Duke of Cornwall's Light Infantry 1st Battalion : 1 January 1916 - 31 August 1917 (First World War, War Diary, WO95/1577)	WD1577	9781474522304	£77.00
5 DIVISION 95 Infantry Brigade Duke of Cornwall's Light Infantry 1st Battalion : 1 April 1918 - 20 April 1919 (First World War, War Diary, WO95/1578)	WD1578	9781474505956	£52.00
5 DIVISION 95 Infantry Brigade East Surrey Regiment 1st Battalion and Devonshire Regiment 1st Battalion : 1 January 1916 - 19 April 1919 (First World War, War Diary, WO95/1579)	WD1579	9781474522311	£75.00
5 DIVISION 95 Infantry Brigade Gloucestershire Regiment 12th (Service) (Bristol) Battalion, Brigade Machine Gun Company and Brigade Trench Mortar Battery : 3 October 1915 - 31 July 1916 (First World War, War Diary, WO95/1580)	WD1580	9781474505963	£35.00

Title	Product Code	ISBN	Price
50 DIVISION			
50 DIVISION Headquarters, Branches and Services General Staff : 19 April 1915 - 31 December 1915 (First World War, War Diary, WO95/2807)	WD2807	9781474527538	£54.00
50 DIVISION Headquarters, Branches and Services General Staff : 1 January 1916 - 30 June 1916 (First World War, War Diary, WO95/2808)	WD2808	9781474527545	£54.00
50 DIVISION Headquarters, Branches and Services General Staff : 1 July 1916 - 31 March 1917 (First World War, War Diary, WO95/2809)	WD2809	9781474527552	£55.00
50 DIVISION Headquarters, Branches and Services General Staff : 1 April 1917 - 31 December 1917 (First World War, War Diary, WO95/2810)	WD2810	9781474527569	£69.00
50 DIVISION Headquarters, Branches and Services General Staff : 1 January 1918 - 30 September 1918 (First World War, War Diary, WO95/2811)	WD2811	9781474527576	£54.00
50 DIVISION Headquarters, Branches and Services General Staff : 1 October 1918 - 19 March 1919 (First World War, War Diary, WO95/2812)	WD2812	9781474527583	£58.00
50 DIVISION Headquarters, Branches and Services Adjutant and Quarter-Master General : 23 April 1915 - 30 November 1918 (First World War, War Diary, WO95/2813/1)	WD2813_1	9781474527590	£30.00
50 DIVISION Headquarters, Branches and Services Commander Royal Artillery : 1 April 1915 - 31 December 1916 (First World War, War Diary, WO95/2813/2)	WD2813_2	9781474527606	£34.00
50 DIVISION Headquarters, Branches and Services Commander Royal Artillery : 1 January 1917 - 30 June 1919 (First World War, War Diary, WO95/2814)	WD2814	9781474527613	£55.00
50 DIVISION Headquarters, Branches and Services Royal Army Medical Corps Assistant Director Medical Services : 17 April 1915 - 20 June 1919 (First World War, War Diary, WO95/2815)	WD2815	9781474527620	£67.00
50 DIVISION Headquarters, Branches and Services Commander Royal Engineers : 16 April 1915 - 31 May 1916 (First World War, War Diary, WO95/2816/1)	WD2816_1	9781474527637	£15.00
50 DIVISION Headquarters, Branches and Services Commander Royal Engineers : 27 May 1916 - 31 May 1919 (First World War, War Diary, WO95/2816/2)	WD2816_2	9781474527644	£19.00
50 DIVISION Headquarters, Branches and Services Royal Army Ordnance Corps Deputy Assistant Director Ordnance Services : 19 April 1915 - 30 May 1919 (First World War, War Diary, WO95/2816/3)	WD2816_3	9781474527651	£15.00
50 DIVISION Headquarters, Branches and Services Royal Army Veterinary Corps Deputy Assistant Director Veterinary Services : 1 July 1915 - 31 March 1919 (First World War, War Diary, WO95/2816/4)	WD2816_4	9781474527668	£27.00
50 DIVISION Divisional Troops A Squadron Yorkshire Hussars : 4 April 1915 - 28 May 1916 (First World War, War Diary, WO95/2817/1)	WD2817_1	9781474527675	£15.00
50 DIVISION Divisional Troops Divisional Cyclist Company : 16 April 1915 - 31 May 1916 (First World War, War Diary, WO95/2817/2)	WD2817_2	9781474527682	£15.00
50 DIVISION Divisional Troops 250 Brigade Royal Field Artillery : 17 April 1915 - 4 July 1919 (First World War, War Diary, WO95/2817/3)	WD2817_3	9781474527699	£25.00
50 DIVISION Divisional Troops 252 Brigade Royal Field Artillery : 5 August 1914 - 31 August 1915 (First World War, War Diary, WO95/2817/4)	WD2817_4	9781474527705	£22.00
50 DIVISION Divisional Troops 251 Brigade Royal Field Artillery : 5 August 1914 - 30 September 1915 (First World War, War Diary, WO95/2818)	WD2818	9781474527712	£59.00

Title	Product Code	ISBN	Price
50 DIVISION Divisional Troops 251 Brigade Royal Field Artillery : 23 February 1916 - 30 June 1919 (First World War, War Diary, WO95/2819)	WD2819	9781474527729	£65.00
50 DIVISION Divisional Troops 253 Brigade Royal Field Artillery : 19 April 1915 - 16 November 1916 (First World War, War Diary, WO95/2820/1)	WD2820_1	9781474527736	£15.00
50 DIVISION Divisional Troops Divisional Trench Mortar Batteries : 19 June 1915 - 31 January 1919 (First World War, War Diary, WO95/2820/2)	WD2820_2	9781474527743	£18.00
50 DIVISION Divisional Troops Divisional Ammunition Column : 5 August 1914 - 30 June 1919 (First World War, War Diary, WO95/2820/3)	WD2820_3	9781474527750	£26.00
50 DIVISION Divisional Troops 7, 446 and 447 Field Company Royal Engineers : 16 April 1915 - 31 May 1919 (First World War, War Diary, WO95/2821)	WD2821	9781474527767	£82.00
50 DIVISION Divisional Troops Divisional Signal Company : 16 April 1915 - 30 April 1919 (First World War, War Diary, WO95/2822)	WD2822	9781474527774	£30.00
50 DIVISION Divisional Troops Royal Irish Regiment 5th Battalion Pioneers : 1 April 1918 - 28 February 1919 (First World War, War Diary, WO95/2823/1)	WD2823_1	9781474527781	£15.00
50 DIVISION Divisional Troops Durham Light Infantry 1/7th Battalion Pioneers : 1 December 1915 - 30 June 1918 (First World War, War Diary, WO95/2823/2)	WD2823_2	9781474527798	£19.00
50 DIVISION Divisional Troops Machine Gun Corps 50 Battalion : 1 April 1918 - 30 April 1919 (First World War, War Diary, WO95/2823/3)	WD2823_3	9781474527804	£15.00
50 DIVISION Divisional Troops 245 Machine Gun Company : 15 July 1915 - 31 March 1918 (First World War, War Diary, WO95/2823/4)	WD2823_4	9781474527811	£15.00
50 DIVISION Divisional Troops Royal Army Medical Corps 1/1 Northumbrian Field Ambulance : 17 April 1915 - 8 June 1919 (First World War, War Diary, WO95/2824/1)	WD2824_1	9781474527828	£36.00
50 DIVISION Divisional Troops Royal Army Medical Corps 2/2 Northumbrian Field Ambulance : 18 April 1915 - 10 July 1919 (First World War, War Diary, WO95/2824/2)	WD2824_2	9781474527835	£36.00
50 DIVISION Divisional Troops Royal Army Medical Corps 1/3 Northumbrian Field Ambulance, Field Ambulance Workshop Unit, 50 Sanitary Section, 1/1 Northumbrian Mobile Veterinary Section and Divisional Train (467, 468, 469, 470 Companies A.S.C.) : 16 April	WD2825	9781474527842	£75.00
50 DIVISION 149 Infantry Brigade Headquarters : 1 June 1915 - 30 April 1917 (First World War, War Diary, WO95/2826)	WD2826	9781474527859	£55.00
50 DIVISION 149 Infantry Brigade Headquarters : 1 May 1917 - 30 June 1919 (First World War, War Diary, WO95/2827)	WD2827	9781474527866	£56.00
50 DIVISION 149 Infantry Brigade Northumberland Fusiliers 1/4th Battalion (Territorials) : 1 August 1915 - 31 July 1918 (First World War, War Diary, WO95/2828/1)	WD2828_1	9781474527873	£29.00
50 DIVISION 149 Infantry Brigade Northumberland Fusiliers 1/5th Battalion (Territorial) : 18 April 1915 - 31 July 1918 (First World War, War Diary, WO95/2828/2)	WD2828_2	9781474527880	£26.00
50 DIVISION 149 Infantry Brigade Northumberland Fusiliers 1/6th Battalion (Territorial) : 20 April 1915 - 31 July 1918 (First World War, War Diary, WO95/2829)	WD2829	9781474527897	£72.00

Title	Product Code	ISBN	Price
50 DIVISION 149 Infantry Brigade Northumberland Fusiliers 1/7th Battalion (Territorials) : 20 April 1915 - 31 January 1918 (First World War, War Diary, WO95/2830)	WD2830	9781474527903	£78.00
50 DIVISION 149 Infantry Brigade Royal Dublin Fusiliers 2nd Battalion : 1 June 1918 - 30 April 1919 (First World War, War Diary, WO95/2831/1)	WD2831_1	9781474527910	£15.00
50 DIVISION 149 Infantry Brigade Royal Fusiliers (City of London Regiment) 3rd Battalion : 1 July 1918 - 31 May 1919 (First World War, War Diary, WO95/2831/2)	WD2831_2	9781474527927	£15.00
50 DIVISION 149 Infantry Brigade Border Regiment 5th Battalion : 29 July 1914 - 27 December 1915 (First World War, War Diary, WO95/2831/3)	WD2831_3	9781474527934	£15.00
50 DIVISION 149 Infantry Brigade Black Watch (Royal Highlanders) 13th (Scottish Horse) Battalion : 1 July 1918 - 6 July 1919 (First World War, War Diary, WO95/2831/4)	WD2831_4	9781474527941	£15.00
50 DIVISION 149 Infantry Brigade, Brigade Machine Gun Company and Brigade Trench Mortar Battery : 6 February 1916 - 31 March 1918 (First World War, War Diary, WO95/2831/5-6)	WD2831_5-6	9781474527958	£40.00
50 DIVISION 150 Infantry Brigade Headquarters : 23 April 1915 - 31 July 1917 (First World War, War Diary, WO95/2832)	WD2832	9781474527965	£38.00
50 DIVISION 150 Infantry Brigade Headquarters : 1 August 1917 - 30 June 1919 (First World War, War Diary, WO95/2833)	WD2833	9781474527972	£46.00
50 DIVISION 150 Infantry Brigade East Yorkshire Regiment 1/4th Battalion : 29 July 1914 - 31 December 1916 (First World War, War Diary, WO95/2834)	WD2834	9781474527989	£42.00
50 DIVISION 150 Infantry Brigade East Yorkshire Regiment 1/4th Battalion : 1 January 1917 - 31 July 1918 (First World War, War Diary, WO95/2835)	WD2835	9781474527996	£53.00
50 DIVISION 150 Infantry Brigade Northumberland Fusiliers 2nd Battalion, Duke of Edinburgh's (Wiltshire Regiment) 7th Battalion, Alexandra, Princess of Wales's Own (Yorkshire Regiment) 4th and 5th Battalion : 1 January 1915 - 31 July 1918 (First World War	WD2836	9781474528009	£41.00
50 DIVISION 150 Infantry Brigade Royal Munster Fusiliers 2nd Battalion : 1 May 1918 - 31 May 1919 (First World War, War Diary, WO95/2837/1)	WD2837_1	9781474528016	£15.00
50 DIVISION 150 Infantry Brigade Durham Light Infantry 1/5th Battalion : 23 January 1914 - 31 January 1918 (First World War, War Diary, WO95/2837/2)	WD2837_2	9781474528023	£15.00
50 DIVISION 150 Infantry Brigade, Brigade Machine Gun Company : 1 February 1916 - 31 March 1918 (First World War, War Diary, WO95/2837/3)	WD2837_3	9781474528030	£22.00
50 DIVISION 150 Infantry Brigade, Brigade Trench Mortar Battery : 11 April 1916 - 31 August 1916 (First World War, War Diary, WO95/2837/4)	WD2837_4	9781474528047	£15.00
50 DIVISION 151 Infantry Brigade Headquarters : 17 April 1915 - 30 April 1917 (First World War, War Diary, WO95/2838)	WD2838	9781474528054	£68.00
50 DIVISION 151 Infantry Brigade Headquarters : 1 May 1917 - 4 June 1919 (First World War, War Diary, WO95/2839)	WD2839	9781474528061	£57.00
50 DIVISION 151 Infantry Brigade Durham Light Infantry 1/5th, 1/6th, 1/7th and 1/9th Battalion : 19 April 1915 - 31 January 1918 (First World War, War Diary, WO95/2840)	WD2840	9781474528078	£54.00

Title	Product Code	ISBN	Price
50 DIVISION 151 Infantry Brigade Durham Light Infantry 1/8th Battalion : 17 April 1915 - 30 September 1917 (First World War, War Diary, WO95/2841)	WD2841	9781474528085	£65.00
50 DIVISION 151 Infantry Brigade Durham Light Infantry 1/8th Battalion : 1 October 1917 - 18 November 1918 (First World War, War Diary, WO95/2842)	WD2842	9781474528092	£48.00
50 DIVISION 151 Infantry Brigade King's Own (Yorkshire Light Infantry) 1st Battalion : 1 July 1918 - 31 May 1919 (First World War, War Diary, WO95/2843/1)	WD2843_1	9781474528108	£15.00
50 DIVISION 151 Infantry Brigade Royal Inniskilling Fusiliers 6th Battalion : 1 June 1918 - 31 May 1919 (First World War, War Diary, WO95/2843/2)	WD2843_2	9781474528115	£15.00
50 DIVISION 151 Infantry Brigade King's Royal Rifle Corps 4th Battalion : 1 July 1918 - 7 June 1919 (First World War, War Diary, WO95/2843/3)	WD2843_3	9781474528122	£15.00
50 DIVISION 151 Infantry Brigade Border Regiment 5th Battalion : 27 December 1915 - 31 January 1918 (First World War, War Diary, WO95/2843/4)	WD2843_4	9781474528139	£15.00
50 DIVISION 151 Infantry Brigade Loyal North Lancashire Regiment 1/5th Battalion (Territorial Force) : 1 February 1915 - 30 December 1915 (First World War, War Diary, WO95/2843/5)	WD2843_5	9781474528146	£15.00
50 DIVISION 151 Infantry Brigade, Brigade Machine Gun Company : 7 February 1916 - 31 March 1918 (First World War, War Diary, WO95/2843/6)	WD2843_6	9781474528153	£15.00

Title	Product Code	ISBN	Price
51 DIVISION			
51 DIVISION Headquarters, Branches and Services General Staff : 1 January 1915 - 30 June 1916 (First World War, War Diary, WO95/2844)	WD2844	9781474528160	£58.00
51 DIVISION Headquarters, Branches and Services General Staff : 1 July 1916 - 30 June 1917 (First World War, War Diary, WO95/2845)	WD2845	9781474528177	£76.00
51 DIVISION Headquarters, Branches and Services General Staff : 1 August 1917 - 20 March 1918 (First World War, War Diary, WO95/2846)	WD2846	9781474528184	£66.00
51 DIVISION Headquarters, Branches and Services General Staff : 19 July 1917 - 31 May 1919 (First World War, War Diary, WO95/2847)	WD2847	9781474528191	£77.00
51 DIVISION Headquarters, Branches and Services Adjutant and Quarter-Master General : 29 July 1914 - 31 December 1916 (First World War, War Diary, WO95/2848)	WD2848	9781474528207	£46.00
51 DIVISION Headquarters, Branches and Services Adjutant and Quarter-Master General : 1 January 1917 - 31 January 1919 (First World War, War Diary, WO95/2849)	WD2849	9781474528214	£55.00
51 DIVISION Headquarters, Branches and Services Commander Royal Artillery : 30 April 1915 - 25 March 1919 (First World War, War Diary, WO95/2850)	WD2850	9781474528221	£67.00
51 DIVISION Headquarters, Branches and Services Royal Army Medical Corps Assistant Director Medical Services : 1 May 1915 - 31 March 1919 (First World War, War Diary, WO95/2851)	WD2851	9781474528238	£70.00
51 DIVISION Headquarters, Branches and Services Commander Royal Engineers : 1 May 1915 - 28 March 1919 (First World War, War Diary, WO95/2852)	WD2852	9781474528245	£50.00
51 DIVISION Headquarters, Branches and Services Royal Army Ordnance Corps Deputy Assistant Director Ordnance Services : 1 May 1915 - 31 January 1919 (First World War, War Diary, WO95/2853/1b)	WD2853_1B	9781474528252	£18.00
51 DIVISION Headquarters, Branches and Services Royal Army Veterinary Corps Assistant Director Veterinary Services : 1 May 1915 - 28 February 1919 (First World War, War Diary, WO95/2853/2b)	WD2853_2B	9781474528269	£15.00
51 DIVISION Divisional Troops D Squadron North Irish Horse : 1 May 1915 - 1 April 1916 (First World War, War Diary, WO95/2854/1)	WD2854_1	9781474528276	£15.00
51 DIVISION Divisional Troops Divisional Cyclist Company : 1 May 1915 - 30 April 1916 (First World War, War Diary, WO95/2854/2)	WD2854_2	9781474528283	£15.00
51 DIVISION Divisional Troops 255 Brigade Royal Field Artillery : 1 June 1915 - 31 March 1919 (First World War, War Diary, WO95/2854/3)	WD2854_3	9781474528290	£15.00
51 DIVISION Divisional Troops 256 Brigade Royal Field Artillery : 2 May 1915 - 25 March 1919 (First World War, War Diary, WO95/2854/4)	WD2854_4	9781474528306	£26.00
51 DIVISION Divisional Troops 258 Brigade Royal Field Artillery : 1 May 1915 - 22 August 1916 (First World War, War Diary, WO95/2854/5)	WD2854_5	9781474528313	£15.00
51 DIVISION Divisional Troops 260 Brigade Royal Field Artillery : 22 October 1915 - 28 February 1917 (First World War, War Diary, WO95/2854/6)	WD2854_6	9781474528320	£15.00
51 DIVISION Divisional Troops Divisional Trench Mortar Batteries : 1 August 1916 - 30 November 1918 (First World War, War Diary, WO95/2854/7)	WD2854_7	9781474528337	£15.00

Title	Product Code	ISBN	Price
51 DIVISION Divisional Troops Divisional Ammunition Column : 17 April 1915 - 31 March 1919 (First World War, War Diary, WO95/2854/8)	WD2854_8	9781474528344	£15.00
51 DIVISION Divisional Troops 400 Field Company Royal Engineers : 21 April 1915 - 10 April 1919 (First World War, War Diary, WO95/2855/1b)	WD2855_1B	9781474528368	£25.00
51 DIVISION Divisional Troops 401 Field Company Royal Engineers : 1 December 1915 - 31 March 1919 (First World War, War Diary, WO95/2855/2)	WD2855_2	9781474528351	£33.00
51 DIVISION Divisional Troops 404 Field Company Royal Engineers. From Jan 1917 previously 2/2 Highland Field Company : 2 May 1915 - 31 March 1918 (First World War, War Diary, WO95/2856/1)	WD2856_1	9781474528375	£15.00
51 DIVISION Divisional Troops Divisional Signal Company : 1 May 1915 - 27 February 1919 (First World War, War Diary, WO95/2856/2)	WD2856_2	9781474528382	£18.00
51 DIVISION Divisional Troops Royal Scots (Lothian Regiment) 8th Battalion Pioneers : 1 December 1915 - 31 March 1919 (First World War, War Diary, WO95/2857/1)	WD2857_1	9781474528399	£31.00
51 DIVISION Divisional Troops Machine Gun Corps 51 Battalion : 19 February 1918 - 28 February 1919 (First World War, War Diary, WO95/2857/2)	WD2857_2	9781474528405	£20.00
51 DIVISION Divisional Troops 232 Machine Gun Company : 13 July 1917 - 28 February 1918 (First World War, War Diary, WO95/2857/3)	WD2857_3	9781474528412	£15.00
51 DIVISION Divisional Troops Royal Army Medical Corps 1/2 Highland Field Ambulance : 29 April 1915 - 31 March 1919 (First World War, War Diary, WO95/2858/1)	WD2858_1	9781474528429	£19.00
51 DIVISION Divisional Troops Royal Army Medical Corps 2/1 Highland Field Ambulance : 2 May 1915 - 10 April 1919 (First World War, War Diary, WO95/2858/2)	WD2858_2	9781474528436	£23.00
51 DIVISION Divisional Troops Royal Army Medical Corps 1/3 Highland Field Ambulance and 51 Sanitary Section : 1 May 1915 - 30 April 1917 (First World War, War Diary, WO95/2859)	WD2859	9781474528443	£68.00
51 DIVISION Divisional Troops Royal Army Veterinary Corps 1/1 Highland Mobile Veterinary Section : 1 November 1916 - 1 November 1916 (First World War, War Diary, WO95/2860/1)	WD2860_1	9781474528450	£15.00
51 DIVISION Divisional Troops Royal Army Service Corps Divisional Train (471, 472, 473, 474 Companies A.S.C.) : 1 April 1915 - 14 April 1919 (First World War, War Diary, WO95/2860/2)	WD2860_2	9781474528467	£37.00
51 DIVISION 152 Infantry Brigade Headquarters : 1 May 1915 - 31 December 1916 (First World War, War Diary, WO95/2861)	WD2861	9781474528474	£62.00
51 DIVISION 152 Infantry Brigade Headquarters : 1 January 1917 - 30 September 1917 (First World War, War Diary, WO95/2862)	WD2862	9781474528481	£52.00
51 DIVISION 152 Infantry Brigade Headquarters : 1 October 1917 - 30 April 1918 (First World War, War Diary, WO95/2863)	WD2863	9781474528498	£44.00
51 DIVISION 152 Infantry Brigade Headquarters : 2 January 1918 - 21 April 1919 (First World War, War Diary, WO95/2864)	WD2864	9781474528504	£44.00
51 DIVISION 152 Infantry Brigade Princess Louise's (Argyll & Sutherland Highlanders) 1/6th Battalion : 1 May 1915 - 30 June 1916 (First World War, War Diary, WO95/2865/1)	WD2865_1	9781474528511	£15.00

Title	Product Code	ISBN	Price
51 DIVISION 152 Infantry Brigade Princess Louise's (Argyll & Sutherland Highlanders) 1/8th Battalion : 5 August 1914 - 17 March 1918 (First World War, War Diary, WO95/2865/2)	WD2865_2	9781474528528	£19.00
51 DIVISION 152 Infantry Brigade Seaforth Highlanders (Ross-shire Buffs, the Duke of Albany's) 5th Battalion Seaforth Highlanders : 1 May 1915 - 15 April 1919 (First World War, War Diary, WO95/2866)	WD2866	9781474528535	£39.00
51 DIVISION 152 Infantry Brigade Seaforth Highlanders (Ross-shire Buffs, the Duke of Albany's) 6th Battalion : 19 April 1915 - 11 April 1919 (First World War, War Diary, WO95/2867)	WD2867	9781474528542	£51.00
51 DIVISION 152 Infantry Brigade Gordon Highlanders 6th Battalion : 1 June 1916 - 30 September 1918 (First World War, War Diary, WO95/2868/1)	WD2868_1	9781474528559	£32.00
51 DIVISION 152 Infantry Brigade Gordon Highlanders 6/7th Battalion : 1 March 1918 - 31 March 1918 (First World War, War Diary, WO95/2868/2)	WD2868_2	9781474528566	£15.00
51 DIVISION 152 Infantry Brigade, Brigade Machine Gun Company : 16 January 1916 - 28 February 1918 (First World War, War Diary, WO95/2868/3)	WD2868_3	9781474528573	£15.00
51 DIVISION 152 Infantry Brigade, Brigade Trench Mortar Battery : 1 August 1916 - 31 August 1916 (First World War, War Diary, WO95/2868/4)	WD2868_4	9781474528580	£15.00
51 DIVISION 153 Infantry Brigade Headquarters : 1 April 1915 - 29 December 1915 (First World War, War Diary, WO95/2869)	WD2869	9781474528597	£52.00
51 DIVISION 153 Infantry Brigade Headquarters : 1 January 1916 - 31 August 1916 (First World War, War Diary, WO95/2870)	WD2870	9781474528603	£73.00
51 DIVISION 153 Infantry Brigade Headquarters : 1 September 1916 - 31 March 1917 (First World War, War Diary, WO95/2871)	WD2871	9781474528610	£50.00
51 DIVISION 153 Infantry Brigade Headquarters : 1 April 1917 - 3 August 1917 (First World War, War Diary, WO95/2872)	WD2872	9781474528627	£51.00
51 DIVISION 153 Infantry Brigade Headquarters : 1 August 1917 - 28 February 1918 (First World War, War Diary, WO95/2873)	WD2873	9781474528634	£50.00
51 DIVISION 153 Infantry Brigade Headquarters : 1 March 1918 - 31 July 1918 (First World War, War Diary, WO95/2874)	WD2874	9781474528641	£58.00
51 DIVISION 153 Infantry Brigade Headquarters : 4 August 1918 - 28 March 1919 (First World War, War Diary, WO95/2875)	WD2875	9781474528658	£55.00
51 DIVISION 153 Infantry Brigade Black Watch (Royal Highlanders) 6th (Perthshire) Battalion (Territorial) : 2 May 1915 - 28 February 1919 (First World War, War Diary, WO95/2876)	WD2876	9781474528665	£52.00
51 DIVISION 153 Infantry Brigade Black Watch (Royal Highlanders) 7th (Fife) Battalion (Territorial) : 1 May 1915 - 15 October 1916 (First World War, War Diary, WO95/2877)	WD2877	9781474528672	£44.00
51 DIVISION 153 Infantry Brigade Black Watch (Royal Highlanders) 7th (Fife) Battalion (Territorial) : 1 November 1916 - 31 March 1917 (First World War, War Diary, WO95/2878)	WD2878	9781474528689	£65.00
51 DIVISION 153 Infantry Brigade Black Watch (Royal Highlanders) 7th (Fife) Battalion (Territorial) : 1 April 1917 - 31 March 1919 (First World War, War Diary, WO95/2879)	WD2879	9781474528696	£68.00
51 DIVISION 153 Infantry Brigade Gordon Highlanders 5th Battalion : 5 June 1915 - 31 December 1916 (First World War, War Diary, WO95/2880)	WD2880	9781474528702	£57.00

Title	Product Code	ISBN	Price
51 DIVISION 153 Infantry Brigade Gordon Highlanders 5th Battalion : 1 January 1917 - 26 January 1918 (First World War, War Diary, WO95/2881)	WD2881	9781474528719	£68.00
51 DIVISION 153 Infantry Brigade Gordon Highlanders 7th Battalion : 29 April 1915 - 5 October 1918 (First World War, War Diary, WO95/2882/1)	WD2882_1	9781474528726	£50.00
51 DIVISION 153 Infantry Brigade Princess Louise's (Argyll & Sutherland Highlanders) 1/6th Battalion : 1 October 1918 - 31 March 1919 (First World War, War Diary, WO95/2882/2)	WD2882_2	9781474528733	£15.00
51 DIVISION 153 Infantry Brigade, Brigade Machine Gun Company : 12 January 1916 - 28 February 1918 (First World War, War Diary, WO95/2882/3)	WD2882_3	9781474528740	£15.00
51 DIVISION 153 Infantry Brigade, Brigade Trench Mortar Battery : 1 March 1916 - 31 August 1916 (First World War, War Diary, WO95/2882/4)	WD2882_4	9781474528757	£15.00
51 DIVISION 154 Infantry Brigade Headquarters : 19 April 1915 - 31 December 1916 (First World War, War Diary, WO95/2883)	WD2883	9781474528764	£44.00
51 DIVISION 154 Infantry Brigade Headquarters : 1 January 1917 - 31 December 1917 (First World War, War Diary, WO95/2884)	WD2884	9781474528771	£44.00
51 DIVISION 154 Infantry Brigade Headquarters : 1 January 1918 - 28 February 1919 (First World War, War Diary, WO95/2885)	WD2885	9781474528788	£58.00
51 DIVISION 154 Infantry Brigade Princess Louise's (Argyll & Sutherland Highlanders) 1/7th Battalion : 1 March 1916 - 31 March 1919 (First World War, War Diary, WO95/2886/1)	WD2886_1	9781474528795	£32.00
51 DIVISION 154 Infantry Brigade Gordon Highlanders 4th Battalion : 1 March 1916 - 31 March 1919 (First World War, War Diary, WO95/2886/2)	WD2886_2	9781474528801	£28.00
51 DIVISION 154 Infantry Brigade King's (Liverpool Regiment) 8th Battalion : 1 May 1915 - 31 December 1915 (First World War, War Diary, WO95/2887/1)	WD2887_1	9781474528818	£15.00
51 DIVISION 154 Infantry Brigade King's Own (Royal Lancaster Regiment) 4th Battalion : 1 May 1915 - 31 December 1915 (First World War, War Diary, WO95/2887/2)	WD2887_2	9781474528825	£15.00
51 DIVISION 154 Infantry Brigade Lancashire Fusiliers 2/5th Battalion : 1 May 1915 - 31 October 1915 (First World War, War Diary, WO95/2887/3)	WD2887_3	9781474528832	£15.00
51 DIVISION 154 Infantry Brigade Loyal North Lancashire Regiment 1/4th Battalion (Territorial Force) : 22 October 1914 - 31 December 1915 (First World War, War Diary, WO95/2887/4)	WD2887_4	9781474528849	£15.00
51 DIVISION 154 Infantry Brigade Royal Scots (Lothian Regiment) 9th Battalion : 1 January 1916 - 31 January 1918 (First World War, War Diary, WO95/2887/5)	WD2887_5	9781474528856	£16.00
51 DIVISION 154 Infantry Brigade Cameronians (Scottish Rifles) 6th Battalion : 21 March 1915 - 31 May 1916 (First World War, War Diary, WO95/2887/6)	WD2887_6	9781474528863	£28.00
51 DIVISION 154 Infantry Brigade Seaforth Highlanders (Ross-shire Buffs, the Duke of Albany's) 4th Battalion : 1 January 1916 - 31 March 1918 (First World War, War Diary, WO95/2888/1)	WD2888_1	9781474528870	£15.00
51 DIVISION 154 Infantry Brigade, Brigade Machine Gun Company : 1 April 1918 - 28 February 1919 (First World War, War Diary, WO95/2888/2)	WD2888_2	9781474528887	£15.00

Title	Product Code	ISBN	Price
51 DIVISION 154 Infantry Brigade, Brigade Trench Mortar Battery : 14 January 1916 - 28 February 1918 (First World War, War Diary, WO95/2888/3)	WD2888_3	9781474528894	£28.00
51 DIVISION 154 Infantry Brigade, Brigade Trench Mortar Battery : 3 September 1916 - 31 December 1916 (First World War, War Diary, WO95/2888/4)	WD2888_4	9781474528900	£15.00

Title	Product Code	ISBN	Price
52 DIVISION			
52 DIVISION Headquarters, Branches and Services General Staff : 1 April 1918 - 30 April 1919 (First World War, War Diary, WO95/2889)	WD2889	9781474528917	£51.00
52 DIVISION Headquarters, Branches and Services Adjutant and Quarter-Master General : 1 April 1918 - 31 May 1919 (First World War, War Diary, WO95/2890/1)	WD2890_1	9781474528924	£33.00
52 DIVISION Headquarters, Branches and Services Commander Royal Artillery : 1 April 1918 - 31 May 1919 (First World War, War Diary, WO95/2890/2)	WD2890_2	9781474528931	£33.00
52 DIVISION Headquarters, Branches and Services Royal Army Medical Corps Assistant Director Medical Services : 1 April 1918 - 30 June 1919 (First World War, War Diary, WO95/2891/1)	WD2891_1	9781474528948	£15.00
52 DIVISION Headquarters, Branches and Services Commander Royal Engineers : 1 April 1918 - 31 May 1919 (First World War, War Diary, WO95/2891/2)	WD2891_2	9781474528955	£15.00
52 DIVISION Headquarters, Branches and Services Royal Army Ordnance Corps Deputy Assistant Director Ordnance Services : 1 April 1918 - 30 April 1919 (First World War, War Diary, WO95/2891/3)	WD2891_3	9781474528962	£15.00
52 DIVISION Headquarters, Branches and Services Royal Army Veterinary Corps Deputy Assistant Director Veterinary Services : 1 April 1918 - 30 April 1919 (First World War, War Diary, WO95/2891/4)	WD2891_4	9781474528979	£15.00
52 DIVISION Divisional Troops Divisional Cyclist Company : 1 April 1918 - 4 May 1918 (First World War, War Diary, WO95/2892/1)	WD2892_1	9781474528986	£15.00
52 DIVISION Divisional Troops 9 Brigade Royal Field Artillery : 1 April 1918 - 30 April 1919 (First World War, War Diary, WO95/2892/2)	WD2892_2	9781474528993	£15.00
52 DIVISION Divisional Troops 56 Brigade Royal Field Artillery : 1 April 1918 - 31 March 1919 (First World War, War Diary, WO95/2892/3)	WD2892_3	9781474529006	£15.00
52 DIVISION Divisional Troops Divisional Trench Mortar Batteries : 1 May 1918 - 27 December 1918 (First World War, War Diary, WO95/2892/4)	WD2892_4	9781474529013	£15.00
52 DIVISION Divisional Troops Divisional Ammunition Column : 1 April 1918 - 31 May 1919 (First World War, War Diary, WO95/2892/5)	WD2892_5	9781474529020	£15.00
52 DIVISION Divisional Troops 410 Field Company Royal Engineers : 1 April 1918 - 31 May 1919 (First World War, War Diary, WO95/2893/1)	WD2893_1	9781474529037	£15.00
52 DIVISION Divisional Troops 412 Field Company Royal Engineers : 1 April 1918 - 31 May 1919 (First World War, War Diary, WO95/2893/2)	WD2893_2	9781474529044	£15.00
52 DIVISION Divisional Troops 413 Field Company Royal Engineers : 1 April 1918 - 31 May 1919 (First World War, War Diary, WO95/2893/3)	WD2893_3	9781474529051	£15.00
52 DIVISION Divisional Troops Divisional Signal Company : 1 April 1918 - 27 May 1919 (First World War, War Diary, WO95/2893/4)	WD2893_4	9781474529068	£15.00
52 DIVISION Divisional Troops Northumberland Fusiliers 17th Battalion (N.E.R. Pioneers) : 1 June 1918 - 30 April 1919 (First World War, War Diary, WO95/2893/5)	WD2893_5	9781474529075	£15.00
52 DIVISION Divisional Troops Machine Gun Corps 52 Battalion : 1 April 1918 - 31 March 1919 (First World War, War Diary, WO95/2893/6)	WD2893_6	9781474529082	£36.00
52 DIVISION Divisional Troops Royal Army Medical Corps 1/1 Lowland Field Ambulance : 19 August 1916 - 30 April 1919 (First World War, War Diary, WO95/2894/1)	WD2894_1	9781474529099	£30.00

Title	Product Code	ISBN	Price
52 DIVISION Divisional Troops Royal Army Medical Corps 1/2 Lowland Field Ambulance : 17 April 1918 - 31 May 1919 (First World War, War Diary, WO95/2894/2)	WD2894_2	9781474529105	£15.00
52 DIVISION Divisional Troops Royal Army Medical Corps 1/3 Lowland Field Ambulance : 17 April 1918 - 31 May 1919 (First World War, War Diary, WO95/2894/3)	WD2894_3	9781474529112	£24.00
52 DIVISION Divisional Troops Royal Army Veterinary Corps 1/1 Lowland Mobile Veterinary Section : 1 April 1918 - 28 February 1919 (First World War, War Diary, WO95/2895/1)	WD2895_1	9781474529129	£15.00
52 DIVISION Divisional Troops Royal Army Service Corps Divisional Train (217, 218, 219, 220 Companies A.S.C.) : 1 April 1918 - 31 May 1919 (First World War, War Diary, WO95/2895/2)	WD2895_2	9781474529136	£42.00
52 DIVISION Divisional Troops 984 Divisional Employment Company : 1 May 1919 - 31 May 1919 (First World War, War Diary, WO95/2895/3)	WD2895_3	9781474529143	£15.00
52 DIVISION 155 Infantry Brigade Headquarters, King's Own Scottish Borderers 4th Battalion, Royal Scots Fusiliers 1/4th Battalion, Royal Scots Fusiliers 1/5th Battalion and Brigade Trench Mortar Battery : 1 April 1918 - 31 December 1918 (First World War,	WD2896	9781474529150	£45.00
52 DIVISION 156 Infantry Brigade Headquarters : 1 April 1918 - 31 March 1919 (First World War, War Diary, WO95/2897/1)	WD2897_1	9781474529167	£33.00
52 DIVISION 156 Infantry Brigade Royal Scots (Lothian Regiment) 4th Battalion : 1 April 1918 - 30 April 1919 (First World War, War Diary, WO95/2897/2)	WD2897_2	9781474529174	£15.00
52 DIVISION 156 Infantry Brigade Royal Scots (Lothian Regiment) 7th Battalion : 1 April 1918 - 3 May 1919 (First World War, War Diary, WO95/2897/3)	WD2897_3	9781474529181	£15.00
52 DIVISION 156 Infantry Brigade Cameronians (Scottish Rifles) 7th Battalion : 1 April 1918 - 31 March 1919 (First World War, War Diary, WO95/2897/4)	WD2897_4	9781474529198	£15.00
52 DIVISION 156 Infantry Brigade, Brigade Trench Mortar Battery : 1 April 1918 - 10 February 1919 (First World War, War Diary, WO95/2897/5)	WD2897_5	9781474529204	£15.00
52 DIVISION 157 Infantry Brigade Headquarters : 17 July 1917 - 25 June 1919 (First World War, War Diary, WO95/2898/1)	WD2898_1	9781474529211	£28.00
52 DIVISION 157 Infantry Brigade Highland Light Infantry 5th (City of Glasgow) Battalion (Territorial) : 30 July 1917 - 5 May 1919 (First World War, War Diary, WO95/2898/2)	WD2898_2	9781474529228	£15.00
52 DIVISION 157 Infantry Brigade Highland Light Infantry 6th (City of Glasgow) Battn. (Territorial) : 28 September 1917 - 31 March 1919 (First World War, War Diary, WO95/2898/3)	WD2898_3	9781474529235	£35.00
52 DIVISION 157 Infantry Brigade Highland Light Infantry 7th (Blythswood) Battalion (Territorial) : 1 April 1918 - 30 April 1919 (First World War, War Diary, WO95/2898/4)	WD2898_4	9781474529242	£15.00
52 DIVISION 157 Infantry Brigade, Brigade Trench Mortar Battery : 1 May 1918 - 31 December 1918 (First World War, War Diary, WO95/2898/5)	WD2898_5	9781474529259	£15.00

55 DIVISION

Title	Product Code	ISBN	Price
55 DIVISION Headquarters, Branches and Services General Staff : 3 January 1916 - 30 June 1916 (First World War, War Diary, WO95/2899)	WD2899	9781474529266	£43.00
55 DIVISION Headquarters, Branches and Services General Staff : 1 July 1916 - 31 August 1916 (First World War, War Diary, WO95/2900)	WD2900	9781474529273	£55.00
55 DIVISION Headquarters, Branches and Services General Staff : 8 September 1916 - 31 December 1916 (First World War, War Diary, WO95/2901)	WD2901	9781474529280	£52.00
55 DIVISION Headquarters, Branches and Services General Staff : 1 January 1917 - 31 May 1917 (First World War, War Diary, WO95/2902)	WD2902	9781474529297	£55.00
55 DIVISION Headquarters, Branches and Services General Staff : 1 June 1917 - 30 September 1917 (First World War, War Diary, WO95/2903)	WD2903	9781474529303	£60.00
55 DIVISION Headquarters, Branches and Services General Staff : 1 October 1917 - 31 December 1917 (First World War, War Diary, WO95/2904)	WD2904	9781474529310	£56.00
55 DIVISION Headquarters, Branches and Services General Staff : 1 January 1918 - 31 March 1918 (First World War, War Diary, WO95/2905)	WD2905	9781474529327	£68.00
55 DIVISION Headquarters, Branches and Services General Staff : 1 May 1918 - 30 September 1918 (First World War, War Diary, WO95/2906)	WD2906	9781474529334	£57.00
55 DIVISION Headquarters, Branches and Services General Staff : 1 October 1918 - 4 April 1919 (First World War, War Diary, WO95/2907)	WD2907	9781474529341	£65.00
55 DIVISION Headquarters, Branches and Services Adjutant and Quarter-Master General : 3 January 1916 - 31 August 1916 (First World War, War Diary, WO95/2908)	WD2908	9781474529358	£75.00
55 DIVISION Headquarters, Branches and Services Adjutant and Quarter-Master General : 1 September 1916 - 31 October 1917 (First World War, War Diary, WO95/2909)	WD2909	9781474529365	£66.00
55 DIVISION Headquarters, Branches and Services Adjutant and Quarter-Master General : 1 November 1917 - 30 April 1919 (First World War, War Diary, WO95/2910)	WD2910	9781474529372	£60.00
55 DIVISION Headquarters, Branches and Services Commander Royal Artillery : 1 October 1915 - 30 December 1915 (First World War, War Diary, WO95/2911)	WD2911	9781474529389	£68.00
55 DIVISION Headquarters, Branches and Services Royal Army Medical Corps Assistant Director Medical Services : 3 January 1916 - 29 March 1919 (First World War, War Diary, WO95/2912)	WD2912	9781474529396	£50.00
55 DIVISION Headquarters, Branches and Services Commander Royal Engineers, Deputy Assistant Director Ordnance Services and Assistant Director Veterinary Services : 1 April 1914 - 10 April 1919 (First World War, War Diary, WO95/2913)	WD2913	9781474529402	£39.00
55 DIVISION Divisional Troops `A' Squadron North Irish Horse, Divisional Cyclist Company, 275 and 276 Brigade Royal Field Artillery: 1 October 1915 - 20 December 1915 (First World War, War Diary, WO95/2914)	WD2914	9781474529419	£67.00
55 DIVISION Divisional Troops 277 and 278 Brigade Royal Field Artillery, Divisional Trench Mortar Batteries and Divisional Ammunition Column : 1 February 1915 - 15 March 1919 (First World War, War Diary, WO95/2915)	WD2915	9781474529426	£55.00

Title	Product Code	ISBN	Price
55 DIVISION Divisional Troops 419, 422 and 423 Field Company Royal Engineers and Divisional Signal Company : 1 January 1916 - 30 April 1919 (First World War, War Diary, WO95/2916)	WD2916	9781474529433	£64.00
55 DIVISION Divisional Troops Prince of Wales's Volunteers (South Lancashire Regiment) 1/4th Battalion Pioneers, Machine Gun Corps 55 Battalion and 196 Machine Gun Company : 1 January 1916 - 31 May 1919 (First World War, War Diary, WO95/2917)	WD2917	9781474529440	£78.00
55 DIVISION Divisional Troops Royal Army Medical Corps 2/1 and 1/3 West Lancashire Field Ambulance : 14 January 1915 - 29 June 1919 (First World War, War Diary, WO95/2918)	WD2918	9781474529457	£44.00
55 DIVISION Divisional Troops Royal Army Medical Corps 2/1 Wessex Field Ambulance, 55 Sanitary Section, 1/1 West Lancashire Mobile Veterinary Section and Divisional Train (95, 96, 97, 98 Companies A.S.C.) : 1 December 1915 - 16 June 1919 (First World War	WD2919	9781474529464	£65.00
55 DIVISION 164 Infantry Brigade Headquarters : 1 January 1916 - 31 July 1917 (First World War, War Diary, WO95/2920)	WD2920	9781474529471	£49.00
55 DIVISION 164 Infantry Brigade Headquarters : 1 August 1917 - 29 April 1919 (First World War, War Diary, WO95/2921)	WD2921	9781474529488	£53.00
55 DIVISION 164 Infantry Brigade King's Own (Royal Lancaster Regiment) 4th Battalion : 1 January 1916 - 30 April 1919 (First World War, War Diary, WO95/2922)	WD2922	9781474529495	£55.00
55 DIVISION 164 Infantry Brigade King's (Liverpool Regiment) 8th Battalion : 1 January 1916 - 31 January 1918 (First World War, War Diary, WO95/2923/1)	WD2923_1	9781474529501	£26.00
55 DIVISION 164 Infantry Brigade Lancashire Fusiliers 2/5th Battalion : 1 January 1916 - 30 April 1919 (First World War, War Diary, WO95/2923/2)	WD2923_2	9781474529518	£53.00
55 DIVISION 164 Infantry Brigade Loyal North Lancashire Regiment 1/4th Battalion (Territorial Force) : 1 January 1916 - 30 April 1919 (First World War, War Diary, WO95/2924/1)	WD2924_1	9781474529525	£49.00
55 DIVISION 164 Infantry Brigade, Brigade Machine Gun Company : 19 February 1916 - 28 February 1918 (First World War, War Diary, WO95/2924/2)	WD2924_2	9781474529532	£15.00
55 DIVISION 164 Infantry Brigade, Brigade Trench Mortar Battery : 1 August 1916 - 2 August 1916 (First World War, War Diary, WO95/2924/3)	WD2924_3	9781474529549	£15.00
55 DIVISION 165 Infantry Brigade Headquarters : 3 January 1916 - 30 April 1919 (First World War, War Diary, WO95/2925)	WD2925	9781474529556	£65.00
55 DIVISION 165 Infantry Brigade King's (Liverpool Regiment) 5th and 6th Battalion : 1 January 1916 - 30 April 1919 (First World War, War Diary, WO95/2926)	WD2926	9781474529563	£48.00
55 DIVISION 165 Infantry Brigade King's (Liverpool Regiment) 7th Battalion : 1 January 1916 - 30 April 1919 (First World War, War Diary, WO95/2927/1)	WD2927_1	9781474529570	£15.00
55 DIVISION 165 Infantry Brigade King's (Liverpool Regiment) 9th Battalion : 1 January 1916 - 28 February 1919 (First World War, War Diary, WO95/2927/2)	WD2927_2	9781474529587	£16.00
55 DIVISION 165 Infantry Brigade, Brigade Machine Gun Company : 26 February 1916 - 28 February 1918 (First World War, War Diary, WO95/2927/3)	WD2927_3	9781474529594	£15.00

Title	Product Code	ISBN	Price
55 DIVISION 165 Infantry Brigade, Brigade Trench Mortar Battery : 2 June 1916 - 20 July 1916 (First World War, War Diary, WO95/2927/4)	WD2927_4	9781474529600	£15.00
55 DIVISION 166 Infantry Brigade Headquarters : 3 January 1916 - 28 February 1919 (First World War, War Diary, WO95/2928)	WD2928	9781474529617	£69.00
55 DIVISION 166 Infantry Brigade Loyal North Lancashire Regiment 1/5th Battalion (Territorial Force) : 1 January 1916 - 31 January 1918 (First World War, War Diary, WO95/2929/1)	WD2929_1	9781474529624	£15.00
55 DIVISION 166 Infantry Brigade Prince of Wales's Volunteers (South Lancashire Regiment) 1/5th Battalion : 1 December 1915 - 31 July 1919 (First World War, War Diary, WO95/2929/2)	WD2929_2	9781474529631	£25.00
55 DIVISION 166 Infantry Brigade King's (Liverpool Regiment) 10th Battalion : 30 September 1916 - 30 September 1919 (First World War, War Diary, WO95/2929/3)	WD2929_3	9781474529648	£18.00
55 DIVISION 166 Infantry Brigade King's Own (Royal Lancaster Regiment) 1/5th Battalion : 1 November 1915 - 31 July 1919 (First World War, War Diary, WO95/2930/1)	WD2930_1	9781474529655	£51.00
55 DIVISION 166 Infantry Brigade, Brigade Machine Gun Company : 8 May 1916 - 28 February 1918 (First World War, War Diary, WO95/2930/2)	WD2930_2	9781474529662	£15.00
55 DIVISION 166 Infantry Brigade, Brigade Trench Mortar Battery : 2 March 1916 - 20 April 1916 (First World War, War Diary, WO95/2930/3)	WD2930_3	9781474529679	£15.00

Title	Product Code	ISBN	Price
56 DIVISION			
56 DIVISION Headquarters, Branches and Services General Staff : 5 February 1916 - 31 August 1916 (First World War, War Diary, WO95/2931)	WD2931	9781474529686	£56.00
56 DIVISION Headquarters, Branches and Services General Staff : 1 September 1916 - 31 December 1916 (First World War, War Diary, WO95/2932)	WD2932	9781474529693	£35.00
56 DIVISION Headquarters, Branches and Services General Staff : 1 January 1917 - 28 February 1917 (First World War, War Diary, WO95/2933/1)	WD2933_1	9781474529709	£15.00
56 DIVISION Headquarters, Branches and Services General Staff : 1 March 1917 - 31 March 1917 (First World War, War Diary, WO95/2933/2)	WD2933_2	9781474529716	£15.00
56 DIVISION Headquarters, Branches and Services General Staff : 1 April 1917 - 30 April 1917 (First World War, War Diary, WO95/2933/3)	WD2933_3	9781474529723	£15.00
56 DIVISION Headquarters, Branches and Services General Staff : 1 April 1917 - 30 April 1917 (First World War, War Diary, WO95/2933/4)	WD2933_4	9781474529730	£15.00
56 DIVISION Headquarters, Branches and Services General Staff : 1 July 1917 - 30 November 1917 (First World War, War Diary, WO95/2934)	WD2934	9781474529747	£62.00
56 DIVISION Headquarters, Branches and Services General Staff : 1 January 1918 - 30 April 1919 (First World War, War Diary, WO95/2935)	WD2935	9781474529754	£34.00
56 DIVISION Headquarters, Branches and Services Adjutant and Quarter-Master General : 5 February 1916 - 31 December 1917 (First World War, War Diary, WO95/2936/1)	WD2936_1	9781474529761	£36.00
56 DIVISION Headquarters, Branches and Services Adjutant and Quarter-Master General : 1 January 1918 - 18 May 1919 (First World War, War Diary, WO95/2936/2)	WD2936_2	9781474529778	£33.00
56 DIVISION Headquarters, Branches and Services Commander Royal Artillery : 1 August 1915 - 10 June 1919 (First World War, War Diary, WO95/2937)	WD2937	9781474529785	£58.00
56 DIVISION Headquarters, Branches and Services Royal Army Medical Corps Assistant Director Medical Services : 6 February 1916 - 17 April 1919 (First World War, War Diary, WO95/2938)	WD2938	9781474529792	£49.00
56 DIVISION Headquarters, Branches and Services Commander Royal Engineers : 5 February 1916 - 18 May 1919 (First World War, War Diary, WO95/2939/1)	WD2939_1	9781474529808	£19.00
56 DIVISION Headquarters, Branches and Services Royal Army Ordnance Corps Deputy Assistant Director Ordnance Services : 5 February 1916 - 30 June 1919 (First World War, War Diary, WO95/2939/2)	WD2939_2	9781474529815	£15.00
56 DIVISION Headquarters, Branches and Services Royal Army Veterinary Corps Assistant Director Veterinary Services : 16 October 1915 - 30 April 1919 (First World War, War Diary, WO95/2939/3)	WD2939_3	9781474529822	£15.00
56 DIVISION Divisional Troops `B' Squadron 2 King Edward's Horse : 2 October 1915 - 13 June 1919 (First World War, War Diary, WO95/2940/1)	WD2940_1	9781474529839	£22.00
56 DIVISION Divisional Troops 280 Brigade Royal Field Artillery : 21 March 1916 - 31 May 1916 (First World War, War Diary, WO95/2940/2)	WD2940_2	9781474529846	£15.00
56 DIVISION Divisional Troops 281 Brigade Royal Field Artillery : 1 September 1915 - 25 May 1919 (First World War, War Diary, WO95/2940/3)	WD2940_3	9781474529853	£22.00

Title	Product Code	ISBN	Price
56 DIVISION Divisional Troops 282 and 283 Brigade Royal Field Artillery, Divisional Trench Mortar Batteries and Divisional Ammunition Column : 1 October 1915 - 28 May 1919 (First World War, War Diary, WO95/2941)	WD2941	9781474529860	£23.00
56 DIVISION Divisional Troops 416 Field Company Royal Engineers : 1 May 1916 - 20 May 1919 (First World War, War Diary, WO95/2942/1)	WD2942_1	9781474529877	£39.00
56 DIVISION Divisional Troops 512 Field Company Royal Engineers : 4 February 1916 - 30 April 1919 (First World War, War Diary, WO95/2942/2)	WD2942_2	9781474529884	£15.00
56 DIVISION Divisional Troops 513 Field Company Royal Engineers : 1 February 1915 - 30 April 1919 (First World War, War Diary, WO95/2942/3)	WD2942_3	9781474529891	£15.00
56 DIVISION Divisional Troops Divisional Signal Company : 1 October 1914 - 31 May 1919 (First World War, War Diary, WO95/2942/4)	WD2942_4	9781474529907	£17.00
56 DIVISION Divisional Troops Cheshire Regiment 1/5th Battalion Pioneers, Machine Gun Corps 56 Battalion and 193 Machine Gun Company : 1 January 1916 - 28 February 1918 (First World War, War Diary, WO95/2943)	WD2943	9781474529914	£71.00
56 DIVISION Divisional Troops Royal Army Medical Corps 2/1, 2/2 and 2/3 London Field Ambulance and 56 Sanitary Section : 29 August 1915 - 31 March 1917 (First World War, War Diary, WO95/2944)	WD2944	9781474529921	£53.00
56 DIVISION Divisional Troops Royal Army Veterinary Corps 1/1 London Mobile Veterinary Section and Royal Army Service Corps Divisional Train (213, 214, 215, 216 Companies A.S.C.) : 5 February 1916 - 31 May 1919 (First World War, War Diary, WO95/2945)	WD2945	9781474529938	£45.00
56 DIVISION 167 Infantry Brigade Headquarters : 5 February 1916 - 31 March 1917 (First World War, War Diary, WO95/2946)	WD2946	9781474529945	£53.00
56 DIVISION 167 Infantry Brigade Headquarters : 1 April 1917 - 31 October 1917 (First World War, War Diary, WO95/2947)	WD2947	9781474529952	£56.00
56 DIVISION 167 Infantry Brigade Headquarters : 1 November 1917 - 30 April 1919 (First World War, War Diary, WO95/2948)	WD2948	9781474529969	£71.00
56 DIVISION 167 Infantry Brigade London Regiment 1st (City of London) Battalion (Royal Fusiliers) and London Regiment 3rd (City of London) Battalion (Royal Fusiliers) : 1 November 1915 - 29 January 1918 (First World War, War Diary, WO95/2949)	WD2949	9781474529976	£66.00
56 DIVISION 167 Infantry Brigade Duke of Cambridge's Own (Middlesex Regiment) 1/7th and 1/8th (T.F.) Battalion, Brigade Machine Gun Company and Brigade Trench Mortar Battery. : 1 February 1916 - 31 August 1916 (First World War, War Diary, WO95/2950)	WD2950	9781474529983	£73.00
56 DIVISION 168 Infantry Brigade Headquarters : 5 February 1916 - 31 May 1917 (First World War, War Diary, WO95/2951)	WD2951	9781474529990	£56.00
56 DIVISION 168 Infantry Brigade Headquarters : 1 June 1917 - 31 December 1917 (First World War, War Diary, WO95/2952)	WD2952	9781474530002	£44.00
56 DIVISION 168 Infantry Brigade Headquarters : 1 January 1918 - 20 May 1919 (First World War, War Diary, WO95/2953)	WD2953	9781474530019	£60.00
56 DIVISION 168 Infantry Brigade London Regiment 4th (City of London) Battalion (Royal Fusiliers) and London Regiment 12th (County of London) Battalion (The Rangers) : 2 November 1915 - 31 January 1918 (First World War, War Diary, WO95/2954)	WD2954	9781474530026	£69.00

Title	Product Code	ISBN	Price
56 DIVISION 168 Infantry Brigade London Regiment 13th (County of London) Battalion (Princess Louise's Kensington Battalion) : 1 February 1916 - 22 May 1919 (First World War, War Diary, WO95/2955)	WD2955	9781474530033	£59.00
56 DIVISION 168 Infantry Brigade London Regiment 14th (County of London) Battalion (London Scottish), Brigade Machine Gun Company and Brigade Trench Mortar Battery : 1 February 1916 - 30 September 1916 (First World War, War Diary, WO95/2956)	WD2956	9781474530040	£49.00
56 DIVISION 169 Infantry Brigade Headquarters : 5 February 1916 - 14 April 1917 (First World War, War Diary, WO95/2957)	WD2957	9781474530057	£63.00
56 DIVISION 169 Infantry Brigade Headquarters : 1 May 1917 - 31 December 1917 (First World War, War Diary, WO95/2958)	WD2958	9781474530064	£54.00
56 DIVISION 169 Infantry Brigade Headquarters : 1 January 1918 - 10 June 1919 (First World War, War Diary, WO95/2959)	WD2959	9781474530071	£54.00
56 DIVISION 169 Infantry Brigade London Regiment 2nd (City of London) Battalion (Royal Fusiliers) : 1 November 1915 - 30 April 1919 (First World War, War Diary, WO95/2960)	WD2960	9781474530088	£59.00
56 DIVISION 169 Infantry Brigade London Regiment 5th (City of London) Battalion (London Rifle Brigade) : 1 February 1916 - 31 July 1917 (First World War, War Diary, WO95/2961)	WD2961	9781474530095	£48.00
56 DIVISION 169 Infantry Brigade London Regiment 5th (City of London) Battalion (London Rifle Brigade) : 1 August 1917 - 24 May 1919 (First World War, War Diary, WO95/2962)	WD2962	9781474530101	£47.00
56 DIVISION 169 Infantry Brigade London Regiment 9th (County of London) Battalion (Queen Victoria's Rifles) : 1 February 1916 - 30 January 1918 (First World War, War Diary, WO95/2963/1)	WD2963_1	9781474530118	£15.00
56 DIVISION 169 Infantry Brigade London Regiment 16th (County of London) Battalion (Queen's Westminster Rifles) : 1 February 1916 - 24 April 1919 (First World War, War Diary, WO95/2963/2)	WD2963_2	9781474530125	£22.00
56 DIVISION 169 Infantry Brigade, Brigade Machine Gun Company : 1 July 1916 - 28 February 1918 (First World War, War Diary, WO95/2963/3)	WD2963_3	9781474530132	£15.00
56 DIVISION 169 Infantry Brigade, Brigade Trench Mortar Battery : 2 March 1916 - 28 August 1916 (First World War, War Diary, WO95/2963/4)	WD2963_4	9781474530149	£15.00

Title	Product Code	ISBN	Price
57 DIVISION			
57 DIVISION Headquarters, Branches and Services General Staff : 7 September 1915 - 31 July 1917 (First World War, War Diary, WO95/2964)	WD2964	9781474530156	£45.00
57 DIVISION Headquarters, Branches and Services General Staff : 1 August 1917 - 31 December 1917 (First World War, War Diary, WO95/2965)	WD2965	9781474530163	£43.00
57 DIVISION Headquarters, Branches and Services General Staff : 1 January 1918 - 31 July 1918 (First World War, War Diary, WO95/2966)	WD2966	9781474530170	£55.00
57 DIVISION Headquarters, Branches and Services General Staff : 1 August 1918 - 27 February 1919 (First World War, War Diary, WO95/2967/1)	WD2967_1	9781474530187	£60.00
57 DIVISION Headquarters, Branches and Services Adjutant and Quarter-Master General : 2 February 1917 - 25 June 1919 (First World War, War Diary, WO95/2967/2)	WD2967_2	9781474530194	£15.00
0	WD2968_1-2	9781474530200	£15.00
57 DIVISION Headquarters, Branches and Services Commander Royal Artillery : 7 February 1917 - 23 March 1919 (First World War, War Diary, WO95/2968/3)	WD2968_3	9781474530217	£63.00
57 DIVISION Headquarters, Branches and Services Royal Army Medical Corps Assistant Director Medical Services : 1 September 1915 - 29 February 1916 (First World War, War Diary, WO95/2969/1)	WD2969_1	9781474530224	£15.00
57 DIVISION Headquarters, Branches and Services Royal Army Medical Corps Assistant Director Medical Services : 12 February 1917 - 23 March 1919 (First World War, War Diary, WO95/2969/2)	WD2969_2	9781474530231	£33.00
57 DIVISION Headquarters, Branches and Services Commander Royal Engineers : 7 September 1915 - 29 February 1916 (First World War, War Diary, WO95/2969/3)	WD2969_3	9781474530248	£15.00
57 DIVISION Headquarters, Branches and Services Commander Royal Engineers : 10 February 1917 - 28 March 1919 (First World War, War Diary, WO95/2969/4)	WD2969_4	9781474530255	£38.00
57 DIVISION Headquarters, Branches and Services Royal Army Ordnance Corps Deputy Assistant Director Ordnance Services : 2 February 1917 - 28 February 1919 (First World War, War Diary, WO95/2969/5)	WD2969_5	9781474530262	£15.00
57 DIVISION Headquarters, Branches and Services Royal Army Veterinary Corps Assistant Director Veterinary Service : 6 February 1917 - 28 February 1919 (First World War, War Diary, WO95/2969/6)	WD2969_6	9781474530279	£15.00
57 DIVISION Divisional Troops Divisional Cyclist Company and 285 Brigade Royal Field Artillery : 12 January 1915 - 30 April 1919 (First World War, War Diary, WO95/2970)	WD2970	9781474530286	£81.00
57 DIVISION Divisional Troops 286 and 287 Brigade Royal Field Artillery, Divisional Trench Mortar Batteries and Divisional Ammunition Column : 4 October 1914 - 31 May 1919 (First World War, War Diary, WO95/2971)	WD2971	9781474530293	£45.00
57 DIVISION Divisional Troops 421 Field Company Royal Engineers : 7 February 1917 - 9 June 1919 (First World War, War Diary, WO95/2972)	WD2972	9781474530309	£69.00
57 DIVISION Divisional Troops 502 Field Company Royal Engineers : 1 February 1917 - 10 June 1919 (First World War, War Diary, WO95/2973/1)	WD2973_1	9781474530316	£21.00
57 DIVISION Divisional Troops 505 Field Company Royal Engineers : 13 February 1917 - 10 June 1919 (First World War, War Diary, WO95/2973/2)	WD2973_2	9781474530323	£20.00

Title	Product Code	ISBN	Price
57 DIVISION Divisional Troops Divisional Signal Company : 1 September 1915 - 25 October 1915 (First World War, War Diary, WO95/2974/1)	WD2974_1	9781474530330	£15.00
57 DIVISION Divisional Troops Divisional Signal Company : 11 February 1917 - 30 April 1919 (First World War, War Diary, WO95/2974/2)	WD2974_2	9781474530347	£47.00
57 DIVISION Divisional Troops Loyal North Lancashire Regiment 2/5th Battalion (Territorial Force) : 1 June 1917 - 31 May 1919 (First World War, War Diary, WO95/2974/3)	WD2974_3	9781474530354	£15.00
57 DIVISION Divisional Troops Machine Gun Corps 57 Battalion : 15 June 1916 - 26 May 1919 (First World War, War Diary, WO95/2974/4)	WD2974_4	9781474530361	£15.00
57 DIVISION Divisional Troops 173 Machine Gun Company : 1 May 1917 - 1 March 1918 (First World War, War Diary, WO95/2974/5)	WD2974_5	9781474530378	£15.00
57 DIVISION Divisional Troops Royal Army Medical Corps 2/2, 2/3 and 3/2 Wessex Field Ambulance, 2/1 West Lancashire Mobile Veterinary Section and Divisional Train (505, 506, 507, 508 Companies A.S.C.) : 30 June 1914 - 30 June 1919 (First World War, War D	WD2975	9781474530385	£46.00
57 DIVISION 170 Infantry Brigade Headquarters : 4 September 1915 - 30 September 1917 (First World War, War Diary, WO95/2976)	WD2976	9781474530392	£70.00
57 DIVISION 170 Infantry Brigade Headquarters : 1 October 1917 - 6 June 1919 (First World War, War Diary, WO95/2977)	WD2977	9781474530408	£75.00
57 DIVISION 170 Infantry Brigade Loyal North Lancashire Regiment 2/4th Battalion (Territorial Force) : 4 November 1915 - 30 April 1919 (First World War, War Diary, WO95/2978)	WD2978	9781474530415	£47.00
57 DIVISION 170 Infantry Brigade Loyal North Lancashire Regiment 1/5th Battalion (Territorial Force) : 1 January 1918 - 7 May 1919 (First World War, War Diary, WO95/2979/1)	WD2979_1	9781474530422	£19.00
57 DIVISION 170 Infantry Brigade Loyal North Lancashire Regiment 2/5th Battalion (Territorial Force) : 8 November 1915 - 29 February 1916 (First World War, War Diary, WO95/2979/2)	WD2979_2	9781474530439	£15.00
57 DIVISION 170 Infantry Brigade Loyal North Lancashire Regiment 2/5th Battalion (Territorial Force) : 8 February 1917 - 30 January 1918 (First World War, War Diary, WO95/2979/3)	WD2979_3	9781474530446	£15.00
57 DIVISION 170 Infantry Brigade Loyal North Lancashire Regiment 4/5th Battalion (Territorial Force) : 22 October 1915 - 29 February 1916 (First World War, War Diary, WO95/2979/4)	WD2979_4	9781474530453	£15.00
57 DIVISION 170 Infantry Brigade Loyal North Lancashire Regiment 4/5th Battalion (Territorial Force) : 11 February 1917 - 31 January 1918 (First World War, War Diary, WO95/2979/5)	WD2979_5	9781474530460	£15.00
57 DIVISION 170 Infantry Brigade King's Own (Royal Lancaster Regiment) 2/5th Battalion : 8 September 1915 - 29 February 1916 (First World War, War Diary, WO95/2979/6)	WD2979_6	9781474530477	£15.00
57 DIVISION 170 Infantry Brigade King's Own (Royal Lancaster Regiment) 2/5th Battalion : 6 February 1917 - 31 March 1918 (First World War, War Diary, WO95/2979/7)	WD2979_7	9781474530484	£15.00
57 DIVISION 170 Infantry Brigade King's Own (Royal Lancaster Regiment) 2/5th Battalion : 1 April 1919 - 30 April 1919 (First World War, War Diary, WO95/2979/8)	WD2979_8	9781474530491	£15.00

Title	Product Code	ISBN	Price
57 DIVISION 170 Infantry Brigade, Brigade Machine Gun Company : 9 February 1917 - 28 February 1918 (First World War, War Diary, WO95/2979/9)	WD2979_9	9781474530507	£15.00
57 DIVISION 171 Infantry Brigade Headquarters : 1 September 1915 - 29 February 1916 (First World War, War Diary, WO95/2980/1)	WD2980_1	9781474530514	£15.00
57 DIVISION 171 Infantry Brigade Headquarters : 13 February 1917 - 31 December 1917 (First World War, War Diary, WO95/2980/2)	WD2980_2	9781474530521	£32.00
57 DIVISION 171 Infantry Brigade Headquarters : 17 October 1917 - 30 April 1919 (First World War, War Diary, WO95/2981)	WD2981	9781474530538	£60.00
57 DIVISION 171 Infantry Brigade King's (Liverpool Regiment) 2/7 Battalion : 1 September 1915 - 29 February 1916 (First World War, War Diary, WO95/2982/1)	WD2982_1	9781474530545	£15.00
57 DIVISION 171 Infantry Brigade King's (Liverpool Regiment) 2/7 Battalion : 1 January 1917 - 28 February 1918 (First World War, War Diary, WO95/2982/2A)	WD2982_2A	9781474530552	£57.00
57 DIVISION 171 Infantry Brigade King's (Liverpool Regiment) 2/7 Battalion : 1 March 1918 - 16 May 1919 (First World War, War Diary, WO95/2982/2B)	WD2982_2B	9781474530569	£55.00
57 DIVISION 171 Infantry Brigade King's (Liverpool Regiment) 2/5 Battalion : 1 September 1915 - 29 February 1916 (First World War, War Diary, WO95/2983/1)	WD2983_1	9781474530576	£15.00
57 DIVISION 171 Infantry Brigade King's (Liverpool Regiment) 2/5 Battalion : 11 February 1917 - 31 January 1918 (First World War, War Diary, WO95/2983/2)	WD2983_2	9781474530583	£15.00
57 DIVISION 171 Infantry Brigade King's (Liverpool Regiment) 2/6 Battalion : 20 September 1915 - 1 February 1916 (First World War, War Diary, WO95/2983/3)	WD2983_3	9781474530590	£15.00
57 DIVISION 171 Infantry Brigade King's (Liverpool Regiment) 2/6 Battalion : 14 February 1917 - 15 May 1919 (First World War, War Diary, WO95/2983/4)	WD2983_4	9781474530606	£48.00
57 DIVISION 171 Infantry Brigade King's (Liverpool Regiment) 8th Battalion : 1 February 1918 - 31 May 1919 (First World War, War Diary, WO95/2983/5)	WD2983_5	9781474530613	£15.00
57 DIVISION 171 Infantry Brigade King's (Liverpool Regiment) 2/8 Battalion : 1 September 1915 - 1 February 1916 (First World War, War Diary, WO95/2983/6)	WD2983_6	9781474530620	£15.00
57 DIVISION 171 Infantry Brigade King's (Liverpool Regiment) 2/8 Battalion : 31 January 1917 - 31 January 1918 (First World War, War Diary, WO95/2983/7)	WD2983_7	9781474530637	£15.00
57 DIVISION 171 Infantry Brigade, Brigade Machine Gun Company : 10 February 1917 - 23 February 1918 (First World War, War Diary, WO95/2983/8)	WD2983_8	9781474530644	£15.00
57 DIVISION 171 Infantry Brigade, Brigade Trench Mortar Battery : 12 February 1917 - 22 March 1919 (First World War, War Diary, WO95/2983/9)	WD2983_9	9781474530651	£18.00
57 DIVISION 172 Infantry Brigade Headquarters : 2 September 1915 - 28 February 1919 (First World War, War Diary, WO95/2984)	WD2984	9781474530668	£63.00

Title	Product Code	ISBN	Price
57 DIVISION 172 Infantry Brigade Royal Munster Fusiliers 1st Battalion : 1 May 1918 - 31 May 1919 (First World War, War Diary, WO95/2985/1)	WD2985_1	9781474530675	£15.00
57 DIVISION 172 Infantry Brigade Prince of Wales's Volunteers (South Lancashire Regiment) 2/5th Battalion : 28 January 1917 - 26 February 1918 (First World War, War Diary, WO95/2985/10)	WD2985_10	9781474530767	£23.00
57 DIVISION 172 Infantry Brigade, Brigade Machine Gun Company : 21 October 1916 - 28 February 1918 (First World War, War Diary, WO95/2985/11)	WD2985_11	9781474530774	£15.00
57 DIVISION 172 Infantry Brigade King's (Liverpool Regiment) 9th Battalion : 1 February 1918 - 10 May 1919 (First World War, War Diary, WO95/2985/2)	WD2985_2	9781474530682	£15.00
57 DIVISION 172 Infantry Brigade King's (Liverpool Regiment) 2/9 Battalion : 6 September 1915 - 24 February 1916 (First World War, War Diary, WO95/2985/3)	WD2985_3	9781474530699	£15.00
57 DIVISION 172 Infantry Brigade King's (Liverpool Regiment) 2/9 Battalion : 1 February 1917 - 31 January 1918 (First World War, War Diary, WO95/2985/4)	WD2985_4	9781474530705	£15.00
57 DIVISION 172 Infantry Brigade King's (Liverpool Regiment) 2/10 Battalion : 10 September 1915 - 24 February 1916 (First World War, War Diary, WO95/2985/5)	WD2985_5	9781474530712	£15.00
57 DIVISION 172 Infantry Brigade King's (Liverpool Regiment) 2/10 Battalion : 30 January 1917 - 4 July 1918 (First World War, War Diary, WO95/2985/6)	WD2985_6	9781474530729	£15.00
57 DIVISION 172 Infantry Brigade Prince of Wales's Volunteers (South Lancashire Regiment) 2/4th Battalion : 2 September 1915 - 24 July 1916 (First World War, War Diary, WO95/2985/7)	WD2985_7	9781474530736	£15.00
57 DIVISION 172 Infantry Brigade Prince of Wales's Volunteers (South Lancashire Regiment) 2/4th Battalion : 2 February 1917 - 31 May 1919 (First World War, War Diary, WO95/2985/8)	WD2985_8	9781474530743	£15.00
57 DIVISION 172 Infantry Brigade Prince of Wales's Volunteers (South Lancashire Regiment) 2/5th Battalion : 13 September 1915 - 24 February 1916 (First World War, War Diary, WO95/2985/9)	WD2985_9	9781474530750	£15.00

Title	Product Code	ISBN	Price
58 DIVISION			
58 DIVISION Headquarters, Branches and Services General Staff : 7 September 1915 - 31 July 1917 (First World War, War Diary, WO95/2986)	WD2986	9781474530781	£65.00
58 DIVISION Headquarters, Branches and Services General Staff : 1 August 1917 - 31 December 1917 (First World War, War Diary, WO95/2987)	WD2987	9781474530798	£59.00
58 DIVISION Headquarters, Branches and Services General Staff : 1 January 1918 - 31 March 1918 (First World War, War Diary, WO95/2988)	WD2988	9781474530804	£51.00
58 DIVISION Headquarters, Branches and Services General Staff : 1 April 1918 - 31 July 1918 (First World War, War Diary, WO95/2989)	WD2989	9781474530811	£46.00
58 DIVISION Headquarters, Branches and Services General Staff : 31 July 1918 - 5 September 1918 (First World War, War Diary, WO95/2990)	WD2990	9781474530828	£32.00
58 DIVISION Headquarters, Branches and Services General Staff : 19 October 1918 - 31 December 1918 (First World War, War Diary, WO95/2991)	WD2991	9781474530835	£53.00
58 DIVISION Headquarters, Branches and Services Adjutant and Quarter-Master General : 3 September 1915 - 28 February 1916 (First World War, War Diary, WO95/2992/1)	WD2992_1	9781474530842	£15.00
58 DIVISION Headquarters, Branches and Services Adjutant and Quarter-Master General : 10 January 1917 - 30 April 1919 (First World War, War Diary, WO95/2992/2)	WD2992_2	9781474530859	£24.00
58 DIVISION Headquarters, Branches and Services Commander Royal Artillery : 13 September 1915 - 29 February 1916 (First World War, War Diary, WO95/2992/3)	WD2992_3	9781474530866	£15.00
58 DIVISION Headquarters, Branches and Services Commander Royal Artillery : 21 January 1917 - 5 December 1918 (First World War, War Diary, WO95/2992/4)	WD2992_4	9781474530873	£17.00
58 DIVISION Headquarters, Branches and Services Royal Army Medical Corps Assistant Director Medical Services : 1 October 1915 - 22 February 1916 (First World War, War Diary, WO95/2993/1)	WD2993_1	9781474530880	£15.00
58 DIVISION Headquarters, Branches and Services Royal Army Medical Corps Assistant Director Medical Services : 1 February 1917 - 30 April 1919 (First World War, War Diary, WO95/2993/2)	WD2993_2	9781474530897	£37.00
58 DIVISION Headquarters, Branches and Services Commander Royal Engineers : 1 September 1915 - 31 January 1916 (First World War, War Diary, WO95/2994/1)	WD2994_1	9781474530903	£15.00
58 DIVISION Headquarters, Branches and Services Commander Royal Engineers : 23 January 1917 - 23 June 1919 (First World War, War Diary, WO95/2994/2)	WD2994_2	9781474530910	£39.00
58 DIVISION Headquarters, Branches and Services Royal Army Ordnance Corps Deputy Assistant Director Ordnance Services : 6 October 1915 - 30 December 1915 (First World War, War Diary, WO95/2994/3)	WD2994_3	9781474530927	£15.00
58 DIVISION Headquarters, Branches and Services Royal Army Ordnance Corps Deputy Assistant Director Ordnance Services : 16 January 1917 - 31 May 1919 (First World War, War Diary, WO95/2994/4)	WD2994_4	9781474530934	£15.00
58 DIVISION Headquarters, Branches and Services Royal Army Veterinary Corps Deputy Assistant Director Veterinary Services : 5 September 1915 - 25 February 1916 (First World War, War Diary, WO95/2994/5)	WD2994_5	9781474530941	£15.00

Title	Product Code	ISBN	Price
58 DIVISION Headquarters, Branches and Services Royal Army Veterinary Corps Deputy Assistant Director Veterinary Services : 24 January 1917 - 31 January 1919 (First World War, War Diary, WO95/2994/6)	WD2994_6	9781474530958	£15.00
58 DIVISION Divisional Troops 290 Brigade Royal Field Artillery : 1 October 1915 - 31 May 1919 (First World War, War Diary, WO95/2995/1)	WD2995_1	9781474530965	£18.00
58 DIVISION Divisional Troops 290 Brigade Royal Field Artillery : 1 October 1915 - 11 February 1916 (First World War, War Diary, WO95/2995/2)	WD2995_2	9781474530972	£15.00
58 DIVISION Divisional Troops 290 Brigade Royal Field Artillery : 20 January 1917 - 8 March 1919 (First World War, War Diary, WO95/2995/3)	WD2995_3	9781474530989	£15.00
58 DIVISION Divisional Troops 291 Brigade Royal Field Artillery : 4 October 1915 - 6 February 1916 (First World War, War Diary, WO95/2995/4)	WD2995_4	9781474530996	£15.00
58 DIVISION Divisional Troops 291 Brigade Royal Field Artillery : 22 January 1917 - 31 May 1919 (First World War, War Diary, WO95/2995/5)	WD2995_5	9781474531009	£15.00
58 DIVISION Divisional Troops Divisional Trench Mortar Batteries : 1 March 1917 - 28 December 1918 (First World War, War Diary, WO95/2995/6)	WD2995_6	9781474531016	£15.00
58 DIVISION Divisional Troops Divisional Ammunition Column : 6 January 1917 - 31 May 1919 (First World War, War Diary, WO95/2995/7)	WD2995_7	9781474531023	£15.00
58 DIVISION Divisional Troops 503 Field Company Royal Engineers : 1 September 1915 - 22 February 1916 (First World War, War Diary, WO95/2996/1)	WD2996_1	9781474531030	£15.00
58 DIVISION Divisional Troops 206 Machine Gun Company : 24 October 1916 - 28 February 1918 (First World War, War Diary, WO95/2996/10)	WD2996_10	9781474531122	£15.00
58 DIVISION Divisional Troops Machine Gun Corps 58 Battalion : 2 March 1918 - 31 May 1919 (First World War, War Diary, WO95/2996/11)	WD2996_11	9781474531139	£15.00
58 DIVISION Divisional Troops 503 Field Company Royal Engineers : 23 January 1917 - 31 May 1919 (First World War, War Diary, WO95/2996/2)	WD2996_2	9781474531047	£15.00
58 DIVISION Divisional Troops 504 Field Company Royal Engineers : 1 September 1915 - 29 February 1916 (First World War, War Diary, WO95/2996/3)	WD2996_3	9781474531054	£15.00
58 DIVISION Divisional Troops 504 Field Company Royal Engineers : 25 January 1917 - 28 June 1919 (First World War, War Diary, WO95/2996/4)	WD2996_4	9781474531061	£16.00
58 DIVISION Divisional Troops 511 Field Company Royal Engineers : 16 November 1915 - 27 February 1916 (First World War, War Diary, WO95/2996/5)	WD2996_5	9781474531078	£15.00
58 DIVISION Divisional Troops 511 Field Company Royal Engineers : 26 January 1917 - 31 May 1919 (First World War, War Diary, WO95/2996/6)	WD2996_6	9781474531085	£15.00
58 DIVISION Divisional Troops Divisional Signal Company : 1 September 1915 - 29 February 1916 (First World War, War Diary, WO95/2996/7)	WD2996_7	9781474531092	£15.00
58 DIVISION Divisional Troops Divisional Signal Company : 25 January 1917 - 25 June 1919 (First World War, War Diary, WO95/2996/8)	WD2996_8	9781474531108	£15.00
58 DIVISION Divisional Troops Suffolk Regiment 4th Battalion Pioneers : 1 February 1916 - 31 July 1919 (First World War, War Diary, WO95/2996/9)	WD2996_9	9781474531115	£15.00
58 DIVISION Divisional Troops Royal Army Medical Corps 2/1 Home Counties Field Ambulance : 1 September 1915 - 29 February 1916 (First World War, War Diary, WO95/2997/1)	WD2997_1	9781474531146	£15.00

Title	Product Code	ISBN	Price
58 DIVISION Divisional Troops Royal Army Medical Corps 2/1 Home Counties Field Ambulance : 23 January 1917 - 13 June 1919 (First World War, War Diary, WO95/2997/2)	WD2997_2	9781474531153	£19.00
58 DIVISION Divisional Troops Royal Army Medical Corps 2/2 Home Counties Field Ambulance : 1 September 1915 - 22 February 1916 (First World War, War Diary, WO95/2997/3)	WD2997_3	9781474531160	£15.00
58 DIVISION Divisional Troops Royal Army Medical Corps 2/2 Home Counties Field Ambulance : 24 January 1917 - 28 April 1919 (First World War, War Diary, WO95/2997/4)	WD2997_4	9781474531177	£20.00
58 DIVISION Divisional Troops Royal Army Medical Corps 2/3 Home Counties Field Ambulance : 22 February 1915 - 22 February 1915 (First World War, War Diary, WO95/2997/5)	WD2997_5	9781474531184	£15.00
58 DIVISION Divisional Troops Royal Army Medical Corps 2/3 Home Counties Field Ambulance : 1 February 1917 - 29 May 1919 (First World War, War Diary, WO95/2997/6)	WD2997_6	9781474531191	£15.00
58 DIVISION Divisional Troops Royal Army Veterinary Corps 58 Mobile Veterinary Section : 25 January 1917 - 28 February 1919 (First World War, War Diary, WO95/2997/7)	WD2997_7	9781474531207	£15.00
58 DIVISION Divisional Troops Royal Army Service Corps Divisional Train (509, 510, 511, 512 Companies A.S.C.) : 1 September 1914 - 21 June 1919 (First World War, War Diary, WO95/2998)	WD2998	9781474531214	£67.00
58 DIVISION 173 Infantry Brigade Headquarters : 3 October 1915 - 31 December 1917 (First World War, War Diary, WO95/2999)	WD2999	9781474531221	£35.00
58 DIVISION 173 Infantry Brigade Headquarters : 1 January 1918 - 18 March 1919 (First World War, War Diary, WO95/3000)	WD3000	9781474531238	£58.00
58 DIVISION 173 Infantry Brigade London Regiment 3/1 Battalion (redesignated as 2/1 Battalion June 1916), 2/1, 3/2, 2/2 Battalion, 3rd (City of London) Battalion (Royal Fusiliers), 3/3 Battalion (redesignated as 2/3 Battalion June 1916), 2/3 Battalion	WD3001	9781474531245	£79.00
58 DIVISION 174 Infantry Brigade Headquarters : 1 September 1915 - 26 February 1916 (First World War, War Diary, WO95/3002/1)	WD3002_1	9781474531252	£15.00
58 DIVISION 174 Infantry Brigade Headquarters : 24 January 1917 - 31 August 1917 (First World War, War Diary, WO95/3002/2)	WD3002_2	9781474531269	£46.00
58 DIVISION 174 Infantry Brigade Headquarters : 1 September 1917 - 31 December 1917 (First World War, War Diary, WO95/3003)	WD3003	9781474531276	£47.00
58 DIVISION 174 Infantry Brigade Headquarters : 1 May 1917 - 19 March 1919 (First World War, War Diary, WO95/3004)	WD3004	9781474531283	£52.00
58 DIVISION 174 Infantry Brigade London Regiment 2/5 Battalion : 1 September 1915 - 22 February 1916 (First World War, War Diary, WO95/3005/1)	WD3005_1	9781474531290	£15.00
58 DIVISION 174 Infantry Brigade London Regiment 2/5 Battalion : 24 January 1917 - 31 January 1918 (First World War, War Diary, WO95/3005/2)	WD3005_2	9781474531306	£15.00
58 DIVISION 174 Infantry Brigade London Regiment 6th (City of London) Battalion (Rifles) : 1 February 1918 - 28 February 1919 (First World War, War Diary, WO95/3005/3)	WD3005_3	9781474531313	£15.00

Title	Product Code	ISBN	Price
58 DIVISION 174 Infantry Brigade London Regiment 2/6 Battalion : 2 September 1915 - 28 February 1916 (First World War, War Diary, WO95/3005/4)	WD3005_4	9781474531320	£15.00
58 DIVISION 174 Infantry Brigade London Regiment 2/6 Battalion : 1 October 1915 - 31 January 1918 (First World War, War Diary, WO95/3005/5)	WD3005_5	9781474531337	£28.00
58 DIVISION 174 Infantry Brigade London Regiment 7th (City of London) Battalion : 1 February 1918 - 30 November 1918 (First World War, War Diary, WO95/3005/6)	WD3005_6	9781474531344	£15.00
58 DIVISION 174 Infantry Brigade London Regiment 2/7 Battalion : 30 January 1915 - 27 February 1916 (First World War, War Diary, WO95/3005/7)	WD3005_7	9781474531351	£15.00
58 DIVISION 174 Infantry Brigade London Regiment 2/7 Battalion : 27 January 1917 - 31 January 1918 (First World War, War Diary, WO95/3005/8)	WD3005_8	9781474531368	£15.00
58 DIVISION 174 Infantry Brigade London Regiment 8th (City of London) Battalion (Post Office Rifles) : 11 November 1916 - 31 March 1918 (First World War, War Diary, WO95/3006/1)	WD3006_1	9781474531375	£26.00
58 DIVISION 174 Infantry Brigade London Regiment 2/8 Battalion : 9 September 1915 - 26 February 1916 (First World War, War Diary, WO95/3006/2)	WD3006_2	9781474531382	£15.00
58 DIVISION 174 Infantry Brigade London Regiment 2/8 Battalion : 26 January 1917 - 28 February 1918 (First World War, War Diary, WO95/3006/3)	WD3006_3	9781474531399	£15.00
58 DIVISION 174 Infantry Brigade 198 Machine Gun Company : 7 December 1916 - 28 February 1918 (First World War, War Diary, WO95/3006/4)	WD3006_4	9781474531405	£15.00
58 DIVISION 175 Infantry Brigade Headquarters : 7 September 1915 - 31 December 1917 (First World War, War Diary, WO95/3007)	WD3007	9781474531412	£42.00
58 DIVISION 175 Infantry Brigade Headquarters : 1 January 1918 - 19 March 1919 (First World War, War Diary, WO95/3008)	WD3008	9781474531429	£68.00
58 DIVISION 175 Infantry Brigade London Regiment 9th (County of London) Battalion (Queen Victoria's Rifles) : 1 February 1918 - 16 February 1919 (First World War, War Diary, WO95/3009/1)	WD3009_1	9781474531436	£15.00
58 DIVISION 175 Infantry Brigade 215 Machine Gun Company : 9 September 1915 - 30 January 1918 (First World War, War Diary, WO95/3009/11)	WD3009_11	9781474531511	£15.00
58 DIVISION 175 Infantry Brigade : 17 March 1917 - 28 February 1918 (First World War, War Diary, WO95/3009/12)	WD3009_12	9781474531528	£15.00
58 DIVISION 175 Infantry Brigade London Regiment 2/9 Battalion : 1 September 1915 - 23 February 1916 (First World War, War Diary, WO95/3009/2)	WD3009_2	9781474531443	£15.00
58 DIVISION 175 Infantry Brigade London Regiment 2/9 Battalion : 4 February 1917 - 31 January 1918 (First World War, War Diary, WO95/3009/3)	WD3009_3	9781474531450	£15.00
58 DIVISION 175 Infantry Brigade London Regiment 2/10 Battalion : 2 September 1915 - 1 March 1916 (First World War, War Diary, WO95/3009/4)	WD3009_4	9781474531467	£15.00

Title	Product Code	ISBN	Price
58 DIVISION 175 Infantry Brigade London Regiment 2/10 Battalion : 3 February 1917 - 31 March 1919 (First World War, War Diary, WO95/3009/5)	WD3009_5	9781474531474	£15.00
58 DIVISION 175 Infantry Brigade London Regiment 2/11 Battalion : 1 September 1915 - 21 February 1916 (First World War, War Diary, WO95/3009/6-7)	WD3009_6-7	9781474531481	£15.00
58 DIVISION 175 Infantry Brigade London Regiment 1/12 Battalion : 19 January 1917 - 30 January 1918 (First World War, War Diary, WO95/3009/8)	WD3009_8	9781474531498	£15.00
58 DIVISION 175 Infantry Brigade London Regiment 2/12 Battalion : 1 February 1918 - 31 May 1919 (First World War, War Diary, WO95/3009/9-10)	WD3009_9-10	9781474531504	£15.00

Title	Product Code	ISBN	Price
59 DIVISION			
59 DIVISION Headquarters, Branches and Services General Staff : 29 September 1914 - 2 December 1917 (First World War, War Diary, WO95/3010)	WD3010	9781474531535	£42.00
59 DIVISION Headquarters, Branches and Services General Staff : 1 January 1918 - 1 September 1919 (First World War, War Diary, WO95/3011)	WD3011	9781474531542	£52.00
59 DIVISION Headquarters, Branches and Services Adjutant and Quarter-Master General : 1 January 1916 - 31 August 1916 (First World War, War Diary, WO95/3012/1)	WD3012_1	9781474531559	£15.00
59 DIVISION Headquarters, Branches and Services Adjutant and Quarter-Master General : 2 February 1917 - 31 August 1919 (First World War, War Diary, WO95/3012/2)	WD3012_2	9781474531566	£58.00
59 DIVISION Headquarters, Branches and Services Commander Royal Artillery : 1 January 1916 - 1 August 1919 (First World War, War Diary, WO95/3013)	WD3013	9781474531573	£37.00
59 DIVISION Headquarters, Branches and Services Royal Army Medical Corps Assistant Director Medical Services : 1 February 1916 - 9 August 1918 (First World War, War Diary, WO95/3014)	WD3014	9781474531580	£46.00
59 DIVISION Headquarters, Branches and Services Royal Army Ordnance Corps Deputy Assistant Director Ordnance Services : 14 February 1917 - 31 July 1919 (First World War, War Diary, WO95/3015/1)	WD3015_1	9781474531597	£15.00
59 DIVISION Headquarters, Branches and Services Commander Royal Engineers : 9 January 1916 - 16 July 1919 (First World War, War Diary, WO95/3015/2)	WD3015_2	9781474531603	£34.00
59 DIVISION Headquarters, Branches and Services Royal Army Veterinary Corps Deputy Assistant Director Veterinary Services : 9 February 1917 - 18 March 1919 (First World War, War Diary, WO95/3015/3)	WD3015_3	9781474531610	£15.00
59 DIVISION Divisional Troops 295 and 296 Brigade, 2/3 North Midland Brigade and 2/4 North Midland Brigade Royal Field Artillery, Divisional Ammunition Column and Divisional Trench Mortar Batteries : 12 December 1915 - 31 January 1919 (First World War, Wa	WD3016	9781474531627	£40.00
59 DIVISION Divisional Troops 467 Field Company Royal Engineers : 1 November 1915 - 27 February 1916 (First World War, War Diary, WO95/3017/1)	WD3017_1	9781474531634	£15.00
59 DIVISION Divisional Troops Machine Gun Corps 25 Battalion : 1 July 1918 - 30 September 1918 (First World War, War Diary, WO95/3017/10)	WD3017_10	9781474531726	£15.00
59 DIVISION Divisional Troops Machine Gun Corps 59 Battalion : 1 March 1918 - 30 April 1918 (First World War, War Diary, WO95/3017/11)	WD3017_11	9781474531733	£15.00
59 DIVISION Divisional Troops Machine Gun Corps 200 Battalion : 1 August 1918 - 31 October 1918 (First World War, War Diary, WO95/3017/12)	WD3017_12	9781474531740	£15.00
59 DIVISION Divisional Troops 200 Machine Gun Company : 14 April 1917 - 28 February 1918 (First World War, War Diary, WO95/3017/13)	WD3017_13	9781474531757	£15.00
59 DIVISION Divisional Troops 467 Field Company Royal Engineers : 2 February 1917 - 16 July 1919 (First World War, War Diary, WO95/3017/2)	WD3017_2	9781474531641	£15.00
59 DIVISION Divisional Troops 469 Field Company Royal Engineers : 1 January 1916 - 29 February 1916 (First World War, War Diary, WO95/3017/3)	WD3017_3	9781474531658	£15.00

Title	Product Code	ISBN	Price
59 DIVISION Divisional Troops 469 Field Company Royal Engineers : 17 February 1917 - 16 July 1919 (First World War, War Diary, WO95/3017/4)	WD3017_4	9781474531665	£15.00
59 DIVISION Divisional Troops 470 Field Company Royal Engineers : 10 January 1916 - 28 February 1916 (First World War, War Diary, WO95/3017/5)	WD3017_5	9781474531672	£15.00
59 DIVISION Divisional Troops 470 Field Company Royal Engineers : 24 February 1917 - 16 July 1919 (First World War, War Diary, WO95/3017/6)	WD3017_6	9781474531689	£15.00
59 DIVISION Divisional Troops Divisional Signal Company : 17 February 1917 - 30 April 1919 (First World War, War Diary, WO95/3017/7)	WD3017_7	9781474531696	£44.00
59 DIVISION Divisional Troops Royal Scots Fusiliers 6/7th Battalion Pioneers : 1 February 1918 - 31 May 1918 (First World War, War Diary, WO95/3017/8)	WD3017_8	9781474531702	£15.00
59 DIVISION Divisional Troops King's Royal Rifle Corps 25th Battalion Pioneers : 1 May 1918 - 31 July 1919 (First World War, War Diary, WO95/3017/9)	WD3017_9	9781474531719	£15.00
59 DIVISION Divisional Troops Royal Army Medical Corps 2/1 North Midland Field Ambulance : 18 February 1916 - 1 August 1919 (First World War, War Diary, WO95/3018/1)	WD3018_1	9781474531764	£45.00
59 DIVISION Divisional Troops Royal Army Medical Corps 2/2 North Midland Field Ambulance : 1 November 1916 - 2 August 1919 (First World War, War Diary, WO95/3018/2)	WD3018_2	9781474531771	£19.00
59 DIVISION Divisional Troops Royal Army Medical Corps 2/3 North Midland Field Ambulance : 2 February 1916 - 1 August 1919 (First World War, War Diary, WO95/3018/3)	WD3018_3	9781474531788	£22.00
59 DIVISION Divisional Troops Royal Army Veterinary Corps 59 Mobile Veterinary Section : 11 January 1916 - 28 February 1916 (First World War, War Diary, WO95/3019/1)	WD3019_1	9781474531795	£15.00
59 DIVISION Divisional Troops Royal Army Veterinary Corps 59 Mobile Veterinary Section : 1 January 1917 - 28 April 1919 (First World War, War Diary, WO95/3019/2)	WD3019_2	9781474531801	£15.00
59 DIVISION Divisional Troops Royal Army Service Corps Divisional Train (513,514,515,516, Companies A.S.C.) : 1 January 1916 - 30 June 1916 (First World War, War Diary, WO95/3019/3)	WD3019_3	9781474531818	£15.00
59 DIVISION Divisional Troops Royal Army Service Corps Divisional Train (513,514,515,516, Companies A.S.C.) : 17 February 1917 - 14 August 1919 (First World War, War Diary, WO95/3019/4)	WD3019_4	9781474531825	£35.00
59 DIVISION 176 Infantry Brigade Headquarters : 1 January 1916 - 29 February 1916 (First World War, War Diary, WO95/3020/1)	WD3020_1	9781474531832	£15.00
59 DIVISION 176 Infantry Brigade Headquarters : 19 February 1917 - 28 June 1919 (First World War, War Diary, WO95/3020/2)	WD3020_2	9781474531849	£61.00
59 DIVISION 176 Infantry Brigade Prince of Wales's (North Staffordshire Regiment) 1/5 Battalion. : 1 February 1918 - 31 May 1918 (First World War, War Diary, WO95/3021/1)	WD3021_1	9781474531856	£15.00
59 DIVISION 176 Infantry Brigade King's (Liverpool Regiment) 25th Battalion : 5 May 1918 - 28 May 1919 (First World War, War Diary, WO95/3021/10)	WD3021_10	9781474531948	£15.00
59 DIVISION 176 Infantry Brigade Royal Sussex Regiment 17th Battalion : 1 May 1918 - 30 April 1919 (First World War, War Diary, WO95/3021/11)	WD3021_11	9781474531955	£15.00

Title	Product Code	ISBN	Price
59 DIVISION 176 Infantry Brigade Royal Welsh Fusiliers 4th Garrison Battalion : 1 May 1918 - 30 April 1919 (First World War, War Diary, WO95/3021/12)	WD3021_12	9781474531962	£15.00
59 DIVISION 176 Infantry Brigade 174 Machine Gun Company : 23 February 1917 - 28 February 1918 (First World War, War Diary, WO95/3021/13)	WD3021_13	9781474531979	£15.00
59 DIVISION 176 Infantry Brigade, Brigade Trench Mortar Battery : 17 February 1917 - 31 December 1918 (First World War, War Diary, WO95/3021/14)	WD3021_14	9781474531986	£15.00
59 DIVISION 176 Infantry Brigade Prince of Wales's (North Staffordshire Regiment) 2/5th Battalion : 1 January 1916 - 29 February 1916 (First World War, War Diary, WO95/3021/2)	WD3021_2	9781474531863	£15.00
59 DIVISION 176 Infantry Brigade Prince of Wales's (North Staffordshire Regiment) 2/5th Battalion : 24 February 1917 - 31 January 1918 (First World War, War Diary, WO95/3021/3)	WD3021_3	9781474531870	£15.00
59 DIVISION 176 Infantry Brigade Prince of Wales's (North Staffordshire Regiment) 2/6th Battalion : 1 January 1916 - 29 February 1916 (First World War, War Diary, WO95/3021/4)	WD3021_4	9781474531887	£15.00
59 DIVISION 176 Infantry Brigade Prince of Wales's (North Staffordshire Regiment) 2/6th Battalion : 2 February 1917 - 31 July 1918 (First World War, War Diary, WO95/3021/5)	WD3021_5	9781474531894	£15.00
59 DIVISION 176 Infantry Brigade South Staffordshire Regiment 2/5th (T.F.) Battalion : 4 January 1916 - 19 February 1916 (First World War, War Diary, WO95/3021/6)	WD3021_6	9781474531900	£15.00
59 DIVISION 176 Infantry Brigade South Staffordshire Regiment 2/5th (T.F.) Battalion : 25 February 1917 - 31 January 1918 (First World War, War Diary, WO95/3021/7)	WD3021_7	9781474531917	£15.00
59 DIVISION 176 Infantry Brigade South Staffordshire Regiment 2/6th (T.F.) Battalion : 26 January 1916 - 26 February 1916 (First World War, War Diary, WO95/3021/8)	WD3021_8	9781474531924	£15.00
59 DIVISION 176 Infantry Brigade South Staffordshire Regiment 2/6th (T.F.) Battalion : 24 February 1917 - 31 July 1918 (First World War, War Diary, WO95/3021/9)	WD3021_9	9781474531931	£15.00
59 DIVISION 177 Infantry Brigade Headquarters : 27 January 1915 - 29 February 1916 (First World War, War Diary, WO95/3022/1)	WD3022_1	9781474531993	£15.00
59 DIVISION 177 Infantry Brigade Headquarters : 17 February 1917 - 31 August 1919 (First World War, War Diary, WO95/3022/2)	WD3022_2	9781474532006	£45.00
59 DIVISION 177 Infantry Brigade Leicestershire Regiment 2/4th Battalion. : 27 October 1915 - 14 February 1916 (First World War, War Diary, WO95/3022/3)	WD3022_3	9781474532013	£15.00
59 DIVISION 177 Infantry Brigade Leicestershire Regiment 2/4th Battalion : 24 February 1917 - 31 May 1918 (First World War, War Diary, WO95/3022/4)	WD3022_4	9781474532020	£15.00
59 DIVISION 177 Infantry Brigade Leicestershire Regiment 2/5th Battalion : 7 January 1916 - 29 February 1916 (First World War, War Diary, WO95/3022/5)	WD3022_5	9781474532037	£15.00

Title	Product Code	ISBN	Price
59 DIVISION 177 Infantry Brigade Leicestershire Regiment 2/5th Battalion : 1 February 1917 - 31 January 1918 (First World War, War Diary, WO95/3022/6)	WD3022_6	9781474532044	£15.00
59 DIVISION 177 Infantry Brigade Lincolnshire Regiment 2/4 Battalion : 4 January 1916 - 29 February 1916 (First World War, War Diary, WO95/3023/1)	WD3023_1	9781474532051	£15.00
59 DIVISION 177 Infantry Brigade Lincolnshire Regiment 2/4 Battalion : 23 February 1917 - 31 January 1918 (First World War, War Diary, WO95/3023/2)	WD3023_2	9781474532068	£15.00
59 DIVISION 177 Infantry Brigade Lincolnshire Regiment 2/5 Battalion : 1 January 1916 - 31 July 1918 (First World War, War Diary, WO95/3023/3)	WD3023_3	9781474532075	£15.00
59 DIVISION 177 Infantry Brigade Durham Light Infantry 2/6th Battalion : 10 January 1918 - 31 August 1919 (First World War, War Diary, WO95/3023/4)	WD3023_4	9781474532082	£15.00
59 DIVISION 177 Infantry Brigade Essex Regiment 15th Battalion : 1 January 1918 - 31 August 1919 (First World War, War Diary, WO95/3023/5)	WD3023_5	9781474532099	£15.00
59 DIVISION 177 Infantry Brigade Prince Albert's (Somerset Light Infantry) 11th Battalion : 6 March 1918 - 31 August 1919 (First World War, War Diary, WO95/3023/6)	WD3023_6	9781474532105	£15.00
59 DIVISION 177 Infantry Brigade, Brigade Machine Gun Company : 23 February 1917 - 28 February 1918 (First World War, War Diary, WO95/3023/7)	WD3023_7	9781474532112	£15.00
59 DIVISION 177 Infantry Brigade, Brigade Trench Mortar Battery : 1 March 1917 - 31 December 1918 (First World War, War Diary, WO95/3023/8)	WD3023_8	9781474532129	£15.00
59 DIVISION 178 Infantry Brigade Headquarters : 28 February 1915 - 31 May 1916 (First World War, War Diary, WO95/3024/1)	WD3024_1	9781474532136	£15.00
59 DIVISION 178 Infantry Brigade Headquarters : 19 February 1917 - 31 October 1918 (First World War, War Diary, WO95/3024/2)	WD3024_2	9781474532143	£62.00
59 DIVISION 178 Infantry Brigade Sherwood Foresters (Nottinghamshire and Derbyshire Regiment) 2/5th Battalion : 16 October 1914 - 3 August 1918 (First World War, War Diary, WO95/3025/1)	WD3025_1	9781474532150	£17.00
59 DIVISION 178 Infantry Brigade Duke of Wellington's (West Riding Regiment) 13th Battalion : 27 May 1918 - 13 September 1919 (First World War, War Diary, WO95/3025/10)	WD3025_10	9781474532242	£15.00
59 DIVISION 178 Infantry Brigade Northumberland Fusiliers 36th Battalion (Territorial) : 18 April 1918 - 31 May 1919 (First World War, War Diary, WO95/3025/11)	WD3025_11	9781474532259	£15.00
59 DIVISION 178 Infantry Brigade 175 Machine Gun Company : 24 October 1916 - 26 February 1918 (First World War, War Diary, WO95/3025/12)	WD3025_12	9781474532266	£15.00
59 DIVISION 178 Infantry Brigade, Brigade Trench Mortar Battery : 13 February 1917 - 30 November 1918 (First World War, War Diary, WO95/3025/13)	WD3025_13	9781474532273	£15.00
59 DIVISION 178 Infantry Brigade Sherwood Foresters (Nottinghamshire and Derbyshire Regiment) 2/6th Battalion : 2 November 1914 - 26 February 1916 (First World War, War Diary, WO95/3025/2)	WD3025_2	9781474532167	£15.00

Title	Product Code	ISBN	Price
59 DIVISION 178 Infantry Brigade Sherwood Foresters (Nottinghamshire and Derbyshire Regiment) 2/6th Battalion : 25 February 1917 - 31 July 1918 (First World War, War Diary, WO95/3025/3)	WD3025_3	9781474532174	£15.00
59 DIVISION 178 Infantry Brigade Sherwood Foresters (Nottinghamshire and Derbyshire Regiment) 1/7th Battalion : 1 February 1918 - 22 August 1918 (First World War, War Diary, WO95/3025/4)	WD3025_4	9781474532181	£15.00
59 DIVISION 178 Infantry Brigade Sherwood Foresters (Nottinghamshire and Derbyshire Regiment) 2/7th Battalion : 14 September 1914 - 28 February 1916 (First World War, War Diary, WO95/3025/5)	WD3025_5	9781474532198	£15.00
59 DIVISION 178 Infantry Brigade Sherwood Foresters (Nottinghamshire and Derbyshire Regiment) 2/7th Battalion : 1 May 1916 - 31 January 1918 (First World War, War Diary, WO95/3025/6)	WD3025_6	9781474532204	£15.00
59 DIVISION 178 Infantry Brigade Sherwood Foresters (Nottinghamshire and Derbyshire Regiment) 2/8th Battalion : 1 November 1914 - 29 October 1916 (First World War, War Diary, WO95/3025/7)	WD3025_7	9781474532211	£15.00
59 DIVISION 178 Infantry Brigade Sherwood Foresters (Nottinghamshire and Derbyshire Regiment) 2/8th Battalion : 25 February 1917 - 30 January 1918 (First World War, War Diary, WO95/3025/8)	WD3025_8	9781474532228	£15.00
59 DIVISION 178 Infantry Brigade Royal Scots Fusiliers 11th Battalion : 8 May 1918 - 26 July 1919 (First World War, War Diary, WO95/3025/9)	WD3025_9	9781474532235	£15.00

Title	Product Code	ISBN	Price
6 DIVISION			
6 DIVISION Headquarters, Branches and Services General Staff : 3 August 1914 - 31 December 1915 (First World War, War Diary, WO95/1581)	WD1581	9781474505970	£35.00
6 DIVISION Headquarters, Branches and Services General Staff : 1 January 1916 - 31 December 1916 (First World War, War Diary, WO95/1582)	WD1582	9781474505987	£42.00
6 DIVISION Headquarters, Branches and Services General Staff : 1 January 1917 - 31 December 1917 (First World War, War Diary, WO95/1583)	WD1583	9781474505994	£42.00
6 DIVISION Headquarters, Branches and Services General Staff : 1 January 1918 - 30 January 1918 (First World War, War Diary, WO95/1584)	WD1584	9781474506007	£52.00
6 DIVISION Headquarters, Branches and Services Adjutant and Quarter-Master General : 4 August 1914 - 31 December 1915 (First World War, War Diary, WO95/1585)	WD1585	9781474506014	£65.00
6 DIVISION Headquarters, Branches and Services Adjutant and Quarter-Master General : 1 January 1916 - 31 December 1917 (First World War, War Diary, WO95/1586)	WD1586	9781474522328	£64.00
6 DIVISION Headquarters, Branches and Services Adjutant and Quarter-Master General : 1 January 1918 - 17 September 1919 (First World War, War Diary, WO95/1587)	WD1587	9781474506021	£60.00
6 DIVISION Headquarters, Branches and Services Commander Royal Artillery : 4 August 1914 - 26 June 1915 (First World War, War Diary, WO95/1588)	WD1588	9781474522335	£84.00
6 DIVISION Headquarters, Branches and Services Commander Royal Artillery : 1 October 1916 - 31 May 1917 (First World War, War Diary, WO95/1589)	WD1589	9781474522342	£67.00
6 DIVISION Headquarters, Branches and Services Commander Royal Artillery : 1 July 1917 - 31 October 1917 (First World War, War Diary, WO95/1590A)	WD1590_A	9781474522359	£56.00
6 DIVISION Headquarters, Branches and Services Commander Royal Artillery : 1 June 1917 - 30 June 1917 (First World War, War Diary, WO95/1590B)	WD1590_B	9781474522366	£47.00
6 DIVISION Headquarters, Branches and Services Commander Royal Artillery : 1 November 1917 - 24 April 1918 (First World War, War Diary, WO95/1591)	WD1591	9781474506038	£52.00
6 DIVISION Headquarters, Branches and Services Royal Army Medical Corps Assistant Director Medical Services : 10 August 1914 - 19 August 1914 (First World War, War Diary, WO95/1592)	WD1592	9781474506045	£58.00
6 DIVISION Headquarters, Branches and Services Royal Army Medical Corps Assistant Director Medical Services : 1 January 1917 - 2 January 1917 (First World War, War Diary, WO95/1593)	WD1593	9781474522373	£67.00
6 DIVISION Headquarters, Branches and Services Commander Royal Engineers : 4 August 1914 - 1 September 1919 (First World War, War Diary, WO95/1594)	WD1594	9781474506052	£43.00
6 DIVISION Headquarters, Branches and Services Royal Army Ordnance Corps Assistant Director Ordnance Services and Royal Army Veterinary Corps Assistant Director Veterinary Services : 29 July 1914 - 31 January 1919 (First World War, War Diary, WO95/1595)	WD1595	9781474506069	£36.00

Title	Product Code	ISBN	Price
6 DIVISION Divisional Troops Headquarters 19 Hussars, `C' Squadron 19 Hussars, `B' Squadron Northamptonshire Yeomanry, Divisional Cyclist Company and 2 Brigade Royal Field Artillery : 4 August 1914 - 31 March 1918 (First World War, War Diary, WO95/159	WD1596	9781474506076	£74.00
6 DIVISION Divisional Troops 12 and 24 Brigade Royal Field Artillery : 4 August 1914 - 29 September 1915 (First World War, War Diary, WO95/1597)	WD1597	9781474506083	£50.00
6 DIVISION Divisional Troops 38 Brigade Royal Field Artillery, Trench Mortar Batteries, 38 Trench Mortar Battery and Divisional Ammunition Column: 4 August 1914 - 31 August 1919 (First World War, War Diary, WO95/1598)	WD1598	9781474506090	£47.00
6 DIVISION Divisional Troops 12 Field Company Royal Engineers, 38 Field Company Royal Engineers and 459 Field Company Royal Engineers : 4 August 1914 - 1 September 1919 (First World War, War Diary, WO95/1599)	WD1599	9781474506106	£35.00
6 DIVISION Divisional Troops 509 Field Company Royal Engineers, 93 Field Company Royal Engineers and Divisional Signal Company : 5 August 1914 - 25 September 1919 (First World War, War Diary, WO95/1600)	WD1600	9781474506113	£46.00
6 DIVISION Divisional Troops Leicestershire Regiment 11th Battalion Pioneers, Machine Gun Corps 6 Battalion and 192 Machine Gun Company : 9 March 1916 - 28 February 1918 (First World War, War Diary, WO95/1601)	WD1601	9781474522380	£78.00
6 DIVISION Divisional Troops Royal Army Medical Corps 16 Field Ambulance : 6 August 1914 - 31 December 1914 (First World War, War Diary, WO95/1602A)	WD1602_A	9781474522397	£57.00
6 DIVISION Divisional Troops Royal Army Medical Corps 16 Field Ambulance : 1 January 1915 - 26 May 1919 (First World War, War Diary, WO95/1602B)	WD1602_B	9781474522403	£38.00
6 DIVISION Divisional Troops Royal Army Medical Corps 18 Field Ambulance, 8 Sanitary Section and 6 Mobile Veterinary Section : 5 August 1914 - 31 August 1919 (First World War, War Diary, WO95/1603)	WD1603	9781474522410	£58.00
6 DIVISION Divisional Troops Royal Army Service Corps Divisional Train (17, 19, 23, 24, Companies) A.S.C : 4 August 1914 - 30 April 1919 (First World War, War Diary, WO95/1604)	WD1604	9781474506120	£54.00
6 DIVISION 16 Infantry Brigade Headquarters : 29 July 1914 - 31 December 1916 (First World War, War Diary, WO95/1605)	WD1605	9781474506137	£54.00
6 DIVISION 16 Infantry Brigade Headquarters : 1 June 1916 - 31 October 1917 (First World War, War Diary, WO95/1606)	WD1606	9781474506144	£42.00
6 DIVISION 16 Infantry Brigade Headquarters : 1 November 1917 - 28 February 1919 (First World War, War Diary, WO95/1607)	WD1607	9781474506151	£55.00
6 DIVISION 16 Infantry Brigade Buffs (East Kent Regiment) 1st Battalion : 29 July 1914 - 20 May 1919 (First World War, War Diary, WO95/1608)	WD1608	9781474506168	£51.00
6 DIVISION 16 Infantry Brigade King's (Shropshire Light Infantry) 1st Battalion : 4 August 1914 - 31 March 1919 (First World War, War Diary, WO95/1609)	WD1609	9781474506175	£56.00
6 DIVISION 16 Infantry Brigade York and Lancaster Regiment 2nd Battalion : 4 August 1914 - 17 April 1915 (First World War, War Diary, WO95/1610)	WD1610	9781474506182	£54.00

Title	Product Code	ISBN	Price
6 DIVISION 16 Infantry Brigade Bedfordshire Regiment 8th Battalion, Leicestershire Regiment 1st Battalion, Brigade Machine Gun Company and Brigade Trench Mortar Battery : 4 August 1914 - 31 August 1916 (First World War, War Diary, WO95/1611)	WD1611	9781474506199	£50.00
6 DIVISION 17 Infantry Brigade Headquarters, Prince of Wales's Leinster Regiment (Royal Canadians) 2nd Battalion and London Regiment 2nd (City of London) Battalion (Royal Fusiliers) : 5 August 1914 - 31 October 1915 (First World War, War Diary, WO95/1612)	WD1612	9781474506205	£49.00
6 DIVISION 17 Infantry Brigade Rifle Brigade (The Prince Consort's Own) 3rd Battalion, Royal Fusiliers (City of London Regiment) 1st Battalion and Prince of Wales's (North Staffordshire Regiment) 1st Battalion : 1 August 1914 - 31 October 1915 (First Wor	WD1613	9781474506212	£37.00
6 DIVISION 18 Infantry Brigade Headquarters : 1 October 1914 - 31 December 1916 (First World War, War Diary, WO95/1614)	WD1614	9781474506229	£49.00
6 DIVISION 18 Infantry Brigade Headquarters : 1 January 1917 - 27 February 1919 (First World War, War Diary, WO95/1615)	WD1615	9781474522427	£69.00
6 DIVISION 18 Infantry Brigade Essex Regiment 11th Battalion, London Regiment 16th (County of London) Battalion (Queen's Westminster Rifles) and Sherwood Foresters (Nottinghamshire and Derbyshire Regiment) 2nd Battalion : 4 August 1914 - 1 November 1915 (	WD1616	9781474506236	£44.00
6 DIVISION 18 Infantry Brigade Durham Light Infantry 2nd and 14th Battalion : 4 August 1914 - 31 January 1918 (First World War, War Diary, WO95/1617)	WD1617	9781474522434	£75.00
6 DIVISION 18 Infantry Brigade East Yorkshire Regiment 1st Battalion, Prince of Wales's Own (West Yorkshire Regiment) 1st Battalion and Brigade Machine Gun Company : 7 August 1914 - 31 January 1918 (First World War, War Diary, WO95/1618)	WD1618	9781474506243	£54.00
6 DIVISION 71 Infantry Brigade Headquarters : 21 August 1915 - 31 December 1918 (First World War, War Diary, WO95/1619)	WD1619	9781474522441	£73.00
6 DIVISION 71 Infantry Brigade Headquarters : 1 January 1918 - 28 February 1919 (First World War, War Diary, WO95/1620)	WD1620	9781474506250	£60.00
6 DIVISION 71 Infantry Brigade Leicestershire Regiment 1st Battalion : 1 December 1915 - 31 December 1917 (First World War, War Diary, WO95/1621)	WD1621	9781474506267	£56.00
6 DIVISION 71 Infantry Brigade Leicestershire Regiment 1st Battalion : 1 January 1918 - 13 May 1919 (First World War, War Diary, WO95/1622)	WD1622	9781474522458	£62.00
6 DIVISION 71 Infantry Brigade Norfolk Regiment 9th Battalion : 21 August 1915 - 30 April 1919 (First World War, War Diary, WO95/1623)	WD1623	9781474522465	£76.00
6 DIVISION 71 Infantry Brigade Sherwood Foresters (Nottinghamshire and Derbyshire Regiment) 2nd Battalion : 2 November 1915 - 31 March 1919 (First World War, War Diary, WO95/1624)	WD1624	9781474506274	£55.00
6 DIVISION 71 Infantry Brigade Suffolk Regiment 9th Battalion and Brigade Machine Gun Company : 22 August 1915 - 31 January 1918 (First World War, War Diary, WO95/1625)	WD1625	9781474506281	£24.00
6 DIVISION 1 Midland Infantry Brigade Headquarters, Brigade Duke of Wellington's (West Riding Regiment) 2/4th Battalion, King's Own (Yorkshire Light Infantry) 2/4 Battalion, King's Own (Yorkshire Light Infantry) 5th Battalion, 2 Midland Infantry Brigade	WD1626	9781474506298	£34.00

Title	Product Code	ISBN	Price
60 DIVISION			
60 DIVISION Headquarters, Branches and Services General Staff : 1 November 1915 - 31 December 1915 (First World War, War Diary, WO95/3026/1)	WD3026_1	9781474532280	£15.00
60 DIVISION Headquarters, Branches and Services Royal Army Ordnance Corps Deputy Assistant Director Ordnance Services : 23 June 1916 - 31 October 1916 (First World War, War Diary, WO95/3026/10)	WD3026_10	9781474532372	£15.00
60 DIVISION Headquarters, Branches and Services Royal Army Veterinary Corps Assistant Director Veterinary Services : 21 June 1916 - 30 November 1916 (First World War, War Diary, WO95/3026/11)	WD3026_11	9781474532389	£15.00
60 DIVISION Headquarters, Branches and Services General Staff : 14 June 1916 - 30 November 1916 (First World War, War Diary, WO95/3026/2)	WD3026_2	9781474532297	£15.00
60 DIVISION Headquarters, Branches and Services Adjutant and Quarter-Master General : 28 December 1914 - 23 March 1915 (First World War, War Diary, WO95/3026/3)	WD3026_3	9781474532303	£15.00
60 DIVISION Headquarters, Branches and Services Adjutant and Quarter-Master General : 1 November 1915 - 31 December 1915 (First World War, War Diary, WO95/3026/4)	WD3026_4	9781474532310	£15.00
60 DIVISION Headquarters, Branches and Services Adjutant and Quarter-Master General : 31 May 1916 - 30 November 1916 (First World War, War Diary, WO95/3026/5)	WD3026_5	9781474532327	£15.00
60 DIVISION Headquarters, Branches and Services Commander Royal Artillery : 9 April 1915 - 30 November 1916 (First World War, War Diary, WO95/3026/6)	WD3026_6	9781474532334	£19.00
60 DIVISION Headquarters, Branches and Services Royal Army Medical Corps Assistant Director Medical Services : 1 November 1915 - 31 December 1915 (First World War, War Diary, WO95/3026/7)	WD3026_7	9781474532341	£15.00
60 DIVISION Headquarters, Branches and Services Royal Army Medical Corps Assistant Director Medical Services : 22 June 1916 - 30 November 1916 (First World War, War Diary, WO95/3026/8)	WD3026_8	9781474532358	£15.00
60 DIVISION Headquarters, Branches and Services Commander Royal Engineers : 1 March 1915 - 30 November 1916 (First World War, War Diary, WO95/3026/9)	WD3026_9	9781474532365	£15.00
60 DIVISION Divisional Troops Divisional Cyclist Company, 300, 301, 302 and 303 Brigade Royal Field Artillery, Divisional Ammunition Column and Divisional Trench Mortar Batteries : 12 April 1915 - 30 November 1916 (First World War, War Diary, WO95/3027	WD3027	9781474532396	£42.00
60 DIVISION Divisional Troops 1/6 London Field Company Royal Engineers : 1 December 1915 - 30 November 1916 (First World War, War Diary, WO95/3028/1)	WD3028_1	9781474532402	£15.00
60 DIVISION Divisional Troops 2/4 London Field Company Royal Engineers : 1 December 1915 - 30 November 1916 (First World War, War Diary, WO95/3028/2)	WD3028_2	9781474532419	£15.00
60 DIVISION Divisional Troops 3/3 London Field Company Royal Engineers : 1 December 1915 - 30 November 1916 (First World War, War Diary, WO95/3028/3)	WD3028_3	9781474532426	£15.00
60 DIVISION Divisional Troops Divisional Signal Company : 4 October 1915 - 31 December 1915 (First World War, War Diary, WO95/3028/4)	WD3028_4	9781474532433	£15.00

Title	Product Code	ISBN	Price
60 DIVISION Divisional Troops Divisional Signal Company : 21 June 1916 - 23 November 1916 (First World War, War Diary, WO95/3028/5)	WD3028_5	9781474532440	£15.00
60 DIVISION Divisional Troops Loyal North Lancashire Regiment 12th Battalion Pioneers : 21 June 1916 - 31 December 1916 (First World War, War Diary, WO95/3028/6)	WD3028_6	9781474532457	£15.00
60 DIVISION Divisional Troops Royal Army Medical Corps 2/4 London Field Ambulance : 1 September 1915 - 31 December 1915 (First World War, War Diary, WO95/3029/1-2)	WD3029_1-2	9781474532464	£15.00
60 DIVISION Divisional Troops Royal Army Medical Corps 2/4 London Field Ambulance : 15 June 1916 - 30 November 1916 (First World War, War Diary, WO95/3029/3)	WD3029_3	9781474532471	£15.00
60 DIVISION Divisional Troops Royal Army Medical Corps 2/5 London Field Ambulance : 1 September 1915 - 28 November 1916 (First World War, War Diary, WO95/3029/4)	WD3029_4	9781474532488	£15.00
60 DIVISION Divisional Troops Royal Army Medical Corps 2/6 London Field Ambulance : 18 September 1915 - 27 November 1916 (First World War, War Diary, WO95/3029/5)	WD3029_5	9781474532495	£15.00
60 DIVISION Divisional Troops 60 Sanitary Division : 29 February 1916 - 30 November 1916 (First World War, War Diary, WO95/3029/6)	WD3029_6	9781474532501	£15.00
60 DIVISION Divisional Troops Royal Army Veterinary Corps 2/2 London Mobile Veterinary Section : 26 June 1916 - 30 November 1916 (First World War, War Diary, WO95/3029/7)	WD3029_7	9781474532518	£15.00
60 DIVISION Divisional Troops Royal Army Service Corps Divisional Train (517,518,519,520 Companies A.S.C.) : 23 June 1915 - 30 November 1916 (First World War, War Diary, WO95/3029/8)	WD3029_8	9781474532525	£19.00
60 DIVISION 179 Infantry Brigade Headquarters : 4 February 1916 - 3 April 1916 (First World War, War Diary, WO95/3030/1)	WD3030_1	9781474532532	£15.00
60 DIVISION 179 Infantry Brigade Headquarters : 6 September 1915 - 30 November 1916 (First World War, War Diary, WO95/3030/2)	WD3030_2	9781474532549	£15.00
60 DIVISION 179 Infantry Brigade London Regiment 2/13 Battalion : 8 September 1915 - 30 November 1916 (First World War, War Diary, WO95/3030/3)	WD3030_3	9781474532556	£19.00
60 DIVISION 179 Infantry Brigade London Regiment 2/14 Battalion : 1 January 1915 - 30 November 1916 (First World War, War Diary, WO95/3030/4)	WD3030_4	9781474532563	£15.00
60 DIVISION 179 Infantry Brigade London Regiment 2/15 Battalion : 4 January 1915 - 30 November 1916 (First World War, War Diary, WO95/3030/5)	WD3030_5	9781474532570	£15.00
60 DIVISION 179 Infantry Brigade London Regiment 2/16 Battalion : 30 September 1915 - 30 November 1916 (First World War, War Diary, WO95/3030/6)	WD3030_6	9781474532587	£15.00
60 DIVISION 179 Infantry Brigade, Brigade Machine Gun Company : 27 March 1916 - 1 December 1916 (First World War, War Diary, WO95/3030/7)	WD3030_7	9781474532594	£15.00
60 DIVISION 180 Infantry Brigade Headquarters (formerly 2/5 London Brigade), London Regiment 2/17, 2/18, 2/19 and 2/20 Battalion and Brigade Machine Gun Company : 1 January 1915 - 14 July 1916 (First World War, War Diary, WO95/3031)	WD3031	9781474532600	£66.00

Title	Product Code	ISBN	Price
60 DIVISION 181 Infantry Brigade Headquarters : 5 October 1915 - 31 December 1915 (First World War, War Diary, WO95/3032/1)	WD3032_1	9781474532617	£15.00
60 DIVISION 181 Infantry Brigade, Brigade Machine Gun Company : 27 June 1916 - 30 November 1916 (First World War, War Diary, WO95/3032/10)	WD3032_10	9781474532709	£15.00
60 DIVISION 181 Infantry Brigade Headquarters : 14 June 1916 - 30 November 1916 (First World War, War Diary, WO95/3032/2)	WD3032_2	9781474532624	£21.00
60 DIVISION 181 Infantry Brigade London Regiment 2/21 Battalion : 1 November 1915 - 30 May 1916 (First World War, War Diary, WO95/3032/3)	WD3032_3	9781474532631	£15.00
60 DIVISION 181 Infantry Brigade London Regiment 2/22 Battalion : 4 October 1915 - 31 December 1915 (First World War, War Diary, WO95/3032/4)	WD3032_4	9781474532648	£15.00
60 DIVISION 181 Infantry Brigade London Regiment 2/22 Battalion : 14 June 1916 - 30 November 1916 (First World War, War Diary, WO95/3032/5)	WD3032_5	9781474532655	£15.00
60 DIVISION 181 Infantry Brigade London Regiment 2/23 Battalion : 4 November 1915 - 31 December 1915 (First World War, War Diary, WO95/3032/6)	WD3032_6	9781474532662	£15.00
60 DIVISION 181 Infantry Brigade London Regiment 2/23 Battalion : 15 June 1916 - 30 November 1916 (First World War, War Diary, WO95/3032/7)	WD3032_7	9781474532679	£15.00
60 DIVISION 181 Infantry Brigade London Regiment 2/24 Battalion : 4 October 1915 - 31 December 1915 (First World War, War Diary, WO95/3032/8)	WD3032_8	9781474532686	£15.00
60 DIVISION 181 Infantry Brigade London Regiment 2/24 Battalion : 24 June 1916 - 30 November 1916 (First World War, War Diary, WO95/3032/9)	WD3032_9	9781474532693	£15.00

Title	Product Code	ISBN	Price
61 DIVISION			
61 DIVISION Headquarters, Branches and Services General Staff : 1 September 1915 - 31 May 1917 (First World War, War Diary, WO95/3033)	WD3033	9781474532716	£54.00
61 DIVISION Headquarters, Branches and Services General Staff : 1 June 1917 - 31 December 1917 (First World War, War Diary, WO95/3034)	WD3034	9781474532723	£59.00
61 DIVISION Headquarters, Branches and Services General Staff : 1 January 1918 - 31 August 1918 (First World War, War Diary, WO95/3035)	WD3035	9781474532730	£53.00
61 DIVISION Headquarters, Branches and Services General Staff : 1 September 1918 - 30 July 1919 (First World War, War Diary, WO95/3036/1)	WD3036_1	9781474532747	£26.00
61 DIVISION Headquarters, Branches and Services Adjutant and Quarter-Master General : 17 November 1915 - 30 July 1919 (First World War, War Diary, WO95/3036/2)	WD3036_2	9781474532754	£45.00
61 DIVISION Headquarters, Branches and Services Commander Royal Artillery : 1 June 1915 - 30 June 1918 (First World War, War Diary, WO95/3037)	WD3037	9781474532761	£56.00
61 DIVISION Headquarters, Branches and Services Commander Royal Artillery : 1 July 1918 - 30 May 1919 (First World War, War Diary, WO95/3038/1)	WD3038_1	9781474532778	£26.00
61 DIVISION Headquarters, Branches and Services Royal Army Medical Corps Assistant Director Medical Services : 2 May 1915 - 31 March 1919 (First World War, War Diary, WO95/3038/2)	WD3038_2	9781474532785	£35.00
61 DIVISION Headquarters, Branches and Services Commander Royal Engineers : 1 September 1915 - 30 June 1917 (First World War, War Diary, WO95/3039)	WD3039	9781474532792	£63.00
61 DIVISION Headquarters, Branches and Services Commander Royal Engineers : 1 July 1917 - 30 June 1918 (First World War, War Diary, WO95/3040)	WD3040	9781474532808	£61.00
61 DIVISION Headquarters, Branches and Services : 1 July 1918 - 15 July 1918 (First World War, War Diary, WO95/3041/1)	WD3041_1	9781474532815	£15.00
61 DIVISION Headquarters, Branches and Services Commander Royal Engineers : 1 July 1918 - 31 July 1919 (First World War, War Diary, WO95/3041/2)	WD3041_2	9781474532822	£28.00
61 DIVISION Headquarters, Branches and Services Royal Army Ordnance Corps Deputy Assistant Director Ordnance Services : 1 December 1915 - 28 June 1919 (First World War, War Diary, WO95/3041/3)	WD3041_3	9781474532839	£15.00
61 DIVISION Headquarters, Branches and Services Royal Army Veterinary Corps Assistant Director Veterinary Services : 1 November 1915 - 31 March 1919 (First World War, War Diary, WO95/3041/4)	WD3041_4	9781474532846	£15.00
61 DIVISION Divisional Troops Divisional Cyclist Company : 1 January 1915 - 31 January 1916 (First World War, War Diary, WO95/3042/1)	WD3042_1	9781474532853	£15.00
61 DIVISION Divisional Troops 305 Brigade Royal Field Artillery : 1 May 1915 - 17 September 1916 (First World War, War Diary, WO95/3042/2)	WD3042_2	9781474532860	£15.00
61 DIVISION Divisional Troops 306 Brigade Royal Field Artillery : 1 September 1915 - 10 May 1919 (First World War, War Diary, WO95/3042/3)	WD3042_3	9781474532877	£40.00

Title	Product Code	ISBN	Price
61 DIVISION Divisional Troops 307 Brigade Royal Field Artillery : 1 September 1915 - 31 March 1918 (First World War, War Diary, WO95/3043)	WD3043	9781474532884	£52.00
61 DIVISION Divisional Troops 307 Brigade Royal Field Artillery : 1 April 1918 - 23 June 1919 (First World War, War Diary, WO95/3044/1)	WD3044_1	9781474532891	£53.00
61 DIVISION Divisional Troops 308 Brigade Royal Field Artillery : 1 January 1916 - 27 January 1916 (First World War, War Diary, WO95/3044/2)	WD3044_2	9781474532907	£15.00
61 DIVISION Divisional Troops Divisional Ammunition Column : 25 May 1916 - 31 May 1919 (First World War, War Diary, WO95/3045/1)	WD3045_1	9781474532914	£15.00
61 DIVISION Divisional Troops Divisional Trench Mortar Batteries : 24 June 1916 - 31 January 1919 (First World War, War Diary, WO95/3045/2)	WD3045_2	9781474532921	£50.00
61 DIVISION Divisional Troops 476 Field Company Royal Engineers : 1 December 1915 - 31 July 1919 (First World War, War Diary, WO95/3046)	WD3046	9781474532938	£53.00
61 DIVISION Divisional Troops 478 Field Company Royal Engineers : 1 December 1915 - 30 November 1917 (First World War, War Diary, WO95/3047A)	WD3047_A	9781474532945	£46.00
61 DIVISION Divisional Troops 478 Field Company Royal Engineers : 1 December 1917 - 31 July 1919 (First World War, War Diary, WO95/3047B)	WD3047_B	9781474532952	£50.00
61 DIVISION Divisional Troops 479 Field Company Royal Engineers : 1 December 1915 - 31 October 1917 (First World War, War Diary, WO95/3048A)	WD3048_A	9781474532969	£49.00
61 DIVISION Divisional Troops 479 Field Company Royal Engineers : 1 November 1917 - 31 July 1919 (First World War, War Diary, WO95/3048B)	WD3048_B	9781474532976	£45.00
61 DIVISION Divisional Troops Divisional Signal Company : 1 December 1915 - 6 June 1916 (First World War, War Diary, WO95/3049/1)	WD3049_1	9781474532983	£15.00
61 DIVISION Divisional Troops Machine Gun Corps 61 Battalion : 7 June 1916 - 26 September 1919 (First World War, War Diary, WO95/3049/2)	WD3049_2	9781474532990	£31.00
61 DIVISION Divisional Troops Duke of Cornwall's Light Infantry 1/5th Battalion Pioneers : 21 May 1916 - 1 December 1919 (First World War, War Diary, WO95/3050)	WD3050	9781474533003	£64.00
61 DIVISION Divisional Troops Royal Army Medical Corps 2/1 South Midland Field Ambulance : 1 September 1915 - 31 July 1919 (First World War, War Diary, WO95/3051/1)	WD3051_1	9781474533010	£30.00
61 DIVISION Divisional Troops Royal Army Medical Corps 2/2 South Midland Field Ambulance : 4 September 1915 - 15 July 1919 (First World War, War Diary, WO95/3051/2)	WD3051_2	9781474533027	£30.00
61 DIVISION Divisional Troops Royal Army Medical Corps 2/3 South Midland Field Ambulance : 1 December 1915 - 28 July 1919 (First World War, War Diary, WO95/3051/3)	WD3051_3	9781474533034	£19.00
61 DIVISION Divisional Troops 61 Sanitary Section : 24 May 1916 - 30 April 1917 (First World War, War Diary, WO95/3052/1)	WD3052_1	9781474533041	£15.00
61 DIVISION Divisional Troops Royal Army Veterinary Corps 61 Mobile Veterinary Section : 24 May 1916 - 31 March 1919 (First World War, War Diary, WO95/3052/2)	WD3052_2	9781474533058	£15.00
61 DIVISION Divisional Troops Royal Army Service Corps Divisional Train (521, 522, 523, 524 Companies A.S.C.) : 4 March 1915 - 12 May 1917 (First World War, War Diary, WO95/3052/3)	WD3052_3	9781474533065	£63.00

Title	Product Code	ISBN	Price
61 DIVISION Divisional Troops Royal Army Service Corps Divisional Train (521, 522, 523, 524 Companies A.S.C.) : 31 May 1917 - 12 August 1919 (First World War, War Diary, WO95/3053)	WD3053	9781474533072	£82.00
61 DIVISION 182 Infantry Brigade Headquarters : 1 October 1915 - 31 December 1917 (First World War, War Diary, WO95/3054)	WD3054	9781474533089	£81.00
61 DIVISION 182 Infantry Brigade Headquarters : 1 January 1918 - 30 September 1919 (First World War, War Diary, WO95/3055)	WD3055	9781474533096	£80.00
61 DIVISION 182 Infantry Brigade Royal Warwickshire Regiment 2/5th Battalion : 1 September 1915 - 20 February 1918 (First World War, War Diary, WO95/3056/1)	WD3056_1	9781474533102	£21.00
61 DIVISION 182 Infantry Brigade Royal Warwickshire Regiment 2/6th Battalion : 1 September 1915 - 22 September 1919 (First World War, War Diary, WO95/3056/2)	WD3056_2	9781474533119	£20.00
61 DIVISION 182 Infantry Brigade Royal Warwickshire Regiment 2/7th Battalion : 1 October 1915 - 29 July 1919 (First World War, War Diary, WO95/3056/3)	WD3056_3	9781474533126	£42.00
61 DIVISION 182 Infantry Brigade Royal Warwickshire Regiment 2/8th Battalion : 1 September 1915 - 22 February 1918 (First World War, War Diary, WO95/3057/1)	WD3057_1	9781474533133	£30.00
61 DIVISION 182 Infantry Brigade Worcestershire Regiment 2/8th Battalion : 2 February 1918 - 30 April 1919 (First World War, War Diary, WO95/3057/2)	WD3057_2	9781474533140	£15.00
61 DIVISION 182 Infantry Brigade, Brigade Machine Gun Company : 16 June 1916 - 28 February 1918 (First World War, War Diary, WO95/3057/3)	WD3057_3	9781474533157	£15.00
61 DIVISION 182 Infantry Brigade, Brigade Trench Mortar Battery : 13 June 1916 - 31 August 1916 (First World War, War Diary, WO95/3057/4)	WD3057_4	9781474533164	£15.00
61 DIVISION 183 Infantry Brigade Headquarters : 1 September 1915 - 31 December 1917 (First World War, War Diary, WO95/3058)	WD3058	9781474533171	£65.00
61 DIVISION 183 Infantry Brigade Headquarters : 1 January 1918 - 31 August 1919 (First World War, War Diary, WO95/3059)	WD3059	9781474533188	£41.00
61 DIVISION 183 Infantry Brigade Gloucestershire Regiment 2/4th (City of Bristol) Battalion, Territorial : 1 September 1915 - 22 December 1917 (First World War, War Diary, WO95/3060/1)	WD3060_1	9781474533195	£16.00
61 DIVISION 183 Infantry Brigade Gloucestershire Regiment 2/6th Battalion (Territorials) : 3 September 1915 - 20 February 1918 (First World War, War Diary, WO95/3060/2)	WD3060_2	9781474533201	£16.00
61 DIVISION 183 Infantry Brigade Worcestershire Regiment 2/7th Battalion : 2 September 1915 - 18 January 1918 (First World War, War Diary, WO95/3060/3)	WD3060_3	9781474533218	£15.00
61 DIVISION 183 Infantry Brigade Worcestershire Regiment 2/8th Battalion : 1 September 1915 - 31 January 1918 (First World War, War Diary, WO95/3060/4)	WD3060_4	9781474533225	£15.00
61 DIVISION 183 Infantry Brigade East Lancashire Regiment 1st Battalion and Gordon Highlanders 5th Battalion : 1 February 1918 - 31 May 1918 (First World War, War Diary, WO95/3061)	WD3061	9781474533232	£45.00
61 DIVISION 183 Infantry Brigade Northumberland Fusiliers 9th Battalion : 1 June 1918 - 3 November 1919 (First World War, War Diary, WO95/3062/1)	WD3062_1	9781474533249	£35.00

Title	Product Code	ISBN	Price
61 DIVISION 183 Infantry Brigade Suffolk Regiment 11th Battalion : 1 June 1918 - 15 November 1919 (First World War, War Diary, WO95/3062/2)	WD3062_2	9781474533256	£15.00
61 DIVISION 183 Infantry Brigade, Brigade Machine Gun Company : 17 June 1916 - 23 June 1916 (First World War, War Diary, WO95/3062/3)	WD3062_3	9781474533263	£15.00
61 DIVISION 183 Infantry Brigade, Brigade Trench Mortar Battery : 2 July 1916 - 15 July 1916 (First World War, War Diary, WO95/3062/4)	WD3062_4	9781474533270	£15.00
61 DIVISION 184 Infantry Brigade Headquarters : 1 September 1915 - 30 September 1917 (First World War, War Diary, WO95/3063)	WD3063	9781474533287	£66.00
61 DIVISION 184 Infantry Brigade Headquarters : 1 October 1917 - 31 July 1919 (First World War, War Diary, WO95/3064)	WD3064	9781474533294	£59.00
61 DIVISION 184 Infantry Brigade Princess Charlotte of Wales's (Royal Berkshire Regiment) 2/4th Battalion : 9 September 1915 - 30 April 1919 (First World War, War Diary, WO95/3065)	WD3065	9781474533300	£59.00
61 DIVISION 184 Infantry Brigade Gloucestershire Regiment 2/5th Battalion (Territorial) and Oxfordshire and Buckinghamshire Light Infantry 2/1st Bucks Battalion : 8 May 1915 - 31 July 1919 (First World War, War Diary, WO95/3066)	WD3066	9781474533317	£74.00
61 DIVISION 184 Infantry Brigade Oxfordshire and Buckinghamshire Light Infantry 2/4th Battalion : 1 December 1915 - 30 April 1919 (First World War, War Diary, WO95/3067/1)	WD3067_1	9781474533324	£35.00
61 DIVISION 184 Infantry Brigade, Brigade Machine Gun Company : 1 January 1916 - 28 February 1918 (First World War, War Diary, WO95/3067/2)	WD3067_2	9781474533331	£21.00
61 DIVISION 184 Infantry Brigade, Brigade Trench Mortar Battery : 5 July 1916 - 31 August 1916 (First World War, War Diary, WO95/3067/3)	WD3067_3	9781474533348	£15.00

Title	Product Code	ISBN	Price
62 DIVISION			
62 DIVISION Headquarters, Branches and Services General Staff : 4 January 1917 - 31 March 1917 (First World War, War Diary, WO95/3068)	WD3068	9781474533355	£65.00
62 DIVISION Headquarters, Branches and Services General Staff : 1 May 1917 - 31 October 1917 (First World War, War Diary, WO95/3069)	WD3069	9781474533362	£64.00
62 DIVISION Headquarters, Branches and Services General Staff : 1 November 1917 - 20 July 1918 (First World War, War Diary, WO95/3070)	WD3070	9781474533379	£77.00
62 DIVISION Headquarters, Branches and Services General Staff : 1 August 1918 - 31 August 1919 (First World War, War Diary, WO95/3071)	WD3071	9781474533386	£48.00
62 DIVISION Headquarters, Branches and Services Adjutant and Quarter-Master General : 22 December 1916 - 31 March 1919 (First World War, War Diary, WO95/3072)	WD3072	9781474533393	£34.00
62 DIVISION Headquarters, Branches and Services Commander Royal Artillery and Assistant Director Medical Services : 23 February 1915 - 31 August 1919 (First World War, War Diary, WO95/3073)	WD3073	9781474533409	£79.00
62 DIVISION Headquarters, Branches and Services Commander Royal Engineers : 2 January 1917 - 31 August 1919 (First World War, War Diary, WO95/3074/1)	WD3074_1	9781474533416	£15.00
62 DIVISION Headquarters, Branches and Services Royal Army Ordnance Corps Deputy Assistant Director Ordnance Services : 8 January 1917 - 31 August 1919 (First World War, War Diary, WO95/3074/2)	WD3074_2	9781474533423	£21.00
62 DIVISION Headquarters, Branches and Services Royal Army Veterinary Corps Assistant Director Veterinary Services and Assistant Provost Marshal : 9 January 1917 - 31 August 1919 (First World War, War Diary, WO95/3074/3)	WD3074_3	9781474533430	£16.00
62 DIVISION Divisional Troops 310 Brigade Royal Field Artillery : 7 January 1917 - 31 August 1919 (First World War, War Diary, WO95/3075/1)	WD3075_1	9781474533447	£15.00
62 DIVISION Divisional Troops 312 Brigade Royal Field Artillery : 5 January 1917 - 31 August 1919 (First World War, War Diary, WO95/3075/2)	WD3075_2	9781474533454	£15.00
62 DIVISION Divisional Troops Divisional Ammunition Column : 12 January 1917 - 31 August 1919 (First World War, War Diary, WO95/3075/3)	WD3075_3	9781474533461	£15.00
62 DIVISION Divisional Troops Divisional Trench Mortar Batteries : 1 February 1917 - 31 March 1919 (First World War, War Diary, WO95/3075/4)	WD3075_4	9781474533478	£15.00
62 DIVISION Divisional Troops 457, 460 and 461 Field Company Royal Engineers and Divisional Signal Company : 8 January 1917 - 30 August 1919 (First World War, War Diary, WO95/3076)	WD3076	9781474533485	£45.00
62 DIVISION Divisional Troops Durham Light Infantry 1/9th Battalion Pioneers, Gordon Highlanders 53rd Battalion, Machine Gun Corps 62 Battalion and 201 Machine Gun Company : 10 February 1917 - 28 February 1919 (First World War, War Diary, WO95/3077)	WD3077	9781474533492	£36.00
62 DIVISION Divisional Troops Royal Army Medical Corps 2/1 West Riding Field Ambulance : 12 January 1917 - 29 August 1919 (First World War, War Diary, WO95/3078/1)	WD3078_1	9781474533508	£15.00
62 DIVISION Divisional Troops Royal Army Medical Corps 2/2 West Riding Field Ambulance : 9 January 1917 - 31 May 1919 (First World War, War Diary, WO95/3078/2)	WD3078_2	9781474533515	£16.00

Title	Product Code	ISBN	Price
62 DIVISION Divisional Troops Royal Army Medical Corps 2/3 West Riding Field Ambulance : 10 January 1917 - 31 August 1919 (First World War, War Diary, WO95/3078/3)	WD3078_3	9781474533522	£15.00
62 DIVISION Divisional Troops Royal Army Veterinary Corps 2/1 West Riding Mobile Veterinary Section : 9 November 1916 - 30 August 1919 (First World War, War Diary, WO95/3078/4)	WD3078_4	9781474533539	£15.00
62 DIVISION Divisional Troops Royal Army Service Corps Divisional Train (525, 526, 527, 528 Companies ASC) : 8 January 1917 - 12 August 1919 (First World War, War Diary, WO95/3078/5)	WD3078_5	9781474533546	£15.00
62 DIVISION 185 Infantry Brigade Headquarters : 21 December 1916 - 31 August 1917 (First World War, War Diary, WO95/3079)	WD3079	9781474533553	£48.00
62 DIVISION 185 Infantry Brigade Headquarters : 1 September 1917 - 31 March 1919 (First World War, War Diary, WO95/3080)	WD3080	9781474533560	£65.00
62 DIVISION 185 Infantry Brigade Prince of Wales's Own (West Yorkshire Regiment) 2/5th Battalion : 28 September 1914 - 15 August 1918 (First World War, War Diary, WO95/3081)	WD3081	9781474533577	£78.00
62 DIVISION 185 Infantry Brigade Prince of Wales's Own (West Yorkshire Regiment) 2/6th, 2/7th and 2/8th Battalion : 9 September 1914 - 31 January 1918 (First World War, War Diary, WO95/3082)	WD3082	9781474533584	£84.00
62 DIVISION 185 Infantry Brigade Prince of Wales's Own (West Yorkshire Regiment) 1/8th Battalion, Devonshire Regiment 5th (P.O.W.) Battalion (Territorials), London Regiment 2/20 Battalion and 212 Machine Gun Company : 28 February 1917 - 28 February 1918 (	WD3083	9781474533591	£61.00
62 DIVISION 186 Infantry Brigade Headquarters : 10 January 1917 - 31 December 1917 (First World War, War Diary, WO95/3084)	WD3084	9781474533607	£44.00
62 DIVISION 186 Infantry Brigade Headquarters : 1 January 1918 - 24 March 1919 (First World War, War Diary, WO95/3085)	WD3085	9781474533614	£48.00
62 DIVISION 186 Infantry Brigade Duke of Wellington's (West Riding Regiment) 2/4th Battalion : 9 January 1917 - 28 February 1919 (First World War, War Diary, WO95/3086/1)	WD3086_1	9781474533621	£15.00
62 DIVISION 186 Infantry Brigade Duke of Wellington's (West Riding Regiment) 2/5th Battalion : 9 October 1914 - 31 January 1918 (First World War, War Diary, WO95/3086/2)	WD3086_2	9781474533638	£15.00
62 DIVISION 186 Infantry Brigade Duke of Wellington's (West Riding Regiment) 1/5th Battalion : 5 August 1917 - 2 May 1919 (First World War, War Diary, WO95/3086/3)	WD3086_3	9781474533645	£24.00
62 DIVISION 186 Infantry Brigade Duke of Wellington's (West Riding Regiment) 2/6th Battalion : 17 September 1914 - 31 January 1918 (First World War, War Diary, WO95/3087/1)	WD3087_1	9781474533652	£15.00
62 DIVISION 186 Infantry Brigade Duke of Wellington's (West Riding Regiment) 2/7th Battalion : 14 October 1914 - 18 June 1918 (First World War, War Diary, WO95/3087/2)	WD3087_2	9781474533669	£18.00
62 DIVISION 186 Infantry Brigade Hampshire Regiment 2/4th (T.F.) Battalion : 1 June 1918 - 28 February 1919 (First World War, War Diary, WO95/3087/3)	WD3087_3	9781474533676	£15.00
62 DIVISION 186 Infantry Brigade 213 Machine Gun Company : 1 March 1917 - 28 February 1918 (First World War, War Diary, WO95/3087/4)	WD3087_4	9781474533683	£19.00

Title	Product Code	ISBN	Price
62 DIVISION 187 Infantry Brigade Headquarters : 12 January 1917 - 30 September 1917 (First World War, War Diary, WO95/3088)	WD3088	9781474533690	£48.00
62 DIVISION 187 Infantry Brigade Headquarters : 1 October 1917 - 31 March 1919 (First World War, War Diary, WO95/3089)	WD3089	9781474533706	£47.00
62 DIVISION 187 Infantry Brigade York and Lancaster Regiment 2/4th (Hallamshire) (T.F.) Battalion and 2/5th (T.F.) Battalion : 3 October 1914 - 3 February 1918 (First World War, War Diary, WO95/3090)	WD3090	9781474533713	£49.00
62 DIVISION 187 Infantry Brigade King's Own (Yorkshire Light Infantry) 2/4th, 1/5th, 2/5th Battalion and 208 Machine Gun Company : 15 July 1916 - 28 February 1918 (First World War, War Diary, WO95/3091)	WD3091	9781474533720	£49.00
62 DIVISION 1 Highland Brigade Headquarters, Princess Louise's (Argyll & Sutherland Highlanders) 10th Battalion, Queen's Own Cameron Highlanders 5th Battalion, Gordon Highlanders 52nd, 4th, 1/5th and 51st Battalion, Black Watch (Royal Highlanders) 6th (P	WD3092	9781474533737	£32.00

Title	Product Code	ISBN	Price
63 (ROYAL NAVAL) DIVISION			
63 (ROYAL NAVAL) DIVISION Headquarters, Branches and Services General Staff : 1 May 1916 - 30 April 1917 (First World War, War Diary, WO95/3093)	WD3093	9781474533744	£89.00
63 (ROYAL NAVAL) DIVISION Headquarters, Branches and Services General Staff : 1 May 1917 - 30 September 1917 (First World War, War Diary, WO95/3094)	WD3094	9781474533751	£48.00
63 (ROYAL NAVAL) DIVISION Headquarters, Branches and Services General Staff : 1 October 1917 - 28 February 1918 (First World War, War Diary, WO95/3095)	WD3095	9781474533768	£56.00
63 (ROYAL NAVAL) DIVISION Headquarters, Branches and Services General Staff : 1 March 1918 - 30 June 1918 (First World War, War Diary, WO95/3096)	WD3096	9781474533775	£70.00
63 (ROYAL NAVAL) DIVISION Headquarters, Branches and Services General Staff : 1 July 1918 - 28 February 1919 (First World War, War Diary, WO95/3097)	WD3097	9781474533782	£56.00
63 (ROYAL NAVAL) DIVISION Headquarters, Branches and Services Adjutant and Quarter-Master General : 21 May 1916 - 31 July 1918 (First World War, War Diary, WO95/3098)	WD3098	9781474533799	£65.00
63 (ROYAL NAVAL) DIVISION Headquarters, Branches and Services Adjutant and Quarter-Master General and Commander Royal Artillery : 1 July 1916 - 31 March 1919 (First World War, War Diary, WO95/3099)	WD3099	9781474533805	£51.00
63 (ROYAL NAVAL) DIVISION Headquarters, Branches and Services Royal Army Medical Corps Assistant Director Medical Services : 1 May 1916 - 30 April 1919 (First World War, War Diary, WO95/3100)	WD3100	9781474533812	£56.00
63 (ROYAL NAVAL) DIVISION Headquarters, Branches and Services Commander Royal Engineers, Deputy Assistant Director Ordnance Services, Assistant Director Veterinary Services and Assistant Provost Marshal : 1 May 1916 - 31 January 1919 (First World War, War	WD3101	9781474533829	£50.00
63 (ROYAL NAVAL) DIVISION Divisional Troops 223, 315, 316, and 317 Brigade Royal Field Artillery, Divisional Ammunition Column and Divisional Trench Mortar Batteries : 24 June 1916 - 1 February 1919 (First World War, War Diary, WO95/3102)	WD3102	9781474533836	£59.00
63 (ROYAL NAVAL) DIVISION Divisional Troops 247, 248 and 249 Field Company Royal Engineers : 1 September 1916 - 30 April 1919 (First World War, War Diary, WO95/3103)	WD3103	9781474533843	£62.00
63 (ROYAL NAVAL) DIVISION Divisional Troops Divisional Signal Company : 1 April 1916 - 30 April 1919 (First World War, War Diary, WO95/3104)	WD3104	9781474533850	£45.00
63 (ROYAL NAVAL) DIVISION Divisional Troops Worcestershire Regiment 14th Battalion Pioneers and Machine Gun Corps 63 Battalion Machine Gun Corps : 20 June 1916 - 24 May 1919 (First World War, War Diary, WO95/3105)	WD3105	9781474533867	£59.00
63 (ROYAL NAVAL) DIVISION Divisional Troops Royal Army Medical Corps 148 Field Ambulance : 1 June 1916 - 30 April 1919 (First World War, War Diary, WO95/3106/1)	WD3106_1	9781474533874	£20.00
63 (ROYAL NAVAL) DIVISION Divisional Troops Royal Army Medical Corps 149 Field Ambulance : 23 May 1916 - 30 April 1919 (First World War, War Diary, WO95/3106/2)	WD3106_2	9781474533881	£37.00

Title	Product Code	ISBN	Price
63 (ROYAL NAVAL) DIVISION Divisional Troops Royal Army Medical Corps 150 Field Ambulance : 14 May 1916 - 28 May 1919 (First World War, War Diary, WO95/3106/3)	WD3106_3	9781474533898	£22.00
63 (ROYAL NAVAL) DIVISION Divisional Troops 63 Sanitary Section, 53 Mobile Veterinary Section and Divisional Train (761, 762, 763, 764 Companies A.S.C.) : 18 May 1916 - 1 April 1919 (First World War, War Diary, WO95/3107)	WD3107	9781474533904	£35.00
63 (ROYAL NAVAL) DIVISION Royal Marine Brigade Headquarters : 26 August 1918 - 12 October 1918 (First World War, War Diary, WO95/3108/1)	WD3108_1	9781474533911	£15.00
63 (ROYAL NAVAL) DIVISION Royal Marine Brigade 9 Chatham Royal Marine Battalion : 26 August 1914 - 12 October 1914 (First World War, War Diary, WO95/3108/2)	WD3108_2	9781474533928	£15.00
63 (ROYAL NAVAL) DIVISION 188 Infantry Brigade Headquarters : 26 May 1916 - 30 November 1917 (First World War, War Diary, WO95/3108/3)	WD3108_3	9781474533935	£62.00
63 (ROYAL NAVAL) DIVISION 188 Infantry Brigade Headquarters : 1 January 1918 - 30 April 1919 (First World War, War Diary, WO95/3109)	WD3109	9781474533942	£67.00
63 (ROYAL NAVAL) DIVISION 188 Infantry Brigade 1 Royal Marine Battalion : 14 May 1916 - 30 April 1919 (First World War, War Diary, WO95/3110/1)	WD3110_1	9781474533959	£15.00
63 (ROYAL NAVAL) DIVISION 188 Infantry Brigade 2 Royal Marine Battalion : 1 June 1916 - 28 April 1918 (First World War, War Diary, WO95/3110/2)	WD3110_2	9781474533966	£26.00
63 (ROYAL NAVAL) DIVISION 188 Infantry Brigade Anson Battalion : 1 June 1916 - 30 April 1919 (First World War, War Diary, WO95/3111/1)	WD3111_1	9781474533973	£22.00
63 (ROYAL NAVAL) DIVISION 188 Infantry Brigade Howe Battalion : 1 May 1916 - 28 February 1918 (First World War, War Diary, WO95/3111/2)	WD3111_2	9781474533980	£20.00
63 (ROYAL NAVAL) DIVISION 188 Infantry Brigade Royal Irish Regiment 2nd Battalion : 1 May 1918 - 2 May 1919 (First World War, War Diary, WO95/3111/3)	WD3111_3	9781474533997	£18.00
63 (ROYAL NAVAL) DIVISION 188 Infantry Brigade, Brigade Machine Gun Company : 31 July 1916 - 28 February 1918 (First World War, War Diary, WO95/3111/4)	WD3111_4	9781474534000	£15.00
63 (ROYAL NAVAL) DIVISION 188 Infantry Brigade, Brigade Trench Mortar Battery : 1 July 1916 - 31 July 1916 (First World War, War Diary, WO95/3111/5)	WD3111_5	9781474534017	£15.00
63 (ROYAL NAVAL) DIVISION 189 Infantry Brigade Headquarters : 23 May 1916 - 31 December 1917 (First World War, War Diary, WO95/3112)	WD3112	9781474534024	£46.00
63 (ROYAL NAVAL) DIVISION 189 Infantry Brigade Headquarters : 1 January 1918 - 28 February 1919 (First World War, War Diary, WO95/3113)	WD3113	9781474534031	£44.00
63 (ROYAL NAVAL) DIVISION 189 Infantry Brigade Drake Battalion : 1 July 1916 - 30 April 1918 (First World War, War Diary, WO95/3114/1)	WD3114_1	9781474534048	£15.00
63 (ROYAL NAVAL) DIVISION 189 Infantry Brigade Hawke Battalion : 4 July 1916 - 24 May 1919 (First World War, War Diary, WO95/3114/2)	WD3114_2	9781474534055	£39.00
63 (ROYAL NAVAL) DIVISION 189 Infantry Brigade Nelson Battalion : 1 June 1916 - 23 February 1918 (First World War, War Diary, WO95/3114/3)	WD3114_3	9781474534062	£15.00
63 (ROYAL NAVAL) DIVISION 189 Infantry Brigade Hood Battalion, Brigade Machine Gun Company and Brigade Trench Mortar Battery : 27 May 1916 - 30 April 1919 (First World War, War Diary, WO95/3115)	WD3115	9781474534079	£63.00

Title	Product Code	ISBN	Price
63 (ROYAL NAVAL) DIVISION 190 Infantry Brigade Headquarters : 1 May 1916 - 30 April 1917 (First World War, War Diary, WO95/3116)	WD3116	9781474534086	£33.00
63 (ROYAL NAVAL) DIVISION 190 Infantry Brigade Headquarters : 1 May 1917 - 28 February 1919 (First World War, War Diary, WO95/3117)	WD3117	9781474534093	£44.00
63 (ROYAL NAVAL) DIVISION 190 Infantry Brigade 1 Battalion Honourable Artillery Company, Bedfordshire Regiment 4th Battalion, King's (Shropshire Light Infantry) 1/4th Battalion and Royal Dublin Fusiliers 10th Battalion : 2 February 1916 - 31 May 1917 (Fir	WD3118	9781474534109	£54.00
63 (ROYAL NAVAL) DIVISION 190 Infantry Brigade Royal Fusiliers (City of London Regiment) 7th Battalion, London Regiment 28th (County of London) Battalion (Artists Rifles), Brigade Machine Gun Company and Brigade Trench Mortar Battery : 13 June 1916 - 30	WD3119	9781474534116	£41.00

Title	Product Code	ISBN	Price
66 DIVISION			
66 DIVISION Headquarters, Branches and Services General Staff : 25 February 1917 - 31 December 1917 (First World War, War Diary, WO95/3120)	WD3120	9781474534123	£60.00
66 DIVISION Headquarters, Branches and Services General Staff : 1 January 1918 - 29 August 1918 (First World War, War Diary, WO95/3121)	WD3121	9781474534130	£38.00
66 DIVISION Headquarters, Branches and Services General Staff : 1 September 1918 - 25 March 1919 (First World War, War Diary, WO95/3122)	WD3122	9781474534147	£43.00
66 DIVISION Headquarters, Branches and Services Adjutant and Quarter-Master General and Commander Royal Artillery : 1 September 1915 - 31 December 1917 (First World War, War Diary, WO95/3123)	WD3123	9781474534154	£46.00
66 DIVISION Headquarters, Branches and Services Commander Royal Artillery : 1 January 1918 - 26 April 1919 (First World War, War Diary, WO95/3124)	WD3124	9781474534161	£61.00
66 DIVISION Headquarters, Branches and Services Commander Royal Engineers : 1 September 1915 - 29 April 1919 (First World War, War Diary, WO95/3125)	WD3125	9781474534178	£52.00
66 DIVISION Headquarters, Branches and Services Royal Army Medical Corps Assistant Director Medical Services, Deputy Assistant Director Ordnance Services and Assistant Director Veterinary Services : 1 September 1915 - 24 March 1919 (First World War, War D	WD3126	9781474534185	£69.00
66 DIVISION Divisional Troops 330 Brigade Royal Field Artillery : 2 September 1915 - 17 May 1919 (First World War, War Diary, WO95/3127)	WD3127	9781474534192	£83.00
66 DIVISION Divisional Troops 331 and 332 Brigade Royal Field Artillery, Trench Mortar Batteries and Divisional Ammunition Column : 1 September 1915 - 24 May 1919 (First World War, War Diary, WO95/3128)	WD3128	9781474534208	£48.00
66 DIVISION Divisional Troops 430 and 431 Field Company Royal Engineers : 1 September 1915 - 30 April 1919 (First World War, War Diary, WO95/3129)	WD3129	9781474534215	£72.00
66 DIVISION Divisional Troops 432 Field Company Royal Engineers, Divisional Signal Company and Gloucestershire Regiment 9th (Service) Battalion Pioneers : 7 September 1915 - 28 February 1919 (First World War, War Diary, WO95/3130)	WD3130	9781474534222	£48.00
66 DIVISION Divisional Troops Royal Army Medical Corps 2/1 and 2/2 East Lancashire Field Ambulance : 1 September 1915 - 26 May 1919 (First World War, War Diary, WO95/3131)	WD3131	9781474534239	£65.00
66 DIVISION Divisional Troops Royal Army Medical Corps 2/3 East Lancashire Field Ambulance : 13 September 1915 - 26 February 1916 (First World War, War Diary, WO95/3132/1)	WD3132_1	9781474534246	£15.00
66 DIVISION Divisional Troops Royal Army Medical Corps 2/3 East Lancashire Field Ambulance : 27 February 1917 - 26 May 1919 (First World War, War Diary, WO95/3132/2)	WD3132_2	9781474534253	£21.00
66 DIVISION Divisional Troops Royal Army Medical Corps 1 South African Field Ambulance : 1 October 1918 - 31 December 1918 (First World War, War Diary, WO95/3132/3)	WD3132_3	9781474534260	£15.00

Title	Product Code	ISBN	Price
66 DIVISION Divisional Troops Royal Army Veterinary Corps 1/1 East Lancashire Mobile Veterinary Section : 1 March 1917 - 15 May 1919 (First World War, War Diary, WO95/3132/4)	WD3132_4	9781474534277	£15.00
66 DIVISION Divisional Troops Royal Army Service Corps Divisional Train (541, 542, 543, 544 Companies A.S.C.) : 19 September 1915 - 3 November 1915 (First World War, War Diary, WO95/3133/1)	WD3133_1	9781474534284	£15.00
66 DIVISION Divisional Troops Royal Army Service Corps Divisional Train (541, 542, 543, 544 Companies A.S.C.) : 22 February 1917 - 18 May 1919 (First World War, War Diary, WO95/3133/2)	WD3133_2	9781474534291	£80.00
66 DIVISION 197 Infantry Brigade Headquarters : 5 October 1915 - 17 February 1916 (First World War, War Diary, WO95/3134/1)	WD3134_1	9781474534307	£15.00
66 DIVISION 197 Infantry Brigade Headquarters : 27 February 1914 - 31 July 1917 (First World War, War Diary, WO95/3134/2)	WD3134_2	9781474534314	£41.00
66 DIVISION 197 Infantry Brigade Headquarters : 1 August 1917 - 31 May 1919 (First World War, War Diary, WO95/3135)	WD3135	9781474534321	£54.00
66 DIVISION 197 Infantry Brigade Black Watch (Royal Highlanders) 10th Battalion, Lancashire Fusiliers 2/6th, 2/7th and 2/8th Battalion : 3 October 1915 - 31 July 1918 (First World War, War Diary, WO95/3136)	WD3136	9781474534338	£36.00
66 DIVISION 197 Infantry Brigade Lancashire Fusiliers 3/5th (T) Battalion : 1 September 1915 - 5 February 1916 (First World War, War Diary, WO95/3137/1)	WD3137_1	9781474534345	£15.00
66 DIVISION 197 Infantry Brigade Lancashire Fusiliers 3/5th (T) Battalion : 28 February 1917 - 13 February 1918 (First World War, War Diary, WO95/3137/2)	WD3137_2	9781474534352	£19.00
66 DIVISION 197 Infantry Brigade 202 Machine Gun Company : 10 February 1917 - 28 February 1918 (First World War, War Diary, WO95/3137/3)	WD3137_3	9781474534369	£15.00
66 DIVISION 197 Infantry Brigade, Brigade Trench Mortar Battery : 24 February 1914 - 27 September 1918 (First World War, War Diary, WO95/3137/4)	WD3137_4	9781474534376	£15.00
66 DIVISION 198 Infantry Brigade Headquarters : 9 September 1915 - 20 February 1916 (First World War, War Diary, WO95/3138/1)	WD3138_1	9781474534383	£15.00
66 DIVISION 198 Infantry Brigade Headquarters : 1 March 1917 - 30 December 1917 (First World War, War Diary, WO95/3138/2)	WD3138_2	9781474534390	£40.00
66 DIVISION 198 Infantry Brigade Headquarters : 1 January 1918 - 21 May 1919 (First World War, War Diary, WO95/3139)	WD3139	9781474534406	£41.00
66 DIVISION 198 Infantry Brigade Royal Inniskilling Fusiliers 5th Battalion : 1 June 1918 - 9 May 1919 (First World War, War Diary, WO95/3140/1)	WD3140_1	9781474534413	£15.00
66 DIVISION 198 Infantry Brigade Royal Dublin Fusiliers 6th Battalion : 1 July 1918 - 29 April 1919 (First World War, War Diary, WO95/3140/2)	WD3140_2	9781474534420	£33.00
66 DIVISION 198 Infantry Brigade Lancashire Fusiliers 6th Battalion : 2 March 1918 - 30 April 1919 (First World War, War Diary, WO95/3140/3)	WD3140_3	9781474534437	£20.00
66 DIVISION 198 Infantry Brigade Lancashire Fusiliers 12th Battalion : 1 July 1918 - 31 July 1918 (First World War, War Diary, WO95/3140/4)	WD3140_4	9781474534444	£15.00
66 DIVISION 198 Infantry Brigade Prince of Wales's Leinster Regiment (Royal Canadians) 6th Battalion : 1 June 1918 - 16 September 1918 (First World War, War Diary, WO95/3140/5)	WD3140_5	9781474534451	£15.00

Title	Product Code	ISBN	Price
66 DIVISION 198 Infantry Brigade East Lancashire Regiment 1/4th, 2/4th and 2/5th Battalion, Manchester Regiment 2/9th and 2/10th Battalion, 203 Machine Gun Company and Brigade Trench Mortar Battery : 1 September 1915 - 3 April 1917 (First World War, War	WD3141	9781474534468	£60.00
66 DIVISION 199 Infantry Brigade Headquarters : 9 September 1915 - 10 February 1916 (First World War, War Diary, WO95/3142)	WD3142	9781474534475	£52.00
66 DIVISION 199 Infantry Brigade Headquarters : 1 January 1918 - 21 May 1919 (First World War, War Diary, WO95/3143)	WD3143	9781474534482	£44.00
66 DIVISION 199 Infantry Brigade Connaught Rangers 2nd and 5th Battalion, King's (Liverpool Regiment) 14th and 18th Battalion, Manchester Regiment 2/5th and 2/6th Battalion : 15 August 1915 - 31 May 1917 (First World War, War Diary, WO95/3144)	WD3144	9781474534499	£72.00
66 DIVISION 199 Infantry Brigade Manchester Regiment 2/7th Battalion : 1 September 1915 - 10 February 1916 (First World War, War Diary, WO95/3145/1)	WD3145_1	9781474534505	£15.00
66 DIVISION 199 Infantry Brigade Manchester Regiment 2/7th Battalion : 6 March 1917 - 31 July 1918 (First World War, War Diary, WO95/3145/2)	WD3145_2	9781474534512	£15.00
66 DIVISION 199 Infantry Brigade Manchester Regiment 2/8th Battalion : 1 September 1915 - 10 February 1916 (First World War, War Diary, WO95/3145/3)	WD3145_3	9781474534529	£15.00
66 DIVISION 199 Infantry Brigade Manchester Regiment 2/8th Battalion : 14 March 1917 - 13 February 1918 (First World War, War Diary, WO95/3145/4)	WD3145_4	9781474534536	£15.00
66 DIVISION 199 Infantry Brigade Manchester Regiment 9th Battalion : 1 March 1918 - 15 May 1919 (First World War, War Diary, WO95/3145/5)	WD3145_5	9781474534543	£19.00
66 DIVISION 199 Infantry Brigade Manchester Regiment 13th Battalion. : 1 July 1918 - 31 July 1918 (First World War, War Diary, WO95/3145/6)	WD3145_6	9781474534550	£15.00
66 DIVISION 199 Infantry Brigade 204 Machine Gun Company : 16 March 1917 - 28 February 1918 (First World War, War Diary, WO95/3145/7)	WD3145_7	9781474534567	£15.00
66 DIVISION 199 Infantry Brigade, Brigade Trench Mortar Battery : 1 August 1917 - 28 February 1918 (First World War, War Diary, WO95/3145/8)	WD3145_8	9781474534574	£21.00
66 DIVISION South African Brigade Headquarters : 1 September 1918 - 28 February 1919 (First World War, War Diary, WO95/3146)	WD3146	9781474534581	£34.00
66 DIVISION South African Brigade 1, 2 and 4 Battalion South African Infantry : 1 September 1918 - 28 February 1919 (First World War, War Diary, WO95/3147)	WD3147	9781474534598	£22.00

Title	Product Code	ISBN	Price
7 DIVISION			
7 DIVISION Headquarters, Branches and Services General Staff : 4 October 1914 - 31 January 1915 (First World War, War Diary, WO95/1627)	WD1627	9781474506304	£57.00
7 DIVISION Headquarters, Branches and Services General Staff : 1 February 1915 - 25 May 1915 (First World War, War Diary, WO95/1628)	WD1628	9781474522472	£66.00
7 DIVISION Headquarters, Branches and Services General Staff : 1 June 1915 - 29 September 1915 (First World War, War Diary, WO95/1629)	WD1629	9781474506311	£54.00
7 DIVISION Headquarters, Branches and Services General Staff : 1 October 1915 - 21 December 1919 (First World War, War Diary, WO95/1630)	WD1630	9781474506328	£44.00
7 DIVISION Headquarters, Branches and Services General Staff : 1 July 1916 - 31 December 1916 (First World War, War Diary, WO95/1631)	WD1631	9781474506335	£60.00
7 DIVISION Headquarters, Branches and Services General Staff : 1 January 1917 - 31 May 1917 (First World War, War Diary, WO95/1632)	WD1632	9781474522489	£65.00
7 DIVISION Headquarters, Branches and Services General Staff : 1 June 1917 - 30 November 1917 (First World War, War Diary, WO95/1633)	WD1633	9781474506342	£57.00
7 DIVISION Headquarters, Branches and Services General Staff Appendices : 11 October 1914 - 30 November 1915 (First World War, War Diary, WO95/1634)	WD1634	9781474506359	£49.00
7 DIVISION Headquarters, Branches and Services Adjutant and Quarter-Master General : 31 August 1914 - 31 December 1914 (First World War, War Diary, WO95/1635)	WD1635	9781474506366	£25.00
7 DIVISION Headquarters, Branches and Services Adjutant and Quarter-Master General : 1 January 1915 - 31 December 1915 (First World War, War Diary, WO95/1636)	WD1636	9781474506373	£68.00
7 DIVISION Headquarters, Branches and Services Adjutant and Quarter-Master General : 1 January 1916 - 30 November 1917 (First World War, War Diary, WO95/1637)	WD1637	9781474506380	£55.00
7 DIVISION Headquarters, Branches and Services Commander Royal Artillery : 10 March 1914 - 31 December 1915 (First World War, War Diary, WO95/1638)	WD1638	9781474506397	£66.00
7 DIVISION Headquarters, Branches and Services Commander Royal Artillery : 1 January 1916 - 30 November 1917 (First World War, War Diary, WO95/1639)	WD1639	9781474506403	£63.00
7 DIVISION Headquarters, Branches and Services Royal Army Medical Corps Assistant Director Medical Services : 7 September 1914 - 30 November 1917 (First World War, War Diary, WO95/1640)	WD1640	9781474522496	£66.00
7 DIVISION Headquarters, Branches and Services Commander Royal Engineers, Deputy Assistant Director Ordnance Services, Assistant Director Veterinary Services, Royal Engineers Headquarters War Diaries and 54th Field Company Royal Engineers : 19 September	WD1641	9781474506410	£61.00
7 DIVISION Divisional Troops A Squadron Northumberland Hussars, Divisional Cyclist Company and 14 Brigade Royal Horse Artillery : 5 August 1914 - 31 March 1917 (First World War, War Diary, WO95/1642)	WD1642	9781474506427	£60.00
7 DIVISION Divisional Troops 22 Brigade Royal Field Artillery and 35 Brigade Royal Field Artillery : 4 October 1914 - 30 December 1917 (First World War, War Diary, WO95/1643)	WD1643	9781474506434	£50.00

Title	Product Code	ISBN	Price
7 DIVISION Divisional Troops 37 Brigade Royal Field Artillery, Divisional Trench Mortar Batteries and Divisional Ammunition Column : 8 September 1914 - 30 November 1917 (First World War, War Diary, WO95/1644)	WD1644	9781474506441	£24.00
7 DIVISION Divisional Troops 54, 55 and 95 Field Company Royal Engineers, 401 (1/2 Highland) Field Company Royal Engineers and 528 (1/3 Durham) Field Company Royal Engineers : 4 August 1914 - 30 November 1917 (First World War, War Diary, WO95/1645)	WD1645	9781474506458	£41.00
7 DIVISION Divisional Troops Divisional Signal Company : 4 October 1914 - 30 November 1917 (First World War, War Diary, WO95/1646/1)	WD1646_1	9781474506465	£22.00
7 DIVISION Divisional Troops Manchester Regiment 24th Battalion : 1 June 1916 - 30 November 1917 (First World War, War Diary, WO95/1646/2)	WD1646_2	9781474506472	£30.00
7 DIVISION Divisional Troops 220 Machine Gun Company : 18 March 1917 - 30 November 1917 (First World War, War Diary, WO95/1646/3)	WD1646_3	9781474506489	£15.00
7 DIVISION Divisional Troops Royal Army Medical Corps 21 Field Ambulance : 4 October 1914 - 30 November 1917 (First World War, War Diary, WO95/1647/1)	WD1647_1	9781474506496	£15.00
7 DIVISION Divisional Troops Royal Army Medical Corps 22 Field Ambulance : 5 October 1914 - 30 November 1917 (First World War, War Diary, WO95/1647/2)	WD1647_2	9781474506502	£45.00
7 DIVISION Divisional Troops Royal Army Medical Corps 23 Field Ambulance : 7 October 1914 - 30 November 1917 (First World War, War Diary, WO95/1648/1)	WD1648_1	9781474506519	£26.00
7 DIVISION Divisional Troops 10 Sanitary Section (2 London Sanitary Company) : 1 August 1916 - 31 March 1917 (First World War, War Diary, WO95/1648/2)	WD1648_2	9781474506526	£16.00
7 DIVISION Divisional Troops Royal Army Veterinary Corps 12 Mobile Veterinary Section : 15 September 1914 - 30 November 1917 (First World War, War Diary, WO95/1648/3)	WD1648_3	9781474506533	£15.00
7 DIVISION Divisional Troops Royal Army Service Corps Divisional Train (39,40,42,86 Companies A.S.C.) : 13 September 1914 - 30 November 1917 (First World War, War Diary, WO95/1649)	WD1649	9781474506540	£37.00
7 DIVISION 20 Infantry Brigade Headquarters : 3 March 1914 - 30 April 1915 (First World War, War Diary, WO95/1650)	WD1650	9781474506557	£31.00
7 DIVISION 20 Infantry Brigade Headquarters : 1 May 1915 - 31 August 1915 (First World War, War Diary, WO95/1651)	WD1651	9781474522502	£61.00
7 DIVISION 20 Infantry Brigade Headquarters : 1 September 1915 - 31 December 1915 (First World War, War Diary, WO95/1652)	WD1652	9781474506564	£61.00
7 DIVISION 20 Infantry Brigade Headquarters : 1 January 1916 - 31 October 1916 (First World War, War Diary, WO95/1653)	WD1653	9781474522519	£66.00
7 DIVISION 20 Infantry Brigade Headquarters : 1 November 1916 - 30 November 1917 (First World War, War Diary, WO95/1654)	WD1654	9781474506571	£65.00
7 DIVISION 20 Infantry Brigade Border Regiment 2nd Battalion : 5 October 1914 - 30 November 1917 (First World War, War Diary, WO95/1655/1)	WD1655_1	9781474506588	£29.00
7 DIVISION 20 Infantry Brigade Devonshire Regiment 8th (Service) Battalion : 17 July 1915 - 30 November 1917 (First World War, War Diary, WO95/1655/2)	WD1655_2	9781474506595	£20.00

Title	Product Code	ISBN	Price
7 DIVISION 20 Infantry Brigade Devonshire Regiment 9th (Service) Battalion and Gordon Highlanders 2nd Battalion : 3 March 1914 - 30 November 1917 (First World War, War Diary, WO95/1656)	WD1656	9781474506601	£43.00
7 DIVISION 20 Infantry Brigade Gordon Highlanders 6th Battalion, Grenadier Guards 1st Battalion, Scots Guards 2 Battalion, Brigade Machine Gun Company and Brigade Trench Mortar Battery : 4 October 1914 - 17 November 1915 (First World War, War Diary, WO95	WD1657	9781474506618	£67.00
7 DIVISION 21 Infantry Brigade Headquarters and Bedfordshire Regiment 2nd Battalion : 4 October 1914 - 31 December 1915 (First World War, War Diary, WO95/1658)	WD1658	9781474522526	£79.00
7 DIVISION 21 Infantry Brigade Queen's Own Cameron Highlanders 4th Battalion, Royal Scots Fusiliers 2nd Battalion, Duke of Edinburgh's (Wiltshire Regiment) 2nd Battalion and Princess of Wales's Own (Yorkshire Regiment) 2nd Battalion : 30 August 1914 - 31	WD1659	9781474506625	£41.00
7 DIVISION 22 Infantry Brigade Headquarters : 7 September 1914 - 28 August 1916 (First World War, War Diary, WO95/1660)	WD1660	9781474506632	£50.00
7 DIVISION 22 Infantry Brigade Headquarters : 1 September 1916 - 30 November 1917 (First World War, War Diary, WO95/1661)	WD1661	9781474506649	£44.00
7 DIVISION 22 Infantry Brigade Honourable Artillery Company 2 Battalion and Royal Irish Regiment 2nd Battalion : 1 June 1916 - 30 September 1916 (First World War, War Diary, WO95/1662)	WD1662	9781474506656	£46.00
7 DIVISION 22 Infantry Brigade Manchester Regiment 20th Battalion, Manchester Regiment 24th Battalion and Royal Scots (Lothian Regiment) 8th Battalion : 13 December 1914 - 31 July 1915 (First World War, War Diary, WO95/1663)	WD1663	9781474506663	£41.00
7 DIVISION 22 Infantry Brigade Queen's (Royal West Surrey Regiment) 2nd Battalion, South Staffordshire Regiment 1st Battalion and Royal Warwickshire Regiment 2nd Battalion : 1 January 1914 - 30 November 1917 (First World War, War Diary, WO95/1664)	WD1664	9781474506670	£55.00
7 DIVISION 22 Infantry Brigade Royal Welsh Fusiliers 1st Battalion, Brigade Machine Gun Company and Brigade Trench Mortar Battery : 4 October 1914 - 31 December 1915 (First World War, War Diary, WO95/1665)	WD1665	9781474506687	£57.00
7 DIVISION 91 Infantry Brigade Headquarters : 3 November 1915 - 31 December 1916 (First World War, War Diary, WO95/1666)	WD1666	9781474506694	£39.00
7 DIVISION 91 Infantry Brigade Headquarters : 1 January 1917 - 30 November 1917 (First World War, War Diary, WO95/1667)	WD1667	9781474506700	£31.00
7 DIVISION 91 Infantry Brigade Manchester Regiment 21st Battalion : 31 October 1915 - 30 November 1917 (First World War, War Diary, WO95/1668)	WD1668	9781474506717	£39.00
7 DIVISION 91 Infantry Brigade Manchester Regiment 22nd Battalion : 8 November 1915 - 30 November 1917 (First World War, War Diary, WO95/1669)	WD1669	9781474506724	£58.00
7 DIVISION 91 Infantry Brigade Queen's (Royal West Surrey Regiment) 2nd Battalion, South Staffordshire Regiment 1st Battalion, Brigade Machine Gun Company and Brigade Trench Mortar Battery : 3 April 1915 - 31 January 1916 (First World War, War Diary, WO95	WD1670	9781474506731	£56.00

7 INDIAN (MEERUT) DIVISION

Title	Product Code	ISBN	Price
7 INDIAN (MEERUT) DIVISION Headquarters, Branches and Services General Staff : 8 August 1914 - 30 April 1915 (First World War, War Diary, WO95/3930)	WD3930	9781474534994	£85.00
7 INDIAN (MEERUT) DIVISION Headquarters, Branches and Services General Staff : 30 April 1915 - 31 December 1915 (First World War, War Diary, WO95/3931)	WD3931	9781474535007	£60.00
7 INDIAN (MEERUT) DIVISION Headquarters, Branches and Services Adjutant and Quarter-Master General : 8 August 1914 - 30 November 1915 (First World War, War Diary, WO95/3932)	WD3932	9781474535014	£47.00
7 INDIAN (MEERUT) DIVISION Headquarters, Branches and Services Commander Royal Artillery : 9 August 1914 - 31 December 1914 (First World War, War Diary, WO95/3933/1)	WD3933_1	9781474535021	£19.00
7 INDIAN (MEERUT) DIVISION Headquarters, Branches and Services Commander Royal Artillery : 1 January 1915 - 31 January 1915 (First World War, War Diary, WO95/3933/2)	WD3933_2	9781474535038	£15.00
7 INDIAN (MEERUT) DIVISION Headquarters, Branches and Services Commander Royal Artillery : 1 March 1915 - 31 March 1915 (First World War, War Diary, WO95/3933/3)	WD3933_3	9781474535045	£15.00
7 INDIAN (MEERUT) DIVISION Headquarters, Branches and Services Commander Royal Artillery : 1 April 1915 - 30 April 1915 (First World War, War Diary, WO95/3933/4)	WD3933_4	9781474535052	£15.00
7 INDIAN (MEERUT) DIVISION Headquarters, Branches and Services Commander Royal Artillery : 1 May 1915 - 31 May 1915 (First World War, War Diary, WO95/3933/5)	WD3933_5	9781474535069	£15.00
7 INDIAN (MEERUT) DIVISION Headquarters, Branches and Services Commander Royal Artillery : 1 June 1915 - 30 June 1915 (First World War, War Diary, WO95/3933/6)	WD3933_6	9781474535076	£15.00
7 INDIAN (MEERUT) DIVISION Headquarters, Branches and Services Commander Royal Artillery : 1 July 1915 - 31 October 1915 (First World War, War Diary, WO95/3934)	WD3934	9781474535083	£54.00
7 INDIAN (MEERUT) DIVISION Headquarters, Branches and Services Royal Army Medical Corps Assistant Director Medical Services, Commander Royal Engineers and Assistant Director Ordnance Services : 10 August 1914 - 10 October 1915 (First World War, War Diary	WD3935	9781474535090	£42.00
7 INDIAN (MEERUT) DIVISION Divisional Troops 4 Cavalry : 9 August 1914 - 30 November 1915 (First World War, War Diary, WO95/3936/1)	WD3936_1	9781474535106	£15.00
7 INDIAN (MEERUT) DIVISION Divisional Troops 4 Brigade Royal Field Artillery : 31 August 1914 - 11 December 1915 (First World War, War Diary, WO95/3936/2)	WD3936_2	9781474535113	£18.00
7 INDIAN (MEERUT) DIVISION Divisional Troops 9 Brigade Royal Field Artillery : 9 August 1914 - 30 November 1915 (First World War, War Diary, WO95/3936/3)	WD3936_3	9781474535120	£61.00
7 INDIAN (MEERUT) DIVISION Divisional Troops 13 Brigade Royal Field Artillery and Divisional Ammunition Column : 31 August 1914 - 24 December 1915 (First World War, War Diary, WO95/3937)	WD3937	9781474535137	£40.00

Title	Product Code	ISBN	Price
7 INDIAN (MEERUT) DIVISION Divisional Troops 3 and 4 Field Company Sappers and Miners, Divisional Signal Company and 107 Pioneers : 26 May 1914 - 31 October 1915 (First World War, War Diary, WO95/3938)	WD3938	9781474535144	£50.00
7 INDIAN (MEERUT) DIVISION Divisional Troops Royal Army Medical Corps 19 and 20 British Field Ambulance, 128, 129 and 130 Indian Field Ambulance, 4 Indian Sanitary Section, Mobile Veterinary Section, Divisional Mule Transport and Divisional Train : 22 J	WD3939	9781474535151	£69.00
7 INDIAN (MEERUT) DIVISION 19 (Dehra Dun) Indian Infantry Brigade Headquarters : 8 August 1914 - 31 December 1915 (First World War, War Diary, WO95/3940)	WD3940	9781474535168	£55.00
7 INDIAN (MEERUT) DIVISION 19 (Dehra Dun) Indian Infantry Brigade Seaforth Highlanders (Ross-shire Buffs, the Duke of Albany's) 1st Battalion. : 9 August 1914 - 31 December 1915 (First World War, War Diary, WO95/3941/1)	WD3941_1	9781474535175	£25.00
7 INDIAN (MEERUT) DIVISION 19 (Dehra Dun) Indian Infantry Brigade Seaforth Highlanders (Ross-shire Buffs, the Duke of Albany's) 4th Battalion. : 2 November 1914 - 31 December 1915 (First World War, War Diary, WO95/3941/2)	WD3941_2	9781474535182	£18.00
7 INDIAN (MEERUT) DIVISION 19 (Dehra Dun) Indian Infantry Brigade 1/9 Battalion Gurkha Rifles : 9 August 1914 - 30 November 1915 (First World War, War Diary, WO95/3941/3)	WD3941_3	9781474535199	£16.00
7 INDIAN (MEERUT) DIVISION 19 (Dehra Dun) Indian Infantry Brigade 2/2 Battalion Gurkha Rifles, 6 JAT Light Infantry and 93 Burma Infantry : 28 June 1914 - 3 November 1915 (First World War, War Diary, WO95/3942)	WD3942	9781474535205	£60.00
7 INDIAN (MEERUT) DIVISION 20 (Garhwal) Indian Infantry Brigade Headquarters : 21 June 1914 - 31 March 1915 (First World War, War Diary, WO95/3943A)	WD3943_A	9781474535212	£60.00
7 INDIAN (MEERUT) DIVISION 20 (Garhwal) Indian Infantry Brigade Headquarters : 1 June 1915 - 31 August 1915 (First World War, War Diary, WO95/3944)	WD3944	9781474535236	£64.00
7 INDIAN (MEERUT) DIVISION 20 (Garhwal) Indian Infantry Brigade London Regiment 1/3 Battalion London Regiment (City of London) and Leicestershire Regiment 2nd Battalion. : 9 August 1914 - 2 December 1915 (First World War, War Diary, WO95/3945/1)	WD3945_1	9781474535243	£34.00
7 INDIAN (MEERUT) DIVISION 20 (Garhwal) Indian Infantry Brigade 39 Garhwal Rifles : 9 August 1914 - 26 November 1915 (First World War, War Diary, WO95/3945/2)	WD3945_2	9781474535250	£30.00
7 INDIAN (MEERUT) DIVISION 20 (Garhwal) Indian Infantry Brigade 2/3 and 2/8 Battalion Gurkha Rifles : 9 August 1914 - 31 October 1915 (First World War, War Diary, WO95/3946)	WD3946	9781474535267	£36.00
7 INDIAN (MEERUT) DIVISION 21 (Bareilly) Indian Infantry Brigade Headquarters : 9 August 1914 - 31 December 1915 (First World War, War Diary, WO95/3947)	WD3947	9781474535274	£67.00
7 INDIAN (MEERUT) DIVISION 21 (Bareilly) Indian Infantry Brigade Black Watch (Royal Highlanders) 2nd and 4th Battalion, 41 Dogras, 58 Rifles, 33 Punjabis and 69 Punjabis : 9 August 1914 - 30 November 1915 (First World War, War Diary, WO95/3948)	WD3948	9781474535281	£54.00

Title	Product Code	ISBN	Price
7 INDIAN (MEERUT) DIVISION 20			
7 INDIAN (MEERUT) DIVISION 20 (Garhwal) Indian Infantry Brigade Headquarters : 1 April 1915 - 31 May 1915 (First World War, War Diary, WO95/3943B)	WD3943_B	9781474535229	£66.00

Title	Product Code	ISBN	Price
74 (YEOMANRY) DIVISION			
74 (YEOMANRY) DIVISION Headquarters, Branches and Services General Staff : 1 May 1918 - 30 November 1918 (First World War, War Diary, WO95/3148/1)	WD3148_1	9781474534604	£27.00
74 (YEOMANRY) DIVISION Headquarters, Branches and Services Adjutant and Quarter-Master General : 1 May 1918 - 30 June 1919 (First World War, War Diary, WO95/3148/2)	WD3148_2	9781474534611	£25.00
74 (YEOMANRY) DIVISION Headquarters, Branches and Services Commander Royal Artillery, Assistant Director Medical Services, Commander Royal Engineers, Deputy Assistant Director Ordnance Services and Assistant Director Veterinary Services : 20 May 1917 - 1	WD3149	9781474534628	£39.00
74 (YEOMANRY) DIVISION Divisional Troops 44 and 117 Brigade Royal Field Artillery, Divisional Trench Mortar Batteries, Divisional Ammunition Column, 5 (Anglesey) Field Company Royal Engineers, 5 (Monmouth) Field Company Royal Engineers, 439 Field Company	WD3150	9781474534635	£45.00
74 (YEOMANRY) DIVISION Divisional Troops Royal Army Medical Corps 229, 230 and 231 Field Ambulance, 59 Mobile Veterinary Section and Divisional Train (447, 478, 479, 450 Companies A.S.C.) : 1 May 1918 - 30 June 1919 (First World War, War Diary, WO95/3151	WD3151	9781474534642	£36.00
74 (YEOMANRY) DIVISION 229 Infantry Brigade Headquarters : 1 May 1918 - 23 June 1919 (First World War, War Diary, WO95/3152/1)	WD3152_1	9781474534659	£16.00
74 (YEOMANRY) DIVISION 229 Infantry Brigade Devonshire Regiment 16th (Royal 1st Devon Yeomanry and Royal North Devon Hussars) Battalion : 1 May 1918 - 31 May 1919 (First World War, War Diary, WO95/3152/2)	WD3152_2	9781474534666	£15.00
74 (YEOMANRY) DIVISION 229 Infantry Brigade Prince Albert's (Somerset Light Infantry) 12th Battalion : 1 May 1918 - 20 June 1919 (First World War, War Diary, WO95/3152/3)	WD3152_3	9781474534673	£15.00
74 (YEOMANRY) DIVISION 229 Infantry Brigade Black Watch (Royal Highlanders) 14th (Fife and Forfar Yeo.) Battalion : 16 December 1915 - 31 May 1919 (First World War, War Diary, WO95/3152/4)	WD3152_4	9781474534680	£15.00
74 (YEOMANRY) DIVISION 229 Infantry Brigade, Brigade Trench Mortar Battery : 1 May 1918 - 27 December 1918 (First World War, War Diary, WO95/3152/5)	WD3152_5	9781474534697	£15.00
74 (YEOMANRY) DIVISION 230 Infantry Brigade Headquarters : 1 May 1918 - 29 May 1919 (First World War, War Diary, WO95/3153/1)	WD3153_1	9781474534703	£16.00
74 (YEOMANRY) DIVISION 230 Infantry Brigade Buffs (East Kent Regiment) 10th Battalion : 1 May 1918 - 1 May 1919 (First World War, War Diary, WO95/3153/2)	WD3153_2	9781474534710	£15.00
74 (YEOMANRY) DIVISION 230 Infantry Brigade Suffolk Regiment 15th Battalion : 1 May 1918 - 24 June 1919 (First World War, War Diary, WO95/3153/3)	WD3153_3	9781474534727	£15.00
74 (YEOMANRY) DIVISION 230 Infantry Brigade Royal Sussex Regiment 16th Battalion : 1 May 1918 - 31 May 1919 (First World War, War Diary, WO95/3153/4)	WD3153_4	9781474534734	£15.00
74 (YEOMANRY) DIVISION 230 Infantry Brigade, Brigade Trench Mortar Battery : 1 May 1918 - 31 December 1918 (First World War, War Diary, WO95/3153/5)	WD3153_5	9781474534741	£15.00

Title	Product Code	ISBN	Price
74 (YEOMANRY) DIVISION 231 Infantry Brigade Headquarters, King's (Shropshire Light Infantry) 10th Battalion, Welsh Regiment 24th Battalion, Royal Welsh Fusiliers 25th Battalion and Brigade Trench Mortar Battery : 1 May 1918 - 28 January 1919 (First World	WD3154	9781474534758	£40.00

Title	Product Code	ISBN	Price
8 DIVISION			
8 DIVISION Headquarters, Branches and Services General Staff : 19 September 1914 - 31 March 1915 (First World War, War Diary, WO95/1671)	WD1671	9781474506748	£48.00
8 DIVISION Headquarters, Branches and Services General Staff : 1 April 1915 - 31 July 1915 (First World War, War Diary, WO95/1672)	WD1672	9781474506755	£40.00
8 DIVISION Headquarters, Branches and Services General Staff : 1 August 1915 - 28 December 1915 (First World War, War Diary, WO95/1673)	WD1673	9781474506762	£58.00
8 DIVISION Headquarters, Branches and Services General Staff : 1 January 1916 - 30 June 1916 (First World War, War Diary, WO95/1674)	WD1674	9781474522533	£66.00
8 DIVISION Headquarters, Branches and Services General Staff : 1 July 1916 - 31 December 1916 (First World War, War Diary, WO95/1675)	WD1675	9781474506779	£56.00
8 DIVISION Headquarters, Branches and Services General Staff : 1 January 1917 - 31 May 1917 (First World War, War Diary, WO95/1676)	WD1676	9781474506786	£58.00
8 DIVISION Headquarters, Branches and Services General Staff : 1 June 1917 - 31 December 1917 (First World War, War Diary, WO95/1677)	WD1677	9781474506793	£57.00
8 DIVISION Headquarters, Branches and Services General Staff : 1 January 1918 - 30 June 1918 (First World War, War Diary, WO95/1678)	WD1678	9781474506809	£46.00
8 DIVISION Headquarters, Branches and Services General Staff : 17 March 1918 - 20 March 1918 (First World War, War Diary, WO95/1679)	WD1679	9781474522540	£62.00
8 DIVISION Headquarters, Branches and Services Adjutant and Quarter-Master General : 19 September 1914 - 31 December 1915 (First World War, War Diary, WO95/1680)	WD1680	9781474506816	£50.00
8 DIVISION Headquarters, Branches and Services Adjutant and Quarter-Master General : 1 January 1916 - 30 June 1917 (First World War, War Diary, WO95/1681)	WD1681	9781474506823	£43.00
8 DIVISION Headquarters, Branches and Services Adjutant and Quarter-Master General : 1 July 1917 - 18 June 1919 (First World War, War Diary, WO95/1682)	WD1682	9781474506830	£54.00
8 DIVISION Headquarters, Branches and Services Commander Royal Artillery : 4 November 1914 - 31 December 1915 (First World War, War Diary, WO95/1683)	WD1683	9781474506847	£50.00
8 DIVISION Headquarters, Branches and Services Commander Royal Artillery : 1 January 1916 - 31 October 1916 (First World War, War Diary, WO95/1684)	WD1684	9781474506854	£38.00
8 DIVISION Headquarters, Branches and Services Commander Royal Artillery : 1 January 1917 - 31 December 1917 (First World War, War Diary, WO95/1685)	WD1685	9781474506861	£42.00
8 DIVISION Headquarters, Branches and Services Commander Royal Artillery : 1 January 1918 - 31 May 1919 (First World War, War Diary, WO95/1686)	WD1686	9781474506878	£41.00
8 DIVISION Headquarters, Branches and Services Royal Army Medical Corps Assistant Director Medical Services : 4 November 1914 - 27 March 1919 (First World War, War Diary, WO95/1687)	WD1687	9781474506885	£57.00
8 DIVISION Headquarters, Branches and Services Commander Royal Engineers : 5 November 1914 - 30 April 1916 (First World War, War Diary, WO95/1688)	WD1688	9781474522557	£74.00

Title	Product Code	ISBN	Price
8 DIVISION Headquarters, Branches and Services Commander Royal Engineers : 1 May 1916 - 9 April 1917 (First World War, War Diary, WO95/1689)	WD1689	9781474522564	£77.00
8 DIVISION Headquarters, Branches and Services Commander Royal Engineers : 1 May 1917 - 31 December 1917 (First World War, War Diary, WO95/1690)	WD1690	9781474522571	£71.00
8 DIVISION Headquarters, Branches and Services Commander Royal Engineers : 1 January 1918 - 31 May 1919 (First World War, War Diary, WO95/1691)	WD1691	9781474522588	£90.00
8 DIVISION Headquarters, Branches and Services Royal Army Ordnance Corps Deputy Assistant Director Ordnance Services and Royal Army Veterinary Corps Assistant Director Veterinary Services : 13 December 1914 - 30 April 1919 (First World War, War Diary, WO9	WD1692	9781474506892	£28.00
8 DIVISION Divisional Troops Northampton Yeomanry, C Squadron, Divisional Mounted Troops, Divisional Cyclist Company and 5 Brigade Royal Horse Artillery : 1 January 1914 - 31 December 1916 (First World War, War Diary, WO95/1693)	WD1693	9781474506908	£33.00
8 DIVISION Divisional Troops 33 Brigade Royal Field Artillery, 45 Brigade Royal Field Artillery and 128 Brigade Royal Field Artillery : 5 August 1914 - 18 May 1915 (First World War, War Diary, WO95/1694)	WD1694	9781474506915	£57.00
8 DIVISION Divisional Troops Anti-Aircraft Section and Divisional Ammunition Column: 9 September 1914 - 30 November 1914 (First World War, War Diary, WO95/1695)	WD1695	9781474506922	£21.00
8 DIVISION Divisional Troops Divisional Trench Mortar Batteries : 25 May 1916 - 31 October 1918 (First World War, War Diary, WO95/1696)	WD1696	9781474506939	£29.00
8 DIVISION Divisional Troops 2 Field Company Royal Engineers : 5 November 1914 - 31 March 1919 (First World War, War Diary, WO95/1697)	WD1697	9781474506946	£49.00
8 DIVISION Divisional Troops 15 Field Company Royal Engineers : 10 September 1914 - 20 April 1919 (First World War, War Diary, WO95/1698)	WD1698	9781474506953	£50.00
8 DIVISION Divisional Troops 490 Field Company Royal Engineers : 19 December 1914 - 31 December 1916 (First World War, War Diary, WO95/1699)	WD1699	9781474506960	£44.00
8 DIVISION Divisional Troops 490 Field Company Royal Engineers : 1 March 1915 - 7 May 1919 (First World War, War Diary, WO95/1700)	WD1700	9781474506977	£61.00
8 DIVISION Divisional Troops Divisional Signal Company : 1 December 1914 - 15 May 1919 (First World War, War Diary, WO95/1701)	WD1701	9781474522595	£57.00
8 DIVISION Divisional Troops Durham Light Infantry 22nd Battalion Pioneers, Durham Light Infantry 1/7th Battalion Pioneers, 218 Machine Gun Company, Machine Gun Corps 8 Battalion and Divisional Works Battalion Royal Engineers: 12 January 1916 - 28 Februa	WD1702	9781474506984	£45.00
8 DIVISION Divisional Troops Royal Army Medical Corps 24 and 25 Field Ambulance : 4 November 1914 - 30 April 1919 (First World War, War Diary, WO95/1703)	WD1703	9781474506991	£60.00
8 DIVISION Divisional Troops Royal Army Medical Corps 26 Field Ambulance, Divisional Field Ambulance Workshop Unit, 14 Sanitary Section and 15 Mobile Veterinary Section : 15 October 1914 - 30 April 1919 (First World War, War Diary, WO95/1704)	WD1704	9781474507004	£49.00

Title	Product Code	ISBN	Price
8 DIVISION Divisional Troops Royal Army Service Corps 8 Divisional Train (41, 84, 85, 87, Companies A.S.C.) : 7 October 1914 - 30 June 1916 (First World War, War Diary, WO95/1705)	WD1705	9781474507011	£52.00
8 DIVISION Divisional Troops Royal Army Service Corps Divisional Train (41, 84, 85, 87, Companies A.S.C.) : 6 July 1916 - 21 February 1919 (First World War, War Diary, WO95/1706)	WD1706	9781474507028	£51.00
8 DIVISION 23 Infantry Brigade Headquarters : 4 November 1914 - 31 May 1916 (First World War, War Diary, WO95/1707)	WD1707	9781474507035	£54.00
8 DIVISION 23 Infantry Brigade Headquarters : 1 June 1915 - 30 June 1916 (First World War, War Diary, WO95/1708)	WD1708	9781474507042	£60.00
8 DIVISION 23 Infantry Brigade Headquarters : 1 July 1916 - 30 June 1917 (First World War, War Diary, WO95/1709)	WD1709	9781474507059	£51.00
8 DIVISION 23 Infantry Brigade Headquarters : 1 July 1917 - 31 December 1917 (First World War, War Diary, WO95/1710)	WD1710	9781474507066	£47.00
8 DIVISION 23 Infantry Brigade Headquarters : 1 January 1918 - 25 June 1919 (First World War, War Diary, WO95/1711)	WD1711	9781474507073	£45.00
8 DIVISION 23 Infantry Brigade Devonshire Regiment 2nd Battalion : 4 November 1914 - 19 April 1919 (First World War, War Diary, WO95/1712)	WD1712	9781474507080	£28.00
8 DIVISION 23 Infantry Brigade Duke of Cambridge's Own (Middlesex Regiment) 2nd Battalion : 5 November 1914 - 30 December 1914 (First World War, War Diary, WO95/1713/1)	WD1713_1	9781474507097	£42.00
8 DIVISION 23 Infantry Brigade Duke of Cambridge's Own (Middlesex Regiment) 1/7th Battalion : 14 February 1915 - 31 March 1915 (First World War, War Diary, WO95/1713/2)	WD1713_2	9781474507103	£15.00
8 DIVISION 23 Infantry Brigade Prince of Wales's Own (West Yorkshire Regiment) 2nd Battalion : 4 November 1914 - 18 April 1919 (First World War, War Diary, WO95/1714)	WD1714	9781474507110	£44.00
8 DIVISION 23 Infantry Brigade Cameronians (Scottish Rifles) 2nd Battalion, Brigade Machine Gun Company and Brigade Trench Mortar Battery: 4 November 1914 - 29 February 1916 (First World War, War Diary, WO95/1715)	WD1715	9781474507127	£49.00
8 DIVISION 24 Infantry Brigade Headquarters : 9 March 1914 - 30 June 1916 (First World War, War Diary, WO95/1716)	WD1716	9781474507134	£40.00
8 DIVISION 24 Infantry Brigade Headquarters : 29 January 1916 - 1 July 1917 (First World War, War Diary, WO95/1717)	WD1717	9781474507141	£46.00
8 DIVISION 24 Infantry Brigade Headquarters : 1 July 1917 - 7 May 1919 (First World War, War Diary, WO95/1718)	WD1718	9781474507158	£57.00
8 DIVISION 24 Infantry Brigade Black Watch (Royal Highlanders) 5th Battalion and East Lancashire Regiment 2nd Battalion : 28 July 1914 - 30 June 1916 (First World War, War Diary, WO95/1719)	WD1719	9781474507165	£33.00
8 DIVISION 24 Infantry Brigade East Lancashire Regiment 2nd Battalion : 1 July 1916 - 31 January 1918 (First World War, War Diary, WO95/1720)	WD1720	9781474507172	£66.00
8 DIVISION 24 Infantry Brigade Sherwood Foresters (Nottinghamshire and Derbyshire Regiment) 1st Battalion : 31 August 1914 - 30 April 1919 (First World War, War Diary, WO95/1721)	WD1721	9781474507189	£45.00
8 DIVISION 24 Infantry Brigade Northamptonshire Regiment 2nd Battalion : 6 August 1914 - 31 March 1919 (First World War, War Diary, WO95/1722)	WD1722	9781474507196	£44.00

Title	Product Code	ISBN	Price
8 DIVISION 24 Infantry Brigade Worcestershire Regiment 1st Battalion : 16 October 1914 - 29 March 1919 (First World War, War Diary, WO95/1723/1)	WD1723_1	9781474507202	£24.00
8 DIVISION 24 Infantry Brigade, Brigade Machine Gun Company : 24 January 1916 - 30 June 1916 (First World War, War Diary, WO95/1723/2)	WD1723_2	9781474507219	£18.00
8 DIVISION 24 Infantry Brigade, Brigade Trench Mortar Battery : 5 June 1915 - 16 March 1916 (First World War, War Diary, WO95/1723/3)	WD1723_3	9781474507226	£15.00
8 DIVISION 25 Infantry Brigade Headquarters : 5 October 1914 - 1 September 1915 (First World War, War Diary, WO95/1724)	WD1724	9781474507233	£58.00
8 DIVISION 25 Infantry Brigade Headquarters : 1 September 1915 - 30 September 1915 (First World War, War Diary, WO95/1725)	WD1725	9781474507240	£65.00
8 DIVISION 25 Infantry Brigade Headquarters : 1 June 1916 - 31 March 1917 (First World War, War Diary, WO95/1726)	WD1726	9781474522601	£76.00
8 DIVISION 25 Infantry Brigade Headquarters : 1 January 1917 - 31 December 1917 (First World War, War Diary, WO95/1727)	WD1727	9781474507257	£74.00
8 DIVISION 25 Infantry Brigade Headquarters : 14 September 1916 - 31 May 1919 (First World War, War Diary, WO95/1728)	WD1728	9781474522618	£73.00
8 DIVISION 25 Infantry Brigade Princess Charlotte of Wales's (Royal Berkshire Regiment) 2nd Battalion and East Lancashire Regiment 2nd Battalion : 22 October 1914 - 30 April 1919 (First World War, War Diary, WO95/1729)	WD1729	9781474522625	£63.00
8 DIVISION 25 Infantry Brigade Lincolnshire Regiment 2nd Battalion, London Regiment 1st (City of London) Battalion (Royal Fusiliers), London Regiment 13th (County of London) Battalion (Princess Louise's Kensington Battalion) and Royal Irish Rifles 1st B	WD1730	9781474507264	£53.00
8 DIVISION 2 Battalion Rifle Brigade. Rifle Brigade (The Prince Consort's Own) 2nd Battalion : 5 November 1914 - 30 April 1919 (First World War, War Diary, WO95/1731)	WD1731	9781474507271	£33.00
8 DIVISION 25 Infantry Brigade, Brigade Machine Gun Company and Brigade Trench Mortar Battery: 5 June 1915 - 1 January 1916 (First World War, War Diary, WO95/1732)	WD1732	9781474507288	£34.00

Title	Product Code	ISBN	Price
9 DIVISION			
9 DIVISION Headquarters, Branches and Services General Staff : 15 May 1915 - 30 September 1915 (First World War, War Diary, WO95/1733)	WD1733	9781474507295	£63.00
9 DIVISION Headquarters, Branches and Services General Staff : 1 October 1915 - 30 June 1916 (First World War, War Diary, WO95/1734)	WD1734	9781474507301	£38.00
9 DIVISION Headquarters, Branches and Services General Staff : 1 July 1916 - 31 July 1916 (First World War, War Diary, WO95/1735)	WD1735	9781474507318	£65.00
9 DIVISION Headquarters, Branches and Services General Staff : 1 August 1916 - 30 September 1916 (First World War, War Diary, WO95/1736)	WD1736	9781474507325	£24.00
9 DIVISION Headquarters, Branches and Services General Staff : 1 October 1916 - 31 December 1916 (First World War, War Diary, WO95/1737)	WD1737	9781474507332	£53.00
9 DIVISION Headquarters, Branches and Services General Staff : 1 January 1917 - 12 April 1917 (First World War, War Diary, WO95/1738)	WD1738	9781474522632	£70.00
9 DIVISION Headquarters, Branches and Services General Staff : 1 May 1914 - 6 June 1917 (First World War, War Diary, WO95/1739)	WD1739	9781474507349	£32.00
9 DIVISION Headquarters, Branches and Services General Staff : 1 June 1917 - 31 December 1917 (First World War, War Diary, WO95/1740)	WD1740	9781474507356	£49.00
9 DIVISION Headquarters, Branches and Services General Staff : 1 January 1918 - 30 June 1918 (First World War, War Diary, WO95/1741)	WD1741	9781474522649	£48.00
9 DIVISION Headquarters, Branches and Services General Staff : 1 July 1918 - 1 October 1918 (First World War, War Diary, WO95/1742)	WD1742	9781474507363	£50.00
9 DIVISION Headquarters, Branches and Services General Staff : 1 November 1918 - 24 October 1919 (First World War, War Diary, WO95/1743)	WD1743	9781474507370	£51.00
9 DIVISION Headquarters, Branches and Services Adjutant and Quarter-Master General : 4 May 1915 - 30 April 1917 (First World War, War Diary, WO95/1744)	WD1744	9781474507387	£55.00
9 DIVISION Headquarters, Branches and Services Adjutant and Quarter-Master General : 1 May 1917 - 24 October 1919 (First World War, War Diary, WO95/1745)	WD1745	9781474522656	£66.00
9 DIVISION Headquarters, Branches and Services Commander Royal Artillery : 6 May 1915 - 30 November 1917 (First World War, War Diary, WO95/1746)	WD1746	9781474507394	£52.00
9 DIVISION Headquarters, Branches and Services Commander Royal Artillery : 28 March 1917 - 30 November 1919 (First World War, War Diary, WO95/1747)	WD1747	9781474507400	£40.00
9 DIVISION Headquarters, Branches and Services Royal Army Medical Corps Assistant Director Medical Services : 10 May 1915 - 24 October 1919 (First World War, War Diary, WO95/1748)	WD1748	9781474507417	£66.00
9 DIVISION Headquarters, Branches and Services Commander Royal Engineers : 11 May 1915 - 27 September 1919 (First World War, War Diary, WO95/1749)	WD1749	9781474507424	£52.00
9 DIVISION Headquarters, Branches and Services Royal Army Ordnance Corps Deputy Assistant Director Ordnance Services and Royal Army Veterinary Corps Assistant Director Veterinary Services : 9 May 1915 - 24 October 1919 (First World War, War Diary, WO95/17	WD1750	9781474507431	£24.00

Title	Product Code	ISBN	Price
9 DIVISION Divisional Troops B Squadron Glasgow Yeomanry, Divisional Cyclist Company and 50 Brigade Royal Field Artillery : 8 May 1915 - 17 September 1919 (First World War, War Diary, WO95/1751)	WD1751	9781474507448	£35.00
9 DIVISION Divisional Troops 51and 52 Brigade Royal Field Artillery : 10 May 1915 - 29 December 1916 (First World War, War Diary, WO95/1752)	WD1752	9781474507455	£40.00
9 DIVISION Divisional Troops 53 Brigade Royal Field Artillery, Divisional Ammunition Column and Divisional Trench Mortar Batteries : 7 May 1915 - 31 January 1919 (First World War, War Diary, WO95/1753)	WD1753	9781474507462	£20.00
9 DIVISION Divisional Troops 63 Field Company Royal Engineers : 11 May 1915 - 30 September 1919 (First World War, War Diary, WO95/1754)	WD1754	9781474522663	£82.00
9 DIVISION Divisional Troops 64 Field Company Royal Engineers : 11 May 1915 - 30 September 1919 (First World War, War Diary, WO95/1755)	WD1755	9781474507479	£34.00
9 DIVISION Divisional Troops 90 Field Company Royal Engineers and Divisional Signal Company : 14 May 1915 - 30 September 1919 (First World War, War Diary, WO95/1756)	WD1756	9781474507486	£42.00
9 DIVISION Divisional Troops 197 Machine Gun Company, Machine Gun Corps 9 Battalion, Seaforth Highlanders (Ross-shire Buffs, the Duke of Albany's) 9th Battalion Pioneers and Highland Light Infantry 16th (Service) Battalion (2nd Glasgow) Pioneers : 9 May	WD1757	9781474522670	£66.00
9 DIVISION Divisional Troops Royal Army Medical Corps 27 Field Ambulance : 7 May 1915 - 31 October 1919 (First World War, War Diary, WO95/1758)	WD1758	9781474522687	£77.00
9 DIVISION Divisional Troops Royal Army Medical Corps 28 and 29 Field Ambulance and 2/1 East Lancashire Field Ambulance : 7 May 1915 - 30 April 1919 (First World War, War Diary, WO95/1758)	WD1759	9781474522694	£40.00
9 DIVISION Divisional Troops Royal Army Medical Corps South African Field Ambulance, Royal Army Medical Corps Field Ambulance Workshop Unit, 20 Sanitary Section and 21 Mobile Veterinary Section : 7 May 1915 - 24 October 1919 (First World War, War Diary,	WD1760	9781474507493	£39.00
9 DIVISION Divisional Troops Royal Army Service Corps Divisional Train (104, 105, 106, 107 Companies A.S.C.) : 6 May 1915 - 14 November 1919 (First World War, War Diary, WO95/1761)	WD1761	9781474507509	£52.00
9 DIVISION 26 Infantry Brigade Headquarters : 11 May 1915 - 31 August 1917 (First World War, War Diary, WO95/1762)	WD1762	9781474507516	£55.00
9 DIVISION 26 Infantry Brigade Headquarters : 1 January 1917 - 29 June 1918 (First World War, War Diary, WO95/1763)	WD1763	9781474507523	£43.00
9 DIVISION 26 Infantry Brigade Headquarters : 1 July 1918 - 31 March 1919 (First World War, War Diary, WO95/1764)	WD1764	9781474507530	£46.00
9 DIVISION 26 Infantry Brigade Seaforth Highlanders (Ross-shire Buffs, the Duke of Albany's) 7th Battalion : 9 May 1915 - 28 February 1919 (First World War, War Diary, WO95/1765)	WD1765	9781474522700	£76.00
9 DIVISION 26 Infantry Brigade Black Watch (Royal Highlanders) 8th (Service) Battalion : 10 May 1915 - 3 March 1919 (First World War, War Diary, WO95/1766)	WD1766	9781474507547	£48.00
9 DIVISION 26 Infantry Brigade Queen's Own Cameron Highlanders 5th Battalion and Gordon Highlanders 8th Battalion : 6 May 1915 - 29 April 1916 (First World War, War Diary, WO95/1767)	WD1767	9781474507554	£38.00

Title	Product Code	ISBN	Price
9 DIVISION 26 Infantry Brigade Princess Louise's (Argyll & Sutherland Highlanders) 10th Battalion, Brigade Machine Gun Company and Brigade Trench Mortar Battery : 9 June 1915 - 11 November 1915 (First World War, War Diary, WO95/1768)	WD1768	9781474507561	£35.00
9 DIVISION 27 Infantry Brigade Headquarters : 11 May 1915 - 30 December 1917 (First World War, War Diary, WO95/1769)	WD1769	9781474507578	£52.00
9 DIVISION Headquarters, Branches and Services Headquarters : 1 January 1917 - 31 December 1917 (First World War, War Diary, WO95/1770)	WD1770	9781474522717	£65.00
9 DIVISION Headquarters, Branches and Services Headquarters : 1 January 1918 - 31 May 1918 (First World War, War Diary, WO95/1771)	WD1771	9781474522724	£64.00
9 DIVISION 27 Infantry Brigade Princess Louise's (Argyll & Sutherland Highlanders) 10th Battalion, King's Own Scottish Borderers 6th Battalion, Royal Scots Fusiliers 6th Battalion and Cameronians (Scottish Rifles) 9th Battalion : 21 March 1915 - 31 March	WD1772	9781474507585	£45.00
9 DIVISION 27 Infantry Brigade Royal Scots (Lothian Regiment) 11th Battalion, Royal Scots (Lothian Regiment) 12th Battalion, Brigade Machine Gun Company and Brigade Trench Mortar Battery : 10 May 1915 - 6 March 1916 (First World War, War Diary, WO95/1773)	WD1773	9781474522731	£77.00
9 DIVISION 28 Infantry Brigade Headquarters : 11 May 1915 - 31 March 1919 (First World War, War Diary, WO95/1774)	WD1774	9781474522748	£88.00
9 DIVISION 28 Infantry Brigade Highland Light Infantry 10th (Service) Battalion, Highland Light Infantry 11th (Service) Battalion, King's Own Scottish Borderers 6th Battalion, Cameronians (Scottish Rifles) 9th Battalion, Royal Scots Fusiliers 2nd Battal	WD1775	9781474507592	£36.00
9 DIVISION 1 Lowland Brigades Headquarters : 1 April 1919 - 25 September 1919 (First World War, War Diary, WO95/1776/1)	WD1776_1	9781474507608	£15.00
9 DIVISION 3 Lowland Brigades Headquarters : 1 April 1919 - 9 September 1919 (First World War, War Diary, WO95/1776/10)	WD1776_10	9781474507691	£15.00
9 DIVISION 3 Lowland Brigades Royal Scots Fusiliers 1/4th Battalion. : 1 April 1919 - 31 August 1919 (First World War, War Diary, WO95/1776/11)	WD1776_11	9781474507707	£15.00
9 DIVISION 3 Lowland Brigades Cameronians (Scottish Rifles) 8th Battalion. : 1 March 1919 - 3 September 1919 (First World War, War Diary, WO95/1776/12)	WD1776_12	9781474507714	£15.00
9 DIVISION 3 Lowland Brigades Queen's Own Cameron Highlanders 9th Battalion. : 1 April 1919 - 30 September 1919 (First World War, War Diary, WO95/1776/13)	WD1776_13	9781474507721	£15.00
9 DIVISION 1 Lowland Brigades Highland Light Infantry 15th (Service) Battalion (1st Glasgow). : 1 April 1919 - 31 October 1919 (First World War, War Diary, WO95/1776/2)	WD1776_2	9781474507615	£15.00
9 DIVISION 1 Lowland Brigades Highland Light Infantry 51st (Grad.) Battalion. : 18 March 1919 - 30 September 1919 (First World War, War Diary, WO95/1776/3)	WD1776_3	9781474507622	£15.00
9 DIVISION 1 Lowland Brigades King's Own Scottish Borderers 5th Battalion. : 1 April 1919 - 31 August 1919 (First World War, War Diary, WO95/1776/4)	WD1776_4	9781474507639	£15.00
9 DIVISION 1 Lowland Brigades Brigade Trench Mortar Battery : 20 April 1919 - 31 August 1919 (First World War, War Diary, WO95/1776/5)	WD1776_5	9781474507646	£15.00

Title	Product Code	ISBN	Price
9 DIVISION 2 Lowland Brigades Headquarters : 1 April 1919 - 6 November 1919 (First World War, War Diary, WO95/1776/6)	WD1776_6	9781474507653	£15.00
9 DIVISION 2 Lowland Brigades King's Own Scottish Borderers 6th Battalion. : 1 April 1919 - 31 August 1919 (First World War, War Diary, WO95/1776/7)	WD1776_7	9781474507660	£15.00
9 DIVISION 2 Lowland Brigades Royal Scots (Lothian Regiment) 5/6th Battalion. : 1 March 1919 - 31 October 1919 (First World War, War Diary, WO95/1776/8)	WD1776_8	9781474507677	£15.00
9 DIVISION 2 Lowland Brigades Royal Scots (Lothian Regiment) 11th Battalion. : 1 April 1919 - 31 October 1919 (First World War, War Diary, WO95/1776/9)	WD1776_9	9781474507684	£15.00
9 DIVISION South African Brigade Headquarters : 4 June 1916 - 30 April 1917 (First World War, War Diary, WO95/1777)	WD1777	9781474507738	£44.00
9 DIVISION South African Brigade Headquarters : 1 May 1917 - 31 December 1917 (First World War, War Diary, WO95/1778)	WD1778	9781474507745	£52.00
9 DIVISION South African Brigade Headquarters : 1 January 1918 - 31 August 1918 (First World War, War Diary, WO95/1779)	WD1779	9781474507752	£44.00
9 DIVISION South African Brigade 1 South African Infantry Regiment : 4 March 1916 - 28 February 1918 (First World War, War Diary, WO95/1780)	WD1780	9781474507769	£15.00
9 DIVISION South African Brigade 2 South African Infantry Regiment : 1 January 1916 - 28 February 1918 (First World War, War Diary, WO95/1781)	WD1781	9781474507776	£33.00
9 DIVISION South African Brigade 3 South African Infantry Regiment : 3 April 1916 - 25 April 1916 (First World War, War Diary, WO95/1782)	WD1782	9781474507783	£18.00
9 DIVISION South African Brigade 3 South African Infantry Regiment : 1 October 1916 - 31 March 1917 (First World War, War Diary, WO95/1783)	WD1783	9781474507790	£29.00
9 DIVISION South African Brigade 3 South African Infantry Regiment : 1 April 1917 - 22 February 1918 (First World War, War Diary, WO95/1784)	WD1784	9781474507806	£52.00
9 DIVISION South African Brigade 4 South African Infantry Regiment : 1 July 1916 - 28 February 1918 (First World War, War Diary, WO95/1785)	WD1785	9781474507813	£21.00
9 DIVISION South African Brigade South African Composite Battalion, Cameronians (Scottish Rifles) 9th Battalion, Royal Scots Fusiliers 2nd Battalion, Brigade Machine Gun Company and South African Trench Mortar Battery : 15 February 1916 - 31 August 1916 (	WD1786	9781474507820	£40.00

Title	Product Code	ISBN	Price
DISMOUNTED CAVALRY DIVISIONS			
DISMOUNTED CAVALRY DIVISIONS Headquarters, Branches and Services General Staff, Adjutant and Quarter-Master General, Commander Royal Artillery, Assistant Director Medical Services, Commander Royal Engineers, Assistant Director Ordnance Services. Divisi	WD1189	9781474521550	£86.00

Title	Product Code	ISBN	Price
GUARDS DIVISION			
GUARDS DIVISION Headquarters, Branches and Services General Staff : 1 September 1915 - 31 December 1915 (First World War, War Diary, WO95/1190)	WD1190	9781474501729	£62.00
GUARDS DIVISION Headquarters, Branches and Services General Staff : 1 January 1916 - 31 May 1916 (First World War, War Diary, WO95/1191)	WD1191	9781474501736	£77.00
GUARDS DIVISION Headquarters, Branches and Services General Staff : 1 June 1916 - 31 December 1916 (First World War, War Diary, WO95/1192)	WD1192	9781474521567	£82.00
GUARDS DIVISION Headquarters, Branches and Services General Staff : 1 January 1917 - 31 December 1917 (First World War, War Diary, WO95/1193)	WD1193	9781474521574	£81.00
GUARDS DIVISION Headquarters, Branches and Services General Staff : 1 January 1918 - 30 March 1918 (First World War, War Diary, WO95/1194)	WD1194	9781474501743	£42.00
GUARDS DIVISION Headquarters, Branches and Services General Staff : 1 June 1918 - 31 October 1918 (First World War, War Diary, WO95/1195)	WD1195	9781474501750	£54.00
GUARDS DIVISION Headquarters, Branches and Services General Staff : 1 November 1918 - 13 March 1919 (First World War, War Diary, WO95/1196)	WD1196	9781474501767	£44.00
GUARDS DIVISION Headquarters, Branches and Services Adjutant and Quarter-Master General. : 29 August 1915 - 30 April 1919 (First World War, War Diary, WO95/1197/1)	WD1197_1	9781474501774	£19.00
GUARDS DIVISION Headquarters, Branches and Services Adjutant and Quarter-Master General. : 20 August 1915 - 31 December 1916 (First World War, War Diary, WO95/1197/2)	WD1197_2	9781474501781	£52.00
GUARDS DIVISION Headquarters, Branches and Services Commander Royal Artillery : 18 August 1915 - 31 August 1916 (First World War, War Diary, WO95/1198)	WD1198	9781474501798	£63.00
GUARDS DIVISION Headquarters, Branches and Services Commander Royal Artillery : 1 September 1916 - 31 July 1917 (First World War, War Diary, WO95/1199)	WD1199	9781474501804	£52.00
GUARDS DIVISION Headquarters, Branches and Services Commander Royal Artillery : 1 August 1917 - 27 December 1918 (First World War, War Diary, WO95/1200)	WD1200	9781474501811	£67.00
GUARDS DIVISION Headquarters, Branches and Services Royal Army Medical Corps Assistant Director Medical Services : 18 August 1915 - 29 April 1919 (First World War, War Diary, WO95/1201)	WD1201	9781474521581	£79.00
GUARDS DIVISION Headquarters, Branches and Services Commander Royal Engineers, Deputy Assistant Director Ordnance Services and Deputy Assistant Director Veterinary Services : 15 August 1915 - 24 April 1919 (First World War, War Diary, WO95/1202)	WD1202	9781474501828	£52.00
GUARDS DIVISION Divisional Troops Household Cavalry Squadron, Cavalry Cyclist Company, 61,74, 75 and 76 Brigade Royal Field Artillery, Divisional Ammunition Column and Divisional Trench Mortar Batteries : 1 August 1915 - 1 March 1919 (First World War, Wa	WD1203	9781474501835	£76.00
GUARDS DIVISION Divisional Troops 76 Brigade Royal Field Artillery, Divisional Ammunition Column and Trench Mortar Batteries : 6 August 1915 - 28 February 1919 (First World War, War Diary, WO95/1204)	WD1204	9781474501842	£45.00

Title	Product Code	ISBN	Price
GUARDS DIVISION Divisional Troops 55, 75 and 76 Field Company Royal Engineers and Divisional Signal Company : 19 July 1915 - 31 March 1919 (First World War, War Diary, WO95/1205)	WD1205	9781474521598	£79.00
GUARDS DIVISION Divisional Troops Machine Gun Corps 4 Guards Battalion and 4 Pioneer Battalion : 17 July 1915 - 1 March 1919 (First World War, War Diary, WO95/1206)	WD1206	9781474521604	£72.00
GUARDS DIVISION Divisional Troops Royal Army Medical Corps 3 Field Ambulance : 1 August 1915 - 24 August 1915 (First World War, War Diary, WO95/1207A)	WD1207_A	9781474521611	£45.00
GUARDS DIVISION Divisional Troops Royal Army Medical Corps 3 Field Ambulance : 1 September 1915 - 31 March 1918 (First World War, War Diary, WO95/1207B)	WD1207_B	9781474521628	£59.00
GUARDS DIVISION Divisional Troops Royal Army Medical Corps 9 Field Ambulance, Divisional Field Ambulance Workshop, 45 Sanitary Section and 46 Mobile Veterinary Section : 24 July 1915 - 24 April 1919 (First World War, War Diary, WO95/1208)	WD1208	9781474501859	£72.00
GUARDS DIVISION Divisional Troops Royal Army Service Corps Divisional Train (11, 124, 168 & 436 Companies A.S.C.) : 19 August 1915 - 31 December 1916 (First World War, War Diary, WO95/1209)	WD1209	9781474521635	£64.00
GUARDS DIVISION Divisional Troops Royal Army Service Corps Divisional Train (11, 124, 168 & 436 Companies A.S.C.) : 1 November 1915 - 31 December 1917 (First World War, War Diary, WO95/1210)	WD1210	9781474501866	£49.00
GUARDS DIVISION Divisional Troops Royal Army Service Corps Divisional Train (11, 124, 168 & 436 Companies A.S.C.) : 1 December 1917 - 6 May 1919 (First World War, War Diary, WO95/1211)	WD1211	9781474501873	£48.00
GUARDS DIVISION 1 Guards Brigade Headquarters : 1 August 1915 - 31 August 1916 (First World War, War Diary, WO95/1212)	WD1212	9781474501880	£65.00
GUARDS DIVISION 1 Guards Brigade Headquarters : 1 September 1916 - 30 September 1916 (First World War, War Diary, WO95/1213/1)	WD1213_1	9781474501897	£28.00
GUARDS DIVISION 1 Guards Brigade Headquarters : 1 October 1916 - 30 November 1916 (First World War, War Diary, WO95/1213/2)	WD1213_2	9781474501903	£15.00
GUARDS DIVISION 1 Guards Brigade Headquarters : 1 December 1916 - 31 December 1916 (First World War, War Diary, WO95/1213/3)	WD1213_3	9781474501910	£15.00
GUARDS DIVISION 1 Guards Brigade Headquarters : 1 January 1917 - 31 January 1917 (First World War, War Diary, WO95/1213/4)	WD1213_4	9781474501927	£15.00
GUARDS DIVISION 1 Guards Brigade Headquarters : 1 February 1917 - 28 February 1917 (First World War, War Diary, WO95/1213/5)	WD1213_5	9781474501934	£15.00
GUARDS DIVISION 1 Guards Brigade Headquarters : 1 March 1917 - 30 March 1917 (First World War, War Diary, WO95/1213/6)	WD1213_6	9781474501941	£15.00
GUARDS DIVISION 1 Guards Brigade Headquarters : 1 April 1917 - 30 April 1917 (First World War, War Diary, WO95/1213/7)	WD1213_7	9781474501958	£15.00
GUARDS DIVISION 1 Guards Brigade Headquarters : 1 May 1917 - 31 May 1917 (First World War, War Diary, WO95/1213/8)	WD1213_8	9781474501965	£15.00
GUARDS DIVISION 1 Guards Brigade Headquarters : 1 June 1917 - 30 June 1917 (First World War, War Diary, WO95/1213/9)	WD1213_9	9781474501972	£15.00
GUARDS DIVISION 1 Guards Brigade Headquarters : 1 August 1917 - 31 March 1919 (First World War, War Diary, WO95/1214)	WD1214	9781474521642	£62.00

Title	Product Code	ISBN	Price
GUARDS DIVISION 1 Guards Brigade Grenadier Guards 2nd Battalion : 1 August 1915 - 31 January 1919 (First World War, War Diary, WO95/1215/1)	WD1215_1	9781474501989	£30.00
GUARDS DIVISION 1 Guards Brigade Coldstream Guards 2 Battalion : 1 August 1915 - 31 January 1919 (First World War, War Diary, WO95/1215/2)	WD1215_2	9781474501996	£15.00
GUARDS DIVISION 1 Guards Brigade Coldstream Guards 3 Battalion : 1 August 1915 -1 February 1919 (First World War, War Diary, WO95/1215/3-4)	WD1215_3-4	9781474502009	£15.00
GUARDS DIVISION 1 Guards Brigade Irish Guards 1st Battalion and Guards Machine Gun Company : 1 August 1915 - 28 February 1918 (First World War, War Diary, WO95/1216)	WD1216	9781474502016	£50.00
GUARDS DIVISION 2 Guards Brigade Headquarters : 19 July 1915 - 31 December 1916 (First World War, War Diary, WO95/1217)	WD1217	9781474502023	£63.00
GUARDS DIVISION 2 Guards Brigade Headquarters : 1 January 1917 - 31 March 1919 (First World War, War Diary, WO95/1218)	WD1218	9781474502030	£58.00
GUARDS DIVISION 2 Guards Brigade Grenadier Guards 3rd Battalion, Coldstream Guards 1 Battalion and Scots Guards 1 Battalion : 26 July 1915 - 31 January 1919 (First World War, War Diary, WO95/1219)	WD1219	9781474502047	£60.00
GUARDS DIVISION 2 Guards Brigade Irish Guards 2nd Battalions and Guards Machine Gun Company : 17 July 1915 - 28 February 1918 (First World War, War Diary, WO95/1220)	WD1220	9781474502054	£39.00
GUARDS DIVISION 3 Guards Brigade Headquarters : 15 August 1915 - 31 December 1916 (First World War, War Diary, WO95/1221)	WD1221	9781474502061	£64.00
GUARDS DIVISION 3 Guards Brigade Headquarters : 1 January 1917 - 31 December 1918 (First World War, War Diary, WO95/1222)	WD1222	9781474502078	£70.00
GUARDS DIVISION 3 Guards Brigade Grenadier Guards 1st and 4th Battalion and Scots Guards 2 Battalion : 1 August 1915 - 24 February 1919 (First World War, War Diary, WO95/1223)	WD1223	9781474502085	£71.00
GUARDS DIVISION 3 Guards Brigade Welsh Guards 1st Battalion : 17 August 1915 - 28 February 1919 (First World War, War Diary, WO95/1224/1)	WD1224_1	9781474502092	£59.00
GUARDS DIVISION 3 Guards Brigade Guards Machine Gun Company : 3 December 1915 - 28 February 1918 (First World War, War Diary, WO95/1224/2)	WD1224_2	9781474502108	£15.00
GUARDS DIVISION 4 Guards Brigade Headquarters : 8 February 1918 - 18 November 1918 (First World War, War Diary, WO95/1225)	WD1225	9781474502115	£46.00
GUARDS DIVISION 4 Guards Brigade Coldstream Guards 3 Battalion : 1 February 1918 - 31 October 1918 (First World War, War Diary, WO95/1226/1)	WD1226_1	9781474502122	£15.00
GUARDS DIVISION 4 Guards Brigade Grenadier Guards 4th Battalion : 2 February 1918 - 31 October 1918 (First World War, War Diary, WO95/1226/2)	WD1226_2	9781474502139	£18.00
GUARDS DIVISION 4 Guards Brigade Irish Guards 2nd Battalions : 1 February 1918 - 31 October 1918 (First World War, War Diary, WO95/1226/3)	WD1226_3	9781474502146	£15.00

Title	Product Code	ISBN	Price
RHINE CAVALRY BRIGADES			
Rhine Cavalry Brigades Dragoon Brigade: Headquarters,1st Dragoons (Royals), 6th Dragoon Guards (Carabineers), 6th Dragoons (Inniskilling), Dragoon Brigade Machine Gun Squadron, Hussar Brigade Headquarters, 3rd (King's Own) Hussars, 10th (Prince of Wales'	WD1166	9781474501330	£30.00

WAR DIARY
SAMPLE PAGES

11th Div.

3/Q1/7

Ref, your SG/Q/51, transport as under is required by Units of this Brigade Group for the move on 2nd September:-

Unit.	Transport extra to existing 1st Line Transport required to accompany Transport on line of march.	Transport required to move Officers valises and Lewis Guns to FREVENT Station.
Bde H.Q.		1 G.S. Wagon.
6/Lincoln R.	2 G.S. Wagons.	2 " "
6/Border R.	5 "	2 " "
7/S.Staffs R.	4 "	2 " "
9/Sh.Fors.	4 "	2 " "
33rd M.G.Co.	4 "	1½ "
33/L.T.M.Batt.	1½ "	
33/Fd.Amb.		1

To report if possible on night of 1st Sept. at H.Q. of above units.

Snellm. C.M
Capt.
Brigade Major.
for G.O.C. 33rd Inf. Brigade.

31/8/15.

1st. Bn. Royal Dublin Fusiliers.   Copy No. 19

OPERATION ORDERS No. 7.

1. The Battalion will be relieved on night of 22/23rd January 1918 by the 7th. Batt. LEINSTER REGIMENT.

2. "Y" Coy will be relieved by "D" Coy. 7th. Leinsters.
   "X" "   "   "   "   "   "C" "   "   "
   "Z" "   "   "   "   "   "A" "   "   "
   "W" "   "   "   "   "   "B" "   "   "

3. Advance parties of Relieving Battalion are due at 3 p.m. Guides for same unnecessary.

4. 1 Guide per Platoon (2 per Coy) and 1 from Battalion Headqrs. to report to 2/Lieut. G. Fisher at Battalion Headquarters 4.30 p.m. All guides to have chits. Guides to be marshalled at Rendevous at F. 16. d. 5.2. by 2/Lieut. Fisher by 5 p.m.

5. The undermentioned will be handed over :-
   TRENCH MAPS, DEFENCE SCHEMES, WORK in PROGRESS,
   Information reference PATROLS, and system of PATROLS.
   Trench Stores, Receipt for same and Sanitation & cleanliness Certificates to be taken. These to be at Battalion Headquarters by 9 a.m. 23rd. January 1918.

6. Blankets to be rolled in bundles of 10 and stacked at DUMP by 4.30 p.m. Officers Kits, Mess Boxes, Camp Kettles, Food Containers etc., to be at DUMPS by 5 p.m. In addition particular care will be taken that all Battalion Petrol Tins are at DUMPS by 5 pm.

7. Completion of relief to be notified in usual way.

8. On being relieved Coys will march to Railway Siding, ST. EMILIE where they will entrain for HAMEL. Guides will meet Coys. on arriving at HAMEL.

9. Quartermaster will arrange an issue of Rum and a hot meal for the men on arrival at Billets.

10. An N.C.O. and Nos. 1 of 2 Lewis Gun Teams of "W" Coy. to report at Battalion Headquarters at 9 a.m. 22nd. instant to proceed to take over A.A. Positions at HAMEL. The two Teams will be met at HAMEL by their Nos. 1 and will proceed to A.A. Positions at K.14.c.7.2. and K. 14. a. 1.9. (Waggon Lines of 177th. Bde. R.F.A). Teams will be rationed by R.F.A.

11. Advance party of 1 officer, N.C.O. and Runner per Coy, and 2/Lieut Spiess, N.C.O. Runner and Signaller from Headqr. Coy. to be at Battalion Hdqrs. by 11 a.m. 22nd. instant. On taking over Billets great care to be taken to check any existant damage there may be. Sanitation and Cleanliness Certificates to be granted and duplicates of same to reach Battalion Headquarters by 9 a.m. 23rd. instant. Officers i/c Coy's Advance party will arrange to meet Coys. on arrival of Battalion at HAMEL.

12. Transport officer will make the following special arrangements
    (a) Water Tank at DUNCAN POST and KEN LANE to be filled.
    (b) Limber with 2 Lewis Guns and magazines from "W" Coy, to proceed to Waggon Lines of 177th. Bde. R.F.A. (K.14.c.7.2.)

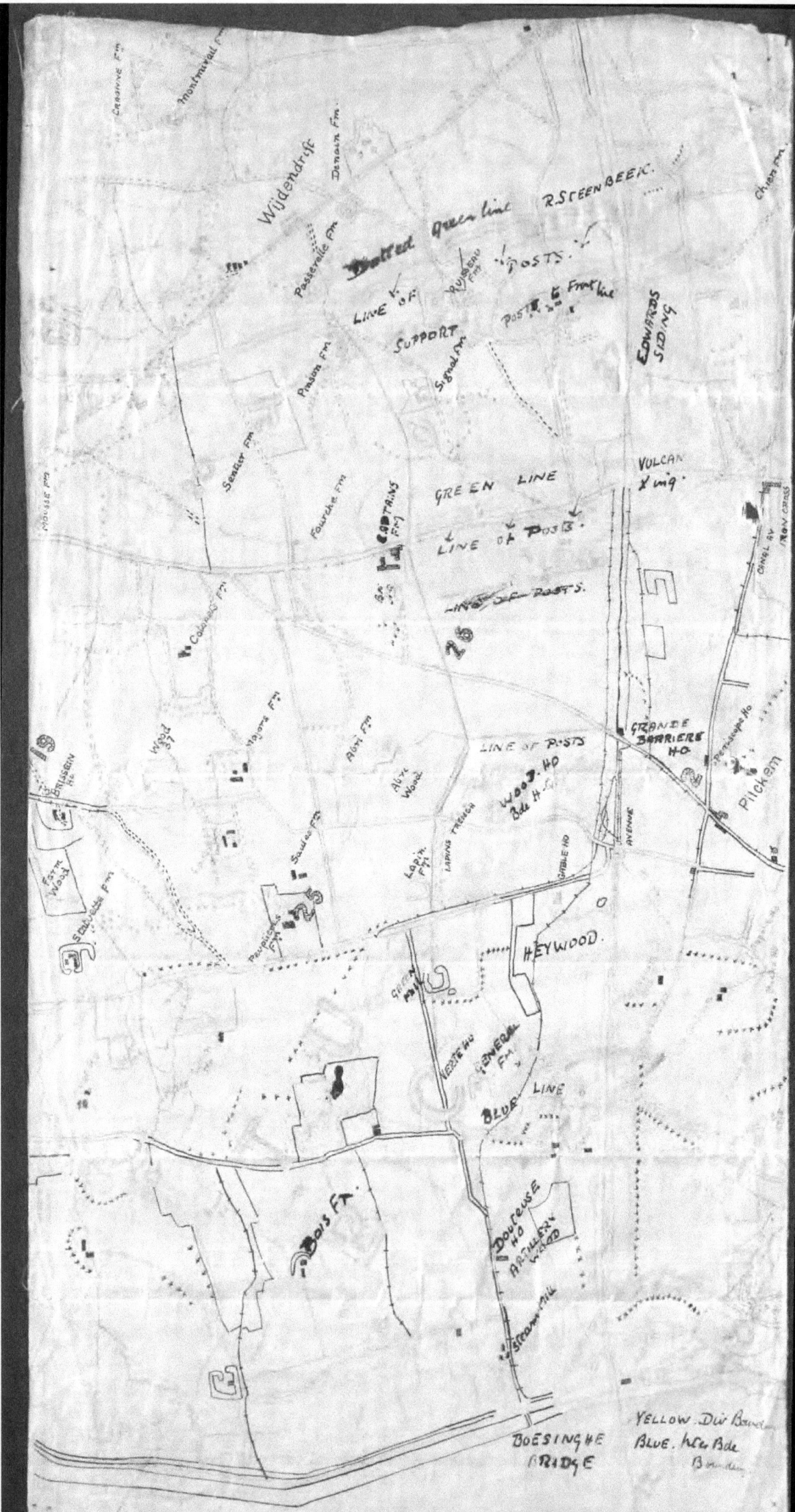

WAR DIARY or INTELLIGENCE SUMMARY

Army Form C. 2118.

Hour, Date, Place	Summary of Events and Information	Remarks and references to Appendices
7-5-15 (continued)	Casualties during the day two men killed 2 men wounded. Major Bridgeman and one man slightly wounded but stuck at duty. 9p.m Capt	
8-5-15	All quiet all day. A 9 C relieved B & D in the fire trenches at 8 p.m. No casualties during relief. Am responsible for issuing gas waves to front line trenches. Casualties during day 1 wounded & 1 slightly wounded. Moncrieff	
9-5-15	All quiet in our front all day. It was reported that the effect of the mine blown last night in trench 37 all along the front had rather further cracks to enemy's trench. If this being sent a working party of 80 be the R.E. to work on a new sap at the front night. 2 Men wounded 1 Moncrieff shot up 6 stranger lights and gas apparatus to the trenches	

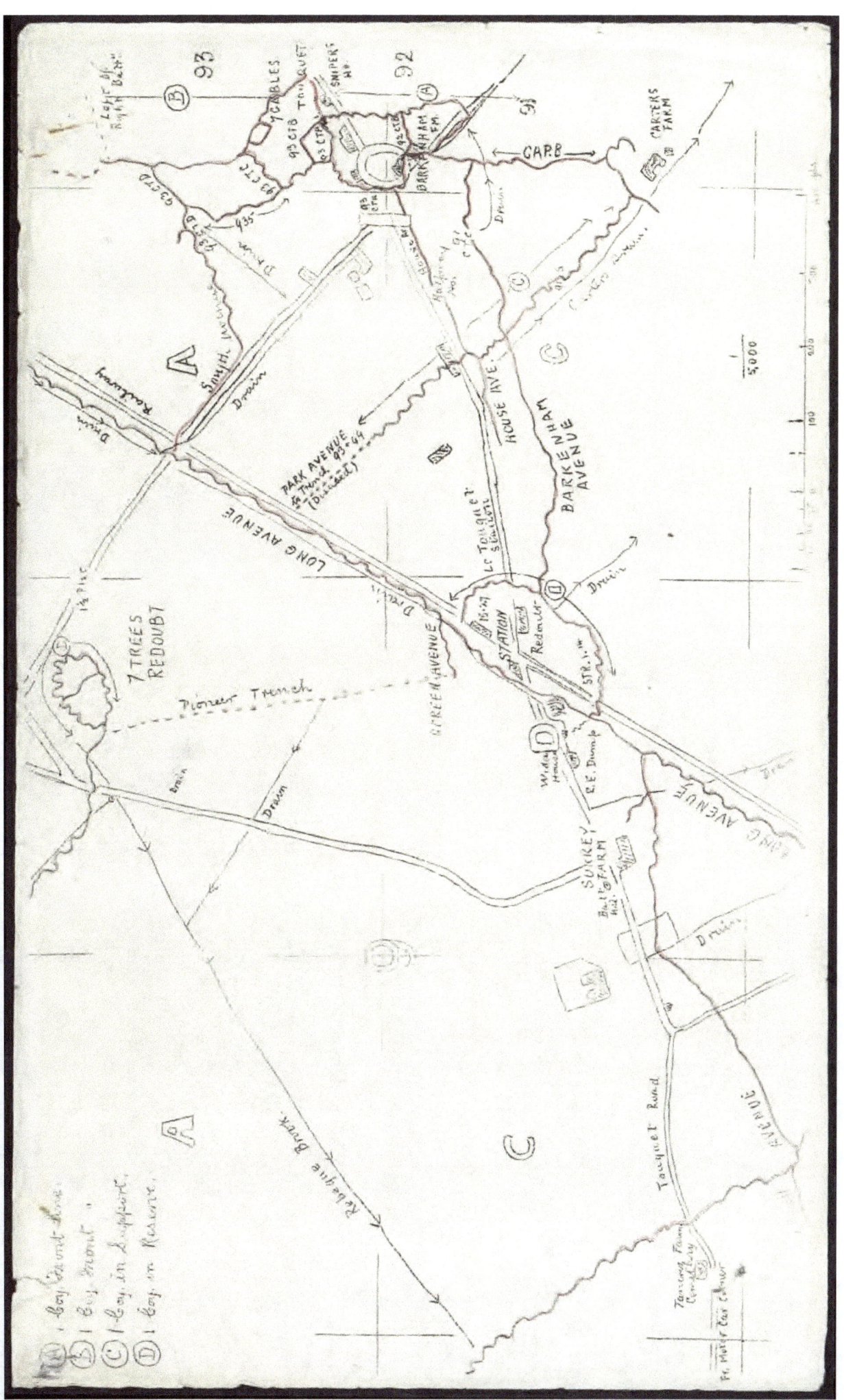

Rough sketch of battle of CERNY
shewing my route in blue pencil
not drawn to scale.

W.R. Warde-Aldam
Capt.
Batt. C/O 4th Cav. Bde.

"A" Form.
MESSAGES AND SIGNALS.

Army Form C. 2121.
(In pads of 100.)
No. of Message................

| Prefix........Code..........m | Words. | Charge. | This message is on a/c of: | Recd. at ......m |
| Office of Origin and Service Instructions. | Sent At......m To...... By...... | | ....Service. (Signature of "Franking Officer.") | Date........ From........ By........ |

TO — TUVI

Sender's Number.	Day of Month.	In reply to Number.	A A A
G636	12		

Please convey Divisional Commanders congratulation to GOFO on smart work last night

8/17.9/4   L

From DEPA
Place
Time 6.45 a
The above may be forwarded as now corrected. (Z)

Censor.   Signature of Addressor or person authorised to telegraph in his name.

Lt Cl

"A" Form.
MESSAGES AND SIGNALS.
Army Form C. 2121.

TO (Cont)

* R97   AAA

Shortly after 11.30 am the enemy fired a few rounds from trench-mortar into our 14b AAA. The trench and wire netting were considerably damaged and are being repaired AAA An N.C.O and man of the 2nd Manchesters who were working in the trench are suffering from shock and superficial wounds AAA Our trench-mortar retaliated with two rounds, the effect of which is not known.
The condition of trenches and wire is very fair; work on the former — especially pumping & cleaning in the centre — has been carried on all day; work on the latter will be continued tonight AAA
At 12.05 am. last night a green

SECRET.   G. 3142.   Headquarters.
                                1st Indian Cavalry Division.
                                   1st September, 1916.

ADMINISTRATIVE INSTRUCTIONS.
Reference O.O.22.

1. **MOVEMENTS OF DISMOUNTED MEN.**

    (1). One lorry per regiment will report at Brigade Headquarters and Jodphur Lancers Headquarters at 7 a.m., on 3rd inst, to carry kits only of dismounted men, to the FROHEN-LE-GRAND billeting area. They should leave units, loaded with the kits and units representatives, by 7-30 a.m., and be released after dumping kits in the new billet, by 10-30 a.m.

    (2). These lorries will then proceed to MANIN Church at 2 p.m., The dismounted men of the Sialkot Brigade will be at MANIN at that hour and go on the lorries to VILLERS L'HOPITAL whence the dismounted men will march to their billets.
    The lorries when released will proceed back to the units whose kits they lifted in the morning

    (3). The D.M., of Lucknow and Mhow Brigades will march to their billeting area.

    (4). In addition 5 lorries will be at Jodphur Lancers H.Q., at Savy at 2 p.m., on the 3rd and will carry their D.M., to billets at BARLEY.

2. On 4th inst, these lorries (one per regiment) will lift the D.M. kits to BUIRE-AU-BOIS, and dump them in charge of the regimental representatives by 8 a.m. when the lorries will be released.
    Dismounted parties will march to BUIRE-AU-BOIS.

3. The dismounted men will remain in BUIRE-AU-BOIS from the 4th inst, during the stay of the Division in the training area.
    Capt H.Clarke, 6th Dragoons will command the D.M., as long as they remain together.

4. POSTAL. Mails will be delivered in new billets each day.

5. There will be no delivery of Ordnance Stores till the 4th inst in the ST RICQUIER area (except for R.H.A Brigade.).

6. Tents that cannot be lifted will be left with Maires and lifted later under Divisional arrangements.
    A report on number of tents left and where left will be furnished to Divisional Headquarters by 4th inst.

7. Notes on FROHEN-LE-GRAND Billeting area are attached.

                                G.R.Maitland
                                        Major.
            D.A.A.&.Q.M.G. 1st Indian Cavalry Division.

To, No 1. Sialkot Bde.   6. Signal Sqdn.   13. Camp Commdt.
       2. Mhow Bde.   7. R.H.A Bde.   14. "G"
       3. Lucknow Bde.   8. O.C.,A.S.C.   15. Third Army.
       4. Jodphur Lrs.   9. A.D.M.S.
       5. Field Sqdn.   10. A.D.V.S
                         11. Liaison Offr.

WAR DIARY
or
INTELLIGENCE SUMMARY.

(Erase heading not required.)

Place	Date	Hour	Summary of Events and Information	Remarks and references to Appendices
ALLOUAGNE	17/3/16		holiday. Brigade Sports, in which the Battalion had its due proportion of successes, were held in the afternoon and at night a successful Battalion concert was held.	
"	18/3/16		The Battalion received a draft of 21 men joining to-day. the assault practised in the morning. In the afternoon classes and drills as usual.	
"	19/3/16		Church Parades. Half the Battalion was employed in work under the Royal Engineers on the ALLOUAGNE - BURBURE road.	
"	20/3/16		Drill and Classes as usual, special attention being given to bombing, it being the aim that every man in the Battalion understands the mechanism of and is practised in throwing live grenades.	
"	22/3/16		The Battalion parade for Assault practice had to be postponed	

Army Form C. 2118.

WAR DIARY
or
INTELLIGENCE SUMMARY.

(Erase heading not required.)

Hour, Date, Place	Summary of Events and Information	Remarks and references to Appendices
1917. Oct 22nd – 31st	The training of Junior NCO is being proceeded with. The Bn. has received one draft of Officers but no draft of O.R. has yet arrived. CASUALTIES and POSTING of OFFICERS during the past month.	
	CAPT THE HON P.J.H. OGILVY Killed in action 9.10.17	
	" R.J.P. RODAKOWSKI do. 9.10.17	
	2 LT A.L. WELLS do. 9.10.17	
	" T.S.V. STONEY do. 9.10.17	
	" H.V. FANSHAWE do. 9.10.17	
	CAPT R.B.S. REFORD Wounded in action 9.10.17	
	LIEUT H.H. MAXWELL do. 10.10.17	
	" N.B. BAGENAL do. 9.10.17	
	" D.S. BROWNE do. 9.10.17	
	2ND LT E.H. DOWLER do. 10.10.17	
	" E.M. HARVEY do. 9.10.17	
	" T. CORRY do. 9.10.17	
	MAJOR R.T.C. BAGGALLAY M.C. JOINED for duty 24.10.17	

WAR DIARY
or
INTELLIGENCE SUMMARY.

(Erase heading not required.)

Army Form C. 2118.

Instructions regarding War Diaries and Intelligence Summaries are contained in F. S. Regs., Part II and the Staff Manual respectively. Title pages will be prepared in manuscript.

Hour, Date, Place	Summary of Events and Information	Remarks and references to Appendices
Aug 14th. Hulluch & Vermelles	Evening patrols found the same as on 13th inst.	
Aug 15th. " "	The 13th left killed in VERMELLES. The relief was not completed until about 6·8pm — 2 platoons starting at 1 before 9pm. There had been some alteration in the line. Nos 2 & 3 coys were to get in. The trenches were held. The new front line of all had been occupied — there were 3 & coys holding the front line right; C coy & center & left coy — 1 platoon named only having 2 platoons up altogether & back in support in CAMBRAY. A. & coys in reserve.	N.C.O. killed in the evening party during right 15th-16th
Aug 16th. Trenches E of LE RUTOIRE y.1	A very quiet day, but a very heavy thunderstorm in the evening. Patrols out not being night. Very heavy mud everywhere.	Lt. Col. Beauchamp is M.A.I. attached for instruction.
Aug 17th. " " "	In front of this coy. A company of 8th Berks is attached to Bn for instruction — one platoon to each coy.	
	3 Patrols went out at 11pm — six from each of the 3 coys. The front line. Capt Ogen Roberts & right reported enemy captains in out the centre refused all quiet — Capt Danell along the MINIVER trifled in on 6 our morning alongside Renaud but heard nothing so cut the wire.	

G. 81. F. y.p. Forms/C. 2118/10.

(7,989) W4141—463. 400,000. 9/14. H.&J.Ltd.

WAR DIARY
or
INTELLIGENCE SUMMARY.

Army Form C. 2118.

Place	Date	Hour	Summary of Events and Information	Remarks and references to Appendices
BOIS DE NOULETTE	Aug 13		Hutchison reported by No 19 team of Section discovered. Bells had broken. Bells's move to LORETTE SPUR cancelled 5 pm.	Paris
	14		Hutchison's Report. Fighting and strong Marshal to LORETTE SPUR relieving DRAKE Battn. stops	Met
ABLAIN ST NAZAIRE	15		at ABLAIN ST NAZAIRE - arrived 11.30 pm (½ mile). Working Party of 2 Officers & 100 O.Rs to Engineers	Met Fine
	16	/10	12 Men sent down to AIX NOULETTE & 3rd Field Coy Engineers. To relieve 12 already there.	Fine
	17		Working party as above. Lewis Guns relieved HAWKE Lewis Guns from SOUCHEZ II	Very heavy rain.
SOUCHEZ II	18		Marched & Relieved HAWKE in SOUCHEZ II throughout the day. Battalion relief complete 12.30 am. 19th Disposition Btt. (½ Coys) on right, NELSON D.Coy centre, tray left each holding F.L. & supports. 2 platoons of B Coy in BATOLLE Pla. other 2 Platoons C Coy in Maison BOIS SIX	Dust
	19		Commenced work on trenches chiefly drainage. Labour carried on throughout period. Construction of a new Support post junction between ROTO & BOSCHE WALK - cleared POSTS WALK when shell had blown in sides. Our artillery bombarded enemy lines between 4.15 and 4.30pm with good effect Retaliation and strong as usual	Fine
	20		Day mostly quiet - work continued on trenches as before. Minenwerfer & Rifle Grenades more sent over between	

WAR DIARY or INTELLIGENCE SUMMARY

Army Form C. 2118.

Vol XII

Place	Date	Hour	Summary of Events and Information	Remarks and references to Appendices
Suez En Rigga	9		The under l'Infant Cleared today from INF RSE to Base 7205 ADAMS W. C Coy Pte & Sgt FLYNN T. A Coy MAJ McQUEEN J. B Coy evacuated out J Div and Sickety. Coy Living +1 Dir had dummy raid 3rd line out Shelling very heavy am. Learn not tonight.	
	10		Two to hospital one from hospital. Day. Envoy May	
	11		Wet today. Two to hospital 49 men sent to Inf Coy evacuated out J Div Area. Above mentioned the following 15892 KIRWAN A. RSIT61 McGRITH J. B Coy 12802 HARTE S. J A Coy 20620 LEONARD P. 16887 DUNNE J. B Coy 26328 BELL J. C Coy and 2/2/10 CLEARY J. D Coy idol 4 wet	
	12		From to hospital one from hospital. Nine men from Inf Base Depot 15701 DUFFY J. C Coy wounded out J Div Area. Struck off strength 9/03 St LEATHAM J. B Coy transferred to Railway Stores Off. Two men Troops sent to D.V Company	

Army Form C. 2118.

WAR DIARY
or
INTELLIGENCE SUMMARY.
(Erase heading not required.)

Instructions regarding War Diaries and Intelligence Summaries are contained in F.S. Regs., Part II. and the Staff Manual respectively. Title pages will be prepared in manuscript.

Hour, Date, Place	Summary of Events and Information	Remarks and references to Appendices
1.5.15. CAMERON E	Orders received in Brigade to take up the line running along Hill 60 and G. edge of SANCTUARY WOOD	LB4
2.5.15 CAMERON H.Q. fd.	We at met C. by kent to HOPPE COPSE - all smiths trench and dug out stores transferred to open trenches in the lines, but the company dug themselves in bell shelter [unclear]	LB4
3.5.15. HOPPE COPSE	A. by in close support of [unclear]. B. by in close support of [unclear]. Firedivn in left section C. by in support to R.I. Firedivn in left section D. bn at SANCTUARY WOOD. Orders received to concentrate in [unclear] 7pm by [unclear] to HOPPE COPSE	LB4
4.5.15 HOPPE COPSE 1.3. oct.	D. by withdraws to the position in the lines, leaving A. and B. companies to [unclear] HOPPE COPSE 7.30 orders only instructions from our brigade that the relief of HOPPE COPSE is to be slept and take over this they situated or [unclear]	LB4
4.5.15. HOPPE & HOPPE	line suffered a serious loss of 2 NCO and [unclear] B by only enough [unclear] fielders in open first dug that [unclear]	LB4

- 5 -

3. All Units will be responsible for the protection of their own headquarters, telephone exchanges, communications, billets, stores, and horse lines.

4. (a) All Units are responsible for assisting to put down fires in their areas, in co-operation with the Local Fire Brigade, taking over the appliances if necessary.
(b) Units will reconnoitre the fire appliances in their area, and Officers and N.C.Os will be detailed to take charge of fire parties.

5. A supply of candles or lamps will be held in reserve in case the Electric lighting supply fails.

13. INSTRUCTIONS AS TO THE EXERCISE OF CONTROL IN THE NEUTRAL ZONE.

1. All persons attempting to cross the boundary between occupied territory and neutral zone, except by the authorised control posts, will be fired upon, whether in occupied territory or not. If individuals are thereby killed or wounded in the neutral zone the British authorities have the right to enter the neutral zone and bring them into occupied territory.

2. (a) German troops forming the garrison of security in the neutral zone will wear yellow brassards.
(b) Other German troops are only allowed within 2 kilometres of the Western boundary of the neutral zone with the previous consent of the British authorities. This does not apply to REMSCHEID, which place they are permitted to enter if required to assist in keeping order.
(c) Local police will wear white brassards. They are allowed to be armed and to be within 2 kilometres of our outpost line in the execution of their duty.

3. British troops are not concerned with riots, strikes, or other disturbances that may take place in the neutral zone, except in so far as they effect the safety of our Troops. Any information that may be obtained as to occurences of this nature should however be forwarded at once to higher authorities.

4. With the exception noted in para 1 British troops are forbidden to cross the boundary line into the neutral zone without reference to the General Staff at G.H.Q.
To meet the case of firing taking place in the direction of our outpost line, or of the safety of our troops being endangered by any action, civil or Military, on the part of the Germans, authority to order troops to enter the neutral zone is delegated to Corps Commanders, who at their discretion may further delegate this authority to subordinate commanders not below the rank of Brigade Commanders. Except in cases of great emergency reference should however, first be made to General Headquarters

5. Any attempt on the part of the Germans to contravene the regulations is to be at once reported to G.H.Q.

(Signed) P.COLIN DUNCAN. Captain,
Adjutant, for Lieut Colonel,
Commanding, 2/4th The Queens Rgt.

DISTRIBUTION.

Copy No. 1 --- War diary.   Copy No. 6. Q.M.
        2 --- O.C. A Coy.   7. S.O.
        3 --- O.C. B Coy.   8. T.O.
        4 --- O.C. C Coy.   9. H.Q.2/Ldn.I.B.
        5 --- O.C. D Coy.   10. O.C.10th Queens
     Copy No. 11 --- O.C. 52nd Royal Warwicks.
             12 --- File.

1/ DORSET REGT.

WAR DIARY or INTELLIGENCE SUMMARY

Army Form C. 2118.

1 Dorset VB
J&46

JUNE 1918

Place	Date	Hour	Summary of Events and Information	Remarks and references to Appendices
	1.		Battn in Line. Fighting patrol from B Coy did good work after a very successful surprise on a German post & capturing a Regt Sergt Major & 1 O.R. Nothing during day ourselves. 1 O.R. very apt on front. Position in line.	
	2		Little shelling. Little Machine Gun fire from Beck rather from shelled Bleux B.Coy on Defences locality compelled to move from H.Q. No officers for 2 hours & fell Clear at 3.30 a.m. 8.5.18. 2 O.R. wounded.	
	3		Battn in Line. Enemy front shelled during morning. Work on support line lifted away to shell fire. Casualties 1 Off (2/Lieut EM LUMSDEN V.C.) & 1 O.R. Killed and 1 O.R. wounded. Brigadier EM LUMSDEN V.C. C.B. D.S.O	
	4		Battn in Line. Day generally quiet. Light shelling harrass support line bat Casualties O.C. B Coy wounded by sniper in L front trench.	
			Unit moved into B.E.R reserve leaving Officers & 2 OR staying at H.Q. Relief P THWAYTES intervening in 2nd BR etc Brigadier General EM LUMSDEN V.C. C.B. D.S.O at RANSART.	

WAR DIARY or INTELLIGENCE SUMMARY

Army Form C. 2118.

JANUARY 1918

1st Guards Brigade Machine Gun Company

Place	Date Jan	Hour	Summary of Events and Information	Remarks and references to Appendices
FAMPOUX H.24 G.9.5	25-26		The Transport aided by fatigue parties from the Details worked on the rotting round the horse lines and then proceeded with this round the Hut. 6 teams relieved by 6 teams of 3rd Guards Brigade Machine Gun Company. Company Headquarters and 10 teams relieved by Company Headquarters and 10 teams of 3rd Guards Brigade Machine Gun Company. Details move from St NICHOLAS to LEWIS BARRACKS.	
Sar/81 B.11. ARRAS	27 28		Routine work resumed – drill and machine gun training. 2/Lt. C.H.EIKHART, 9th Guards joined the Company on 31st January. Lt. C.S.V HERBERT M.G. Guards Brigade left the Company & went on duty at KORAN, CAMIERS on 30 January. Casualties during the month – nil. Honours and Rewards. Military Cross. Lt. S.S. HARRISON, 9th Guards. Croix de Guerre (Belgian) 1193 C.S.M. C.J WHERELL Distinguished Conduct Medal. 4198 Sgt. (a/SSM.) A. FALCOVER Military Medal. 1148 Pte. (L/Cpl.) T.W. M°LBONE 575 Pte. (L/Cpl.) JACKSON 10 Pte. (L/Cpl.) F. ASH 730 Pte. R. WICHERSS	

J. Stern Capt.
Comdt. 1st Guards Bde. M.G. Coy.

Army Form C. 2118.

Sheet 5.

1st BATTALION COLDSTREAM GUARDS :—
WAR DIARY
for
MAY, 1918.
INTELLIGENCE SUMMARY.
(Erase heading not required.)

Place	Date	Hour	Summary of Events and Information	Remarks and references to Appendices
FRONT LINE N. of AYETTE	22nd		In No 3 Coy Capt Barcly,M.C. 2nd Lt. Richie took the place of Lt.Roderick and 2nd Lt. Somerset, and Capt. Salisbury-Jones and Lt.Smith in No 4 Coy took over from Capt. Fellowes and 2nd Lt.Gladstone M.C. There was great activity by our artillery all the night; and the Canadians upon our left, (the next Division but one) carried out a raid. German attack imminent.	
	23rd		Another uneventful, cloudless, midsummer day, and very hot indeed. In the early morning a small patrol of No 1 Coy (1N.C.O. and 2 men) in charge of Cpl Jones succeeded in capturing a German (452nd Regt), who died of wounds. A very useful identification, and one much needed. Our artillery, especially the Heavies, kept up an incessant harrassing fire throughout the day and night. The Brigadier on our right carried out a raid, and the one prisoner secured knew nothing of the coming offensive ; an ignorance apparently shared by our G.H.Q. 2nd Lieut. E.B.O. Woodbury joined the details at ST.AMAND. The Battalion received orders to wear gas masks an hour a day. There was one casualty - wounded.	
			The weather turned cooler, and a S.W. wind got up. Patrolling proceeded,(no results) and a certain amount or wiring was done. The Front Line posts were linked up in places by shallow (4ft 6ins) trenches. Our artillery was again very active. The German reply was only spasmodic.	
	24th		A wet day, unmarked by any particular incident. The Germans put a short barrage on our front line Coys at 3.30 a.m., and also fired a good deal upon our Reserve Coy, in this latter bombardment the percentage of "dud" shells was as high as eighty.	
	25th		A very marked increase in German artillery activity; Not only did he put barrages upon our front lines, early in the morning and in the middle of the night, but he also shelled the roads further back heavily throughout the day. Hostile aeroplanes were also more active, with the result that our A.A. Guns did not fire. A good deal of wiring and digging was done by us.	

Army Form C. 2118.

WAR DIARY FOR FEBRUARY, 1918.
1st BATTALION COLDSTREAM GUARDS.
INTELLIGENCE SUMMARY.
(Erase heading not required)

Place	Date	Hour	Summary of Events and Information	Remarks and references to Appendices
FRONT LINE	1st	1918	Day very quiet, except for rather unusual activity of enemy Machine Guns.	
	2nd		Unusual activity of German Trench Mortars. We asked the artillery for retaliation, which they gave. It had a most quieting effect on the enemy. An enemy patrol approached our lines, but was fired on and scattered. A patrol of 1 Officer, 1 Corporal and 1 Other rank went out to investigate No Man's Land opposite the German Salient "The Nose". They found nothing but a mass of derelict trenches and saps and shell holes full of wire and old tins which made a lot of noise, on an otherwise quiet night.	Lieut. C.G.Barclay to Lewis Gun course at LE TOUQUET.
	3rd		A quiet day. In the evening the Battalion was relieved by the 2nd Battalion Irish Guards, and returned to the Support Line; Companies going to their former lines, No 1 in CHICKEN RESERVE and HUMID trench, No 4 in HARRY, No 3 in HUSSAR and No 2 in CADIZ Reserve.	
SUPPORT LINE	4th		Nothing to report. A very quiet day. Companies engaged in work on their lines. In most cases they found that little had been done in their absence.	Lieut. J.R.Saunders returned from a Gas Course.
	5th		After a quiet day the Battalion was relieved by 3rd Battalion Grenadier Guards, and left the line for ARRAS, after a tour of 18 days without a break. The support line only differed from the front line in this respect that it was not trench mortared and machine gunned. The men were just as much confined to trenches and had as much work to do on them as in the front line, in addition to fatigues, such as carrying rations and R.E. material for the front line Battalion. The Battalion was billetted in Lewis Barracks, ARRAS, and Headquarters and Company Messes in the rue des Louez Dieu.	

WAR DIARY or INTELLIGENCE SUMMARY

Army Form C. 2118

Place	Date	Hour	Summary of Events and Information	Remarks and references to Appendices
GINCHY	15th Sept 1916		The attack was then re-organized as well as possible, and the front and left flanks hung by that time up in line the advance was carried onto the next objective. All this time the 6th Division on our right had failed to make any progress at all, and we were suffering heavy casualties from M.G. fire from high ground on our right. In spite of this the advance continued and the second line of enemy trenches was taken. Our position was not then so many [yet?] the enemy surrendered. By this time nearly all of the Officers of the Battalion had become casualties and the Batt. was very much split up and having lost direction somewhat had joined the other Battalions on their left. A party of about 13 Battalion under the highest [Sergt Digby] kept their positions, and with the remnants of 2 other Irish and Canadian now occupied what they took to be the second objective, but which was really the 1st according to the scheme. There, they consolidated and held on, though under heavy M.G. and rifle fire from their right flank and rear. Another party of about 40 1st Battalion under Lt. R.d Baugh had gone off further to their left and were joined by about 1st Brigade who had also joined this objective, and still another party of about 30 under Lt. Sinclair were now under the command of Lt Col F Campbell who had pressed on and joined another trench reached slightly in advance and who now contemplated advancing to attack Lesboefs, which was the final objective. However they too, had lost their direction and gone off too much to the left and were now on the second objective or they supposed but in a second none 200 yds short of it. As the night grew near

SECRET

39 Vol 2

Army Form C. 2118

116th Bde. Trench Mortar Battery
August

WAR DIARY

INTELLIGENCE SUMMARY
(Erase heading not required.)

Instructions regarding War Diaries and Intelligence Summaries are contained in F. S. Regs., Part II. and the Staff Manual respectively. Title Pages will be prepared in manuscript.

Place	Date	Hour	Summary of Events and Information	Remarks and references to Appendices
Givenchy	7.8.16	5.30 a.m.	Operations. In Givenchy section from 6.8.16 to 10.8.16. 60 shells fired from 3 guns on points A.10.c.2½.2. A.10.c.1½.1½. A.9.d.9½.5. Casualties. Killed 14360 Pte Yeager J. 14th Hants 13004 " Killing R. 14th Hants 1676 " Baugtley J. 12th Royal Sussex 1387 " Lambert G. 12th Royal Sussex } Attached to 116th Brigade L.T.M.B. Wounded 12747 Pte Decker E.J. 14th Hants 12878 " Bower H.J. 14th Hants	
Hamel Section	30.8.16			

S. Farver
2nd Lieut.
116/T.M.B⁄y

WAR DIARY or INTELLIGENCE SUMMARY

Army Form C. 2118.

Place	Date	Hour	Summary of Events and Information	Remarks and references to Appendices
GREENLAND HILL Trench Map	Feb 27-28 1918	12.25 mn	2nd Gordons Bite raided enemy trenches in I.7.c. Nos 3 & 4 guns fired from zone K + 6 as part of gun distribution S. of Rly. 1000 rounds fired — Raid successful (prisoners & guns). Enemy barrage 10 minutes after zero on trench & support trench, district in front of but chiefly enemy (?) of 505. This was left or Reserve line — saw shell Dist front —	
	28		Gun positions in CLYDE shelled. 6 HA gun moves from C.6/7 to new gun pit at enemy's position in Rly. Embankment at I.13 c 3.6 with enfilade fields of fire on our N. flank of CHÂTEAU Strong Point. Another gun also put in immediately Reserve section from ARRAS Faubourg de ... to be ready to meet any enemy pushing up to dry water defences at eastern approaches & walking of Scarpe to Rly. positions. 2 guns H.17.A.1.6 firing S.E. along main Arras (these fields of fire are being opened by demolition of houses in Champagne Faubourg with gun wests covering ETC.) 2 guns battery known at H.17 & h.h covering towards slopes of hill & Northern outskirts Arras.	

WAR DIARY
INTELLIGENCE SUMMARY.

Army Form C. 2118.

11th (S) Batt. Northumberland

Hour, Date, Place	Summary of Events and Information	Remarks and references to Appendices
GREVILLERS. 22 April	Battn. engaged in burial of Infantry dead around BAPAUME. Main P.G.R.N.O.B.Y.C.K. grave from 30 to 115 D.	
" " 23.	Battn. engaged in burying officers of BAPAUME. Proceeded to reconnoitre roads which Battn. will occupy tomorrow. Capt. E.C. SPRAY was severely wounded by shell splinter whilst returning. Enemy aeroplanes were active over our front during the day which was a fine day. 2/Lieut. N. DARBY assumes command of S. Coy in succession to hospital.	
" 24	Preparing to move to positions 34th Brigade are in Divisional Reserve. Battn. moved off by Companies with 15 mins interval commencing with H.Q. Coy at 5.15 p.m. On arrival at FREMICOURT rations were issued and Battn. continued to the front. By Batns the relief was completed by 10-20 p.m. Work was commenced at 12 MN. B. & am not much of defences owing to lack of materials. Occasional shelling Batter in vicinity of Battn. area during day no casualties incurred. Fine day.	
Positions in Bde. Reserve near MORCHIES – BEAUMETZ.	Battn. occupy positions in sunken roads near a line of X roads running from Left to Right. From a point about 300 yards due west of MORCHIES (centre) 300 N of MORCHIES thence in a South Westerly direction. Fn/Front Right half Bery abouts 1000 x 7	E.P.Connor Capt.

WAR DIARY
INTELLIGENCE SUMMARY

Army Form C. 2118.

Place	Date	Hour	Summary of Events and Information	Remarks and references to Appendices
HIGHLAND RIDGE. REF. NINE WOOD. 1/10,000. SHT. 57C.	29/12/16		Reconnaissance made of Dugouts in Sector area occupied by Bn. Three found – all with one entrance. C & D Coys working on NAVAL RESERVE. [R.9. NINE WOOD.] from 4 p.m. to 8 p.m. Party of 20 men working making dugouts at A.18.b.4.9. R.18.b.5.9. ARTY	
OPERATIONS IN COUNTER ATTACK.	30/31st		From 11.30 a.m. to 7.30 p.m. This party was at work until dug outs are completed. HIGHLAND RIDGE. Shelled during night by 5.9" & 4.2". SUB LIEUT. MT. BOYS – wounded.	
		6.30 a.m.	A heavy enemy barrage was laid by enemy apparently on whole of Divisional Front.	
		[Both] 7.25 a.m.	Orders received to reinforce to DRAKES with one coy. The enemy had penetrated our front line system of trenches but for the time was held up by the Drakes.	
		10.25 a.m.	Orders received from H.Q. to man NAVAL RESERVE with remainder of Batt B.H.Q. being in Ravine at R.8.C.9.0. Completed by 2.30 p.m.	
		2.15 p.m.	In accordance with orders from O.C. Drakes. C Coy (Nelson) counter-attacked for WELSH SUPPORT. R.15a.85.70 to R.9.b.46.00. from NAVAL R. over the top – No artillery barrage. After men succeeded in gaining objective, but the right was held up by machine gun fire. At the same time a bombing party bombed up FARM. AVE. at R.15a.6.9. towards the right end of WELSH SUPPORT, meeting considerable opposition. SPLENDID GALLANTRY was shown by SUB LIEUT. CLERK. D.C.(Clery.	

WAR DIARY
INTELLIGENCE SUMMARY

Army Form C. 2118.

Place	Date	Hour	Summary of Events and Information	Remarks and references to Appendices
	1918			
	1		The enemy attempted to raid one of our posts on "C" Coy front but was successfully driven off leaving two prisoners in our hands. We suffered only one casualty (wounded). "B" & "D" Coy relieved "A" & "C" Coy in the line. "B" Coy on the right flank and "D" Coy on the left. "C" Coy became Right support Coy and "A" Coy left support Coy.	
	2		Instructions were received early in the morning to send out fours fighting patrols to establish posts in the enemy 2nd line. Two patrols from "A" Coy under 2/Lt Q L Robertson and two patrols from "C" Coy under 2/Lt C M Humphries and 2/Lt E R Belfast and 2/Lt H Y K Widdowson left our trenches at 4·30 a.m. and proceeded towards the enemy lines. The Commanding Officer moved up to Railway Keep to receive reports from the patrol leaders. No reports came in up to 6·15 a.m. when at this period he advanced thro' moved up to Right front Coy HQrs. The first reports came in about 10·5 a.m. stating one patrol had been held up by the enemy and the remainder had lost direction and had returned but caused [several] hurried out again. Three men were 3 casualties. This included killed, wounded and missing 2/Lt E R Belfast, missing believed killed	

D.D. & I., London, E.C.
(A19263) Wt W3500/P733 750,000 2/18 Sch. 52 Forms/C2118/16.

Wednesday May 5th 1915 @ GORRE & LA BEUVRIERE
Battalion was relieved by 8th Battalion City of
London Rifles on the Reserve billets @ GORRE at
2h.m. Battn then marched to LA BEUVRIERE
by Coys @ 15 minutes intervals. Battn
took over billets and reported all correct at 4.30 p.m.

Thursday May 6th. 1915 @ LA BEUVRIERE
No change.

Friday May 7th 1915 @ LA BEUVRIERE
Battalion received orders to be ready to move
at 4 minutes notice. Battalion ready but did
not move off

Saturday May 8th 1915 @ LA BEUVRIERE & ESSARS.
Battalion still in readiness to move. Battalion
moved off with 1st line transport @ midnight
and marched via CHOCQUES and BETHUNE
to ESSARS. Arrived and took over billets
about 4 a.m. 9/5/15 Battalion attached to
2nd Division under Major General Horne.

Sunday May 9th 1915 @ ESSARS & LA TOURET
At 5 a.m. Battalion in First Army Reserve
during the attack on the enemies lines
Battalion evacuates billets @ ESSARS and marches
from to LA TOURET at 9 p.m. Everyone in billets &
all correct at 11.50 p.m.

Monday May 10th 1915 @ LA TOURET and LA COUTURE
Battalion received orders to change billets and to be there by
4 p.m. Battalion took over new billets and HQ at
LA COUTURE. Battalion still part of First Army Reserve.

Tuesday May 11th. 1915 @ LA COUTURE & LE FALON
Battalion received orders to move M.G. from S. of
LA COUTURE to E. of LACON. Batt still in reserve.
Battalion M.G. evacuated a Van and seas and descents
taken over.

Wednesday May. 12th. 1915 @ LE FALON & BEUVRY
Battalion received orders re change of billets. Left (7 a.m.)
LACON and marches in column of route to
BEUVRY. New designation of 2nd London Division
to 47th (London) Division and 5th London Infantry Bde.
to 141st Infantry Brigade. Battn refers to 4th (J.a.)
Division.

Army Form C. 2118.

WAR DIARY
or
INTELLIGENCE SUMMARY.
(Erase heading not required.)

Instructions regarding War Diaries and Intelligence Summaries are contained in F. S. Regs., Part II. and the Staff Manual respectively. Title pages will be prepared in manuscript.

Place	Date	Hour	Summary of Events and Information	Remarks and references to Appendices
LANCASHIRE TRENCH	13.10.15	—	Attack by 8th Division – 35th and 37th Inf Bde – Objective 25th Brigade. The Quarries West of CITE ST. ELIE. HQ a and 3 companies attached to 35th Inf Bde – One company to 37. – Order from 35 Inf Bde Lg four attacking bomb rounds THE QUARRIES. Further attack completed Orders from 37 B'de to consolidate any trenches gained and to dig communication trenches between own front line and the quarries enough – Attack commenced at 2PM – 37th Inf Bde and French company consolidated – 35th Inf Bde attack not being [?] successful so companies could not come out owing to bleaking in communication trench, also not reach from the trenches till 2 am the 14th when they [?] down [?] covered by German shell fire – Five men killed – one missing – Twenty nine [?] wounded 9 Cpls	
"	14.10.15	—	All companies returning to their trenches damaged by shell fire and working in front of first lines. One NCO killed – Five NCO's and men wounded # CP Capts	
"	15.10.15	—	Companies moving along the front of the Division (re.along positions gained by 35th and 37th Infantry Brigade.) It is found in advance where enemy's trenches are too near to use rifle & french wire is removed as well. One has men are too fix it to the ground with stakes. The [?] of [?] attacking in heidle attacks too much attention – One man wounded on 13th man dies of wounds. One men killed – seven NCO's and men wounded. 4 CP Capts	
"	16.10.15	—	Same as 15th – One man died of wounds – Four men wounded #9 Cpls	
"	17.10.15	—	Same as 16th – Two men wounded # CP Capts	
"	18.10.15	—	Three companies with 35th Inf Bde B'de wiring – Company with 37th Brigade returning trenches damaged by shell fire – Five men wounded # CP Capts	

Army Form C. 2118.

WAR DIARY
or
INTELLIGENCE SUMMARY.
(Erase heading not required.)

Hour, Date, Place	Summary of Events and Information	Remarks and references to Appendices
27th January 1916 LAVENTIE	Alarm about possibility of attack by enemy as it was the anniversary of the Kaiser's birthday. Great preparations against a gas attack by enemy.	2nd Lt Fields (No. 4 Coy) 2nd Lt Warrington (No. 2 Coy) 2nd Lt Irvine (No. 1 Coy) join the Battalion.
28th January 1916	All quiet. Expected to relieve 2nd Bn Irish Guards but relief cancelled and tour extended to 3 days instead of two.	
29th January 1916 LAVENTIE	Relieve 2nd Bn Irish Guards in the trenches near PICANTIN about 6.30 p.m. Quick relief & trench found to be in a very much better condition than we expected. Found Headquarters RED HOUSE. Trenches much drier than usual owing to very little rain having fallen lately.	2nd Lt A.D. Bridge goes on leave. Capt Hon. E.F.J. Morl comes off leave.
30th January 1916 Trenches near PICANTIN	Patrols sent out from the two centre companies.	Capt Smythe R.A.M.C. goes on leave. Buffam Martyn R.A.M.C. comes in his stead. (permanently)
31st January 1916	Bombardment of the German lines on our right provoked heavy enemy retaliation much to our surprise.	

Army Form C. 2118.

WAR DIARY
of
INTELLIGENCE SUMMARY.
(Erase heading not required.)

Place	Date	Hour	Summary of Events and Information	Remarks and references to Appendices
			Lieut.Col.R.V.Pollok.D.S.O. Wounded (Gas) 8-4-18 Not to Hospital.	
			Capt.F.R.Moodhouse.M.C. -- do --	-- do --
			(R.A.M.C.attached)	
			Lieut. J.N.Ward. -- do --	-- do --
			2/Lieut.C.L.Browne. Wounded in Action 13-4-18.	
			2/Lieut.J.G.Maclachlan. -- do -- 29-4-18.	
			Capt.A.F.L.Gordon.M.C. Transfd. to 2nd Battn. 26-4-18.	
			3 Other Ranks Killed in Action.	
			41 -- do -- Wounded in Action.	
			4 -- do -- Declared Deserted.	
			10 -- do -- Struck off Strength.	
			26 -- do -- Evacuated (ill)	
			84	
			Honours & Rewards	
			No.1767. Sgt. P.Joyce. Awarded Military Medal (A.R.O.1/24-4-18)	
			6273.L/Cpl. F.Boyle. -- do --	
			10200. " D. Deveney. -- do --	

Lieut. A.H.Buller. Joined B'ttn. for duty. 10-4-18.
Lt.(a/Capt).W.Joyce. -- do -- 10-4-18.
Lieut.Hon.B.A.A.Ogilvy. -- do -- 10-4-18.
2/Lt. T.B.Maughan. -- do -- 10-4-18.
" P.R.J.Barry. -- do -- 10-4-18.
" H.J.Lofting. -- do -- 10-4-18.
" J.G.Maclachlan. -- do -- 10-4-18.

112 Other Ranks joined for duty 5-4-18.
40 -- do -- 16-4-18.
4 -- do -- 18-4-18.
14 -- do -- 21-4-18.
6 -- do -- 28-4-18.
13 -- do -- 29-4-18.
___
189
===

	Officers.	O.R.
Approximate Fighting Strength 1-4-1918.	20	827
Joined during month. ...	7	190
	27	1017
Left during month. ...	3	84
Approximate Fighting Strength 30-4-1918.	24	933

WAR DIARY
or
INTELLIGENCE SUMMARY
(Erase heading not required.)

Army Form C. 2118

Place	Date	Hour	Summary of Events and Information	Remarks and references to Appendices
LINE BEFORE LES BOEUFS	20th		and rain - The relief taking in all 12 hours.	
	21st		The Company "side slipped" with the whole Bde and relieved the 3rd Wilts Bde M.G. Company in the Line just N. of the LES BOEUFS - GINCHY Rd.	
	23rd		2 Lts M. ARNOLD FOSTER & grenadier S/S and 2nd Lt F.Y. BURGESS join the Company.	
	24th	9.30 p.m.	The Company move to their assembly positions for the attack the following day. Two sections dug in behind the grouping Off Line, one in the Cable detailed to occupy the 3rd Objective on its capture (point beyond LES BOEUFS) and 2 Guns of the other East flank, detailed to occupy the 2nd Objective (point to N side of LES BOEUFS). One section in reserve in the SWITCH LINE.	
	25th	12.35 a.m.	The Bde attacked with the 1st 13th Gren Gds on the right and the 1st B" Irish Gds on the left, the 2 Coldstream Bns in support. The M.G. sections were not attached to Bns but chose their own Lines of advance. The M.G. Coy. Hd. Qrs. were with the 3rd B" Coldstream Gds. The attack was highly successful and the M.Gs. continued to support the objective in front of them. Captured the Objective in front of them.	

WAR DIARY
or
INTELLIGENCE SUMMARY.
(Erase heading not required.)

Army Form C. 2118.

Place	Date	Hour	Summary of Events and Information	Remarks and references to Appendices
LINE	21st		**Artla** The 1st WAVE will consist of TRENCH MORTARS, the VICKERS GUNS, & Germans & sting pimts. On arrival at objective OS C Coys will form carrying dumps of Tools. (Sgd) C. Marten Lt Col Cmdg 13th Bn Essex Regt	
LINE	22nd			
LINE	23rd	7am	The Battalion was formed up on their jumping off position without any hitch occurring about 2 am in spite of heavy shelling. Companies were organized in three platoons, one platoon of each company representing 1st 2nd & 3rd waves each had consisting of two lines. 1st Line Bombers & Riflemen 2nd Line Lewis Gunners & Rifle Bombers Moppers up for each wave were formed up in rear of the 3rd line carrying picks & gunsacks for clearing points were found up in rear of the 3rd wave. At H.d. had gained well the Highland Light Infantry, the 17th Middlesex and 1st Royal Marine Light Infantry	
		4.25 am	At 4.25 am ns an barrage came down and at 4.38 am the 1st wave crossed the enemy front line Trench, with the exception of the extreme right of	

WAR DIARY
or
INTELLIGENCE SUMMARY.

(Erase heading not required.)

Army Form C. 2118.

Place	Date	Hour	Summary of Events and Information	Remarks and references to Appendices
LINE	28th		the Battalion, which was held up by machine gun fire and not that heavily from machine gun fire in endeavouring to get through it. At the point took us entirely into with the Royal Marine Light Infantry on our RIGHT, and the maintained liaison. The 13th Essex & 17th Middlesex but our right with the Highest Light Infantry who were in the LEFT & 17th Middlesex. The advance continued into the terrage & the line & the formation touched in C.13.d. further end of OPPY WOOD and touch in C.Y.C at the faced a party of German snipers attacked our RIGHT FLANK. Heavy machine gun fire, a rifle fire took place from OPPY village and large numbers of the enemy were advancing down the SUNKEN ROAD at the CROSSES.	
		5.50am	We noticed one company of the Kings Royal Rifle Corps (who company was sent up by the 6th Infantry Bde as support) to advance and form a defensive flank from B.18 d 3.5 to SOUTH and of possibly further than the British front line along the Battalion was much machine gun fire. About this time our line line the Battalion was not LEFT (17th Middlesex) were heavily attacked	

Original

Army Form C. 2118.
Sheet 7

WAR DIARY
INTELLIGENCE SUMMARY
of 6th (S) Bn
The Royal Irish Regiment
June 1916

(Erase heading not required.)

Instructions regarding War Diaries and Intelligence
Summaries are contained in F.S. Regs., Part II.
and the Staff Manual respectively. Title pages
will be prepared in manuscript.

Place	Date	Hour	Summary of Events and Information	Remarks and references to Appendices
LOOS	23/6/16		Rof Sheet 36c decided to postpone the attack.	
	25/6/16		Casualties :- 2 OR wounded	
	24/6/16		Preparations were again made to carry out the gas attack but it had again been postponed on account of the wind.	
			Casualties :- 2 OR killed, 3 OR wounded.	
	26/6/16		2 OR wounded.	
	27/6/16	12.15 AM	Following on the explosion of 2 mines the 7th Leinsters on our right carried out a successful raid on the enemy trenches taking one prisoner and killing some hundreds of the enemy. During the raid the two craters were consolidated and to raiding party returned at dawn. The provoked some retaliation from the enemy all along our front causing some casualties.	
			Casualties :- Lieut. J.H. Falls and Lieut. O. Crosbie wounded also 9 OR killed and 13 OR wounded	
	28/6/16	1 AM	It was decided to carry out the gas attack at 1 am at the last moment however the officer responsible for liberating the gas decided that the wind was not suitable and no gas was liberated	

WAR DIARY or INTELLIGENCE SUMMARY

Army Form C. 2118.

Place	Date	Hour	Summary of Events and Information	Remarks and references to Appendices
M/2 R00 b5-	1/11/17		Maj Scott Clark visits the guns in the afternoon. 2nd Lt Bey & Lt Hemsley arrive and take over guns to reconnoitre the ground for Lt Pierce's departure to Cantiers on a course. Situation normal. Right Section engaged several times.	
	2/11/17		Maj Scott Clark visits the guns in the left sub section. 2nd Lt Jeffries 2 O.C. Lancaster Reg't 5th Bn open gas can discharges from our lines. Night firing carried on. Situation normal. The distribution of premises was very complete & the reports sent stated that there was no by Lt Entony's Serasergeno was where it. Lt C R W Richards left for transport line.	
	3/11/17		Maj Lou the Clark visits the guns when ordered. The situation is very quiet & C is hard. Pemberton (L.P.) Lt Williams (N.Z) Lt Parnell (M.G.C) No practice available for Scout. Two wire found cut and langing from the night sub first line. Situation normal & Night firing carried on by Section returned "B" on left in back line. Lt Annis S.C. proceeds to Tournehem Lane for duty. Lt CO Se & Oz took on Sting 2nd in Company. Major Scott Clark visits O.C. Ministers.	
	4/11/17		Situation normal. Withdrew supports Sect & caravan from line. Soyecourke Sent. Arnold, Pt Branham & Illingworth went on M.C. Course. Cpl Connell went to Brussels Course. Pt Holland went for gas course. Lt Annis S.C. and Lt Parnell	
	5/11/17		Maj Scott Clark visits the guns in conjunction with the Div M.G.O. Capt Fowler C.E. & MG Bde	

WAR DIARY
INTELLIGENCE SUMMARY

Army Form C. 2118.

Place	Date	Hour	Summary of Events and Information	Remarks and references to Appendices
M12 B00-65	1/11/17		Maj Foster, Clark visited the guns on the right with Lt Selby & Lt Hennessey who was taking over owing to arrangement being made for Lt Ricardo's departure to Cavalry on Course. Situation normal. Night firing.	
	2/11/17		Maj Foster Clark visited the guns on the left, also visited O.C. 4th Bn's & O.C. Bombers Regt at 6pm. Gas was discharged from our lines. Night firing continuous. Situation normal, with exception of position being very completely & thoroughly searched but been thrown on by the enemy's trench mortars, was a result. Lt C.D.W Richards left for transport lines.	
	3/11/17		Maj Foster Clark visited the guns, also went round the front line & examined equipment & ect. Was at Pemberton (L.P.) Lt Williams (L.2) Lt Pratt (M.C.) No parties available for work. Saw enemy found moving many guns & night work front line. Situation normal. Night firing continuous. "B" on left on front line. Lt Annis SG repairs at Transport lines for duty. Lt C.O Selby look over duty by 2nd Bn. Company. Maj Foster Clark visited O.C. Manchesters.	
	4/11/17		Situation normal. Whitehouse reported sick & remained in. Reynolds Scott Archer, Pte Brashaw & Illingworth went on A.M. Course. Cpl Connell wound to Casualty Corner, Pte Holland wound for Gas Course. L Corpl S.G. Avent to Lt Pratt's.	
	5/11/17		Maj Foster Clark visited the Guns in conjunction with the Div M.G.O. Col Foster (Bridge) 2nd Batt.	

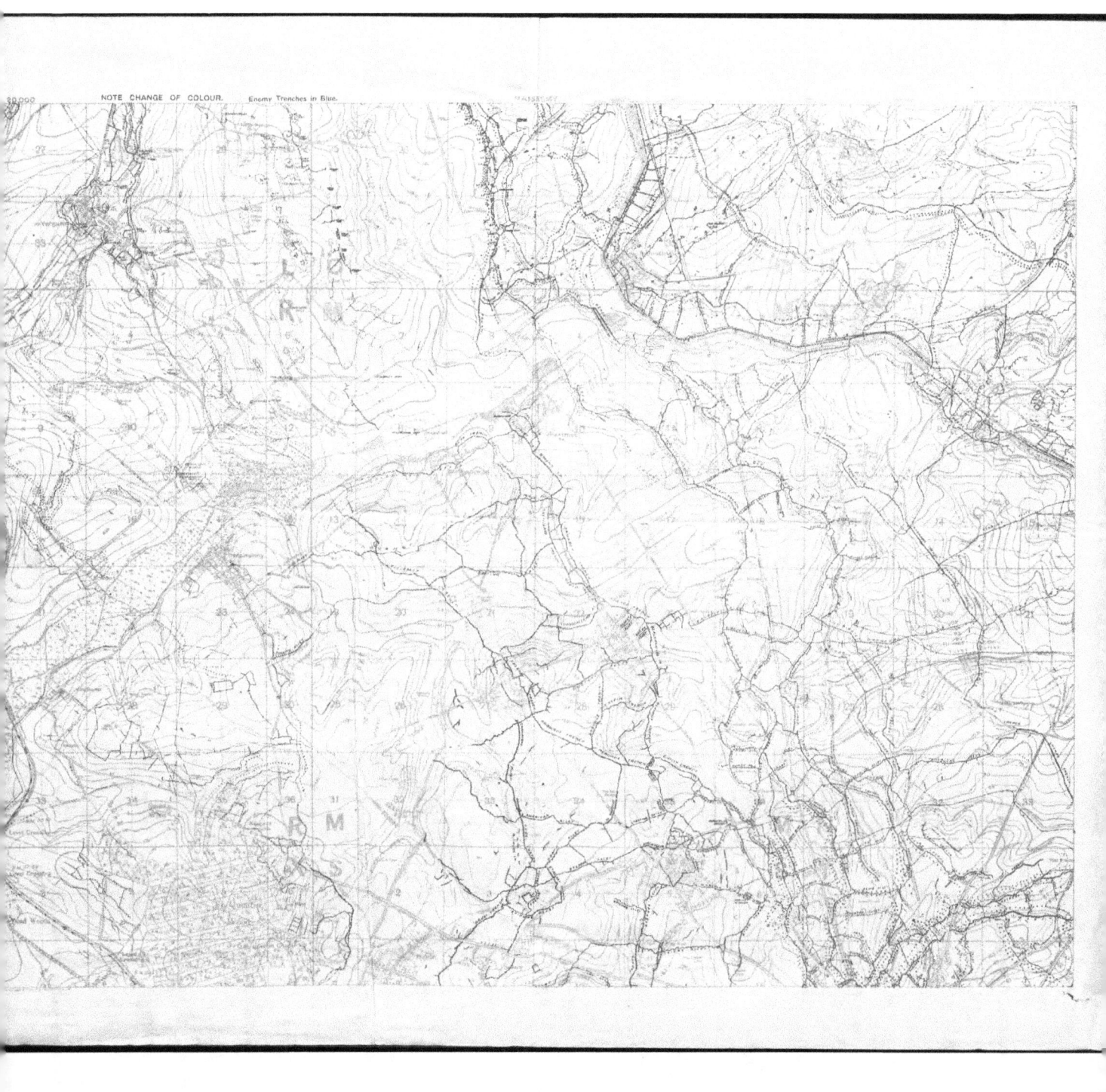

Army Form C. 2118

WAR DIARY
or
INTELLIGENCE SUMMARY 11th (S) Bn. Manr. Regt.
(Erase heading not required.)

Instructions regarding War Diaries and Intelligence Summaries are contained in F.S. Regs., Part II. and the Staff Manual respectively. Title Pages will be prepared in manuscript.

Place	Date July	Hour	Summary of Events and Information	Remarks and references to Appendices
MARSEILLES	9.	10.00	Battn. Left Docks for Camp. FOURNIER (about 2 miles)	
		13.30	Ship was closed and all Battn. marched to camp.	
	10		Still at camp FOURNIER. Ordinary orders so military or only route marches.	
	11 to 13.	10.30	Battn. entrained at Marseilles and left at 10.30. In the train until arrival at St. Pol. at 16.00 on the 13th. Thence by march route to MAIZIERES. Arrived about 20.00 and billeted for the night. 2Lt	
MAIZIERES	14 & 15.		In Billets at MAIZIERES. Coys route marching etc. Edt	
	16.	10.00	Battn. left MAIZIERES by march route to GRAND RULLECOURT arriving about 12.00. Went into Billets. 5/6?	
GRAND RULLECOURT	17.		Still in Billets. Transport arrangements Batt. Comdg. Officer & Coy. Comdrs. proceeded to Capt M WOOD and Capt A.F. SOUTHON proceeded to Divl. French mortar school & Coy. RP. & PIGGINBOTTOM GRAND RULLECOURT by march Trenches	
	18.	9.30 AM	Battn. Coo four platoons left GRAND RULLECOURT by march route and arrived at BEAUMETZ about 1-45 p.m. and went into Billets. Four platoons (one per Coy) left GRAND RULLECOURT by motor lorry and arrived at BEAUMETZ about 5-30 p.m. Thence by march route to trenches (F sector WAILLY) 2/Lt R.P. HIGGINBOTTOM to 3rd Army for school.	
			Battn. proceeded to the trenches to relieve 4th Kings Liverpool Rgt. Coys leaving BEAUMETZ one hour interval. Relief was completed at about 12 midnight. During relief Battn. had 1 casualty, 1 man being slightly wounded. 2Lt A.D. Roberts & Sgt. BREAKLEY to hosp. sick. Capt M. Alop.	
	10.			E.R.O'Connor

WAR DIARY
or
INTELLIGENCE SUMMARY.
(Erase heading not required.)

Army Form C. 2118.

Instructions regarding War Diaries and Intelligence Summaries are contained in F. S. Regs., Part II. and the Staff Manual respectively. Title pages will be prepared in manuscript.

Place	Date	Hour	Summary of Events and Information	Remarks and references to Appendices
MISC 3.3.	1/10/18		A Coy attacking with Bedfords whose task was to push through and push forward, on the left and form defensive flank. A Coy attacked (objective) Bois Quesnoy wood. The C.O. was wounded at CAUDRY CAMBRAI Quarries. C Coy with 9 Platoon in support to A Coy through SW EPEHY/VENDHUILE. The S.O. was wounded. WIDCAST. Wood at m 19 b1. Reorganized. Diary with A/Adjt.	
MISC 3.3.	2/10/18		A Coy still attacking with 15 Bde. B, C & D Coys still resting and refitting. Reorganising.	
MISC 3.3.	3/10/18		Many still carrying out refit. C Coy with the Bde moved up to forward the Forborough Line Position. B & D Coys retaining while the remainder Highlanders (Scovey ?) artillery employed as Battalion Reserve. Bivouac in field. Hostile Shelling of Boves position.	
MASSEMY	4/10/18		Bivouacs. Resting. C Coy returned to MASSEMY. A Coy returned to the Brewery and moved back to YERMANDOIS. C Coy followed to Coy of Highlanders MGC in the vicinity of HUT 718. Hereon holding was much reduced and almost "T" Trench was fixed. B & D Coys resting & training. C Coys returned. Entr'd with German prisoners recaptured by the Bn & BELLANGLISE.	
MASSEMY	5/10/18		The battalion resting, refitting and cleaning. New buttons issued in Bulgate out. From within ABLETT Coys. The Brigade was reported respectably. Off the quality of the New Men Orderly of the BN was inspected by the Army Cmdr. General Colyer de Lisle at which admirable speech he made addressing the Battalion. Said he considered that they were amongst the best Battalions and Brigades.	
MASSEMY	9/10/18		Coys moved out to prepare dinner and Brittanion war departed. Battalion moved SE HB Coy moved with advance to HAPAINCOURT. Dbn repaired &ery in SaPPlo group the southern Coy cleared of Civilians.	
MASSEMY LAMPAGNIE	10/10/18 11/10/18		Battalion still resting, and honored to a few at old areas. Bn was moved to LAMPAGNIE. Evening - the Brigade - on the HINDENBURG LINE. Training with Tanks.	

Army Form C. 2118.

6th (S) BATTALION NORTHAMPTONSHIRE REGT. (MORESB)

WAR DIARY
or
INTELLIGENCE SUMMARY.
(Erase heading not required.)

Instructions regarding War Diaries and Intelligence Summaries are contained in F. S. Regs., Part II. and the Staff Manual respectively. Title pages will be prepared in manuscript.

Place	Date	Hour	Summary of Events and Information	Remarks and references to Appendices
Near Eriis.	1917 Mar. 14		'A' Coy in position to hope turgid commenced to make trenches more east in Gross St including Bogum. GOMIECUS & VILLERS-GUISLAIN 'B' Coy in attack to work on VILLERS-GUISLAIN - PESSIERES road, commenced firing on trench wire in VILLERS-GUISLAIN. 'C' 'D' Coys same as before.	
	15th		'A' Coy commenced clearing VILLERS-GUISLAIN - GONNELIEU ROAD and continued clearing round entry on same. 'C' Coy commenced digging latrines on HINDI-BURG KREUZE ROAD.	
	16th		'C' Coy dug latrines in PESIERES. Beyambin same work. All companies to Ancre Ancienne. 'A' & 'B' Coys to Railway embankment - W. 23. 5A (57). 'C' 'D' Companies to shelters in PESIERES.	
Near PESIERES	17th		All companies continued same work 2 days. H.Q. moved to shelters on railway embankment Beyambin 2 days.	
	18th		'A' 'B' Coys same work. 'C' 'D' Coys clean CAMBRAI Road up to Support Line.	
	19th		'A' 'B' Regts did no work. 'C' 'D' Coys continued clearing CAMBRAI Road. Thus companies moved into Village in the Reserve Line.	
	20th		At 6.30 a.m. III Corps attacked went 12th Division on our right, 2 divisions front 35th Lt. Bde. Brigade on our right, 36th Lt. Bde. on our left, 2. 35th Bde. were two Companies retain tenders same day. At 4 p.m. Loys Coy moved up to front line to follow on the Camera Road to 4 roads at R.21.d.4.6. (57.c) - Thence up to LAVACQUERIE. 2 O.R. killed 10 or wounded.	
	21st		'A' 'B' Coys continued work on New C.T. investigating them to form a line transport stores cut 'C' 'D' Coys continued alignment mining Cambrai Road from 4 roads at R.21.d.w.w towards BONAVIS. No casualties.	
	22nd		all companies same work.	
	23rd		'A' 'B' Coys moved up into position in the Reserve line. 'A' Coy went to Relation opposite on road between 4 roads at R.21.d.w.w. to LAVACQUERIE advancing planning one Platoon carried on backing same working and about C.T. Friz to 20 of 'B' Coy lost. Platoon working to village at R.21.d. wu. One Platoon obtaining wire on road from GONNELIEU working C.T. aug on 20th. 'C' 'D' Coys same work as before. French boundary	

WAR DIARY or INTELLIGENCE SUMMARY

Army Form C. 2118.

1st Batt. Grenadier Guards

Place	Date	Hour	Summary of Events and Information	Remarks and references to Appendices
Near LES BOEUFS	1916 SEPT 15th		Road, in accordance with the orders, and marched to a pt. 85 yds in rear, they proceeded to dig in, and patrols were sent forward to keep in touch with the enemy who were invisible in small bodies, from which, however, indiscriminate ill-fortunately our further barrage attacks have dropped direct on the line and when the 2IC Coys were digging in, and it failed to lift forward for at least 15 minutes (the 2 in the A.LI.R.) a desperate report was sent through this line. Capt. L. T. HARGREAVES was so severely wounded that he died while being carried back, and there were other casualties including Capt. DRURY-LOWE, Commanding 1st Batt. Grenadier Guards, which was digging in on our left. The 2nd Batt. Grenadier Guards were 100 yds on the Right, though practically without any Company Officers left, but certainly was able double, except for the 2nd while 3rd Companies of the 1st Batt. Grenadier Guards subsequently, however, a defensive flank was formed at right angles to the S.E. Guards Brigade facing GUEDECOURT, where the attack had been held up. Battalion although not moved forward before 8pm to the Brown Line, and	24

Copy No. 2

Operation Order No.5
by
Brigadier-General, H.C.Lowther, C.V.O., C.M.G., D.S.O.
Commanding 1st Guards Brigade.

Reference BETHUNE Map.
1/40,000

BETHUNE.
18th May 1915.

1. The Brigade will march to-day as follows, to relieve 58th French Division in Section Y (3rd Brigade have taken over Section Z on our left)
   (a). 1st Coldstream Guards at 2.15 p.m. to billets in SAILLY LABOURSE.
      1st Black Watch at 4.30 p.m. to billets in SAILLY LABOURSE.
      1st Scots Guards at 5 p.m. to relieve the right of the French Y.1
      London Scottish at 5.15 p.m. to relieve the centre of the
         French Y.2
      1st Cameron Highlanders at 6.30 p.m. (to march behind London
         Scottish) to relieve the left of the French in Y.3
   (b). East of the cross roads in L.4.c.5.6 Battalions will march in small parties at intervals of 200 yards on each side of the road during daylight. Carts will go down singly.

2. (a) On arrival at SAILLY LABOURSE the 1st Coldstream Guards will at once send 2 companies to VERMELLES. These companies will be marched up in parties of not more than 12 men, and at intervals of 200 yards. Each party to go direct to it's billets and remain in them till the relief is completed.
   (b). They will take 5 S.A.A.Carts with them, and dump the ammunition at Bde Headquarters Advanced Reporting Centre (G.8.a.5.2). Carts to go up at intervals of ½ mile and return singly to SAILLY LABOURSE immediately they have dumped the ammunition.
   (c). This ammunition will be Brigade Reserve, and the ½ Battalion in Brigade Reserve at VERMELLES will find a guard over this.

3. The three Battalions going into the trenches will take up their 5 S.A.A.Carts, dump the ammunition and then send the carts back to SAILLY LABOURSE.

4. 1st Line Transport will march immediately in rear of units, and will all be billeted at SAILLY LABOURSE.

5. The Lowland Field Company R.E. is allotted to Y Section and will be billeted in SAILLY LABOURSE.

6. No.3 Field Ambulance will form an Aid Post in VERMELLES.

7. No.2 Coy.Train and baggage Section will be at FOUQUIERES LES BETHUNE H.21.a.5.7.

8. Brigade Headquarters will be in NOYELLES LES VERMELLES L.11.b.5.

9. 1st Coldstream Guards will find a Control Post at cross roads L.11.c.9.5. Orders for Control Posts attached.

Major,
Brigade Major, 1st Guards Brigade.

Copy No.1 Office.
Copies Nos. 2 to Coldstream, 3 to Scots Gds, 4 to Black Watch, 5 to Camerons,
   6 to London Scottish, 7 to No.2 Coy Train.

(c) Further orders will be issued regarding the move of 20th Trench Howitzer Battery and Divisional Ammunition Column.

7. Brigadiers will retain command of the trench line until the relief of battalions in the trenches is complete.

8. Field Companies R.E., Field Ambulances, and Companies of Train will accompany Brigades.
The 57th Field Company, R.E. will be withdrawn to a position near LOCRE on the night 19th/20th.

9. Pigeon men will remain in charge of pigeons until relieved by experts.

10. Brigade Mining Sections will remain in charge of mines until relieved. Further orders will be issued.

11. Trench stores will be handed over to incoming battalions. The C.R.E. will issue instructions regarding tools in workshops and any other stores it is proposed to move.

12. Cable and airline communications will be left in position.

13. Acknowledge.

                                                             Lieut-Colonel,
                                                            General Staff.

Issued at 6.30 p.m. to

A.A. & Q.M.G. (2)	By hand.
C.R.A.	By Motor Cyclist.
C.R.E.	By Orderly.
137th Infantry Brigade.	By Motor Cyclist.
138th do	do
139th do	do
Divisional Train.	do
A.D.M.S.	By Orderly.
A.D.V.S.	do
Camp Commandant.	do
D.O. Signals.	do
War Diary. (2)	
A.P.M.	By Orderly.
50th Division.	By Motor Cyclist.

acknowledged.

Operation Orders by Lt. Col. R.J. Morris D.S.O.
Comdg. RAIM?
25th June 1917.

1. The Battn. will be relieved in the Right Subsector by the 2/HAC tonight 25/26th.

2. Coys. will be relieved as follows:-
   No.1 Coy will be relieved by "A" Coy 2/HAC On the Right.
   2 Coy.   "   "   "   "   "   "B" "   In the Centre.
   4 Coy.   "   "   "   "   "   "C" "   On the Left.
   3 Coy.   "   "   "   "   "   "D" "   In Support.

3. Platoon guides will be at Bn. HQ by 9:30 pm.

4. Completion of relief will be reported to Bn. HQ. by code word SPRAT.

5. On completion of relief Coys will move independantly to Camp in B.27.d.18. C.Q.M.Sgts. will meet Coys in vicinity of Camp.

6. Coy. Mess Boxes will be sent to Bn. HQ. by 10 pm.
   Lewis Gun limbers will meet Coys near the Four Willows at fork tracks in C.8.d.47.

7. All empty petrol tins will be carried out of the line and left on Lewis Gun limbers.

8. One Officer per Coy; 1 NCO + 1 Lewis Gunner per platoon will remain in the line for 24 hours after relief, when they will rejoin their own Coys. at MORY.

Continued........

REFERENCE.

□ Area occupied by "A" Coy.

□ Area occupied by "B" Coy.

□ Area occupied by "C" Coy.

□ Area occupied by "D" Coy.

◁ Gun positions and close defence lines.

◁ Guns of 35th Div.

◁ AT - Anti-tank guns.

◁ Guns of 4th Belgian Div.

○ S.O.S. lines.

○ Help Right lines

○ Help Left lines

○ Retaliation targets.

The black dots show the exact aiming points of guns.

Sheet. 1.
Army Form C. 2118.

1st BATTALION COLDSTREAM GUARDS
WAR DIARY
FOR MAY, 1918.
INTELLIGENCE SUMMARY.

Place	Date	Hour	Summary of Events and Information	Remarks and references to Appendices
RESERVE (Rabbit Wd) X.19.c.	1st		A quiet day, spent chiefly in resting. No 3 Coy had a certain amount of difficulty with their Billets. In a Boxing Competition at ST. AMAND, organized by the 1st Bn. Scots Guards, 10 entries by the details produced 8 winners in the 1st round.	
	2nd		Rounders were played, especially by No 2 Company. At St. AMAND, boxing continued, the details providing 1 runner up in the Finals. ST. AMAND Church received a direct hit from a H.V. Shell. The details were beaten by R.F.A. by 9 - 1.	
FRONT LINE between BOIRY AYETTE left Bn. " Bde.	3rd		Major Hon E.K.Digby,M.C., Capt. C.G.Barclay,M.C. and Capt. Fellowes; 2nd Lieuts. P.P.Mallam, A.D.Keith-Cameron, H.V.F.Somerset, H.D.Ritchie, C.I.F.Vincent and Lieut. Little, relieved the Commanding Officer, Lieut. Gamble, Capt Salisbury-Jones, 2nd Lieuts. A.J.Maxwell-Stuart, W.H.Wilson, Lieut.Roderick 2nd Lieuts. Rowlatt, W.H.Gladstone,M.C. J.Campbell-Young. The Rev. W.H.M.Secker, M.C. returned to details. The Battalion relieved Scots Guards X, in the left sub-sector of the left Brigade in Divisional Front. No 1 Coy in Right Front. 2 = " Reserve. 4 = " Support 3 = " Left Front.	
			The Battalion front extended about 1200 yds facing SS.E., and was held by a line of 10 posts in the front line, with the same number in rear. Battalion Headquarters in the bed of the COJEUL River, 1500'South of BOIRY.ST.MARTIN (X.24.c.2.0.) No casualties in relief; a warm sunny day. German attack imminent.	
	4th		One of the patrols sent out by No 1 Company (right) was fired on, and challenged in English (S.2.c.3.5.) - During the evening a working party of No 2 Company had one man killed, and 5 wounded by shell fire. A fine day - colder - German attack still imminent.	
	5th		2nd Lt. Headlam relieved Lt.Cazenove and 2nd Lt. Kent came up to help No 3 Coy. 2nd Lieut Keith-Cameron (No 1 Coy) was wounded in the thigh by Machine Gun fire. The usual patrols, but nothing of importance was reported. A good deal of rain fell during the day. German attack still imminent.	

WAR DIARY
or
INTELLIGENCE SUMMARY.
(Erase heading not required.)

Army Form C. 2118.

Instructions regarding War Diaries and Intelligence Summaries are contained in F.S. Regs., Part II. and the Staff Manual respectively. Title pages will be prepared in manuscript.

Place	Hour, Date	Summary of Events and Information	Remarks and references to Appendices
Right Subsector Sailly-au-Bois Section	3pm 3/10/16	Battalion relieved by the 1st Bn. Gordon Highlanders and took over billets at BERTRANCOURT.	A
Bertrancourt	4/10/16 5/10/16 6/10/16	Battalion found various Working Parties.	A
	H.15pm 7/10/16	Battalion moved to new billets at PUCHEVILLERS, a distance of about 8 miles.	A
Puchevillers	8/10/16 9/10/16 14/10/16	Battalion engaged in practising Division- al attack on Trenches	A
	18/10/16	Battalion moved to new billets at BERTRAN COURT.	A
Bertrancourt	19/10/16 20/10/16	Working parties supplied by Battalion	A
	9 am 21/10/16	Battalion moved to MAILLY-WOOD. EAST and took over Huts nts vacated by 2nd Bn Royal Fusiliers.	A

WAR DIARY
or
INTELLIGENCE SUMMARY.
(Erase heading not required.)

Army Form C. 2118.

Hour, Date, Place	Summary of Events and Information	Remarks and references to Appendices
1915 May 9 4.6 p.m. [RUE du BOIS] RICHEBOURG	2nd Lieut Sharod and some men tried to rush the guns but were put on hold but one gun was disabled by a shot into the lock mechanism fired by Pte Mannion. Sergt Graham took charge of this platoon of C.Coy 2nd Lieut Gray's platoon was on the left of Sergt Graham but he was hit whilst on the parapet by a bullet from the 2nd line On the extreme left 2nd Lieut Scott with his platoon of C apparently broke right through the first German line. As [soon as] the left of the "Batt" was unsupported owing to massive [fire] fire being stopped the C.O. of Camerons the third line of C.Coy leaving the whole of A line from the London Divn to oppose [the losses] (R2) and (R6) held by the last 2 platoons of B Coy and the 4 machine guns of the Battalion. The Germans who were in the first breastwork ran down a communication trench from (R2) and met their reinforcements coming up amidst much confusion so that our men carried fire who the main advance some worked up through our men and began to [enemy] trenches. 2nd Lieut Wardles sent a flag message	

WAR DIARY or INTELLIGENCE SUMMARY

Army Form C. 2118.

Place	Date	Hour	Summary of Events and Information	Remarks and references to Appendices
SUPPORT LINE	4/3/18 5/3/18		Day & night passed quietly. The Bn. continues to find parties for R.E. & New Zealand Tunnelling Company	
SUPPORT LINE to FRONT LINE	6/3/18	2.40 am	On 2.40 am the 2⁰ B: G.Gds. moved into relief. Relief to retaliation by enemy on the Bn. Trenches. No casualties.	
		5 pm	On 5 pm B: Commenced to relieve 2⁰ B: G.Gds. in the Front line. Bn. a relief completed by 3.15 pm. Dispositions & H.Q. were as follows: No.1 Coy right front line (pts 2 & 3) from June 5-8 to I.14.a.77 2 Platoon front line. 2 Section about junction of CROW ALLEY & CORONA SUPT. One platoon Coy H.Q. Coy H.Q. by B. Strong point about I.13.d.5.2 No.3 Coy, 2 platoons front line from (pts 6,7,8) left of No.1 Coy to T.8.C.10.25 (less 1 Section of No.1 Coy). COLD ALLEY & CUPID SUPT. One platoon One Section junction of COLD ALLEY in COLD ALLEY about I.13.a.4.8 Coy H.Q. in COLD ALLEY to T.7.d.95.95. No.2 Coy (left front) from left 8 No.3 Coy to T.7.d.95.95. 2 platoons in front line (pts 24-29). 2 sections about junction of CURLEY SPT & CASH ALLEY, one platoon + 2 sections at D Strong point. Coy H.Q. in CASH ALLEY No.4 Coy in CASE RESERVE at junction of CURLY SPT & CASH ALLEY. Bn.H.Q & trenches in CADIZ RESERVE H.13.6.5.8	

WAR DIARY
INTELLIGENCE SUMMARY

1st Royal Dublin Fusiliers

Army Form C. 2118.

Place	Date	Hour	Summary of Events and Information	Remarks and references to Appendices
RAILWAY Right Support 7.40 C. 3 Rue S.P.S.W.	20th	continued	In month of November 1917. Work splendidly, making repeated journeys backwards & forwards to the Exchange position with wire for X Coy. The G.O.C. Bde expresses his entire satisfaction with the work done by the Batt & in Bde orders very complimentary references are made to its excellence. This wiring carried out by the 2 companies of the Batt. The 16th Divl Scheme in all 670 ammunition panniers. Casualties very considerable. Amongst the Wounded The front Number of Wounded prisoners is unknown but that it was high. Casualties were very slight. 2/Lt BWARD X Coy Inde behaved very gallantly & was killed. he was first shot through his wrist but carried on, Cpl WALL D.C.M. of X Coy was also killed, Capt DUTTON M.C. & 2/Lt W.A. MCWILLIAM were wounded also 4 ORs — Capt LENDRUM was slightly wounded in the face but re-mained with unit. W&X upon Batt about 10 a.m.	
— " —	21st		Batt at various times 'stood to' in expectation of a counter attack. Bde Pipers 9.0R & 1 OR from 10 Batt completed Intake in Strength.	59-807.
— " —	22nd		Batt move up & relieve 2nd Batt 10th Batt R.D. from Exchange positions.	59-817

WAR DIARY
or
INTELLIGENCE SUMMARY.
(Erase heading not required.)

Army Form C. 2118.

Instructions regarding War Diaries and Intelligence Summaries are contained in F. S. Regs, Part II. and the Staff Manual respectively. Title pages will be prepared in manuscript.

Hour, Date, Place	Summary of Events and Information	Remarks and references to Appendices
25-8-14	and after some engagement retired under cover of darkness to COUDRY. Enemy did not pursue but shelled the town of SOLESMES.	Hotch ms
26-8-14	Battle of COUDRY — LE CATEAU. WILTS held N. & E. of COUDRY the whole morning were heavily shelled and attacked by infantry and suffered 80 k 100 casualties. The following officers were wounded Lieut Loder-Symonds, Brown and Carrington. When retirement was ordered WILTS fell back to BEAUREVOIR.	Hotch ms
27-8-14	At 2 a.m. retired to HARICOURT where halted a few hours and then retired to VERMAND, halted for five hours and then continued retirement to HAM. WILTS found advanced guard during night march	Hotch ms

Army Form C. 2118.

WAR DIARY
or
INTELLIGENCE SUMMARY.
(Erase heading not required.)

Instructions regarding War Diaries and Intelligence Summaries are contained in F. S. Regs., Part II. and the Staff Manual respectively. Title pages will be prepared in manuscript.

Hour, Date, Place.	Summary of Events and Information.	Remarks and references to Appendices.
NOVEMBER 10th. Trenches E. of FESTUBERT.	A quiet day in trenches. New fire trench improved. Captain E.B HENDERSON, Adjt. wounded among night, whilst conveying a message to unit on our left. One man wounded. No. III & IV bays still occupy Trenches N.W. of GIVENCHY.	Wⁿ
11th	About 2 a.m. No. I bay. occupied new fire trench prepared about 150 yds in rear of old position. No. II. bay. retired to Support trenches. Quiet in trenches all day. 1 man killed; Sgt Mayor Johnstone, 2 L/Sgts, Corpls 6 other Ranks wounded by Shrapnel whilst unloading Rations in FESTUBERT. Nos III & IV bays still at GIVENCHY	Wⁿ

WAR DIARY
or
INTELLIGENCE SUMMARY

(Erase heading not required.)

Army Form C. 2118.

8th Batt.
Graham Grieve

Place	Date	Hour	Summary of Events and Information	Remarks and references to Appendices
TRONES WOOD	1916 Sept 24th	9pm	Battalion left to bivouac in TRONES WOOD at 9PM 24th and after a somewhat difficult march across the ground, when not long the action of the 15th/16th reached its final trenches about midnight without many further casualties. No 1 Coy (Captain S.R. Clarkson) and No 2 Coy (Captain D.C. Ogilvy) were in the front line, the latter on the right. No 3 Company (2/Lieut A.M. Blay) and No 4 Company (Capt R. Y. St. John Rotenburgh) in a second line about 150 yards in rear, with Battalion Headquarters in a diagonal communication trench.	
	25th		There was some shelling during the night and following morning but the trenches being Germans casualties were not numerous. It unfortunately included 2nd Lt C. Strick who was hit dying the march, and was replaced in No 3 Coy by 2nd Lieut J.S.M. McMahon, who had been left in reserve. Is took all 4th to the Battalion was to take 3 structures afforded by the 3rd Battalion Coldstream Guards, who were to consolidate	

Army Form C. 2118.

WAR DIARY
or
INTELLIGENCE SUMMARY.
(Erase heading not required.)

Instructions regarding War Diaries and Intelligence Summaries are contained in F. S. Regs., Part II. and the Staff Manual respectively. Title pages will be prepared in manuscript.

Place	Date	Hour	Summary of Events and Information	Remarks and references to Appendices
GRANDA CAMP 2nd B 10th inf	20/3/18		[illegible handwritten entry]	
"	21/3/18		[illegible handwritten entry]	
"	22/3/18		[illegible handwritten entry]	
"	23/3/18		[illegible handwritten entry]	
TURCO FARM HUTS M 111 d 2.2	24/3/18		TURCO FARM HUTS [illegible]	
"	25/3/18		[illegible handwritten entry]	
"	26/3/18		[illegible handwritten entry]	
"	27/3/18		[illegible handwritten entry]	
"	28/3/18		[illegible handwritten entry]	
"	29/3/18		[illegible handwritten entry]	

Army Form C. 2118.

WAR DIARY
or
INTELLIGENCE SUMMARY.
(Erase heading not required).

13 Essex
Vol II

CONFIDENTIAL

WAR DIARY

of

13th (S) BATTN THE ESSEX REGT

FROM MAY 1st 1916 TO MAY 31st 1916

Army Form C. 2118.

WAR DIARY
or
INTELLIGENCE SUMMARY
(Erase heading not required.)

Instructions regarding War Diaries and Intelligence Summaries are contained in F. S. Regs., Part II. and the Staff Manual respectively. Title pages will be prepared in manuscript.

Place	Date	Hour	Summary of Events and Information	Remarks and references to Appendices

Confidential

WAR DIARY

OF

61ST MACHINE GUN COMPANY.

FEBRUARY 1st — FEBRUARY 28th. 1918.

VOL. III. PAGE 7.

R.O.

Army Form C. 2118

WAR DIARY
INTELLIGENCE SUMMARY

(Erase heading not required.) 1st Battn. SCOTS GUARDS.

Place	Date	Hour	Summary of Events and Information	Remarks and references to Appendices
WARLUS	18th Oct.		Weather being unit entirely favourable went to the alternative in the afternoon Battery Contests between representations of the 1st and 2nd Battns were held. Result: 2nd Battn. — Winners. 1st Battn. — Minus 2. Rev. F.W. HEAD (C.F.E.) gave a lecture in the evening, subject :— "The Causes of the Present War". Frequent heavy showers.	
— do —	19th.		Company parades and training of trained Snipers and Lewis gunners. Work with frequent heavy showers.	
— do —	20th.		Battalion practised bomb throwing. Snipers and Lewis Gunners were under the orders of their respective officers. R.F. had the use of the Brigade Baths at TAILLY. Battalion Sports were held in the afternoon. Results :— Trial.	

	Finals	Semis	Thirds	Total
L.F	3	5	4	12
B	4	2	3	9
C	4	3	1	8
R.F.	1	1	2	4

| | | | In the Officers' Race Capt. C.I. Drew (R.A.M.C.) M.O., took first place; Capt. Sir Iain Colquhoun Bt. D.S.O. second; and Pte. W.E.D. SHORTT third. Cinema Entertainment in the evening. Sharp frost in the early morning; then much warmer of day. | |
| — do — | 21st. | | Some programme of work carried out. B and C Coys. battns. Officers v Sergts. Football Match :— Result — 3-1 in favour of Sergeants. Snowing with light frost in the air. | |

www.ingramcontent.com/pod-product-compliance
Lightning Source LLC
Chambersburg PA
CBHW080857230426
43663CB00013B/2566